9XM Talking

9XM Talking

∾

WHA Radio and the Wisconsin Idea

Randall Davidson

THE UNIVERSITY OF WISCONSIN PRESS
TERRACE BOOKS

The University of Wisconsin Press
1930 Monroe Street
Madison, Wisconsin 53711

www.wisc.edu/wisconsinpress/

3 Henrietta Street
London WC2E 8LU, England

Library of Congress Cataloging-in-Publication Data
Davidson, Randall, 1959–
9XM talking : WHA Radio and the Wisconsin Idea /
Randall Davidson.
p. cm.
Includes bibliographical references and index.
ISBN 0–299–21870–8 (cloth : alk. paper)
1. Public radio—Wisconsin—History. 2. Educational radio stations—
Wisconsin—History. 3. WHA (Radio station : Madison, Wis.)—History.
I. Title. II. Title: Nine XM talking. III. Title: WHA Radio and
the Wisconsin Idea.
HE8697.95.U6D38   2006
384.5409775'83—dc22   2006008875

Contents

Illustrations

Preface

This book covers a topic that has received relatively little serious attention: the history of educational radio. While several books on early radio networks and some pioneer commercial broadcast stations have appeared, it is rare to find historical works on non-commercial "educational" radio stations, which typically were run by colleges and universities in the early days. Commercial and financial pressures in the 1930s took a heavy toll, and only a handful of the more than two hundred AM stations licensed to educational institutions since 1922 are still on the air as non-commercial broadcasters. WHA at the University of Wisconsin in Madison is one of these survivors.

As an industry, broadcast radio has been a mediocre steward of its history. Happily, WHA Radio has been an exception. Its continuous association with the University of Wisconsin is certainly a factor, but much of the credit has to go to the early staff members at WHA. It is obvious that many of them recognized the pioneering nature of their work and made real efforts to document their activities. A breathtaking amount of material has been preserved from the station's early decades. The papers of WHA manager Harold B. McCarty alone fill ninety-four records boxes at the Wisconsin Historical Society Archives.

Like most works in history, this one owes much to the efforts of earlier researchers. One work of scholarship is worthy of special mention: a remarkable 1959 doctoral dissertation by University of Wisconsin student John Stanley Penn. It traces the first quarter-century of WHA's history, from its earliest days as experimental station 9XM. It is a fine record of the period, and Penn's references pointed to sources that I might have otherwise overlooked. As part of his research, Penn sent queries to many early WHA staff members and former University of Wisconsin students who were involved with the radio operation. Their responses are preserved at the Wisconsin Historical Society Archives and provide fascinating anecdotes about the station's early days. Individual WHA programs have also been the focus of academic research over the years.

I used some unique reference material in this research. One such source, the University of Wisconsin *Press Bulletin,* was a single sheet of newsprint that featured news items about the university for republication by newspapers and wire services. It was produced from 1909 to 1943, bracketing the formative years of the university's radio operation. Its particular value is that the staff at the radio station in the earliest years relied on the publication as keeper of the station's historical record and believed that its writers were supporters of the station. Items from the *Press Bulletin* were also broadcast on WHA beginning in 1922, one of the early efforts in news programming. Also useful in my research were the regular in-house newsletters that WHA published from 1943 through 1968.

UW–Madison's student newspaper, the *Daily Cardinal,* was another valuable resource, but local newspapers have less historical value than one might think. Early on, many papers stopped including news about local radio outlets but would list the schedules for distant big-city stations. The problem was exacerbated in Madison after the local papers began operating radio stations of their own; from that point forward, they rarely mentioned WHA, which was now competing with their stations for listeners. Newspaper information is much better for WHA's affiliated station WLBL in Stevens Point. The *Stevens Point Daily Journal* did not operate its own radio outlet during this era and seemed to regard state-owned (and non-commercial) WLBL less as competition and more as a public service. The paper cooperated with the station on many projects and often put news items about the station on the front page. The paper even published the next day's program schedule on or near its editorial page from 1933 to 1950.

Sadly, the research notes and personal papers of WHA founder Earle M. Terry are not available. After he died in 1929, his widow disposed of all this material. Only fragments of Terry's writings remain, usually carbon copies of letters he wrote to equipment suppliers and other researchers, memos sent within the university, and correspondence with the federal government when he was negotiating for radio frequencies and licenses.

This story uses a minimal amount of engineering detail. However, the nature of radio in its early days requires that some be included. I have converted the radio wavelengths to kilohertz. The government did not begin to identify AM radio stations by kilocycles or kilohertz, rather than wavelength, until mid-1923, and the wavelengths continued in popular discourse for some time thereafter. Whenever a wavelength is given, I have included its equivalent frequency in kilohertz. Many frequencies are actually below the "bottom" of today's AM dial, some as low as 120 kHz. I have rounded them off as well: 360 meters appears as 833 kHz and 485 meters appears as 618 kHz.

This work is organized mostly in chronological order. However, so much was going on simultaneously during the early years of WHA that I have devoted separate chapters to each of the mainstays of the WHA schedule: the *Farm Program, The Homemakers' Program,* the Wisconsin School of the Air, the Wisconsin College of the Air, and *Chapter a Day.* The history of WLBL is so interesting that it warrants a separate chapter as well.

This book takes the story of WHA and the state FM stations through the end of 1978. It is a good point at which to end: on January 1, 1979, some stations began using their current identification, Wisconsin Public Radio. Later that year National Public Radio programming really came into its own with the debut of *Morning Edition* and the start of satellite distribution for its programs. The final chapter briefly discusses some highlights of Wisconsin Public Radio operations through to the present day.

This research debunks several persistent and well-loved legends about WHA and its programs. Even the 9XM/WHA historical marker at the entrance to the Madison headquarters of Wisconsin Public Radio appears to contain errors, despite WHA promotions manager Harold Engel approving its text in 1958. The postscript examines the accuracy of WHA's claim to be "oldest station in the nation." It reviews the arguments of earlier academic researchers and adds to them documentary evidence that has only recently become available in public archives and that other researchers have therefore missed.

Several findings from this new research are noteworthy. One is the challenge that Earle Terry faced in keeping the station afloat in the early days and how he managed to persevere despite inadequate support from his academic department and the university. Scholars recognized Terry's struggles a generation ago, but the importance of his contribution has dimmed over time. Wisconsin Public Radio has conference rooms, a performance studio, and even an FM station named in honor of various former staff members but nothing that recognizes Terry, who was once accorded the title "Father of Educational Radio." I am pleased that this book will give the public a renewed appreciation for the pivotal role that this scientist played in the early days of the radio operation.

Another finding is the important work done by radio operator–announcer Malcolm Hanson during the early years of 9XM and WHA. He too has received some credit over the years, but the archival material makes clear that it was largely through Hanson's devotion and sacrifice that Terry's public service vision was realized. Hanson also was one of the first of thousands of university students who become so caught up in the excitement of a campus radio station that they neglect their coursework. Hanson never did complete his degree and was at one point dropped from the university rolls for failing grades. Hanson's papers have been preserved at the Wisconsin Historical Society, and much of the collection from his early days at the university consists of letters he wrote to his mother in Milwaukee. Somewhat surprisingly, they are all in Danish. Thankfully, an earlier researcher translated them into English and included the translations in the collection.

The other major discovery is the rich and heretofore mostly unexplored history of the "other" AM station, WLBL, which was licensed to the Wisconsin Department of Agriculture and Markets. From the perspective of WHA in Madison, the "up north" station was always a bit of an anomaly in the state radio network, and its local programming was the source of puzzlement, bemusement, and often outright disdain. However, in many ways it was equal to or slightly ahead of WHA in some programming innovations. This was even more remarkable given that the station was located in a small city, was not operated by educators, and did not have direct access to the University of Wisconsin resources that were available to WHA. It was also one of the very few non-commercial AM stations from the 1920s not owned by an educational institution. As a result, it is omitted from standard reference works chronicling educational radio.

I would like to thank the staff at the University of Wisconsin Archives, where the bulk of the historical materials reside. Their Iconography Division provided most of the photographs that illustrate this book. I also wish to thank the staff at the Archives Division of the Wisconsin Historical Society for use of its collections, which include the papers of several early WHA staff members. The archives at the University of Wisconsin–Stevens Point hold an interesting collection of material about WLBL; the station's studio was located on that campus from 1938 to 1951, and its predecessor institution was involved with the station as early as 1925. An additional rich collection of documents, some of which date from 1932, was found in the WLBL transmitter building, the oldest structure still in use by Wisconsin Public Radio.

Special thanks also go to Professor Samuel Sauls at the University of North Texas. As one of the early academic reviewers of this work, he offered many useful suggestions and the final product is much improved because of his efforts. I also wish to thank Jean Feraca, humanities producer and program host for Wisconsin Public Radio. During her own negotiations with the University of Wisconsin Press, she mentioned my interest in the history of WHA and prompted my connection with the publisher. I also wish to thank my brother Brad, who provided computer assistance with the illustrations included in this work.

Finally, I would like to thank the many WHA, WLBL, and State Radio Council employees who over the years had the foresight to preserve materials that provide a record of their accomplishments.

9XM Talking

After Marconi reported the results of the Kingstown Regatta from a tugboat at sea for the *Dublin Daily Express,* the *New York Herald* invited Marconi to report the International Ocean Yacht Races off Sandy Hook, New Jersey, in October 1899. Marconi and his backers accepted the invitation and used the opportunity to approach the U.S. Navy about using the technology. The navy officials were impressed by the possibilities. Marconi also used the trip to incorporate the Marconi Wireless Company of America.[5]

In the earliest years of radio, dots and dashes were all that wireless could manage, but the dream of transmitting the actual sounds of voice and music persisted. Common use of the term *radio* was still in the future; rather, people referred to the *wireless telephone* to describe this hoped-for development. In Britain the term *wireless* persisted and was the common term for regular radio broadcasting for many years.

One man who attempted throughout his life to be known as the father of radio was Lee de Forest. His contribution to voice transmissions was the Audion vacuum tube in 1906. It traced its development to experiments with the light bulb. Thomas Edison noted that current would flow from a light bulb filament to a plate placed near it in the bulb. English researcher John Ambrose Fleming found this device worked well as a detector for reception of wireless signals and he received a patent in 1905 for this device, known as the Fleming Valve. To this, de Forest added a third element, a grid, which controlled this current flow between the filament and the plate and is the basis for amplification. Whether de Forest really understood the importance of the modification remains a matter of debate, this three-element vacuum tube is the technical basis for radio and television. De Forest also did some early experimental voice broadcasts in New York City, including a January 1910 broadcast of a performance by the Metropolitan Opera.[6]

A Canadian-born engineer and former Edison employee, Reginald Fessenden, is credited with the earliest advances in transmitting speech. He had experimented with Hertzian waves while a professor of electrical engineering at Western University, now the University of Pittsburgh. After Marconi's demonstrations the Weather Bureau of the U.S. Department of Agriculture hired Fessenden to explore how wireless could be used in weather forecasting.

Fessenden had the idea to go beyond Marconi's "discontinuous wave," which was an interrupted wave or series of bursts. Rather, Fessenden envisioned a "continuous wave" that could have a human voice or music superimposed on it. On December 23, 1900, while still working for the weather bureau, Fessenden transmitted his voice by using such a wave. He soon had a falling-out with the agency and withdrew from the weather research project. With backing from two Pittsburgh financiers, he set up his own firm, the National Electric Signaling Company.

He turned to General Electric in Schenectady, New York, to build the type of radio generator that he needed for voice transmissions. The initial response from its engineering staff was to dismiss his ideas as unworkable, but a new GE employee from Sweden, Ernst F. W. Alexanderson, took up the challenge and managed to construct the equipment that Fessenden needed. Fessenden then installed it at his wireless station at Brant Rock, Massachusetts. In October 1906 he successfully made an experimental transmission of voice over a distance of ten miles.

On Christmas Eve 1906 Fessenden sent a wireless telegraphic message alerting all receivers to prepare for a general message. Wireless operators on ships in the Atlantic, who were accustomed to listening for the buzzing of dots and dashes through their headphones, were then astonished to hear a voice reading Bible passages, the playing of a phonograph record (Handel's "Largo"), as well as Fessenden himself playing "O Holy Night" on the violin and wishing the listeners a merry Christmas. Fessenden made a similar transmission on New Year's Eve.[7] He also asked anyone receiving the transmission to contact him by mail.

A man named Edward Bennett was on Fessenden's staff during some of his experiments at Brant Rock during 1905–6. He later worked for an electric utility in Colorado and then joined the electrical engineering department at the University of Wisconsin as a professor.[8] He had not lost his interest in wireless, and in 1914 he set up some apparatus on the Madison campus. To comply with the regulations set forth in the federal Radio Act of 1912, Bennett applied to the Department of Commerce's Bureau of Navigation for an experimental wireless license.

The government assigned Bennett the call letters 9XM.

CHAPTER 1

❧

Early Wireless Experiments at the University of Wisconsin

1909–16

These antennae wires pick up the disturbances in the aerial medium.

In the decade before World War I, experimentation with wireless telegraphy was underway at many U.S. colleges and universities, including those in Wisconsin. Beloit College in far southern Wisconsin began experiments with wireless in the summer of 1908. Less than a year later, on May 8, 1909, Charles Culver, a Beloit physics professor, performed a public demonstration in Beloit during a track meet. He sent wireless telegraph reports of the event from the athletic field to receivers on campus and one at the office of the *Beloit Daily News*. Once the University of Wisconsin began experimenting with wireless telegraphy, Culver would assist in tests of the transmissions.

By 1910 a 1,000-watt wireless station was in daily operation at Beloit. On February 3, 1913, Beloit began regular transmission of time signals from the college's observatory, and college administrators claimed that Beloit "had taken a step ahead of all other educational institutions in the world" by doing so. Within a week of the first such transmissions, twenty wireless-equipped high schools in Wisconsin, Illinois, and Indiana had applied to the college to be recipients of these time "broadcasts."[1] After the Radio Act of 1912, licenses were required for all wireless land stations. The initial Department of Commerce list of licensed wireless land stations, dated July 1, 1913, shows that Beloit College was assigned the designation 9XB.

Commercial wireless operations were also underway in the state, with two in Milwaukee and one in Manitowoc by late 1909.[2] These commercial "stations" transmitted private telegraphic messages from point to point for a fee (a point-to-point communication is essentially a conversation between two parties, albeit

7

not a private one when conducted by radio waves; its opposite is a broadcast, which is a one-way communication to all who are listening).

A real burst of interest in wireless followed the sinking of the *Titanic* in the spring of 1912. The role that wireless telegraphy played in both the distress call and the rescue operation caught the public's fancy and demonstrated that it was more than just a toy for hobbyists.

At the University of Wisconsin some experimentation with wireless was underway in 1909, although some references cite classroom wireless experiments as early as 1902. In 1914, Professor Edward Bennett of the electrical engineering department assembled an amateur wireless telegraphic set and applied to the Department of Commerce for an experimental license. The license assigned Bennett the call letters 9XM: 9 for the north central region of the United States, X for experimental, and M for Madison.

Shortly thereafter, physics professor Earle M. Terry approached Bennett and said he wished to "borrow" the license for some experimental wireless telegraph equipment that he and his students had begun building in the spring of 1915. Bennett recognized the value of the license to the experiments and gave it to Terry. In June 1915 the license was transferred to the university. The July 1915 *Radio Service Bulletin,* published by the Navigation Bureau of the U.S. Department of Commerce, is the first issue that shows the University of Wisconsin as holding the license for 9XM.

Terry became the driving force behind the wireless operation at the University of Wisconsin. He was born in 1879 on a farm near Battle Creek, Michigan, and arrived in Madison in 1902 after receiving his undergraduate degree from the University of Michigan at Ann Arbor. During his student days Terry studied the classics, giving him an unusually broad education (years later he was still able to tutor his son in Latin).[3] As a graduate student in Madison, he was first a graduate assistant and advanced to instructor after he earned his master's degree in 1904. While in graduate school he met A. Hoyt Taylor, a colleague in the physics department who shared his interest in wireless. In 1908 Taylor took a year's leave of absence to pursue postgraduate work in Germany. He received his doctoral degree in 1909 and became head of the physics department at the University of North Dakota at Grand Forks. He and Terry stayed in touch. In the years to come the two scientists would send many wireless transmissions between their respective campuses to test their equipment.

Terry earned his doctoral degree in 1910 and was promoted to assistant professor. That same year he began directing the basic physics course required of all engineering students, in addition to teaching advanced courses in magnetism and electricity. In the spring of 1915 Terry began teaching a course in radio.

Terry was an acknowledged expert in several fields, particularly electricity and magnetism. However, the attitude of his physics department colleagues toward his radio work could best be described as indifferent, particularly in later years. Although the senior members of the department respected Terry's ability as a physicist, they regarded his wireless work as taking him more in the direction of applied science or engineering rather than pure research, which was their preferred focus. Some went so far as to dismiss wireless as a mere plaything. Younger staff members in the department were not as critical of Terry, but self-interest kept them from displaying much enthusiasm for his activities with wireless.[4] The prevailing attitude meant that Terry's wireless operation could not be at the expense of the department's other laboratory activities, and Terry and his students assembled much of the early wireless equipment from

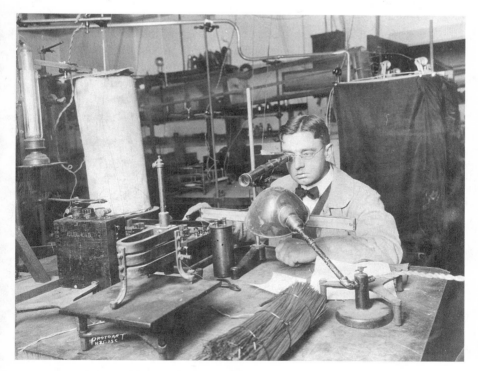

The founding father, Earle M. Terry, professor of physics at the University of Wisconsin Terry was a graduate student in Madison from 1902 to 1910 and taught in the physics department from 1910 until his death in 1929. He founded the university's radio operation and nurtured it through the 1920s. (University of Wisconsin Archives series 3/1, negative 48447-C)

ordinary material in the laboratory and whatever they could scrounge. Terry's former students remembered him as an unpretentious and modest person who did not tell his students of his own successes. They also remarked on his skill as a teacher and his wry sense of humor. He seems to have been a favorite of his students'.

During the spring of 1915 the wider university community was introduced to the technology of wireless telegraphy. The university exposition was held that March, and Commendant P. G. Wrightson of the University Cadet Corps arranged for the display of a temporary wireless transmitter and receiver. It was used to demonstrate long-distance reception and "every visitor to the Exposition will have an opportunity to send a wireless telegram to any station within 500 miles." An article in the *Press Bulletin* said, "The antennae wires which will pick up and transmit the messages will be four in number and will be swung from the flagstaff of the YMCA Building to the flagstaff of the University gymnasium. After these antennae wires pick up the disturbances in the aerial medium, the messages will be transported into the University gymnasium and recorded in the Electrical Engineering exhibit."

The original wireless equipment was assembled by the physics department in the basement of Science Hall in what is now room 55; this would be the

Display of wireless telegraphy at the University of Wisconsin
The electrical engineering exhibit at the University Exposition in March 1915 featured this demonstration of wireless telegraphy. (University of Wisconsin Archives series 11/3, negative M74)

home of 9XM until 1918. The antenna was a wire strung from the tower of the building to the chimney of the adjacent Mining and Metallurgy Laboratory building, which had once been the university's heating plant.

The transmitter had a power of 5,000 watts and transmitted wireless telegraphic signals at 475 and 750 meters (631 kHz and 400 kHz). Terry built the station with the assistance of students Carl Kottler, a former commercial wireless operator, and Malcolm Hanson. The equipment was operating as early as the spring of 1915, but the public did not become aware of it until the fall. A November 3 *Press Bulletin* article described the apparatus and said that it was receiving signals from as far away as the Arlington Naval Station in Virginia. The powerful Arlington station had been on the air since 1912 and operated at 2,500 meters (120 kHz) with the call letters NAA. One regular midday transmission from Arlington was a signal that provided a standard time reference. The original function of these telegraphic time signals (for five minutes at 10:55 a.m. Central Time) was to synchronize clocks aboard ocean vessels for navigation purposes. Various navy facilities had sent the time signals since

Earle M. Terry at early 9XM apparatus (University of Wisconsin Archives series 3/1, negative 8245-C-1)

1905, and they were popular among wireless enthusiasts. Also, these transmissions had led to the development of a nonhobbyist market for wireless receivers. Equipment manufacturers were marketing simple receivers to jewelers so they could use these signals to offer the exact time when setting the clocks and watches of their customers.

Terry had a personal reason to tune in to the signals: his hobby was building precision grandfather clocks. Always the scientist, part of Terry's interest was in making the timepieces as accurate as possible, even going so far as to account for the effect that changes in temperature would have on the pendulum. To check the quality of his work, he would use the 9XM equipment to receive the daily wireless time signals.[5]

The day-to-day operation of the station was the responsibility of a half-dozen physics and engineering students who came to be known around campus as the "wireless squad." They were avid wireless enthusiasts, and most ended up with careers in communications or electronics. The squad worked mostly in the evening and overnight hours because the noise from the equipment interfered with other teaching and scientific activities in the building.[6] At this time, 9XM was using a rotary spark gap transmitter, which generated electromagnetic waves by interrupting a current flow in a wire. This apparatus had a motor-driven disk with electrodes around its edge. Sparks were generated between fixed electrodes and the electrodes on the disk and the speed of the motor controlled the wavelength of the transmission. This type of transmitter was known for producing a deafening sound and dangerous voltages.

Through this early period the 9XM transmitter was used solely for point-to-point messages and only in the dots and dashes of wireless telegraphy. On December 30, 1915, Arthur Ford, a professor in the electrical engineering department at the State University of Iowa at Iowa City, sent a letter to the University of Wisconsin. Ford wanted to use his university's wireless station, 9YA, and Wisconsin's 9XM to report the results of an upcoming basketball game between the two schools scheduled for January 10, 1916. However, the plan was not for play-by-play nor for "broadcast" to a general audience. Instead, wireless operators at each campus would take turns sending telegraphic messages to each other until the final result of the game was in. Operators at the Iowa station planned to "call" Madison for five minutes at 8:25 p.m., 8:35 p.m., and 8:45 p.m. at 750 meters (400 kHz), with 9XM operators calling the Iowa station for five minutes at 8:30 p.m., 8:40 p.m., and 8:50 p.m. at 2,000 meters (150 kHz).[7] Of course, a postgame telephone call from Iowa City to Madison could have provided the score as well.

∽

CHAPTER 2

Early Broadcasts from 9XM

1916–17

You can't tell how many are listening.

As experimentation with wireless telegraphy continued, two views emerged as to how the technology could be used. The majority opinion, held by industry and the government, was that it would be useful only for point-to-point, private communications. Business people and government officials envisioned its use for the military, maritime applications, and in other instances where wired communication was impractical, such as to and from moving trains. However, early private wireless transmissions were, of course, heard by others. Part of the fun for amateur wireless enthusiasts was listening in to the Morse code messages sent from point to point. This led some to believe that the true value of wireless telegraphy was to use this eavesdropping phenomenon to efficiently send a single message to many people at once. The student operators at 9XM occasionally experimented with this concept when they were testing the equipment. As part of some point-to-point transmissions, they would ask anyone who heard the message to respond. In addition to providing valuable information about the performance of the transmitter, the number of responses suggested that many amateurs were listening in. This helped reinforce the notion that wireless could indeed be used for broadcasting a message. The term *broadcasting* predates wireless and had been appropriated from agriculture, where it meant a scattering of seeds—casting them over a broad area. The navy had begun using the term around 1912 to describe telegraphic messages meant for all ships or for anyone listening; previously, they had used the term *radiating*.[1] Some experiments with wireless telegraphic "broadcasts" had already been attempted. The *New York Herald* was sending out telegraphic "newscasts" for reception by wireless enthusiasts as early as 1915.

Some foreign wireless operations had been thinking along the same lines. During World War I the German government used wireless for what some claim were the first propaganda broadcasts. From powerful transmitters in Nauen, Eilvese, and Norddeich, the German government offered special telegraphic newscasts several times a day, fully expecting that radio hobbyists in the United States and other neutral countries would hear them.[2] On March 3, 1916, 9XM received "war news from Berlin."[3] Student Carl Kottler was at the 9XM apparatus when he listened in to a message as it was being sent from Eilvese to Tuckerton, New Jersey.[4] Another example of the potential for broadcasting came on June 18, when a commercial wireless station in Milwaukee sent a general message: "Serious trouble on border. Wisconsin National Guard ordered to mobilize and be in readiness for instant service." At 9XM Malcolm Hanson of the student wireless squad happened to be monitoring the airwaves when the message came in late in the evening.[5] Hanson kept odd hours at the station, and Terry had entrusted him with a key to the room.[6]

In the fall of 1916 Terry decided to rebuild the station to use a different wavelength. The 9XM transmitter had been operating regularly at 900 meters (333 kHz) but was encountering interference from a commercial wireless station in Milwaukee. The rebuilt equipment would allow transmissions at 1,700 meters (176 kHz), and it was ready for operation by mid-November.[7]

Because the equipment had been modified, the station had to get a new license. However, because the university itself now held the license for 9XM, the relicensing had to go through the office of the university president, Charles Van Hise, who contacted Benjamin W. Snow, chair of the physics department, for information. Snow referred Van Hise to Terry, adding that "the establishment and installation of our wireless station are due entirely to Terry's initiative and interest, and I am certain that he can give you, much better than I, the information you desire." Snow even invited Van Hise to drop by Science Hall to get a demonstration of the 9XM equipment. He wrote: "I hope you may be able to come down some afternoon and see what [Terry] has done, and have him explain to you, as he has many times to me, the mechanisms by which the marvelous achievement of wireless transmission is made possible."[8] After meeting with Terry, Van Hise gave his approval for the application. The new license was issued in December and continued to use the 9XM designation.

Terry had wanted to operate the new transmitter on a regular schedule to provide some material that would be of use to the general public. He decided the weather forecast would be easy to obtain and would have value to many listeners, especially the state's farmers. Several farmers who had wireless receivers had already contacted Terry to say they'd heard an experimental transmission he had made from 9XM to the wireless operation at the University of North Dakota.[9] The *Wisconsin State Journal* of March 6, in the article that told of receiving the war news from Europe, also mentioned Terry's interest in building a wireless operation for weather "broadcasts."

By this time others had begun experimenting with sending out weather information by wireless telegraphy. As early as 1900 the U.S. Weather Bureau (then a division of the Department of Agriculture) had been interested in the possibility of using wireless for collecting meteorological data as well for as transmitting weather warnings and forecasts. The agency hired wireless pioneer Reginald Fessenden to conduct wireless experiments. Wireless telegraphy of weather information began July 15, 1913, when the naval wireless stations at Arlington,

A member of the wireless squad at work University of Wisconsin student wireless operator Gustav Blomquist, class of 1918, at the 9XM equipment in Science Hall, 1916. (University of Wisconsin Archives series 23/24/1)

Virginia, and Key West, Florida, started their regular telegraphic broadcasts. On June 1, 1914, the Arlington station added material for the Great Lakes during the lake navigation season, and in April 1917 this forecast was transferred to the radio facility at the Great Lakes Naval Station north of Chicago.[10]

Some university-based wireless operators were transmitting Morse code versions of the weather forecast as well. In January 1914 the University of North Dakota had begun wireless telegraphic weather reports from their station 9YN (later 9XN), an operation under the supervision of former University of Wisconsin physicist A. Hoyt Taylor. The station had made arrangements with nine amateurs in the state who agreed to distribute the weather information in their areas, although it could of course be heard by anyone with receiving equipment.[11] Also in 1914 Nebraska Wesleyan University's station, 9YD, began a daily transmission of weather and news by wireless telegraph.[12] By 1916 the University of Nebraska was offering regular wireless telegraphic transmissions of weather forecasts, farm market information, and road condition reports from its station, which would later operate with the call letters 9YY.[13]

Another factor in the decision to transmit the weather forecast was enthusiastic support for the idea from the Madison office of the U.S. Weather Bureau. Since 1908 the bureau's local meteorologist had been Eric R. Miller, one of Terry's former students. Miller had a keen interest in the potential for wireless and requested approval for the broadcasts from his superiors in Washington. As early as September 1915 Miller was writing to Washington, telling officials there that the new university wireless station would be put at the disposal of the weather bureau for broadcast of the weather forecast. However, he warned that the agency would have to pay for the cost of the operator, since the university at the time had no staff member assigned on a regular basis.[14] Officials at the weather bureau initially rejected the proposal but approved it the following year, once 9XM had student operators available and there would be no charge to the agency. Miller's involvement in the project went beyond his meteorological duties: he was the force behind publicizing the first broadcasts. His efforts paid off: a short item announcing the beginning of telegraphic weather broadcasts made the front page of Madison's *Wisconsin State Journal* on December 1, 1916.

The first telegraphic broadcast of weather information over 9XM came at 11 a.m. on Monday, December 4, 1916. This date can legitimately be cited as the first regular broadcast by the station that would one day become WHA. Wisely, it was decided to schedule this program at a time when many amateurs would be tuned in: "Immediately after the sending of the time signals by the Naval Wireless Station at Arlington at 11 a.m. each day, except Sunday."[15]

Eric Miller, chief of the Madison weather bureau, 1908–44
Miller's enthusiasm for broadcasting the weather by wireless
telegraphy helped make a name for 9XM in its earliest days. This
photo was taken around 1938, the year that Miller's office in North
Hall was equipped with a microphone and line to the radio station,
which by then was WHA. This allowed Miller to announce the
forecast himself; he was probably the second radio weatherman in
the United States. (University of Wisconsin Archives series 23/24/1,
negative 15872-C)

The 9XM transmitter used its new wavelength, 1,700 meters (176 kHz), for the weather transmission. The wording of an item in the *Wisconsin State Journal* of December 1 showed how unfamiliar nonenthusiasts were with the jargon of wireless. It said: "If other stations tune the machines to this strength, it will be possible for them to hear the report." The telegraphic weather message included the forecast received from the Chicago weather bureau office and the temperature changes predicted for the next thirty-six hours. The *Press Bulletin* of December 16 said: "The strength of the sending apparatus is such that the messages may be picked up in the most remote part of the state" and quoted Terry, who said that "an amateur anywhere in the state would be able to get these forecasts very easily." The article also said that the simple equipment required to receive the information would cost no more than ten dollars, and, according to Terry, "very much less if the amateur constructed part of it himself."

The new service rated a puzzling mention in the *New York Times,* which carried a short item with a Chicago dateline. It read: "State officials of Wisconsin have sent out a proposal that every farmer in Wisconsin shall install wireless telegraph apparatus to receive weather reports from the University of Wisconsin. The service will be free."[16] No record has been found for an official state mandate of this kind.

After a couple of weeks of successful broadcasts, Miller sent a letter to the weather bureau office in Milwaukee, reporting the date of the first broadcast and the potential size of the audience for the service. He said a Department of Commerce directory listed about five hundred wireless receiving "stations" in Wisconsin, and he noted that all were "possible recipients" of the forecast. In his December 16 letter to the *Milwaukee Journal,* he described the nature of wireless telegraphy as akin to a rural telephone system in that "you can't tell how many are listening, only more so, since there is no chorus of clicks when receivers are put up. The only way that we can find out is to ask recipients to write and tell us." He reported that Terry had already received unsolicited letters from amateurs in the Wisconsin communities of Mount Horeb, Racine, and Wausau. They reported that the 9XM weather transmissions were "coming in strong." Miller continued his efforts to publicize the service, keeping the staff of the *Press Bulletin* apprised so the writers could provide updates and releases to newspapers and to various magazines catering to the growing ranks of wireless hobbyists. He hoped that a substantial audience would develop for the 9XM wireless weather reports. (Some records of the weather bureau incorrectly report that these telegraphic forecasts from 9XM began on October 1, 1916; it could be that this earlier date was when Miller's request for the broadcasts was officially granted.)[17]

Staff members at 9XM were not content to simply send out their regular weather message and hope for gradual growth in the number of listeners. Instead, they actively sought to manufacture an audience for their service by making it possible for more people to acquire receiving equipment. Shortly after the telegraphic weather broadcasts began, a notice in the *Press Bulletin* of December 12 told readers that university physics personnel would assist beginners who wanted to build a receiving set. Before the end of the year, they had mailed out instructions and diagrams in response to the first of what would soon become a flood of requests.

The weather broadcasts continued for about three weeks, until a broken condenser took the transmitter off the air until mid-January 1917. By January 31 the *Press Bulletin* was reporting that 9XM was being received clearly at various points in the East, including Trenton, New Jersey, and Albany, New York. The report claimed that 9XM had the strongest sending apparatus of any experimental station in the Midwest, adding that an all-night test was planned for the first week of February between 9XM and stations in Chicago and North Dakota to further test the signal strength.

On February 17, 1917, 9XM operators attempted the telegraphic broadcast of a college basketball game between the University of Wisconsin and Ohio State. The broadcast included not only what today would be called play-by-play action but also a summary of the contest written by a reporter from the university's student newspaper, the *Daily Cardinal*. The summary was transmitted telegraphically five minutes after the conclusion of the game, sort of an early version of a postgame show. The *Daily Cardinal's* February 19 story about the broadcast reported that the wireless reports of the game "were received by Buckeye fans as fast as the plays were made" and said the experimental broadcast was so successful "that other games will doubtless be reported in the same manner." It is not clear from the accounts whether the wireless operator was physically at the game. It is more likely that the plays were telephoned to Science Hall or that relays of student runners were used as the University Armory gymnasium was only a block from the Science Hall home of 9XM (Wisconsin won the contest, 40 to 15). The *Daily Cardinal* was cooperating with the wireless operation in other ways as well. By early April it had begun a telegraphic news exchange service with a few other colleges over 9XM.[18]

Experimentation in broadcasting sound rather than code continued, and the first non-telegraphic transmission was made sometime in the first three months of 1917. Shortly after putting his original 1915 transmitter into service, Terry grasped the limitations of the spark gap technology and began experimentation with the three-element vacuum tube. Tubes designed and built by

Terry were tested in the transmitter during the 1916–17 school year and were likely used for these first telephonic transmissions.[19] During this period Terry invited some guests to his home for what he termed the "first broadcast," a special transmission during which phonograph records would be played over the air. Terry gathered his guests around the receiving equipment in his home and then phoned student operator Malcolm Hanson at Science Hall to begin the broadcast. To Terry's disappointment his guests (including other professors and some university deans) were unimpressed with the stunt. One person at the gathering recalled years later that the first piece of music played was "Narcissus."[20] This was a popular piano tune written by Ethelbert Nevin and may have been selected because listeners would have recognized it immediately. Hanson's involvement means that the broadcast occurred before March 21, 1917, the day he left Madison for service in the navy.[21]

John S. Penn, who was researching the station's history in the 1950s, believed this particular broadcast was probably not truly the first, because Terry would not have attempted such a public demonstration without first making successful test transmissions.[22] Indeed, an amateur in Madison recalled tuning in for the Arlington time signals in early 1917 and being surprised to hear music over 9XM. His puzzlement that there had been no prior announcement of the broadcast is evidence that it was an experiment.[23] These unscheduled music broadcasts happened from time to time over some wireless stations. Back in November 1913 Arlington station NAA had also surprised listeners with a music transmission.[24] Local legend has it that the University of Wisconsin band performed the school song "On Wisconsin" over the air on 9XM during this period,[25] but there is no documentary evidence for this, nor is it likely that the band members could have squeezed themselves into the wireless room in the basement of Science Hall. However, a recording of the song might have aired, or perhaps the band members assembled themselves behind the building, and the 9XM operator just opened the window and positioned a microphone near it.

Others around the country were experimenting with telephonic broadcasts, and sometimes they asked the 9XM staff for help. In early March 1917 Chicago entrepreneur Austin Howard wrote to Terry at the suggestion of A. Hoyt Taylor. Howard was a dealer in wireless equipment made by de Forest. As an adjunct to his business, Howard had set up a transmitter and in the past month had received an experimental license for it with the call sign 9XG.[26] Howard asked Terry to try to pick up 9XG on the evening of March 9. Howard planned an evening of telephonic broadcasts at 800 meters (375 kHz) featuring Victrola music, voice, and continuous wave telegraph signals. Howard wanted Terry's opinion about the quality of the transmission. He thought Terry would have no problem receiving the station, although Howard said he had thus far not had any reception reports from more than ninety miles away.[27]

Further advances in wireless telegraphy and wireless telephony seemed imminent but the United States would soon enter the war in Europe. The conflict would temporarily suspend wireless research at most universities and the activities of amateurs as well. However, the 9XM wireless operation at the University of Wisconsin was granted special permission from the government to remain in operation. The result was that research into wireless moved forward at Wisconsin, while amateurs, most of the industry, and nearly all other universities were silenced for the duration of the war.

CHAPTER 3

❧

Wartime Radio Experiments at the University of Wisconsin

1917–18

You will immediately dismantle all aerial wires and radio apparatus, both sending and receiving.

With the entry of the United States into World War I, President Woodrow Wilson issued an executive order shutting down all wireless stations in the country, including radio receiving sets. The fear was that the long-distance capability of wireless telegraphy could result in Germany gaining some vital information by monitoring U.S. wireless traffic. This was a genuine concern: in 1915 a wireless hobbyist in New Jersey named Charles Apgar heard curious wireless messages being sent from a German-owned station at Sayville, Long Island, to station POZ at Nauen, Germany, near Berlin. The messages were odd, such as "ship 300,000 shovels express C.O.D.," "Myra has dyptheria," or "send always invoice before shipping knives." Apgar, who was also a Marconi employee, thought this suspicious and connected an Edison Dictaphone to his receiving set to make cylinder recordings of the wireless traffic from Sayville. He took the recordings to the local radio inspector, who in turn informed the Secret Service. An investigation revealed that the transmissions contained coded espionage messages. The result was a suit against the German wireless company charging it with violating the neutrality of the United States. Ultimately, the Sayville station was taken over by the U.S. government.[1] (Apgar also used his rudimentary set-up to record some 1915 telegraphic "newscasts" from the *New York Herald;* some copies of these recordings survive in the hands of collectors.)[2]

In the Midwest the order to shut down wireless operations was dated April 7, 1917, and came from J. F. Dillon, the U.S. radio inspector with the Department of Commerce's Navigation Service at Chicago. The *Wisconsin State Journal* of April 10 said copies of the order were received in Madison that day by George Crownhart, an amateur wireless operator and a former second lieutenant in

22

the University Signal Corps. He was supposed to forward the copies to other wireless operators in the area. The article said the stations in the Madison area to be dismantled included "those at the university and high school and ten or twelve others."

The specific and ominous wording of the order: "In accordance with the order of the President of the United States . . . , promulgated in a letter of instructions from the Commandant of the Great Lakes Naval District, you will immediately dismantle all aerial wires and radio apparatus, both sending and receiving, and place the same out of commission until further notice. . . . Also, please notify all other stations with which you are in communication as the purport of this order, and use your best endeavor to have them comply with same. In any case, the dismantling of the station must be completed within forty-eight hours after the receipt of this notice. This measure is considered necessary for the defense of the country, and the Navy Department has ample authority to deal with any case of failure to comply according to military procedures. Please acknowledge receipt, and report your action in the premises."[3]

In response the 9XM staff began disassembling the station's equipment. Most other early university stations were forced to do the same, but some were allowed to remain in operation for such military purposes as training radio operators and engineers. Station 3XJ at St. Joseph's College in Philadelphia was briefly allowed to operate as a receiving-only station to monitor the airwaves for espionage transmissions and for copying messages from German stations. The station was shut down once this activity was transferred to the radio operation at the Philadelphia Navy Yard.[4]

9XM was one of the few private (nongovernment) stations granted permission to resume operation during the ban, largely through Terry's lobbying efforts. After the wireless ban was announced, he had contacted several officials to get special approval for 9XM to resume operation. On April 21 he wrote to Dillon in Chicago. Terry said that one ongoing activity at the Madison radio operation was experimental work in developing a "sight receiving apparatus for aeroplanes." He had been trying to find a way to convert sound waves into visual images in order to send telegraphic messages to airplane pilots. The idea was that pilots would see a wireless message as light flashes rather than hear it as dots and dashes—which was important because early aircraft were so noisy that even loud telegraphic signals could not be heard.[5] Clearly, this research required some sort of radio transmitter in operation. Dillon replied that he did not have the authority for the "installation of stations," but would forward the information to the Commissioner of Navigation with a recommendation that it be sent on to the appropriate department for authorization. Dillon's response was encouraging, and he ended the letter by saying: "I sincerely trust that the permission will be granted, as a sight receiver would undoubtedly be of great value in the aeronautical radio service."[6]

Terry also contacted his long-time colleague A. Hoyt Taylor. Taylor had just left his teaching post at the University of North Dakota to join the navy and was now stationed at the Great Lakes Naval Station in Illinois as the district communication superintendent. Terry proposed that 9XM resume its experimental work and said he believed that the station could be of service to the country by working with the navy to provide communications between the Wisconsin campus and the Great Lakes station. Taylor found the idea acceptable, forwarded his recommendation to his superiors in Washington, and the idea was approved. Whether the experiments with light-receiving apparatus for airplanes influenced the government's decision is not known.

On May 8, 1917, Taylor wrote to Van Hise, authorizing Wisconsin to put its radio apparatus back into operation for both sending and receiving. The order said the transmitter output was not to exceed 2 kilowatts, a tremendous amount of power for the era. There were two conditions: transmissions from Wisconsin could be interrupted at any time if "naval work in the vicinity of Great Lakes requires such action," and Van Hise, as president of the university, had to assume full responsibility for use of the station's antenna.[7] Van Hise responded the next day, agreeing to the conditions.[8]

Terry's public explanation for 9XM's being returned to operation was that it had to work on "a special war problem," the *Daily Cardinal* reported on May 10. Moreover, the navy said it would provide money for equipment. Terry undoubtedly welcomed this news, given the shoestring nature of his wireless operation in the previous years. The exact focus of the 9XM research was not disclosed until after the war, when it was revealed that the experiments tested radio reception by submerged submarines. Telegraphic and telephonic transmissions from Madison were received using a submerged antenna at the Great Lakes station.[9]

Taylor's wireless operation at North Dakota did not fare as well. The government ban, as well as Taylor's navy service, meant the suspension of wireless activities at the Grand Forks campus, which did not have a voice broadcast station until August 1923.[10] Taylor never returned to the academic world and remained in the navy until his retirement.

With permission to operate in hand, Terry and his students had the station reassembled and ready for use by May 16. Their speed was all the more remarkable because four of the six members of the wireless squad had left campus for the navy. Malcolm Hanson and William T. Lewis were posted almost immediately to the government wireless station at Mackinac Island, Michigan, while Charles T. Schrage and Richard J. Oetjen were sent to the Great Lakes Naval Station, according to the *Press Bulletin* of May 23. These four young men received minimal naval training, probably because of Taylor's interest in starting wireless experiments as soon as possible. Hanson received the *Daily Cardinal* by mail at Mackinac Island and read with interest that Terry was back in business. Hanson wrote to his mother about the Wisconsin wireless operation, saying, "They are really the only private station in the whole country now, and it will be wonderful to hear our station again, even though we are far away."[11] While stationed at the remote outpost, Hanson and Lewis adopted two stray dogs: they named them Radio and Sparks.[12]

From his experience as an amateur and with the homemade equipment at the University of Wisconsin, Hanson had developed a knack for getting the most out of wireless apparatus. By August 1917 long-distance tests showed that he had made the Mackinac Island station the most efficient such facility on the Great Lakes. His superiors were so impressed that they were considering putting him in charge of building another station in the Great Lakes region.[13] By the autumn Hanson was told he was in line for a promotion, perhaps to be assigned to teach wireless courses for the navy at Harvard University.[14] He never did get to Harvard, but he was put in charge of a new naval wireless operation at Manistique on Michigan's Upper Peninsula. Several other Wisconsin wireless operators enlisted in 1918 and were stationed at Great Lakes. The result was that government radio operations at Madison, Great Lakes, Mackinac Island, and Manistique all were staffed by operators trained at the University of Wisconsin by Terry.[15]

A device for the detection of submarines was another wartime development that Terry was involved with. Fellow Wisconsin physicists J. R. Roebuck and Max Mason also worked on the project, which used Terry's research and a submarine detection device that he had designed. The navy called their device the "MV tube."[16] Shortly before the armistice the navy pronounced the program a success, and the *Daily Cardinal* reported on October 2, 1918, that "every submarine chaser, every transport and every destroyer is now equipped with the Wisconsin device for detection." The value of the device was that it filtered out the sounds of the ship on which it was mounted. For his contribution to the project Terry received a letter of appreciation from Franklin D. Roosevelt, acting secretary of the navy.[17]

While the work with the navy was getting underway in late 1917, the University of Wisconsin received a request from the U.S. Army Signal Corps to establish an experimental radio station on the campus. Once again a prewar academic connection was a factor: the request came from Charles Culver, the Beloit College physics professor who was now a U.S. Army captain in the Office of the Chief Signal Officer. The signal corps planned to establish "a series of important special radio stations at various points throughout the United States," including the Madison campus. The signal corps would provide standard apparatus so that it had comparable data from the stations. The corps wanted the university to provide a room for the project, four radio operators capable of receiving code transmissions at twenty words per minute, and a faculty member to "assume general supervision and operation of the station." Four operators also meant that the station could be on the air around the clock.[18]

Physics department chair Benjamin Snow consulted with Terry and asked whether the signal corps project could be coordinated with the ongoing work for the navy. Terry felt the two projects were compatible, could be done simultaneously with existing equipment, and would require only limited additional staffing. Snow informed Van Hise that the department would take on the project and, moreover, would assign it a room especially designed for radio work in the basement of the new physics building. The building, then nearing completion, would be named Sterling Hall. (After the war the basement room would be the home of 9XM and WHA for six years.) The university appropriated $1,200 to pay the four operators, the first specific appropriation by the university's Board of Regents for any sort of radio operation.[19]

Although the signal corps project originally called for just the reception of wireless messages, the Wisconsin transmitter was soon being used for testing transmissions over long distances. Terry had continued his research into the use of vacuum tubes and had a new tube transmitter in operation by the fall of 1917.[20] One student operator during the period recalled that a signal corps officer would be at a station in a nearby state and would try to pick up the signal from Madison; then the officer would contact Terry with a report about the quality of the signal. Terry would then adjust or modify the transmitter or antenna to improve the range or clarity of the transmission. The tests were at preset times, lasted thirty minutes, and used telegraphic keying as well as some voice transmissions.[21] Although the purpose for the exercise was not revealed, it is believed to have been related to the use of radiotelephone service to communicate with aircraft.[22]

While serving with the navy Hanson reported hearing about several telephonic broadcasts from the University of Wisconsin station. There is evidence that telegraphy was used to identify the music broadcasts and help those monitoring the transmission find the weaker telephonic signals.[23]

Another war-related wireless activity at the University of Wisconsin was training operators for the signal corps. On August 8, 1917, Van Hise wrote to Snow with a proposal that had come from Lieutenant Colonel L. D. Wildman of the signal corps. Wildman had asked that the university open its courses in telegraphy to any nonstudent who wished to enroll. Van Hise wanted Snow to consider the matter and report to him on its feasibility, so the regents could respond to the offer.[24]

It was a year before the training of radio operators began. Terry did teach a small course in wireless for university credit during the fall semester in 1917. In early 1918 Van Hise chose Terry to represent the university at conference in Washington, D.C., called by the signal corps to discuss the training of wireless personnel. The army needed radio operators who were also technicians, and Terry began making arrangements to provide an appropriate course through the university's physics department.[25] On October 18, 1918, the *Daily Cardinal* reported that more than 450 men would be sent to the Madison campus for radio training.

In the early weeks of 1918 9XM had moved its operation to the new physics building. For several months during the transition period wireless operations were carried on simultaneously from the old location in Science Hall and the new station in the physics building. This allowed the navy experiments to continue without interruption and made it possible to send messages, some telephonic, between the two wireless operations on campus. One physics student of the era recalled that she had broadcast from Science Hall to the new physics building, and another remembered "the thrill we had when we took the instruments over the 'hill' and listened to the 'phonograph' in the Physics Building over the 'wireless.'"[26]

The new antenna was made up of wires strung from a thirty-foot steel pipe on the roof of the physics building to a similar mast uphill from the station behind the university's Main Hall, now called Bascom Hall. Terry told the *Daily Cardinal* of January 10, 1918, that this three-hundred-foot antenna would have a range of fifteen hundred miles for sending and four thousand miles for receiving. As the experiments continued and new equipment was tried out, it frequently became necessary to change the configuration of the antenna. Some antenna installations were wires strung between the two wings of the building.[27]

In late May 1918 Terry received a letter from Culver, the former Beloit professor. Culver was still in the army at the War Department in Washington and had been promoted to major. Culver's "personal and unofficial" request was that Terry consider joining government service in Washington at once. Culver said that Terry would be in charge of the "research work on anti-static devices and agencies, and special long-distance tests." He added that Terry could enter the service as a civilian employee at a salary comparable to his university pay and after two or three months would be recommended for a commission as a captain.[28] Terry declined and remained a university-based researcher and educator. In some postwar correspondence with Culver, Terry lamented that private industry was luring so many of their colleagues away from their universities and said he occasionally "felt the pull" as well.[29] A. Hoyt Taylor also tried to recruit Terry, to work at the U.S. Naval Research Laboratory at Anacostia near Washington, D.C.[30] A former student recalled that RCA of Canada offered Terry a position with a yearly salary of $25,000, but Terry chose to remain in Madison for one-fifth that amount. Terry told the student that he liked the setup at Wisconsin and, besides, "a man can live on $5,000."[31]

The Army Signal Corps work in 1918 increasingly used wireless telephony as the equipment improved. The army may have decided on this course once it saw how advanced the university's operation was. Frederick W. Nolte, one of the operators during this period, recalled that most of the work was done during daylight hours on an irregular schedule, at times designated by the army. "We used to play records, frequently repeating our station call letters and counting," he said.[32] This format suggests that the experiments were designed to test clarity of the signal and that some successful voice transmissions were made before the armistice in 1918.

CHAPTER 4

Telephonic Broadcasting by 9XM

1919–20

The first clear speech was transmitted last week.

After World War I ended on November 11, 1918, work at the Wisconsin radio operation continued, benefiting from the research performed during the conflict. However, the general ban on civilian wireless activity remained in effect for six months, keeping everyone not previously affiliated with government projects off the air. This brief period afforded the University of Wisconsin wireless operators the luxury of experimenting with their equipment without the limitations imposed by military projects. The university's role in wartime experiments paid off: government stations familiar with the Wisconsin operation were willing to help it with tests. The end of the war also increased the inventory of radio equipment at the Madison campus. The military deemed much of the navy and army gear on campus to be surplus and the physics department acquired it at low cost.

Many WHA references and historical works list February 1919 as the beginning of regular voice broadcasts: all refer to an article in the *Press Bulletin* of March 5, 1919, which reported the first clear voice transmission the previous month. The article stated that "wireless telephonic communication with Great Lakes Naval Training Station is now carried on by the University of Wisconsin wireless station after some months of experimentation. The first clear speech was transmitted last week."[1] Further evidence is provided by a letter from R. D. McPherson of the U.S. Naval Communication Service in which he relates the success of a test transmission between Madison and the Great Lakes Naval Station on February 17, 1919: "Audibility on Radio Phone 800—Voice Clearer and generator noises less than during previous tests."[2] Tests on voice transmissions had been underway since the previous year, but for whatever reason Terry had not felt comfortable with releasing the information to the public. However, this could hardly be termed a broadcast because it was point-to-point communication, nor is it known if it could be considered regular. Moreover, civilians were not supposed to be using receivers at this time, so the only people in the United States who could legally hear these voice messages were government operators.

The government lifted its ban on operating a personal wireless receiver on April 15, 1919. Now 9XM could direct its experimental telephonic broadcasts to a wider audience of local amateurs, who were finally allowed to reassemble their receiving equipment. Experimentation continued as well. Terry enlisted the help of Charles Culver, who was back at his prewar post in the physics department at Beloit College, about forty-five miles from Madison. Terry was looking forward to the collaboration. In a letter of March 25, 1919, Terry told him, "We are still working on radio telephony problems and would appreciate it very much if you would test out with us occasionally. Some time ago, I obtained permission to test with the Great Lakes station and we have availed ourselves of the privilege several times. However, I realize that they are very busy and I would like to test much oftener and for longer than we have done so far."[3] Culver agreed to help. Once his wireless equipment was in place, he would listen to various test broadcasts from 9XM and offer his opinion to Terry. After one such test on June 4, 1919, Culver reported that 9XM's telegraphic wave came through strongly and was "entirely commercial"—comparable to the quality of the signal put out by a commercial wireless station. However, Culver said that while the wave of the telephonic broadcast was strong, the speech "was not at all satisfactory," and the test was "not nearly as satisfactory as the one we made last fall." This is further evidence that some successful telephonic experiments were carried out in late 1918, perhaps after the armistice. Culver also asked Terry to have the 9XM operator send the telegraphic message more slowly, as "my speed of reception is limited."[4]

9XM inadvertently benefited from a new federal requirement forcing all wireless transmissions onto two frequencies. With the lifting of the wireless ban, the Department of Commerce had designated 485 meters (618 kHz) for all government broadcasting and 360 meters (833 kHz) for all private broadcasting. The decision shows that the federal government thought the future of wireless was for point-to-point communication rather than broadcasting. Having only two frequencies available for the entire country would not allow multiple stations to operate simultaneously in the same area, nor would it allow listeners to tune in to distant stations. The good news for 9XM was that it could continue to use the frequencies assigned to it for military experiments and remain clear of the two new frequencies. 9XM continued to use 1,000 meters (300 kHz) for code and 1,300 meters (231 kHz) for voice. This helped 9XM develop a regular audience: wireless enthusiasts found they could receive the Wisconsin station clearly at great distances without the interference that affected transmissions on the two authorized frequencies.

Madison weather bureau chief Eric Miller was watching these advances with interest. He recognized that the technology of wireless telephony would solve the problem of getting timely weather information to farmers. Although the prewar telegraphic weather broadcasts on 9XM had worked as planned, their value was limited to those who understood Morse code, regardless of how slowly the message might be sent. In a May 1919 letter to the chief of the U.S. Weather Bureau in Washington, Miller outlined a plan that accurately predicted the concept of radio broadcasting. He wrote: "I am informed that any Bell telephone can be very cheaply converted into a receiving station for wireless telephone messages. The wireless station at the University of Wisconsin has already been converted to a sending station for wireless telephony, and has talked plainly to Chicago. Similar installations will doubtless be available in every state. Would it not be most advantageous to take this prblem [sic] up with the engineers of the American Telephone and Telegraph Company, with the object of inducing the commercial companies to provide for the broadcast distribution of weather information by wireless telephone?"[5]

Despite the limited successes, voice and music broadcasts remained an experimental and irregular feature of 9XM. Reception reports from amateurs tell of some telephonic transmissions during the summer of 1919.[6] Madison resident William Steuber recalled listening to 9XM voice broadcasts in 1919 at the home of a fellow eighth grader who had a wireless receiver.[7] (Decades later, several of Steuber's books were read over WHA on *Chapter a Day*). During the fall of 1919 the station presented experimental music transmissions during evening hours, and physics department faculty or students who could wield any kind of musical instrument would find themselves pressed into service. Former student Grover Greenslade recalled playing his harmonica over the air, as well as several occasions when Terry asked him to recite Lincoln's Gettysburg Address.[8] When the operators could find no live performer, they played phonograph records. These were supplied from the collection at Terry's home or purchased by him for the experiments. Accounts from this early period tell of persistent problems with distortion during 9XM music broadcasts. The recordings that seemed to transmit the clearest were those featuring Hawaiian guitar music, since the station "sounded sort of twangy anyway."[9] This wasn't the worst possible development, since Hawaiian music was enjoying fad status among the record-buying public during this era. On one occasion a recording of the school fight song "On Wisconsin" was transmitted repeatedly while Terry and his students were making equipment tests and adjustments. A listener who had grown weary of the monotonous broadcast contacted 9XM and offered to provide the station with a different record.[10]

There is also evidence that 9XM sent out both weather and farm market reports telegraphically during this time. One postwar member of the wireless squad recalled that Terry assigned him this task in the fall of 1919.[11] L. L. Nettleton said he "was one of those who had certain days to go into the station at the noon hour and pound out the market and weather reports by international code."[12] The addition of the market report is possible in that the Wisconsin Department of Markets started sending out a mimeographed market newsletter on a regular basis beginning on October 17, 1919.[13] Agriculture departments at colleges and universities were on the mailing list, so that may have been where the 9XM operators got their copy of the material, if not directly.

Years later another former student, C. M. Jansky Jr., said that a fairly regular schedule of voice weather broadcasts was in place on 9XM in the fall of 1919; although he said that these were well established by that time (perhaps as part of the evening music transmissions), no additional documentation has been found. He was certain of the year being 1919, because he left for a position at the University of Minnesota on January 1, 1920.[14]

More regular telephonic broadcasts from 9XM led to the identification of several problems. One was the need to move the microphone and announcer out of the noisy transmitter room. This had not been a problem for wireless telegraphy, but the station would have to address the idea of a "studio" for voice broadcasts. Another problem was ensuring the availability of program materials and performers on a regular basis. A third problem was finding a way to make radio receivers available to the general public, as commercial radio sets were still not available.

Terry wanted to move toward a formal schedule for 9XM again and decided to reinstitute the regular broadcast of weather information, this time including transmission by voice. Meteorologist Eric Miller again enthusiastically offered his assistance. To reach as many people as possible, Terry decided to provide the weather by both wireless telegraph and voice. By early 1920 the telephonic equipment was evidently ready to use, but the broadcast schedule was delayed because the telegraphic apparatus needed work.[15] Some research hints that this equipment had not been used much since the end of the wartime experiments with the navy. The Department of Commerce issued a new experimental license for 9XM on February 11, 1920.[16]

The telegraphic service continued at 1,000 meters (300 kHz), and the planned voice broadcasts were to continue using 1,300 meters (231 kHz).[17] The transmitting equipment was the same used for the experimental telephonic broadcasts of 1919. The telegraphic broadcast was scheduled between 9:50 and 10 a.m., transmitting the state weather forecast issued by the weather bureau each morning at 9:30 a.m. Weather bureau records show that this service was in operation by February 1, 1920.[18] The forecast covered a period of thirty-six hours, and in describing the service meteorologist Miller said the material "is often of critical importance to the farmer, as for instance in haying." He added: "It is sent very slowly so that beginners can copy it after very little experience." Miller said there was much more available to the wireless listener than just the weather from the Madison station, "for the air is full of wireless telegraphy, especially at night. The correct time is sent out twice a day from Arlington."[19]

It is not clear whether any regular voice broadcasts were made in the months before the university's summer vacation, perhaps because the equipment was not available. In a mid-May letter to his supervisors Eric Miller wrote: "Prof. Terry is planning to experiment with the sending of the forecast by wireless telephone, using a vacuum tube of his own invention, but up to this time, the necessary auxiliary apparatus has been needed for other purposes. Prof. Terry's vacuum tube has been successfully used in talking to Great Lakes, Ill., and when applied to the sending of the forecast should be audible in the apparatus ordinarily used by amateurs in wireless telegraphy, throughout the southern half of Wisconsin."[20]

Word of the experiments with voice was getting out. Miller got a letter from Lee Yorkson at the Civic and Commerce Association in Waupaca, Wisconsin, asking: "Has your wireless telephone worked out satisfactorily [sic] as yet? We are anxious to install a receiving set and receive the weather report by this method. Will you kindly advise us if you are now using the wireless telephone for sending out these reports, and what stations are receiving this service?"[21] Miller responded that they would have to wait: "All our vacuum tubes have so far failed to work. We are making three new ones and hope to get satisfactory results out of these."[22] Yorkson's organization would soon apply for a license for its own radio station, WIAA (which was never built), and would later play a role in lobbying the Wisconsin Department of Markets to establish its radio operation in Waupaca.

Terry decided to discontinue what little voice service 9XM was providing in order to concentrate on building a new higher-power transmitter. It would incorporate improvements he had achieved in the design of transmitter tubes.

Prewar "wireless squad" member Malcolm Hanson had returned to the university after his stint in the navy and enrolled as a student to continue his work toward his undergraduate degree. He arrived in late June 1920 and Terry asked him to help construct a permanent station for telephonic broadcasting.

Terry had always recognized Hanson's passion for wireless and realized that, with his three years of experience as a navy radio operator, he would now be even more useful to the Wisconsin operation. Hanson had also acquired something the previous summer that would make him especially valuable: a commercial first-grade radio operator's license.[23] Despite his years of experience, Terry had only an experimental operator's license. He managed to secure an appointment for Hanson as a student assistant, at the rather large sum of $500 for the

The 9XM staff
Student operator Malcolm Hanson (left) and physics professor Earle M. Terry were the key players in the operation of 9XM during the earliest years of voice broadcasts. This photo was taken outside Sterling Hall sometime in the early 1920s. It has been published before, but because the original was damaged, it has always been cropped. It is shown here in complete form. (University of Wisconsin Archives series 23/24/5)

1920–21 school year; his assigned duties were the operation of 9XM and building the new transmitter. Hanson's pay as a student assistant is the first salary item to appear in the physics department budget for the wireless operation.[24]

During the summer of 1920 meteorologist Eric Miller continued his efforts to make telephonic weather broadcasts a reality. He understood that radio receivers would have to be commercially available for the broadcasts to be of value. He wrote to Western Electric, trying to interest the firm in the idea of designing and building a simple receiver to market to farmers. He told of the tobacco industry in southern Wisconsin and how these growers needed immediate notice of frost when the crop was ripening. Miller mentioned not only the successful telegraphic weather transmissions from 9XM but also their limitations: "The service does not, however, reach those to whom it would be of most account, because they have not the skill to use wireless telegraphy." He recounted Terry's success in communicating with the Great Lakes Naval Training Station by wireless telephone and by using "one of his own bulbs," which Miller said "suggests the practicability of using wireless telephony for the dissemination of the weather predictions." He asked: "Will you kindly let me know what you think of this? Whether your company is in a position to develop a suitable receiving apparatus, and market it to farmers, is of course a critical consideration. If you could develop a fool-proof sending apparatus, with a radius of about fifty miles, and a receiving apparatus that would be within the means of the more prosperous farmer, I am sure that it would be of the greatest value all over the country, not only for the sending of wireless weather reports, but for the transmission of market reports and of news generally."[25] There is no record of the firm's response to Miller, who clearly saw the future possibilities for radio broadcasting. However, in later years Miller said he had no recollection of any discussions with Terry about radio's potential.[26]

Terry did have a vision of the potential for the new technology. At one point he was said to have made the bold prediction that one day radio receivers would be as common in Wisconsin homes as bathtubs.[27] A colleague, Professor J. R. Roebuck, said that Terry foresaw the great implications of radio in society. According to Roebuck, Terry also correctly predicted the difficulties that would arise when business interests understood the commercial possibilities of the new medium.[28]

When 9XM resumed operation after the university's summer break in 1920, it offered only the wireless telegraphic broadcasts, now at 10:30 a.m. and on the same 1,000-meter wavelength that the station had used earlier in the year. People were continuing to write in to ask when they could expect the telephonic broadcasts. Miller wrote to a listener that the "wireless phone is still in the experimental stage. It can be received, when in operation, with the ordinary set used for wireless telegraphy (head phone etc.)." He continued: "I will keep your letter on file and will let you know when we are ready to begin sending by wireless phone and the wave length that will be used."[29]

In the summer and fall of 1920 other pioneer stations were making their first regular telephonic broadcasts. On August 20 Detroit amateur station 8MK made its first broadcast, which featured recorded music. (*Detroit News*–owned WWJ traces its ancestry to this broadcast.) On November 2 Westinghouse-owned KDKA in East Pittsburgh debuted its regular broadcast schedule with the results of the Harding-Cox election, an event usually cited as the beginning of radio broadcasting in the United States. KDKA's predecessor operation, 8XK, had been offering regular broadcasts as early as October 17, 1919, with twice-weekly programs of music from phonograph records. The music broadcasts from 8XK were well known among wireless enthusiasts and were almost certainly received in Madison by the staff at 9XM. WWJ and KDKA continue to operate today.

Meanwhile, Hanson continued work on the new transmitter. In a letter to his mother on September 27, 1920, he excitedly related his hopes for the telephonic service. He told her that "wireless telephone will be the main work, very interesting, and if successful, it will give us a name over the whole country. I expect to have it done in about three weeks."[30] By mid-October 9XM was still sending only the telegraphic transmission of the weather.[31] The 10:30 a.m. broadcast was moved to 12:30 p.m. at the request of many listeners, who wanted to tune in while they were home for lunch at midday.[32]

The new transmitter was completed in late October or early November 1920. During testing Hanson reported successful two-way transmissions of radio-telephone service, including several of great distance, to the naval air station at Anacostia, near Washington, D.C., and several other locations. Hanson had a close call while working alone during one such nighttime test:

> I well remember one of these tests with Texas, when I had established good communication late one night, after a busy day and was making some adjustment. Fully aware of the high voltage, 2,000 volts, I carefully stood on an insulated stool before touching the dangerous parts of the circuit, but forgot to lay down the grounded microphone transmitter which I held in my left hand. As I touched the high voltage wires with my right hand, my muscles doubled up so that I was unable to remove my hands, and apparently was caught while the current burned some gashes into my fingers. Fortunately, I was able to kick myself over backwards with my knees, thus tearing the wires and interrupting the circuit. Attracted by

the odor of "fried chicken," the night watchman who was making the rounds found me a few minutes later, partially dazed on the floor but not much worse for the experience. He always made it a point to look into the radio room after that, and I from this experience learned a lesson in greater caution which has stayed with me.[33]

On November 2, the evening that KDKA made its debut broadcast with the results of the Harding-Cox election, 9XM may also have been on the air, albeit only telegraphically. That evening an amateur in Ohio received election returns by wireless telegraphy from various states, including Wisconsin.[34] Given the range of the new 9XM transmitter, it is likely that it was the station that the Ohioan heard. Whether these transmissions featured locally gathered returns from Wisconsin or were telegraphic relays of material received from KDKA is not known.

As 1920 drew to a close, a new telephonic transmitter designed by Terry and built with the help of Hanson and other students was finished and had undergone testing. Hanson recalled that some regular programs of phonograph music were offered beginning about November 1920, "about the same time that the Westinghouse station KDKA in East Pittsburgh commenced broadcasting."[35] Burton Miller, a graduate student who succeeded Hanson as WHA operator in 1924, remembered Hanson's saying to him on several occasions that the University of Wisconsin station missed being the first in the regular broadcasting field by only five days, presumably a reference to KDKA's debut.[36] This would make November 7, 1920, the first day of regular noncode broadcasts on 9XM. The 9XM music programs may have been only weekly efforts and perhaps after midnight. November 7, 1920, was a Sunday, and throughout the early 1920s it was common for the Madison station to test its equipment by playing records over the air in the early Sunday morning hours. However, on at least two occasions in December 1920, Terry responded to letters asking about telephonic weather broadcasts and said they'd start after the holidays.[37] In both letters he mentioned the ongoing telegraphic service but made no mention of any telephonic service at all. Because Terry had a reputation for not being a "night owl," he may have been unaware of these phonograph programs. Alternatively, if they had been primarily for testing purposes, he may have dismissed them as not being regular programming.

A new experimental license for 9XM was issued in December 1920 and specified 475 meters (631 kHz) for code and 800 meters (375 kHz) for voice.[38] With the start of the new year, the staff at 9XM would use the new transmitter to begin voice broadcasts on a regular schedule.

CHAPTER 5

Regular Voice Broadcasts on 9XM

1921

Stand by one minute for our weekly radiophone concert.

Regularly scheduled programming began on 9XM on Monday, January 3, 1921, providing the weather forecast by both voice and Morse code at 12:30 p.m. six days a week. Records of the weather bureau show that these were the first voice broadcasts of weather in the United States.[1] Only three weeks earlier Terry had been telling interested people that when the telephonic service began, it would air immediately after the 9:55 a.m. telegraphic weather broadcast. He must have reconsidered during the holidays and decided a midday broadcast time would be more advantageous.[2] The original wavelength for the weather forecast was 800 meters (375 kHz). Reports came in during the first few weeks from Texas, Kansas, New Jersey, and points along the Canadian border, where amateurs reported the 9XM wireless telephone transmissions were being clearly heard. As had been the case with the telegraphic weather reports, those receiving the telephonic reports were asked to transcribe and post them for the benefit of the public. The station had also begun assisting the astronomers at the university's observatory, who now began regulating their clocks with the Arlington time signals received by 9XM instead of with star observations.[3]

By the end of January 1921 the station had added a regular program of live or recorded music to Friday evenings at 7 p.m. The *Press Bulletin* of January 26 reported that the Friday music offerings were "among the new experiments tried by the wireless station at the University of Wisconsin," adding that "Victrola music and music by various instruments will be played. It is expected that the music will be clearly heard at long distances." The idea for the program was Terry's, based on the response to earlier 9XM experimental music broadcasts and perhaps encouraged by the popularity of the regular music broadcasts from

8XK near Pittsburgh the previous year. The scheduling of a program in the evening suggests that Terry and his staff were looking to expand the listenership beyond the intended farm audience of the midday weather broadcasts.

The staff at the *Press Bulletin* continued to demonstrate its skill at attracting publicity: a nearly verbatim version of the item about the Friday concerts ran in the *New York Times* on February 6, despite the fact that New Yorkers would not in theory be able to hear the programs. The report said the broadcasts were available "within a probable radius of 200 miles."

To host the music program, Terry enlisted the assistance of Professor Edgar B. Gordon, a music educator from the university's Extension Division. Gordon was pleased to help, and it marked the beginning of thirty-four years of work with the station. Gordon recalled that Terry had approached him and asked that he provide some musical programs from time to time. He said that Terry wanted to provide additional programming and the response to some previous musical programs indicated they would be popular.[4] At the time Gordon and meteorologist Eric Miller were the only people involved with the station who were not affiliated with the physics department.

Reception of the evening music broadcast of February 11, 1921, was reported in Juneau, Wisconsin, about forty miles northeast of Madison. The February 18 *Juneau Independent* carried a headline that read: "Music in the Air Wafted Here from Madison Friday Evening." Two city employees had used the wireless set at the community's powerhouse to listen to the evening broadcast. They told the paper that "a Victrola, a piano and other instruments were heard as clearly as if the musicians had been in the room."

The 9XM staff soon found it difficult to arrange for live performers each week and began to rely on playing phonograph records. This presented several problems. One was that no electronic method was yet available for playing records over the air. Instead, the microphone was simply placed in front of the Victrola's speaker horn. Terry tried for some time and without success to develop a usable electronic phonograph pickup. The other problem was the lack of a record library at the station. Malcolm Hanson had the idea to approach Madison's Albert E. Smith Music Company at 215 State Street and arrange for the store to lend records to 9XM in exchange for an on-air acknowledgement.[5] This might be the very first example in non-commercial broadcasting of what today would be called an underwriter statement and a "tradeout" one at that. Some modern underwriter statements on public radio stations (and advertisers on commercial stations, for that matter) are not in exchange for cash, but are "traded-out" for goods or services of use to the station. Years later Albert E. Smith recalled that his store lent records to the station for "a considerable period" but that it had no formal arrangement with 9XM or the university. Smith said: "We simply allowed them to use such records from our stock as they wished."[6]

Hanson may have gotten the idea for the alliance with the record store from the phonograph programs of other early broadcasters, some of which had similar agreements. Beginning in 1920, KDKA predecessor's, 8XK, had an arrangement with the Hamilton Music Store, a record dealer in Wilkinsburg, Pennsylvania.[7] The dealer was pleased to find that the records played over the station sold better.[8] Recent research has shown that Charles Herrold's early station in San Jose, California, had an arrangement with the local Sherman Clay & Co. music store to borrow records for the station's regular Wednesday night *Little Hams Program.* The store's owners found that the records played over the air would sell out following the broadcast.[9]

Also in January 1921, 9XM was involved in a complicated sports broadcast of sorts. The plan was to transmit play-by-play reports from the Wisconsin–Minnesota basketball game of January 29 from the gymnasium in Minneapolis to the offices of the *Daily Cardinal* in Madison. A person at the game would relay details to the radio laboratory at the University of Minnesota, and the operators there would transmit the material to Madison by wireless. Hanson would receive it in Sterling Hall and telephone it to the *Cardinal* offices, and students could call the paper to receive updates. The link between Minneapolis and Madison was telegraphic, because the University of Minnesota's station, 9XI, did not begin voice broadcasts until later in the spring. A press report said "faster handling of the news from the game will be possible in this way . . . and it is expected that these reports will arrive considerably in advance of any wire messages." The article added, "students wishing to obtain the latest 'dope' from the game Saturday evening may obtain these reports by calling either of the Cardinal offices."[10] The station also planned to relay the information by telephone to the *Capital Times,* the student union, and the Morgan Brothers' billiard parlor and cigar store on nearby State Street. In the latter two locations, announcements about the game would be made to the assembled sports fans. Madison fans also would be able to send messages of encouragement to the Wisconsin team at halftime in Minneapolis.[11] Of course, any amateur who understood Morse code and happened upon the Minneapolis-to-Madison telegraphic transmission would get the game information first hand. Minnesota had attempted wireless telegraphy broadcasts of football games as early as 1912, and by the fall of 1921 its station was doing football broadcasts telephonically, with student relays carrying play-by-play notes from the sidelines to the studio.[12]

9XM continued to receive reception reports, and from surprisingly great distances. An amateur in New Rochelle, New York, wrote in to say he'd heard the 9XM sign-off message the previous evening: "Station 9xm, University of Wisconsin located at Madison Wisconsin. We are preparing for our concert to be given tomorrow night. This is 9xm signing off." He described his receiving equipment and said, "The reception of your station beats all previous radiophone long distance receiving of my outfit." He also wished to know whether he was the most-distant listener to report having received 9XM, adding as a postscript that the distance between New Rochelle and Madison is approximately nine hundred miles.[13] A busy Hanson found time to write to his mother and report on his activities during the first few weeks of the 9XM telephonic broadcasts. He told her : "Getting along fine with the wireless telephone, our concerts are heard in Boston, Texas, North Dakota, and a lot of places."[14] There is some evidence that in early 1921 the station added a Saturday noontime program of phonograph records as well as a weekly broadcast of road conditions furnished by the Wisconsin State Highway Commission.

During this time transmitter tubes were not commercially available, so Terry and others in the physics department were responsible for their construction, doing everything from assembling the electrical components to actually blowing the glass tube itself. Although the university employed its own glassblower, events forced Terry to learn glassblowing techniques, and he soon became expert at it. The Terry-designed tubes became well known among other experimenters, and Terry and his staff were regularly called upon to produce tubes for other early radio operations.

Achieving a vacuum in the tube was an arduous process. First, they had to pump air out of the tube at room temperature. Then, while the vacuum pump continued to run, they placed an oven around the tube to heat it. Finally, they lit the filaments in the tube and heated them almost to the melting point, a necessary step to drive the accumulated gases out of the components. The process sometimes took twenty hours. A tube would often fail at the very end of the process, because a plate in the tube melted, a filament burned out, or the glass of the tube cracked as it was being removed from the vacuum pump. Hanson recalled that the transmitter required five tubes, and the station was sometimes "one or two ahead," but accidents and failures often caused the staff to stay up all night to have enough tubes for the next day's broadcast. Hanson and Terry devised many safety devices in the transmitter equipment that would automatically open the circuits to protect the precious tubes if anything went wrong. Wisconsin Public Radio still has one of the hand-built tubes from this era on display. It was part of a collection of early tubes that was once displayed in Radio Hall.

Despite the safety precautions, Hanson admitted to some nervousness and to being "on edge" whenever the transmitter was in operation, particularly because he did his announcing in the same room. The transmitter tubes sometimes failed in spectacular fashion, showering the area with sparks and melted components. Hanson recalled "one occasion when we had 'fire works' and the student assisting me appeared too slow in drawing the switch. My rather loud exclamations were not intended to go out by radio, but were heard by altogether too many people with the result that I added a push button to the microphone to prevent anything going out unless the button was pressed."[15] At the time the standard 9XM microphone was an ordinary candlestick-style desk telephone.

In February 1921 the station staff announced a plan to receive the March 4 inaugural address by President Warren G. Harding and to rebroadcast it on 9XM. In addition, Terry and the staff were planning to set up two wireless receivers for the benefit of the public: one in the State Capitol so legislators could hear the event, and another in the auditorium in Sterling Hall to allow students and faculty to listen in.[16] At least one other local radio operator

Preparing transmitter tubes for 9XM, ca. 1921
Hanson and Terry constructing transmitter tubes for 9XM in the laboratory.
(University of Wisconsin Archives series 23/24/2)

planned to tune in: the principal at Madison High School had planned to use the school's wireless set so students could hear the broadcast.[17] The *Press Bulletin* reported that "President Harding's words will be heard in Madison about one-fifth of a second after they are spoken in Washington."[18] This was inaccurate because the speech was not going to be broadcast live. The actual plan called for recording the speech on transcription records, which would be played for the broadcast that evening. The *New York Times* reported that the idea was abandoned after it became apparent that the speech "would not be finished in time to have it placed on phonograph records."[19] Terry was forced to announce the cancellation of the broadcast. This must have been a disappointment for the 9XM staff, who lost a great opportunity to demonstrate the capabilities of the new radio operation to state lawmakers and a wider audience of the university community.

Despite this setback, innovations continued. By the next week Hanson was busy stringing a temporary broadcast line from the Sterling Hall studio to the university's Music Hall to carry a live concert by the University Glee Club for the station's first remote broadcast. Hanson released an advance announcement of the March 11 event, which was printed in the *Daily Cardinal*. The broadcast was a success, and an early reception report came in from Independence, Missouri.[20]

Also in the spring of 1921 some additional spoken-word material became an irregular feature of the broadcast schedule, with "reports of athletic events and communication of University news."[21] Andrew W. Hopkins, a professor in the Department of Agricultural Journalism, provided some of this material under an arrangement with Hanson, who had sought Hopkins's assistance. Hopkins recognized the possibilities for using radio to broadcast agricultural information, because many farmers were already tuning in to the telephonic weather broadcasts. Hopkins and other members of the College of Agriculture prepared material specifically to be read on air (by Hanson, of course). These talks on agriculture were the first hint of the station's service to the Wisconsin farm community in the years to come.

In April 1921 the 9XM staff presented a public demonstration of wireless telephony, broadcasting phonograph music from the studio at Sterling Hall that was received at the University Exposition, where it was played through an amplified loudspeaker.[22] Another Midwestern university followed 9XM's lead that month and began telephonic broadcasts of weather forecasts. Station 9XY at the St. Louis University (later WEW) started its voice weather broadcasts on April 26. By July 1, 1921, the U.S. Weather Bureau reported there were twelve "radiophone stations" in seven states presenting weather information.[23]

9XM had added another wavelength to the noon weather transmission; it was now sent at 350 meters (857 kHz) at 12:30 p.m. and then repeated at 800 meters (375 kHz).[24]

In late spring 9XM received a letter from Dallas, where a group had used the broadcast of the Friday radiophone concert as the music for its dance.[25]

In this era before even rudimentary radio ratings services were available, the staff at 9XM had no idea how many people might be listening to the broadcasts. While some listeners contacted the station with reception reports, the number who never did was unknown. One day during the weather broadcast Hanson asked regular listeners to contact the station. The results were encouraging: 205 amateurs responded from seventy towns—fifty in Wisconsin, with the rest in Minnesota, Iowa, and Illinois.[26]

As in the early years, 9XM shut down in June for the university's summer vacation. When broadcasts resumed in September, the station added a new program feature: the farm market reports. The Wisconsin Department of Markets had begun exploring the idea of using the new medium to better provide market data to farmers in Wisconsin and elsewhere in the region. Terry had approached the agency during the summer to propose that 9XM transmit the material along with the weather during the noon hour. The agency began providing market information to 9XM on September 19, 1921, paying the station fifty dollars per month to include the information in its midday broadcasts, both by voice and telegraphically. The money paid for Hanson's services as operator. Adding the market report brought another person to the 9XM operation: Max M. Littleton, a Department of Markets employee with the title of "wireless expert." The Department of Markets installed a leased market telegraph wire in its office in the State Capitol, where Littleton would compile the information as a daily market report for Hanson to broadcast at midday. Given his telegraphy skills, Littleton may also have filled in for Hanson as the 9XM operator from time to time.

On September 23, 1921, 9XM operators asked listeners to contact the station with reception reports and offered to mail them blank forms for recording the new farm market information. A listener from a hardware concern about eighty miles away in Coloma, Wisconsin, wrote in for the blanks and reported clear reception. He said he had been transcribing the weather forecast for the past three or four months and was giving it to the local telephone exchange, which "broadcast" it to its subscribers. He said, "I can assure you it is appreciated by the farmers of this section."[27] Sharing the 9XM material with others was common during this era, and encouraged. A bulletin from the university's Extension Division said, "Most of these receiving stations post the reports in conspicuous places for the information of the public; many of the receiving operators have made arrangements to furnish all or a portion of the information received daily to their newspapers, banks, county agents, farmers and other people especially interested."[28] The midday broadcast once included a message asking who among the listeners would be willing to post it for others or otherwise distribute it. Thirteen amateurs in Wisconsin responded, as did seventeen from Minnesota, Iowa, and Illinois. Noting this, Miller wrote to his superiors in Washington, D.C., for permission to include forecasts for those three states in 9XM's broadcast.[29]

The 9XM staff continued its earlier efforts to get radio receivers into the hands of potential listeners. Terry began to distribute galenite crystals and wires for crystal sets, sending them free of charge to those who asked for them. Terry also enlisted the Burgess Battery Company of Madison to build an inexpensive receiver that Hanson had designed. The first ten sold as soon as they were completed, and the company began building one hundred more to sell at forty dollars each.[30] The availability of a simple and affordable receiver was a development long sought by Miller. He reported to his superiors that comparable ready-made units then on the market sold for about $130 and the comparatively low cost of the Madison-built receiver "will bring the service within the means of any farmer." Miller also reported that he had used one of the Madison receivers to listen to a concert from "the Westinghouse Company" in Pittsburgh (KDKA). Miller proudly pointed out that "hearing it at Madison is ordinarily possible only with the most sensitive apparatus."[31] Hanson wrote to his mother that one of his radios was in daily use and was working wonderfully. He also said that as the designer of the set, he was hoping to negotiate a 2 percent royalty for each sold.[32]

On Saturday, October 1, 1921, Max Littleton and two other employees of the Department of Markets traveled the forty miles from Madison to Janesville to demonstrate the value of the 9XM broadcasts in distributing market information. Another reason for the trip was to determine whether one of the inexpensive Hanson receivers could pick up the message at that distance. They set up a receiver at the *Janesville Gazette* and listened to the regular midday market report sent out by 9XM. The paper gave the event Page One coverage that day, including a transcription of the first message received: "Chicago. Potato market, 323 cars on track. Demand and movement good. Market slightly stronger. Wisconsin round White U.S. Number one, $1.80 to $2.00, mostly $1.85 to $2.00. Ungraded, $1.50 to $1.70."

The paper said it was the "first wireless phone message in history of city." After the demonstration Littleton and his colleagues left the radio receiving set at the *Gazette* office so the newspaper staff could receive the football scores that would be transmitted that evening. Whether these would also come from 9XM or from another broadcaster is not known. Hanson wrote to his mother the next day, telling her that the Bureau of Markets personnel were very enthusiastic about the results of their test trip.[33]

9XM added a new staff member in the fall of 1921 to help with programming. William H. Lighty had been a social worker in St. Louis and arrived at the University of Wisconsin in 1906 to organize the first section of what would become the university's Extension Division. Its main function, then as now, was to bring the resources and services of the university to residents of Wisconsin. This concept is often called the Wisconsin Idea, which says, "the borders of the University are the borders of the state." One of the first to articulate the Wisconsin Idea was university president Charles Van Hise, who was once quoted as saying: "I shall never rest content until the beneficent influence of the University of Wisconsin shall be available in every home in the state."[34]

Lighty's two adolescent sons were both wireless hobbyists and had built a homemade receiver that had caught the interest of their father.[35] One reference says that Lighty had originally stumbled on the 9XM operation by accident. He was walking on campus with his sons one day, when they noticed flashes of light coming from the basement of Sterling Hall. They dropped in at the 9XM studio to investigate, and Lighty immediately grasped the educational potential of the radio operation.[36] Lighty's son Paul recalls that the noise of the rotary spark gap equipment was such that it could be heard outside the building when it was operating.[37] Student operator Reeve Strock remembered the staff's joking about the noise of the rotary spark gap apparatus, saying it "had a sure range of 10 miles, and if we opened the window we could get 5 miles further."[38] In a paper that the senior Lighty wrote shortly after the spark transmitter was decommissioned, he recalled its "emitting its fierce and angry noises from the north window of Sterling Hall." He added wistfully: "It contributed picturesqueness and romance in the radio station sending outfit."[39]

Lighty was a strong believer in adult education as a vehicle for improving the lives of people and saw radio broadcasting as an opportunity to further this work. He suggested that lectures by faculty members be added to the Friday evening broadcasts. One problem he faced was the unwillingness of some faculty members to actually speak on the air, as they considered radio to be undignified. Lighty was able to convince some to prepare scripts, which Hanson or Lighty himself read over the air. Lighty's role at 9XM was essentially that of program director, which allowed Terry and Hanson to focus more on the station's maintenance and operation. Lighty also had a flair for publicity and managed to both increase the audience for 9XM and raise the station's standing among the faculty. A bit of an eccentric, he commuted to campus on horseback well into the automobile age. When he finally did go horseless, he did so by acquiring an ancient and outmoded air-cooled Franklin automobile.[40]

In October 1921, 9XM expanded on the success of the spring glee club concert and made ambitous plans to broadcast five classical music performances presented under the auspices of the Wisconsin Union Board. The series of evening concerts would take place in the University Armory, known to today's students as the Old Red Gym. Tickets were available at the Alfred E. Smith Music Company, the same store that had lent records for 9XM's weekly program of music from phonograph records.

To get the audio of the concerts from the armory to Sterling Hall for broadcast, Hanson, student Ross Herrick, and "several students from the military department" installed a line of field telephone cable through the heating tunnels under the campus. Because the armory was also the university's gymnasium, having a permanent line in place would make it possible to broadcast college basketball games, as well as convocations and graduation ceremonies. Hanson even devised a way to make the line bidirectional so that the station staffer at the armory and the transmitter operator at Sterling Hall could communicate.[41] A permanent line to Music Hall was installed at about the same time. (Wisconsin Public Radio today has broadcast lines to numerous campus locations that are strung through the same heating tunnels.)

The first concert in the series was broadcast on October 20, 1921, featuring soprano Mabel Garrison. In the days following the broadcast, Terry received letters from listeners throughout Wisconsin as well as from Ohio, New York, Minnesota, Missouri, Illinois, Iowa, and Nebraska. The *Press Bulletin* reported: "A number of concerts will probably be transmitted by the radio station of the University physics department this winter because of the widespread interest in them."[42]

In late October 1921 the 9XM staff came up with yet another innovation: a program guide for general distribution. A single copy remains in the university's archives, and it is one of the earliest examples of such a promotional publication. It was preserved only because a listener in Vermont had used its blank reverse side to send in a reception report.[43] It was typed on a standard sheet of paper and formatted horizontally. Its grid used dashes for horizontal lines and colons for vertical lines. It was sent out with a two-page cover letter labeled "Circular #1" dated October 28 that appears to have been written by Hanson. The station sent the guide to all listeners who had contacted the station with reception reports; its availability was also announced on air.

The letter and program guide together provide a good description of 9XM's broadcast procedures. The midday broadcasts were transmitted at a wavelength of 800 meters (375 kHz) and began at 12:15 p.m. with the telegraphic transmission of the farm markets at ten words per minute. At 12:35 p.m. the weather forecast went out telegraphically, first at eighteen words per minute and then repeated at seven words per minute for the benefit of those less adept at deciphering code transmissions. Hanson said another reason for the differing speeds was to provide amateurs with an opportunity to practice receiving code.[44] Following the code broadcasts, the operator read the weather report, repeating it three times. Finally, at 12:50 p.m. the operator read the market information that had gone out by code earlier in the broadcast. If all went well, the broadcast was concluded by 1 p.m., when time signals were given. The order of the segments was deliberate: code-only listeners could tune in for only the first half of the broadcast, and "telephonic" listeners could tune in for the last half.

```
            R A D I O   S T A T I O N   9 X M
    DEPARTMENT OF PHYSICS, UNIVERSITY OF WISCONSIN.   OPERATING SCHEDULE FOR 1921 - 1922.
```

NATURE OF WORK	DAYS	TIME (Std.Cent)	SET USED	WAVE-LENGTH	SPEED OF TRANSMISSION	REMARKS
U.S. Weather Forecast for Wisconsin	Daily exc.Sun.	12:35 PM	4KW Spk. and Phone	800 800	First 18 then 7 w.p.m; - - -	Speech repeated 3 times
Wis.Dept.of Markets Market Report	Daily exc.Sun.	12:15 PM 12:50 PM	4KW Spk. Phone	800 800	10 wds.p.min - - -	Special Code used; Forms MI-20 and MI-22. Speech alphabet code.
Radiophone Concert (See Note.)	Fridays	7:30 PM 8:15 PM	Phone Phone	800 375	- - - - - -	Special Selections on Edison phonograph.
College News Exchange with other Univ.	Mondays	9:00 to 11:30 PM	Spark or C.W.	375 375	About 20	Special Schedules
Relay Message Traffic	Tues.& Thurs. Fridays	10 to 12pm 9 to 12pm	Spark C.W.	330 375	Variable Variable	Work with amateurs. Messages and tests.

    NOTE: It is contemplated, (dependent upon the consent of the artist), to send
    out, by radiophone, the following local concerts by famous artists, which will be
    given at the University Armory, under the auspices of the Wisconsin Union Board:
            Nov. 15, 1921,   Ferenc Veesey, famous European Violinist.
            Nov. 25, 1921,   Joseph Lhevinne, the great pianist.
            Feb. 14, 1922,   Pablo Casals, great Master of the Cello.

        For these concerts, beginning at about 8:30 PM, we will employ a wavelength
    of 800 meters, and will change to 375 meters wavelength beginning 9:30 PM, standard
    central time.
        Our Edison phonograph concerts will be omitted those weeks during which above
    mentioned three events take place.

9XM program schedule, 1921–22
9XM issued this typewritten program schedule on October 28, 1921. It is one of the earliest examples of a radio program guide for the general public. (WHA Radio and Television Records/University of Wisconsin Archives)

Hanson handled the code and voice transmissions of the midday programming. The market information was prepared by Max Littleton, and the weather forecast was provided by Eric Miller. One regular feature of the midday broadcasts was announcements of special broadcasts of athletic contests and other "notices of general interest." These were sent right before the weather forecast "on each of the two preceding days."

The guide shows that the Friday evening music program was the only other telephonic (nontelegraphic) offering on the schedule. It was now called the *Radiophone Concert* and aired from 7:30 to 9 p.m. The guide said it offered "Special Selections on Edison Phonograph." This program had to contend with what today would be considered an awkward problem: the need to change frequencies halfway through the broadcast from 800 meters (375 kHz) to 375 meters (799 kHz). This program was presented in two half-hour segments to deal with this requirement, transmitting on 800 meters from 7:30 to 8 p.m. and on 375 meters from 8:30 to 9 p.m.[45] 9XM had also switched music suppliers and was now borrowing phonograph records from the local Edison Phonograph distributor, the Hook Brothers Piano Company at 101–103 State Street. They provided 9XM with "some of the latest and best selections every week."[46]

Other evening programs were transmitted only by Morse code and were listed in the program guide at the 375-meter wavelength. The *College News Exchange* aired on Mondays from 9 to 11:30 p.m., transmissions on "special schedules" with other universities at a speed of "about 20" words per minute. After the *Radiophone Concert* on Fridays and continuing up through midnight, the station allotted time for telegraphic messages, tests, and relay traffic; these were scheduled at "variable" code speeds. Similar telegraphic relay work was done on Tuesdays and Thursdays from 10 p.m. to midnight specifically for amateurs and at a different wavelength, 330 meters (908 kHz).

Noted at the bottom of the guide are three special live broadcasts featuring classical music artists. The guide lists the Ferenc Vecsey concert of November 15, the Josef Lhevinne concert of November 29 (incorrectly listed as November 25), and an upcoming concert on February 14, 1922, featuring the "great Master of the Cello," Pablo Casals (another error: the concert was actually on February 17). Following the concert listings is this note: "It is contemplated (dependent upon the consent of the artist), to send out, by radiophone, the following local concerts by famous artists, which will be given at the University Armory, under the auspices of the Wisconsin Union Board. For these concerts, beginning at about 8:30 PM, we will employ a wavelength of 800 meters, and will change to 375 meters wavelength beginning at 9:30 PM, standard central time." The guide added: "Our Edison phonograph concerts will be omitted

those weeks during which above mentioned three events take place." This latter program deviation might have been to give Malcolm Hanson a breather:
after running the midday programming six days a week, handling station correspondence, teaching, maintaining the equipment, and engineering the live
concerts, he was a busy fellow.

The next live music broadcast, on November 1, 1921, was the most ambitious yet: a Madison concert appearance by the Cincinnati Symphony Orchestra, conducted by Eugene Ysaye. The concert was a challenge for Hanson
because he was using only a single microphone. This is likely the first live radio
broadcast of a symphony orchestra concert in the United States. Most reference
works erroneously give that honor to a February 10, 1922, concert by the
Detroit Symphony over WBL in Detroit (later WWJ),[47] and WWJ makes that
claim in its publicity materials today.

In a 1950 interview the concertmaster of the orchestra, violinist Emil Heermann, recalled that members of the symphony were excited about the broadcast because "it was a new experience for all of them." Heermann also said
that the musicians were told that "the President of the United States, Warren
Harding, would be among the listeners."[48] Although it's never been verified,
the Ohio-born president may have indeed tried to tune in this orchestra from
his home state. It is known that Harding had the first radio receiver installed
in the White House, but that did not occur until February 8, 1922,[49] so perhaps someone temporarily supplied the president with a radio for that evening
or he sought out a location that had one available. The *Press Bulletin* said the
concert was heard as far away as New York and that "the wireless concerts from
the University are now becoming widely known among wireless operators, as
are the daily market and weather reports."[50]

The next concert was scheduled for November 15, 1921, a fund-raiser for the
planned student union building. It featured Hungarian violinist Vecsey, who
had performed two weeks earlier at Carnegie Hall.[51] The concert of November 29 featured the Russian-born pianist Lhevinne and generated tremendous
listener response. It generated even more listener response than the Cincinnati
Symphony broadcast. Reports came in from twenty-six Wisconsin cities, eighteen states (including Texas, Georgia, North Carolina, and New York), and two
locations in Saskatchewan.[52]

One letter came from a listener in the small community of Stenen near the
Manitoba–Saskatchewan border. He wrote: "I am pleased to inform you that
I spent an enjoyable evening, (last night) listening to your Radio Concert. Your
voice and music came in very clearly, and I was using only a one-step amplifier, with a home made single coil short wave tuner. I would surely be pleased

to have you forward me your program list, (which you mentioned last night) which gives the date and hour of the concerts you will be broadcasting in the future. Also please state what power you are using. It seems remarkable to me that the voice and music comes in so clear at that distance, considering the Receiver I was using." At the bottom of the letter is a note initialed by Hanson: "P.S., Stenen is over 1000 miles from Madison MPH."[53] The station prepared a map that showed the reception locations reported from the Lhevinne concert and used it regularly for publicity purposes.

Another letter came in from the Holmes News Service, a subscription news agency in downtown Madison. It was signed by fifteen people who had gathered there to hear the concert broadcast with a rare accessory for the era: a loudspeaker. The writer said that by using "one step of amplification and a Vocaloud the concert was heard in wonderful style all over the building." Among those

Reception reports received at 9XM
The 9XM staff prepared this map of locations that received the broadcast of the Josef Lehvinne concert on November 29, 1921. Note the concentration of reports from western Pennsylvania. Pittsburgh station KDKA had been on the air with a regular schedule of programs for more a year and its predecessor, 8XK, had been offering regular programs since October 1919. The popularity of the 8XK broadcasts had prompted even nonhobbyists in the area to acquire radio receivers. (Wisconsin Historical Society Archives series PH 3461, image WHi-23495)

signing the letter were Wisconsin governor John Blaine and his wife, several city officials, and George Crownhart, the radio enthusiast who had received notice of the ban on wireless back in 1917 and who was now co-owner of the Holmes News Service.[54]

This was not the first time that Crownhart had brought his radio equipment to the office. Some weeks earlier he brought a receiver in to show the managing editor of *La Follette's Magazine* how radio worked. Crownhart told of the experience in an article in the November 1921 issue of the magazine, which was a forerunner of the *Progressive*. He wrote:

> Do you live in Wisconsin? Then if you had one of the "magic boxes," this is what you could hear in your own home by simply turning one switch. Every noon at 12:45 you could hear Malcolm P. Hanson at the University of Wisconsin tell you what the weather would be for the next 24 hours. Three minutes after that he would tell you exactly what are the latest market reports from every large stock, grain and produce market center in the country. By the time you have had supper Friday night and the table is cleared, just turn that switch again and you will hear all the latest Edison records broadcasted by the University of Wisconsin.
>
> . . . In many communities in Wisconsin today, there is but one wireless telephone receiving set, often operated by a young boy. Every noon he copies these reports on forms that are supplied free and then immediately turns them over to the local rural telephone exchange. Here Central calls all the subscribers at one time and reads the reports which have come "via Marconi" through the ether.

Crownhart also told of the live Cincinnati Symphony concert over 9XM, the nightly two-hour music program from KDKA, and the 9 p.m. time signals from Arlington, Virginia. He had brought groups into the office to hear the Friday 9XM concerts, and he said their reaction was "'of course I knew it could be done but I wanted to see it.'" He also described hearing a member of Congress speak on "Labor and the Press" on KDKA and how the Pittsburgh station planned to bring candidates for Congress to the microphone in the coming election year. Crownhart predicted similar political uses for radio in Wisconsin. He correctly anticipated that within five years, nearly every home would have a receiver and that music, speeches, and world news would be available to listeners. Crownhart ended the article by enthusiastically urging readers to buy a receiving set, saying, "Grasp it and it will grasp you forever."[55]

In addition to the Crownhart article, the efforts of Hanson, Miller, and Lighty to publicize the station were beginning to pay off. On November 20, 1921, the *Milwaukee Journal* ran a long item under the headline "500 Radio

Stations in State 'Pull' Music From Air; Hear Market Reports." One of the photos with the article featured Hanson speaking into a microphone, while the other showed Max Littleton of the Department of Markets wearing a headset while sitting at a "typical wireless and wireless telephone receiving set." Also in the article was a map showing Wisconsin locations receiving 9XM. The subheading "Noted Artists' Concerts Are Farm Treats" emphasized the rural clientele of the station.

The story said, "For many years amateurs have shown their friends their wireless sets and let them listen to buzzing dots and dashes which were the messages being hurled through the air by commercial stations. It is hard to become enthusiastic over listening to dots and dashes, but it is an eighth wonder to listen to jazz and speech come floating through the ether to your ears, to listen to music played at East Pittsburgh or to a symphony concert at the University of Wisconsin. That is what hundreds of wireless amateurs in this state are doing." The report continued: "Every noon, except Sunday, 9XM, the powerful radio station of the university, sends out by wireless and then by wireless telephone the market reports direct from the state bureau of markets and also the weather report. Every Friday night, the station sends out a wireless telephone concert consisting of the latest phonograph records and when noted musicians come to Madison to entertain the university town their music is connected to the radio set. While you are eating your lunch, while you are seeing the latest movie, and while you are sleeping, the ether waves are penetrating your room that with a few instruments might be turned into music or speech." The article noted that receivers were reasonably priced and information on the sets "may be secured from the physics department of the university." Since he was being interviewed for a Milwaukee newspaper, operator Malcolm Hanson told the reporter there were forty-one known regular 9XM listeners in Milwaukee. Amazingly, the newspaper article listed the name and address of each one.

The article also includes a transcription of what was the "station identification" at the time. The article said "messages like this come to amateur radio stations: 'Nine XM talking, department of physics, University of Wisconsin. Stand by one minute for our weekly radiophone concert.'"[56]

Another transcription of actual on-air presentation appeared in the Crownhart article from *La Follette's Magazine.* He said: "As I put on the phones I heard the University of Wisconsin saying: '9XM speaking, University of Wisconsin, Madison, Wisconsin. Stand by one minute for the daily weather report. Weather for Wisconsin. Snow tonight and Friday with cold north winds. Falling temperature will bring heavy frost. Cloudy and colder in northern Wisconsin.

That's all. Stand by three minutes for radiophone market report.'" Crownhart said that his business partner listened to this particular forecast and because of the frost warning, went home early to harvest his cabbages.[57]

Another news article appeared four days later in the *Wisconsin Farmer,* a weekly statewide newspaper of agriculture news. Its front page story carried the headline "Reaching Wisconsin Farms by Wireless." The article showed a Wisconsin map of the number of licensed amateur radio stations in each county. Also included was a photo of Hanson and Littleton. The article said that "farm outfits" could be easily installed "by attaching one wire to the ground and taking another to the aerial mast on silo or windmill, and following printed instructions, the messages should come in clearly."

This article offered a detailed description of the preparation and sending of the noontime broadcast: "First, in the forenoon M. M. Littleton, department of markets operator, receives over the leased telegraph wires his full reports of the current markets. Potato markets come from Chicago and Waupaca, chiefly; butter and cheese reports from New York, Chicago and Fond du Lac. Special cheese quotations come once a week on Mondays from the Plymouth board and the farmers' call board. Live stock messages come from Chicago, Omaha, and St. Paul, and truck crop notes from Chicago, Milwaukee and elsewhere in the shipping zones. About this same time the weather bureau, Eric Miller, chief is making up its high-average 'guesses' as to the possible turn of the weather and whether Medicine Hat is brewing trouble again. Frost warnings, storms, cold snaps and such contingencies all are assembled. Thereupon both Mr. Littleton and Mr. Miller send their detailed messages by phone or by special code forms to the University wireless operator, Malcolm Hanson."[58]

Fan letters continued to pour in. An employee of the Onsgard State Bank in Spring Grove, Minnesota, reported that the 9XM weather forecasts were posted in the bank lobby and were "creating much interest in this community."[59] A theater owner in Portage, Wisconsin, wrote: "I intend to give the audience of this theater the pleasure of listening to future concerts of the physics department."[60] A firefighter at the Central Fire Station in Freeport, Illinois, had a receiving set and posted both the weather forecast and the market report in front of the building for the benefit of the public. He wrote, "You'd be surprised to see the number of people who stop and read it."[61] This location and others used special card holders and blank U.S. Forecast cards that Eric Miller had secured from the weather bureau. These had been regularly distributed to those correspondents who were receiving weather material telegraphically and by mail. Miller felt that the requests for the blanks and holders were one way to gauge who was listening.[62] A fan letter from an unexpected source arrived late in the year. Astronomers at the University of Chicago's Yerkes Observatory in Williams Bay, Wisconsin, wrote to say that they had found the forecasts useful in planning their evening's work. They also wanted to know particulars about the forecast and whether it could be regarded as more reliable than the ones printed in the Chicago newspapers.[63] The Department of Markets also reported many appreciative comments from farmers with receiving sets.[64]

The mail brought more than just praise, however. In mid-December 1921 a letter arrived from L. R. Schmitt of the Office of the Radio Inspector in Chicago. It informed Terry that 9XM was not licensed to use the 800-meter wavelength for "broadcasting" under its experimental license and said that if the station wished to carry on "broadcasting service such as musical concerts, etc., it will necessary to apply for a 'Limited Commercial License' and you will be given a wave length of 360 meters for this purpose." Schmitt went on to say that if 9XM wished to continue to broadcast weather and market reports, the Navigation Service of the Department of Commerce would require letters granting permission from the chief of the weather bureau and the chief of the Bureau of Markets. Schmitt said that the wavelength of 485 meters (618 kHz) would be assigned for that material exclusively and that the station could use that frequency for no other purposes.[65] The term *commercial* here did not mean that the station would become a commercial operation. Rather, this word drew the distinction between experimental or amateur facilities and the new category in which the federal government was placing these broadcast operations. For want of a better place to put them, they were grouped with shore telegraph stations that transmitted messages to ships for a fee. The only difference was a rider on the license limiting operation to 485 meters or 360 meters for broadcasting "news, concerts, lectures and like matter." Officials at the Department of Commerce had become concerned that too many amateur and experimental stations were making broadcasts intended for the general public. As of December 1, 1921, the agency had adopted regulations that restricted this "public" broadcasting activity to those stations that met the standards of this newly created broadcast service classification. Being licensed in this category also meant that 9XM would be forced onto the same frequencies used by all other broadcasters.

A contrite Terry responded immediately, confirming that 9XM was indeed using the 800-meter wavelength, and he appealed for permission to continue using it "until we can make necessary changes in our equipment." He pointed out that "the broadcasting of the market and weather reports has become a very important part of the University's service to the State. There are about 300 stations listening regularly for our reports. These include a number of daily papers which have installed receiving sets and depend upon this service for their daily market and weather quotations. A number of telephone companies have also installed receiving sets and are taking our reports and then sending them out to rural subscribers by wire phone." Terry noted that while the concert broadcasts were important and that the university's Extension Division was "planning on making use of this service for lectures and talks concerning the programs before they are sent out," he did say that 9XM would agree to discontinue the broadcasting of concerts. He also said that the University of Wisconsin would, as suggested, apply for a limited commercial license.[66]

Miller also wrote to the radio inspector, perhaps hoping to appeal to his sense of interagency cooperation. Miller pointed out that the weather broadcasts were valuable not only to the public but, if continued, "will result in both increased efficiency and diminished cost of this form of government service." He said that the weather bureau was then "spending hundreds of thousands of dollars for wire telegraphy in the distribution of weather forecasts that do not easily or quickly reach farmers." He listed the communities where amateurs were receiving the forecasts and then distributing them to the public; it included twelve locations in Wisconsin, six in Illinois, and three each in Iowa and Minnesota. Miller also said that the weather bureau chief and "your Chief" were conferring in Washington about the appropriate power and frequency for 9XM. He echoed Terry's request that 9XM be allowed to continue broadcasts on the 800-meter wavelength.[67]

The letters did not sway radio inspector Schmitt, who replied that while he had no objection to 9XM's continuing to broadcast until a new license was issued, the station must immediately discontinue service on the 800-meter wavelength. He took care to point out that 800 meters was reserved for radio compass work, which is so important that "nothing will be allowed that can possibly interfere with them." Somewhat diplomatically, he added that it would be "very easy for a station with the power of the University of Wisconsin's station to interfere on the coast these winter nights." Given the reception reports that 9XM had been receiving for months, it must have seemed a reasonable argument. Schmitt also said that 9XM was not alone in having to make changes, although none of the other affected operators was using 800 meters. All was not lost, however. Schmitt did say that 9XM could switch to 485 meters (618 kHz) immediately for weather broadcasts.[68]

Terry and the 9XM staff moved fast: by December 23 Schmitt had received a description of the station's apparatus as part of the application for a limited commercial license. Under "nature of service," the form states, "Broadcasting Weather, Markets, and special concerts. Not exceeding two concerts each week.

Also official communication with various college station" (*sic*). Applicants for a "limited" license were required to list any other stations with which they were in regular correspondence. 9XM's application lists "Universities of Minnesota, Purdue, Michigan, Illinois, Missouri, Texas, Iowa, Texas M.&A. college, Union College (NY), Billings (Mont) Polytechnic Inst., and others to be added from time to time."

The application also listed new wavelengths with handwritten notations alongside each one. As expected, 485 meters was "for broadcasting weather + market information only," 360 meters (833 kHz) "for broadcasting music + like material only," and 410 meters (731 kHz) "for intercommunication." This was for handling relay traffic between universities, which inspector Schmitt said was not covered by the experimental license. He added that if the 410-meter wavelength could not be issued, the station should be allowed to use its former evening wavelength of 375 meters (799 kHz) for this purpose. Written across the face of the form, evidently by the radio inspector, were the words *Provisional Limited Commercial* and below the serial number were the letters WHA.[69] If the call letters were written on the license at that time, it marks the first association of this designation with the University of Wisconsin radio operation. The call letters are not believed to have had any particular meaning; they were merely an available three-letter combination. It would be a few years before the Department of Commerce began to allow stations to request call letters with special meaning or promotional value. Still, legends persist that the call letters might stand for "Wisconsin, Heartland of America"[70] or "Wisconsin Hails All." More likely, the call letters were assigned and then attempts were made to find a slogan that fit. Terry wrote to Schmitt to say that Hanson would go to Chicago to get the station's license materials in order, adding that Hanson had to make the trip anyway to take the test for a new radio operator's license.[71] Hanson's personal "Commercial First Class" license, issued by the Chicago office, carries the same December 23 date as the license for the university's radio station.[72]

While the controversy about wavelengths and licensing was occupying the attention of the 9XM staff, yet another favorable article appeared, this time in the *Milwaukee Sentinel*. The Sunday edition of December 18, 1921, carried an illustrated article under the headline "Nation 'Listens In' on Radio Concerts at Badger Capital." Under the heading "Flashing Music to Distant Audiences" was a photo of Terry and Hanson in the laboratory, constructing and testing transmitter tubes. Below it was the map they had prepared after the Lhevinne concert the previous month (see pages 42 and 51). The story included some listener reports from the concert: "'Your concert was heard in

Mars very fine,' was the startling letter received a few days after the concert. After rubbing their eyes the university operators found it was only Mars, Pa., but nevertheless the concert was heard there in excellent style on a homemade set." The article also told of a group that gathered for the concert at the central firehouse in Freeport, Illinois, as related by Captain E. L. Kahley of the station: "'We had an audience of forty to fifty people,' reported Capt. Kahley, 'and we get the market and weather report every noon. The people here in Freeport did not pay much attention to wireless until we put this set in our fire station but now they are all very much interested.'"

The article described the noonday broadcasts of weather and market reports and the "observatory" time signal at 1 p.m., which was said to be accurate "within one second," and continued: "This is not all. Friday night the university transmits two phonograph concerts of half an hour each. When Mabel Garrison sings in Madison, when the Cincinnati symphony gives a concert, or Ferenc Vecsey his famous violin recital, wireless amateurs and their friends 'hear' those concerts just as though they were in the same room."

The value of the market reports was touted, claiming "the farmer with a receiving set in Wisconsin is now on an equal basis with the buyer who may have leased telegraph wires." The Saturday program schedule was also given: "Every Saturday noon, after the market and weather reports have been given and everyone has set his watch, Mr. Hanson gives a fifteen or twenty minute lecture on some phase of radio, followed by the playing of two or three records."

The article said that improvements were in the offing: "Mr. Hanson has announced that the efficiency has just been increased 40 per cent and that within three weeks the power of the sending station will be increased three times over the present power used." Although the article noted that 9XM was usually silent on Sundays, it concluded by promoting a broadcast later that very day: "When the famous first regimental band of the university gives the first of its popular Sunday afternoon concerts on Dec. 18, radio amateurs all over the state will hear the music."[73]

In all, 1921 was a successful year for the station. It saw the beginning of the regular schedule, the first remote broadcasts, the addition of the market reports, and lots of positive publicity.

CHAPTER 6

‿

WHA Begins

1922–29

This is the University Extension Instruction Service by Radio Broadcast.

On January 13, 1922, the new broadcasting license for the radio station at the University of Wisconsin took effect. The license assigned the station the call letters WHA, which remain to this day. On the same day the federal government issued a license for station WLB at the University of Minnesota, now KUOM-AM. These two licenses were the first in the new "limited commercial" category issued to universities for educational broadcasting.[1] The 9XM call letters remained in effect until 1926 for the experimental work in wireless code and telephonic transmissions, and the station used the designation 9DW (later W9DW, then W9YT) for point-to-point work with amateurs.[2] The number of radio stations also increased dramatically in 1922. At the beginning of the year the United States had only twenty-eight licensed radio broadcasting stations; by December the nation had nearly six hundred.

WHA's new licensed frequency required new equipment, including a new antenna. A T-type four-wire cage antenna was installed atop Sterling Hall; its wires were mounted in a large wooden frame. A later modification to the station was the development of a broadcast booth to isolate the speakers. Before it was built, announcers had worked next to the transmitter. Malcolm Hanson built a five-by-five-foot booth from scrap material and lined it with quilts to prevent reverberation. Because the booth had no window, the operator communicated with the speaker using a device of Hanson's invention, a flat box about a foot square and about six inches deep. It had compartments covered in frosted glass with messages etched into them, and the transmitter operator could activate lights in each compartment (see photo on page 78).

Hanson reported: "As long as everything went along all right, we would

illuminate the compartment marked 'O.K.' However, it was often necessary to
flash on the signs marked 'Faster,' 'Slower,' 'Louder,' 'Too Close,' or even 'One
Minute Please,' etc." Hanson added, "It is not surprising that occasionally our
speakers would suffer from a case of microphone fright or become disgusted
with the relentless flashing of the signs, in which case it was usually my job to
complete the task with as good an imitation of the speaker's voice as I could
muster."[3] Hanson was able to finish the speeches because all those giving presentations on WHA during this era were required to provide the station with
a copy of their planned remarks. Harold McCarty, who served as WHA manager from 1931 to 1967, preserved copies of most speeches from the 1920s.

One early guest was Dr. Charles E. Brown, curator for the State Historical
Society. He recalled: "I will never forget the little box into which I was asked
to enter. Heavy curtains were draped on all sides of this 'telephone booth,' no
air, no sound, no hope was available for him who entered here. Once inside
lights began to dance merrily, dictating the procedure. They flashed 'Begin'—
'Faster'—'Slower'—'One minute'—'End,' etc., until the poor mortal who had
thought he was reading a well prepared script was not sure whether he had
read in an intelligent fashion or mumbled it to an unseen friend or foe. Weak
with nervous exhaustion and heavy perspiration, I stepped limply from the
ordeal, hoping that never again would I be called upon to participate in this
strange new field of broadcasting." Some regular participants on WHA during
these early years took to calling the booth "the padded cell."[4]

Hanson also had begun using a particular recording as a theme song for the
midday broadcasts. Its title was "Mystery," probably the 1919 composition by
Joseph Cirina.[5] At least two commercial recordings of this work were available, both from 1920.[6]

Three days after the new license went into effect, Hanson wrote to Herbert
Whittemore of the U.S. Bureau of Standards to ask about the procedure for
patenting a device that he had devised to determine the efficiency of modulation of a radio telephone transmitter. Hanson said he had never seen so much
as a description of such an item, adding that one was needed to adjust equipment for the highest efficiency.

Of most interest in the correspondence, however, are Hanson's comments
about the radio station in Madison. He wrote: "It looks as tho I will have to
devote my entire time to radio development work, at least during the next year
or so, until we can get our special radio appropriation out of the legislature when
they meet a year from now. Until then, constant development and publicity
work is necessary, in order to bring home the possibilities of radio phone broadcasting to the people of the state, and incidentally other states, who are waking

up and following us." Hanson added that when the station got that funding, it would be able to hire someone to replace him and he would be able to again focus on his studies. He thought that after getting his degree, he could get a good job in the radio industry and perhaps return to Madison to "run things for the State or the University for a while."[7] This is the first recorded hint that the station staff was actively looking beyond the university for funding and fully expected an appropriation. It also shows that the station's continuous efforts to promote itself were aimed at more that just building an audience—they were calculated to also generate political support for the radio operation. Hanson's final comment leaves one to wonder how the Wisconsin radio operation would have been different if he had indeed run the station in the decades ahead. In a letter to his mother on March 9, 1922, Hanson also said he planned to return to his studies once he could be confident "that neither the University of the state or Government is going to give up the work which we are going to build up."[8]

In late January 1922, WHA took part in the Farmers' Week on campus, an event presenting the latest in agricultural techniques and research. To demonstrate the value of the daily market broadcasts, the staff set up a receiver with a loudspeaker in the auditorium of the Agriculture Building about two blocks from the studio. Farmers attending the event got to hear the noon-hour weather and market broadcast over WHA. A sign near the radio receiver said that radios cost $35 to $200, and a farmer contemplating a radio purchase should figure on spending about one dollar for each mile of distance between his farm and Madison.

On February 1, 1922, representatives of the *Milwaukee Journal* visited Terry. Officials at the paper were impressed by the university radio operation and wanted to develop a working relationship with the station. In a letter to Edward A. Birge, who had succeeded Van Hise as university president in 1918, Terry outlined the newspaper's proposal. He said the paper would contribute $5,000 to increase the power of WHA "to an extent sufficient for a dependable daytime range, covering the entire state." The paper would also contribute a sum of money to pay an operator and for maintenance during the two years the agreement would be in effect. In return WHA would broadcast material furnished by the paper "three or more times per week, according to a definite schedule." The material would consist of "musical concerts, lectures and talks by well-known persons," similar to that "furnished by the Westinghouse Company, the *Chicago Tribune* and others." The paper intended to advertise the service as a cooperation between the university and the *Milwaukee Journal.* At the end of the two years all the radio equipment purchased by the paper for the project would become the permanent property of the university.[9]

Although the offer was attractive on several levels, Terry wanted to turn it down. He believed that the station should steer clear of any commercial relationship as a general policy. In a written response to H. J. Grant, the paper's publisher, Terry said that Birge had informally brought up the topic for discussion at a meeting of the Board of Regents. The feeling was "that since the university is a state institution and its facilities must, accordingly, be available to all citizens of the state without discrimination, it is hardly at liberty to accept funds from any group of individuals to enter upon any agreement whereby a particular group may secure privileges not available to the citizens of the state at large." Terry went on to say that if the agreement could be modified so that

Radiophone Demonstration, January 31 - 1922, at "Farmer's Week." A sign reads "Wisconsin was the first state to employ the wireless telephone for market reports and is still leading all others." Receiver is displayed at right.

WHA demonstration at the 1922 Farmers' Week
WHA's value to Wisconsin's agricultural community was demonstrated during the Farmers' Week on the University of Wisconsin campus in 1922. Market reports broadcast by WHA were received on the radio at the far right and the day's prices were written on the blackboard. (University of Wisconsin Archives series 23/24/3)

after the power increase WHA would still be free to broadcast material from other newspapers, the arrangement with the *Milwaukee Journal* might be acceptable, but he assumed that "exclusiveness is one of the features which makes the proposition of value to you." On behalf of Birge, Terry thanked Grant for the generosity of the offer and diplomatically said the university was in no way discriminating against the paper. He said other offers had come in to the university and were rejected for similar reasons.[10] Grant replied that the paper understood the university's position and had decided not to pursue the matter further.[11] The newspaper eventually would enter the broadcast business with its own station, and relations between the paper and WHA would not be nearly so cordial.

Lighty, the new program director, continued his efforts to promote the station. He began to send newspapers regular press releases about the program schedule. On February 8, 1922, the *Press Bulletin* included the schedule for the first time, a lineup similar to what had been in effect the previous fall. The weekday market reports and weather continued as before, but on Saturdays the market report was followed at 1:15 p.m. by a fifteen-minute program of music from phonograph records and a brief lecture on some topic having to do with radio. The Friday night *Radiophone Concert* was now thirty minutes long and the only program at 360 meters (833 kHz); the rest of the schedule was at 485 meters (618 kHz).

Lighty had more programming innovations in mind. A February 1922 circular by Hanson that was issued through the Extension Division said the station planned to augment the concerts with "lectures, political speeches and several phases of University Extension work."[12]

On February 17, 1922, the station broadcast its fifth live concert from the armory, featuring the cellist Pablo Casals. The *Daily Cardinal* of February 22 said: "From the microphone, the sound was run through a amplifier which intensified it 50 times. From here, the sound traveled through a line placed in the university heating tunnel to the station, where it was again amplified 50 times and sent out from the radiophone." By early the next week the station had received nearly one hundred letters from listeners in the Midwest, as well as Texas, Alabama, West Virginia, and New York. More remote broadcasts were in the offing, as the station also had an audio line to the university's Music Hall. Charles H. Mills, a music professor, said that the station would air as many concerts as it could from the Music Hall or the armory; these would include performances by the glee club, bands, orchestras, the Choral Union, and Mills himself on the organ.

Another addition to the schedule was a regularly scheduled newscast with university news, activities, and information, the *University Press Bureau Radio-phone Report.* The program was to debut the evening of March 10, but WHA found itself involved with news earlier in the day, when the Randall State Bank in Madison was robbed. Hanson went on the air to broadcast a description of the suspects and their car. Twenty miles away in Sauk City, the message was heard over the receiver at the high school and the information relayed to the police. As a result, two men who matched the description were detained for questioning.[13]

The new weekly offering of university news featured material from the *Press Bulletin,* which reported: "The Badger university is the first to utilize wireless telephone to disseminate its news." The program's content recognized the per-ishable nature of news, in that "the items broadcasted will be selected for the widest interest. Because 'spot news' is likely to be old in a weekly service, more general items and special features will make up the service."[14] By mid-April the program had been moved to 8 p.m., just ahead of the *Radiophone Concert,* which now began at 8:20 p.m.[15]

The *Radiophone Concert* was also modified. Edgar Gordon became its full-time host as of the March 10 program. He abandoned the playing of phono-graph records and managed to schedule live performers each week.

During the first two programs Gordon offered short comments about the music. Response from listeners was positive, and Gordon changed the format again to formalize his comments as a lecture. On March 24 the lecture series *Appreciation of Music* was born, one of the nation's first attempts to use radio for education. Gordon began the program by saying: "This is the University Exten-sion Instruction Service by Radio Broadcast on the appreciation of music."[16] The series continued through the end of July.

At 9:15 p.m. a special presentation, a proclamation from Wisconsin gover-nor John J. Blaine, followed the new newscast and *Radiophone Concert* on March 10. Blaine probably did not read the address on the radio himself, as an advance notice in the *La Crosse Tribune* two days earlier noted that "if Gover-nor Blaine is unable to deliver the proclamation in person, it will be broadcasted by chief operator Malcolm P. Hanson of the University." Given the lack of press coverage after the event, it is likely that Hanson did indeed step in. But Blaine nonetheless holds the title as first Wisconsin governor to speak on the station, since his appearances on WHA programs later in his term were documented.

Lighty made another addition to the station schedule in March: a program of "concerts or talks" at 4:30 p.m. on Tuesday and Thursday afternoons. The station's broadcast schedule was still limited to times it would not interfere with classes and other laboratory activities nearby in Sterling Hall. Lighty also came up with the idea of announcing upcoming programs on the air and holding to a definite schedule.[17]

WHA got more valuable publicity a few days later. University of Wisconsin economics professor Alfred Haake spoke over WHA on the afternoon of March 15, during a time of day when the station was usually off the air. He had been scheduled to address the Wisconsin Credit Men's Association convention, underway eighty miles away in Oshkosh, but was unable to make the trip. To present his address, he used WHA and the convention attendees listened to him over a receiving set. How his use of WHA came about is not known, but someone arranged to record the occasion with a photograph. It made the front page of the next morning's *Wisconsin State Journal,* accompanying a short story that related: "A telegram received from the association congratulated Prof. Haake upon the address. It was distinctly heard by the delegates." Professor Lighty was no doubt thrilled with the publicity. Here was a distinguished

Economics professor Alfred Haake
Haake was one of the first University of Wisconsin professors to speak over WHA, shown here making an address on March 15, 1922. The station used this photo at least twice for publicity. A cropped version ran in a Madison newspaper the next morning, and this full version ran later that year in *Popular Radio* magazine. (University of Wisconsin Archives series 3/1)

faculty member talking over the radio on an academic topic in his area of expertise, and getting front-page coverage in the local newspaper.

The plan for using the new radio operation to present an organized educational series was formally announced in mid-March. Lighty had worked on the project for some months and had recruited faculty members from different departments. He outlined his vision for using radio in the classroom and for his personal goal, adult education, ideas that served as the basis for the Wisconsin School of the Air and Wisconsin College of the Air. Lighty's plan called for encouraging high schools to install radio receivers, much as the Extension Division had encouraged them to purchase "motion picture and stereoptican machines" for visual instruction. The midday programs were to be five to ten minutes long and begin at 1:05 p.m., after the noon-hour weather and markets broadcasts. The schedule followed a regular pattern:

Monday: facts and reports interpretive of the university
Tuesday: four-minute addresses by university men
Wednesday: health notes and comments
Thursday: facts for the promotion of the idea of being mentally and
physically fit and the promotion of high standards and ideals in athletics
and sports
Friday: examples of artistic expression in music, readings and other forms that
lend themselves to radio broadcasting.

The evening programs consisted of Gordon's established music appreciation course on Friday, along with a new program at 8 p.m. on Tuesday, when a university professor would broadcast a twenty-minute lecture "on a subject of general interest." The first Tuesday of the month would feature a talk on current events, the second week's talk would be on civic and municipal information, the third week would be devoted to a women's club program, and the fourth week would offer a community program or a program from the PTA.[18]

Lighty had met with Birge to get approval to serve as program coordinator. An outgrowth of this meeting was that on March 27 Birge appointed a radio committee, which lent prestige to the endeavor. It was chaired by Lighty, and its members included Terry and Gordon. Some historians have suggested that Lighty stacked the committee with faculty members who would be most likely to contribute programs and whose stature would influence their colleagues to participate.[19] The involvement of the committee may also have allayed some of Birge's reservations about the radio operation. Lighty recalled that Birge believed that radio was not sufficiently dignified to be a university project and was concerned about public statements by people officially identified with the institution. Lighty suggested that faculty members prepare their scripts in advance, with a copy sent to Birge for approval. This procedure appears to have remained in effect for all of 1922 and for a time thereafter. One unintended benefit is that many on-air presentations from this era are preserved in written form, long before sound recording was available at WHA.

Once again, the staff of the *Press Bulletin* managed to get news of the radio station into the *New York Times*. On April 1, 1922, the paper carried an item about Lighty's program and Gordon's music appreciation lecture on Friday evenings. The *Noon-Day Educational Radio Broadcasts* began the week of May 29, 1922:

Monday: The Wisconsin Spirit—Prof. Gardner
Tuesday: An Address—President Birge
Wednesday: The Medical Clinic—Dr. Evans
Thursday: Spring Sports—T. E. Jones
Friday: Literary Readings—Dean Roe

The first Tuesday evening offering in the series of *Evening University Lectures* was a professor of neuropsychiatry at the medical school and a major in the U.S. Army. As had been the case for weeks, Gordon gave his music appreciation program on Friday.[20]

Lighty wrote introductions for the talks and read them on air himself or gave the task to Hanson. Some professors just sent prepared lectures that Lighty read on the air. Lighty was bemused that some professors suffered "mike fright." He thought it ironic that these same professors had no problem in a large lecture hall filled with students but would freeze up when faced with what he called "this little tin box."[21]

A dramatic example of how the radio could be used for education came in a letter from a group of people in the small town of Hayes Center, Nebraska, which they described as "20 miles from the railroad and 300 miles from a city." They were getting together to listen as a group to Gordon's Friday evening music appreciation program.[22]

The Nebraska group was not the only one to gather for Gordon's lectures. A listener in Bradford, Illinois, said five to fifteen people gathered weekly to hear the program.[23] In Watertown, Wisconsin, the city's Chamber of Commerce hosted a community listening session that attracted seventy people, and a listener in Beaver Dam, Wisconsin, was hosting a "wireless Friday night" at the area's country club to which one hundred people had been invited.[24]

The reports of group listening prompted Gordon to try something new that summer. On the evening of July 4, 1922, he asked those listening to stand in their homes and join him in singing "America." Within days he received letters from people who had participated. It was a hint of Gordon's future: beginning in 1931, he would host a weekly music education program for schools and lead thousands of unseen schoolchildren in song.[25] Gordon's 1922 music appreciation program also developed an odd sort of studio audience. On Friday evenings Madison residents would line up outside Sterling Hall and file in to silently peek through the door into the basement studio during the broadcast.[26]

Merchants also wrote in to say that they were playing WHA in their stores and that the practice was attracting customers. A Madison radio dealer called

The Radiophone Marching Band
Little information is available about the Radiophone Marching Band pictured here. It marched in a St. Patrick's Day parade in 1922, the date hinted at by the WHA and 9XM call letters on the drumhead. The group carries storage batteries and a radio receiver on the "stretcher," as well as speakers and an antenna wire, evidently to march along to music broadcast by WHA. (Wisconsin Historical Society Archives series PH3461, image WHi-23491)

Hanson at lunchtime one day to ask that he deviate from the regular broadcast schedule to play a record after the market report. The *Wisconsin State Journal* of April 23 reported that the dealer told Hanson: "I have nearly got a set sold and just need that music."

People continued to request instructions for building their own receiving set. In fact, the demand was overwhelming WHA. The station finally announced that the Extension Division would assume the responsibility for publishing the instructional bulletins in the future.[27]

WHA staffers directed the mail to the most appropriate person for response. Lighty took letters involving the Extension Division, while others went to Miller, Gordon, and Hopkins, the UW agricultural journalism professor. Hanson also answered many letters.[28] Lighty made certain to immediately forward one WHA fan letter to Birge. After complimenting WHA on a particular program, the listener wrote: "The writer has long been an admirer of the University of Wisconsin and expects to have his boy attend your school at the close of his high school, which will be in two years hence."[29]

The boom in radio during the early months of 1922 meant a growing audience for the university station. By the end of July a compilation of station correspondence showed that more than one thousand receiving stations in Wisconsin and nearby states were regularly tuning in to WHA.[30]

Regular broadcasting also had a price. It was too much for Hanson, a part-time operator, to handle alone. Terry asked Lighty and Hopkins, the UW agricultural journalism professor, to jointly take charge of the program schedule. Terry and Hanson would be responsible for the technical side of things. Lighty was in charge of most of the programming with Hopkins responsible for agricultural materials. By April Terry also was appealing to the university for more funding. He told Birge that the station had become a matter of "general university interest," and its support should not be borne entirely by the physics department budget. Terry asked for $500, which was enough to pay two student assistants $250 each and keep the station afloat for another year, but it would not, as he said, "permit us to make extensions which I feel are justified by the opportunities that radio offers for making the university of service to the state." Birge approved the amount for the 1922–23 school year.[31]

Also during the early part of 1922, Lighty suggested to Hanson that he organize an on-air correspondence course in building and maintaining radio sets. Hanson came up with a six-part course by April. The course was to be offered again in the fall, and by early October more than one hundred people had signed up.[32]

On the evening of April 14, 1922, Madison residents in the downtown area

near the State Capitol were treated to a technological innovation that also
promoted WHA. B. B. Jones and Max Littleton of the Department of Markets displayed an automobile that they had outfitted with a radio receiver and
loudspeaker, powered from the car's battery. They claimed it was the first radio-
equipped auto in the state, and they played WHA's regular Friday evening music
appreciation program for curious spectators. In a description of the event people today would find familiar, Jones reported they were able to play the music
"so loud we were able to throw it out on a loud speaker over nearly a block."
The aerial was Littleton's invention, 130 feet of copper wire that he ran from
the radiator cap to the rear of the roof. Littleton said he also used the body of
the car itself as a "counterpoise," and "the results exceeded my expectations."
Not only was the WHA programming heard through the speaker, but onlook-
ers who used the headphones on the set were able to hear "every word and strain

The first automobile in Wisconsin with a radio
Max Littleton (center) of the Department of Markets outfitted this automobile with
a radio and stretched the antenna wires from the radiator cap to the top of the
windshield and over the roof. Pictured with Littleton are fellow agency employees
Harry Tunstall (left) and B. B. Jones. The photo was taken on the grounds of the
Wisconsin State Capitol in April 1922. (Wisconsin Historical Society Archives
series PH3461, image WHi-23508)

of music from WWJ at Detroit, KDKA at Pittsburg, and even WJZ at Newark." Jones predicted, "I do not think it will be long before the wireless aerial will be a common sight on automobiles." He pointed to the success of radio receivers on passenger trains and said a radio would be of value to the "automobile tourist-camper" in the future.[33]

The same article describing the car radio claimed that "wireless for the pedestrian is coming" and told of a factory in Paris that was turning out an umbrella that concealed an antenna and "in the lady's purse is a little battery and in her hair a small receiver." The writer predicted it would be seen on the streets of Madison within a year.[34]

Lighty continued his efforts to promote the station. He convinced public libraries around the state to prominently post the weekly WHA schedule and sent representatives from the Extension Division to speak to community and civic groups about the value of WHA. He even enlisted the visual aids section of the Extension Division and commissioned a promotional film about WHA. Called *Broadcasting a University*, it toured forty Wisconsin cities beginning in May 1922. The film showed the building and installation of a receiving set as well as scenes of WHA in operation. No print of the film is known to have survived, but one frame from it accompanied a story about the film in the *Wisconsin State Journal* on April 30. It shows a farm wife listening to WHA through headphones in her kitchen.

In June 1922 WHA had a display at the Milwaukee Radio Show and provided special broadcasts to demonstrate the station's service. One segment broadcast was an address by Terry himself. He began by commenting on how strange it was to be addressing listeners at that distance. He saved his typed copy of the speech, and more than any other existing document, the text outlines Terry's belief in non-commercial, educational broadcasting.

He spoke of "the possibility of simultaneous reception of signals at a large number of widely separated points [which] makes such service especially applicable to the dissemination of weather forecasts, market quotations, news, description of criminals, timely and useful information of all sorts from centers of activity to remoter regions to which such information seldom penetrates." He also told of how the state universities were the first to sense the possibilities of radio broadcasting.

Terry went on to describe a meeting in Washington called by President Harding earlier that year. The goal of this first conference on radio telephony was to revise the rules for controlling broadcasting. Attending the conference were representatives of government, educational institutions, and amateurs, but no one from commercial broadcasting. Terry said the conference attendees called for government control of radio telephone service as the only solution to "the present chaos of interference." He said the conference called for all wavelengths from 0 to 6,000 meters (everything above 50 kHz) to be reserved for radiotelephony. He said the conference had specified twenty-one different "wave bands" over this range, seventeen of which were between 0 and 2,000 meters (everything above 150 kHz). Further, he said the conference recommended that broadcasting be given first consideration for assignments within this band.

Looking ahead, Terry noted that the recommendations called for at least eleven of the twenty-one wave bands to be under federal, state, or municipal control, which he said was suggestive of the future control of radio broadcasting. Terry evidently thought the conference was to be the last word on regulation and felt that because it called for prohibiting direct advertising by radio,

The WHA/9XM display at the Milwaukee Radio Show
The June 1922 Milwaukee Radio Show featured this promotional display from the University of Wisconsin. (Wisconsin Historical Society Archives, Classified series 86619, image WHi-23505)

private companies would be in the field only as long as indirect advertising value existed. He said that, ultimately, broadcasting would become a public or governmental responsibility, "par excellence for eliminating the effects of geographic differences, and for the creation of greater national and even international harmony. It will provide increased facilities for widespread dissemination of educational matter aiding in advancing the average of intellectual attainments. By the increased distribution of finer products of the musical art, it will stimulate popular appreciation of and increase the sensitiveness to the less materialistic aspects of living. By increasing familiarity with phenomena of science, it will necessarily tend to produce a much needed keenness of perception and power of logical reasoning."[35]

On June 28, 1922, WHA found that it had competition in Madison, as the city's first commercial station went on the air. WGAY was operated by the North Western Radio Company, which ran a radio sales and service shop on State Street. It too was authorized to operate at 360 meters (833 kHz) and was in operation for about a year. The building in which it was located remained a radio store for years thereafter and still stands in Madison. (In a nice example of continuity of use, part of the building later became home to Madison's downtown Radio Shack outlet.)

On July 1, 1922, the Department of Markets announced the temporary suspension of the market reports through the end of August. To take their place during the summer session, WHA announced the addition of a new daily talk "on agriculture and country life" by experts from the College of Agriculture. This formalized the agriculture college's offerings, which had been short remarks accompanying the market reports, and made them into more of a regular program.[36] This service to the state's farm listeners would be part of the noon hour for decades to come. The new schedule continued until the station shut down as usual with the start of the university summer break at the end of July.

Littleton had been urging his supervisors in the markets department to establish a separate station for market reports. By mid-July it was reported that the number of regular recipients of the market reports had grown to a thousand.[37] B. B. Jones of the Department of Markets met with Terry during the summer to discuss ways to improve the service, with particular attention to improving the poor reception of the station in far northern Wisconsin. Terry said he had just completed a study and said the rebuilt transmitter should be able to send a strong signal to the entire state. Based on the meeting, the Department of Markets decided to continue its operation with WHA.[38]

The next month Jones wrote Terry to say that the agency was interested in having the market reports on the station four times a day, six days a week, and he asked what WHA would charge for the additional broadcasts.[39] Along with the additional work, the request meant the station would be operating outside the midday-evening-weekend schedule it had maintained to avoid interfering with other activities in the building. On the back of the letter are Terry's blue-pencil calculations of the cost of another operator and the cost of tubes, based on how rapidly the transmitter was consuming them. Terry responded that the proposal would cost WHA $4,014 for the 1922–23 school year. Part of the additional cost would be for WHA to acquire its own motor generator set to power the transmitter. Up to this point, the station had been using one from the physics department. This was another reason that the schedule was limited: the station was on the air during hours when the physics department did not need its generator for laboratory work. Terry noted that during the previous year, the payments from the Department of Markets had covered only Hanson's time and contributed nothing toward the cost of operating the station. Terry said he thought it fair that the Department of Markets pay half the additional cost for the station, or $2,000 ($200 per month for ten months).[40] This was much more than the fifty dollars per month the station had charged for the first year of the broadcasts. The increase evidently caused some reevaluation at the Department of Markets and made the concept of its own station more appealing. Equipment problems forced the station to delay resumption of broadcasting in the fall, which also frustrated the markets officials. Finally, they decided to go ahead with their own station in Waupaca in central Wisconsin and closed the Madison markets office. The agency's Waupaca operation was ready by November, and Max Littleton moved there as well. He would oversee the installation of the department's new radio station and serve as its manager for more than a year. (See chapter 18 for a detailed discussion of the agency's station, WPAH, which later became WLBL.)

While station was off the air, Lighty submitted a report to Birge that summarized the first season of educational broadcasts. Lighty said the radio committee had convinced a number of faculty to participate and that "these broadcasts were participated in by almost every college, school or course in the university." In the first eight weeks of the programs, thirty-five individuals from twenty university departments had participated. The only one who appeared more than twice was T. E. Jones, a professor in the physical education department, who gave talks about college athletics.[41]

The fall broadcasting season was delayed several times. Accidents to the transmitting tubes continued to affect the operation, keeping the station off the air until November 1, 1922. Once back on the air, it was announced that WHA would make its first broadcast of a college football game when the Badgers played their homecoming game against Illinois on November 11. This would be a good contest to present, because fans in both Wisconsin and Illinois were within range of WHA. Unfortunately, the broadcast was never made. On November 9, the *Daily Cardinal* reported that an equipment breakdown and need for repairs would keep the station off air "for about two weeks." The period of silence was much longer, until January 8, 1923. Repairs were delayed because the university's glassblower, James B. Davis, had injured his hand in an automobile accident and was unable to immediately assist in making new tubes. Although Terry was by this time capable of making the tubes himself, his teaching load kept him from doing so until the Christmas break. Someone once asked Terry about some tubes he'd made that had the glass used for sealing the tube colored red. He replied: "You see I started making those particular tubes on Christmas day and I used red sealing-in glass by way of celebrating a little."[42] A colleague noted Terry's presence in the laboratory on Christmas Day one year and said Terry told him that because it was a holiday, he'd close up shop a bit early: 4 p.m.[43]

While WHA was off the air, two milestones in radio were recorded. On October 3, 1922, KFBU in Laramie, Wyoming, began operations. Now all forty-eight states had broadcasting stations. On November 14 station 2LO in London made its first broadcast, marking the beginning of what would become the British Broadcasting Corporation.

WHA's 1923 broadcast year began on Monday, January 8. The station was still on the air Monday through Saturday and featured a brief program of time signals at 11:59 a.m., followed by the weather at noon, both at 485 meters (618 kHz). The weather was followed at 12:07 p.m. by an agricultural broadcast. After changing frequencies to 360 meters (833 kHz), the daily educational lecture was delivered, beginning at 12:20 p.m. The station also made a regular transmission from 11 p.m. Friday until 3 a.m. Saturday to run tests of signal strength.[44]

While WHA was off the air, a postcard of complaint arrived from a regular correspondent. Several postcards and letters remain in WHA files from a W. C. Shumaker of the Orangeville Radio Club; Orangeville is just south of the Wisconsin border near Freeport, Illinois. Some letters are on letterhead, with Shumaker referring to himself as a "consulting radiotrician." Regardless of form, all are critical of WHA to the point of insult. In response to the announcement of the temporary shutdown, he sent a card that said, "So glad you are going to 'shut up' for a while. Wish it was forever. It will sure be a relief at that. We are all rejoicing. Orangeville Radio Club."[45] Shumaker had also complained the previous year about WHA music programs, which he said were vastly inferior to those on KYW, the Westinghouse commercial station in Chicago. For their first year of operation, KYW had but one program format: live opera. It soon evolved into a typical broadcast outlet of the period with phonograph records, news bulletins, and the like. Still, Shumaker wrote: "K.Y.W. plays 19 pieces of music in their hour, it takes them 20 seconds to announce. If you play 4 pieces in an hour you do good, too much talk, too much W.H.A. W.H.A. W.H.A. W.H.A. W.H.A. W.H.A. just like a parrot. Lord knows, everyone knows who you are."[46]

With WHA back on the air, Schumaker immediately resumed his complaints. He started by saying, "Your old mill sounds just as rotten, as it did when you quit last fall." He was also displeased that WHA would be on in the evening, and on the 360-meter wavelength, thereby interfering with distant stations he wanted to hear. Unaware he was actually paying a compliment to Hanson, he did praise the telegraphy heard over WHA, citing "perfect letters, something you don't hear often these days."[47]

Hanson decided that, with the station back on the air, he could take the time to respond to Schumaker. A carbon copy of his response was retained in the WHA archives, dated January 9, 1923; it shows Hanson's mischievous streak, and it's unknown if he received permission from Terry or Lighty to send it. It fairly drips with sarcasm:

My dear Mr. Shumaker:

Please accept our apologies for our long-standing failure to acknowledge all the interesting letters and valuable suggestions we have received from you in the past. For some time we have been wondering what had become of you and whether you would be able to enjoy your receiving set while our station, WHA, was closed. We have been anxiously awaiting the day when we were ready to start up again and when we could hear from all our old friends who faithfully have listened day after day for the return of WHA. We were not disappointed when we found your kind note among the first letters of congratulation to reach us, and we are glad that you are still interested as ever and are helping us with your suggestions and criticisms. Among our great audience of enthusiastic listeners, we have few if any who have the refreshing sense of humor which you bring to bear in your letters, and we wish to thank you for many a hearty laugh which you have afforded us.

From your letterhead, we gather that perhaps you might be persuaded to come to Madison for a day or two to assist us with your advice in securing an even more perfect adjustment of our transmitter. We would appreciate to hear from you in regard to this matter as soon as possible as we desire to have the best station in this part of the country. Please advise what salary you would charge and how soon you could make the trip. We are all looking forward to meeting you in person.

Yours for perfect radio,

Operating Staff WHA[48]

Schumaker fired a letter back, bemused by Hanson's response. He began: "At last you have shown some signs of being human, at least you have a sense of humor." The pleasant tone didn't last, however. Schumaker complained that a recent talk on WHA about a soil survey had been broadcast by other stations weeks earlier and that a health lecture was a repeat of one given the previous year. He also complained about dead air and that the time signal given by WHA was four seconds off from the one given by Arlington. He grudgingly acknowledged that WHA sounded better, but he turned down the sarcastic invitation to come to Madison, saying, "Any suggestions I could give would go over your head."[49] Most of the Schumaker letters in the file have the word "freak" scrawled across them.

The noontime schedule remained in effect only through February 3. Sometime in February WHA apparently stopped sending out material by code and became a telephonic-only operation. During the week of February 10 the educational broadcast was moved to 7 p.m., again at 360 meters (833 kHz). The evening program began with a repeat of the weather forecast, then featured university speakers. There is evidence that the forecast and educational talk together took about twenty minutes, as "specials" during this period were often scheduled for 7:20 p.m. Other specials occasionally followed the noontime weather forecast. The lineup of 7 p.m. programs for the week of March 5, 1923, was as follows:

Monday March 5: "Understanding and Contracts: The Strength of the Organization" by Professor Theodore Macklin

Tuesday March 6: "The Significance of the Engineer's Survey" by Professor R. S. Owen

Wednesday March 7: "Diptheria Control Among Children" by W. D. Stovall

Thursday March 8: "Physical Education" by Professor T. E. Jones

Friday March 9: "Good Architecture in Wisconsin" by Arthur Peabody

Saturday March 10: "The Relation Between the Broadcast Listener and the Transmitting Amateur" by M. P. Hanson[50]

By March 1923 the Monday and Thursday broadcasts included "government agriograms," added to compensate for the loss of the markets reports.

The *Press Bulletin* had reported on January 10, 1923, that the station would be adding bulletins from the U.S. Department of Agriculture. The regular Saturday broadcast also included an announcement of the topics to be presented during the upcoming week. Because the Saturday educational broadcast was always about radio, Hanson was often the speaker, but on March 31 Terry himself was featured. He was listed with the title "Director of the University of Wisconsin Radio Station" and his topic was "Some Recent Developments in Radio."[51] Unfortunately, Terry's script is not among those preserved from this period.

Terry also continued his research into the science of radio. He presented the results of some studies to the executive committee of the American section of the International Union for Scientific Radio Telegraph. He told of his Wisconsin research to "determine the direction of prevailing static disturbances, to measure variations in strength of the signals of stations, and to measure the variations in the apparent direction of stations in the United States."[52]

Earle Terry and W. H. Lighty
Lighty, WHA's first program director, is standing at the lectern at right in the Sterling Hall studio in June 1923. Relaxing at left is a dapper Terry. (University of Wisconsin Archives series 23/24/2)

The WHA workplace was improved during this period. The station now took up two basement rooms in Sterling Hall. The radio equipment was in room 38, and room 37 was equipped with an illuminated speaker's table and a special microphone "about the size of a large teacup." Although the signal box remained, the "studio" now had a small loudspeaker near the table so the lecturers could hear the announcements and introduction before their presentation. One additional benefit of the new arrangement was that the quilt-lined booth was retired.[53]

The early months of 1923 brought another long-awaited new feature: live play-by-play broadcasts of college basketball games from the armory, using the steam tunnel audio lines that ran to Sterling Hall. WHA aired five home contests that spring, beginning with a game against the University of Michigan on February 19. The *Daily Cardinal* reported on March 2 that the station collected more than five hundred letters from thirty-four states and Canada after the first two basketball broadcasts. An often-published photo shows a broadcast in progress from what appears to be a raised platform. The games were very popular with listeners around the country, and WHA received hundreds of letters from those who "told the station of this pleasure of 'seeing the game' by wireless." A reception report even came in from Garrochales, Puerto Rico, where a listener had picked up the Wisconsin–Purdue basketball broadcast on March 3.[54] That spring, WHA added another sports feature, broadcasting the championship game of the state high school basketball tournament on March 24.[55]

The day after the first basketball broadcast, the station used the lines to the armory again, this time for another live classical music broadcast. Pablo Casals, who had performed over WHA a year earlier, was back in Madison for another concert. Since the previous year the growing popularity of radio had become a cause for concern on the part of some musicians. Casals's manager regarded radio as a threat to his client's livelihood and had enjoined the artist from broadcast performances. However, WHA had cleared the broadcast with Casals's student manager, had the equipment in place, and had promoted the concert on air. When Casals walked on stage, he spotted the WHA microphone, which had been concealed in a decorative palm. The famous cellist gave Ross Herrick, the on-site student engineer, a severe "bawling out" and said that he was not allowed to broadcast. Herrick communicated this to the transmitter operator, and they quickly agreed to not call it a broadcast but simply a test for experimental purposes. This fine point of semantics was communicated to Casals, and he agreed to proceed. The engineers then switched on the microphone and transmitter during the concert, and WHA's audience heard much of Casals's performance. However, Casals evidently suspected something was

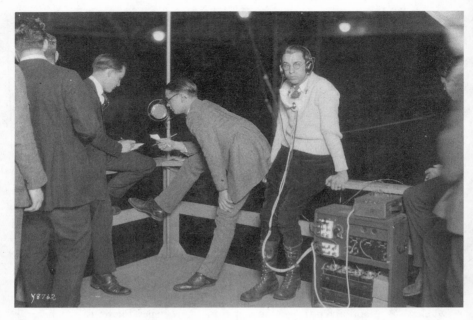

WHA student operators at college basketball broadcast
Reeve O. Strock (facing the camera) is engineering a live broadcast of a basketball
game in this photograph from 1923. That year WHA broadcast five home games as
well as the state high school basketball championship. (University of Wisconsin
Archives series 23/24/5)

up, since each time he reappeared on stage, he moved a bit farther from the
microphone. By the end of the broadcast listeners could hear the piano accom-
paniment and little else.[56]

Through this early period Terry and the other members of the WHA staff
firmly held to their policy of non-commercial, educational broadcasting. However, as the public became more acquainted with radio, requests began arriving
from businesses and various other organizations to use the station for "commercial" purposes. Usually, the station was able to reject the requests without
any consequences, but Don Mowry, the secretary of the Madison Chamber
of Commerce, complained directly to Birge after being turned down. After
meeting with Lighty and Terry for explanation, Birge told Terry to write a
letter to Mowry and try to mollify him. Terry did so, telling Mowry that the
station was "merely following . . . the only consistent policy [that] can be
adopted by an educational institution."[57]

WHA was authorized to broadcast at night, when AM radio signals can normally travel great distances, due to changes in the ionosphere after sundown. However, there were now hundreds of other radio stations on the same frequency. In the summer of 1922 the federal government had added a third authorized frequency for broadcasting, 400 meters (749 kHz). However, with six hundred stations sharing the three frequencies, interference was a severe problem. The *Daily Cardinal* of February 15, 1923, commented on the situation, saying the nighttime airwaves were "a regular frog pond because of perpetual interference."

Some special programs augmented the evening schedule that spring, including a rare Sunday operation to air a special address and music for Mothers' Day. But the Saturday evening programs were discontinued after the first week in April. Special programs were offered during the university's Farmers' Week, and during the week of June 4–9, 1923, WHA pulled out all the stops with special programs for Better Homes Week. Each evening's program began with a musical prelude arranged by Gordon, followed by introductory remarks from Evelyn Jensen, assistant professor of home economics with the Extension Division. Many speakers on the programs were Extension Division personnel, and most others were affiliated with the University of Wisconsin. On the first evening Governor Blaine discussed the value of the Better Homes in America movement.

The programs included a banker-turned-mathematics professor who spoke about financing a home, a discussion by the state architect about how to choose a home site and its relation to architecture, a presentation about landscape design by another professor; a talk by a nursing professor called "Health in the Home," a philosophy professor's discussion of moral education in the home, and a talk on recreation by a professor of physical education.[58]

After the Better Homes Week broadcasts the station returned to its regular weekday evening schedule for one week and then began a Monday-Wednesday-Friday evening schedule, with the weather continuing at noon Monday through Saturday. The printed listings for the first week of the new schedule showed the cancellation of the Wednesday and Friday offerings and the Monday program of the following week. That week also saw the start time of the programs moved to 7:30 p.m. For several weeks that summer, the Friday evening program was a formalized reading hour, and "readings from literature" were a semi-regular Friday feature through 1926. The three-day schedule continued through August 1, 1923, when the station shut down for summer break.[59]

The 1923 fall broadcasting season for WHA began on October 1, continuing the three-night schedule. The second week's schedule shows ongoing problems: on Wednesday, October 10, the program list has the notation "failed to show up" next to a guest's name, and beside Friday, October 12, someone noted, "Machine broke down."[60]

WHA expanded its sports offerings with the new broadcast season, adding live broadcasts of University of Wisconsin football games; the October 6, 1923, home opener against Coe College may have been the first game broadcast, according to letters from listeners, who wrote in with suggestions and criticisms. One listener said the microphone was too close to the crowd, with the "roar from the crowd of rooters" obscuring the announcer's comments. He also said there was "too much of an intermission between announcements." The writer pointed out that the football broadcasts on KYW-Chicago the previous year were much easier to understand, which he attributed to the announcer's location atop the press stand, away from the crowd. Further, he noted that the KYW announcer kept up a steady account of the game, which made it easy to follow.[61]

A capacity crowd was expected for the October 27 homecoming match-up with the University of Minnesota, with a dozen chartered trains bringing sports fans to Madison from various cities. Curiously, there was very little advance publicity of the broadcast of this contest or any of the season's games: so little, in fact, that at least one researcher mistakenly puts the first football broadcasts four years later.[62] Perhaps the WHA staff was reluctant to publicize the broadcasts given the cancellation of the widely promoted Wisconsin–Illinois game broadcast the previous year. Some letters written by listeners after that game remain in WHA files. One from a self-described "old football player" was complimentary but complained that "your operator or announcer at the sending station spent too much time real often in telling us who was broadcasting and what and where. Several times he cut off the wire from the field and we missed one and sometimes two plays right in an important place. Have him make these announcements between quarters or when someone takes out time."[63] The constant interruption of the play-by-play announcer by the transmitter operator also irked another listener, who said he found the announcing so disjointed that it was impossible to follow the action. He went on to say: "The announcer seems to hold a running conversation with some of his friends, discussing the various plays as they would play them if they were on the field. In these conversations with his friends, the visiting team is criticized. Furthermore, his choice of language would not be considered entirely proper should there be ladies listening in to these games, which, no doubt, there are. Especially toward the end of the Minnesota–Wisconsin game, he went beyond the bounds of decency in expressing his thought aloud over the microphone." Despite the complaints, this listener expressed appreciation for the broadcasts and asked that the WHA managers "accept this criticism as broad mindedly as possible."[64]

The Wisconsin Electric Sales Company in Janesville, which sold radios, took out a newspaper advertisement that referenced the games: "If You Had a Radio—You would have kept in touch with the big Wisconsin game, play by play. Install a radio and have your fingers on the pulse of the world."[65]

The station tried something new for the evening broadcasts during the week of November 19, 1923. Each evening educational broadcast had three guests instead of one. The first part of each broadcast was devoted to a topic in education, as this was American Education Week. In the second part professors who had been in Europe during the previous year discussed their observations, and during the last part of each program a professor from the Department of Economic Entomology spoke on various aspects of beekeeping.

During this period, if one of the evening presentations could not be made because the speaker failed to show up or the station was down for repairs, the guest would be rescheduled to another day and that broadcast would feature two speakers in sequence. Also, some guests were no longer turning in advance copies of their remarks. The broadcast schedule shows the notation "spoke from notes" with many of the listings. The talks were generating favorable responses. A November 26 lecture entitled "The Place of the Inspirational in Teaching," by Stephen W. Gilman, a business professor, generated more than three hundred letters of appreciation.[66]

Sometimes the WHA staff was asked to cancel the evening broadcast if another station had scheduled a special program. On October 24, 1923, H. F. Wilson, a professor in the Department of Economic Entomology, found his scheduled talk on the honeybee bumped to the following week. Madison residents had contacted WHA and said they wanted to tune in KDKA that evening for a broadcast by David Lloyd George, the wartime prime minister of Great Britain.[67] WHA also canceled its regular broadcast on December 10, 1923. The note on the program sheet says: "no broadcast tonight due to President of the U.S. broadcasting."[68] That evening President Coolidge made a speech from the White House memorializing Warren Harding, who had died on August 2. The address was carried at 8:30 p.m. Eastern Time over WEAF–New York, WCAP-Washington, and WJAR-Providence.[69] Coolidge had made his broadcast debut six days earlier with an address to the nation over those three stations and KSD–St. Louis, WDAF–Kansas City, and WFAA-Dallas, all part of the fledgling AT&T network. Listeners a thousand miles from Washington, D.C., reported that this broadcast was so clear that they could hear the Coolidge turn the pages of his manuscript.[70] WHA had received no request to remain off the air for this earlier broadcast as they were silent on Tuesdays anyway.

The first two weeks of February 1924 were hectic at WHA. During the first week WHA was on each evening at 8 p.m. with special programs for Farmers' Week on campus. One evening the station broadcast the event's banquet, which featured a toast by Governor Blaine.[71] The next week the station made special remote broadcasts from the university's Stock Pavilion to mark the university's seventy-fifth anniversary.[72] In the middle of this busy week a severe snowstorm disrupted communication in the Midwest, knocking out telegraph and telephone service. Madison's *Wisconsin State Journal* was able to use the receiving equipment at WHA to get press association reports from Chicago. The *Press Bulletin* boasted on February 13: "This is not the first time the powerful university station has been used for the dispatch and receipt of news matter, and on occasion it has been used in the pursuit of criminals." The article also said that since the beginning of the broadcast year in October, WHA had received more than twenty-five hundred letters from listeners and from every state except Utah. Reception had also been reported in Cuba and Alaska.

In early 1924 WHA received another offer to cooperate with a commercial enterprise. Sears, Roebuck and Company contacted Dean H. L. Russell of the College of Agriculture. Sears wanted to know whether WHA would be interested in cooperating with a station it was building in Chicago, and it offered to connect the two stations by leased wire so WHA could carry material from the Chicago operation. Russell seemed interested, but Hopkins, Terry, and Lighty all opposed the plan, and it was dropped.[73] The Chicago operation signed on for testing March 21, 1924, as WBBX, and after briefly using the call letters WES it officially went on the air April 12 at 345 meters (869 kHz) with the call letters WLS, honoring its owner as the World's Largest Store. WLS was later sold to *Prairie Farmer* magazine and for years served the rural audience of the Midwest and beyond.

Other broadcasting ideas were rejected as well. A wide variety of amateur performers were now contacting WHA, seeking airtime. WHA's strict adherence to its educational status gave the managers a diplomatic way to turn down these requests. The official policy was modified the following spring when high school bands from Richland Center, Sauk City, and Janesville were permitted to perform on separate occasions.[74] Some involvement by high school groups had already occurred by this time: in May 1924, WHA had broadcast the winners for the state high school lyceum contest.[75] These events not only appealed to listeners but had the added value of promoting the university among area high school students.

Through the early months of 1924, WHA remained on the three-night schedule, occasionally adding special broadcasts on Tuesdays or Thursdays for recitals or public speeches. One night per week, the scheduled speaker was followed by the *University Radiophone Press Bulletin,* the weekly news program. The station aired some special weekend programs in June, including the alumni banquet on June 21 and Birge's baccalaureate address on June 22.[76]

That summer Malcolm Hanson's neglect of his studies because of his involvement with the radio station finally caught up with him. He had been placed on academic probation in June 1921 and actually was dropped from the rolls of the College of Engineering in February 1922, after dropping three classes the previous fall and failing the remaining two. In a letter to Hanson's mother, Edward Bennett, a professor of electrical engineering, wrote: "I presume you are already familiar with the situation which has led to this extremely unsatisfactory record. It is that Malcolm is so interested and has devoted himself so whole heartedly to the work he is doing in radio that his studies receive very little consideration."[77] Terry had been Hanson's salvation, securing him a position as an instructor in the physics department even as he was failing courses as an electrical engineering student. Hanson recognized his addiction to radio and chastised himself for being unable to get away from it. He even asked friends for advice about "how to get out of my terrible habit."[78] Lida Hanson called her son's interest in radio "a jealous mistress who demanded all of his time." She said that this affected not only his studies but everything else as well, from friends to sports to books. She convinced her son to register as a senior in September 1923 and to devote himself full time to his studies in order to get his degree.[79] He even officially resigned from the station, replaced temporarily by student Robert V. Ray, a former commercial wireless operator who had graduated from the electrical engineering program at the University of Illinois.[80] Still, WHA kept pulling Hanson back. In June 1924 the university informed the twenty-nine-year-old undergraduate that he would not receive a diploma.

After he left the campus Hanson entered government service and worked on the development of radar in the Electronic Research Bureau of the U.S. Navy. His appointment to the bureau was made possible by A. Hoyt Taylor, the former Wisconsin and North Dakota physicist. Hanson later served as the radio operator for Admiral Byrd's fourteen-month expedition to Antarctica in 1929–30. (Antarctica's Mount Hanson was named by Byrd in honor of the radio engineer.) In August 1942, while on active duty with the navy, Hanson was killed when the military plane in which he was riding crashed into a mountainside in Alaska.

Hanson's permanent replacement as WHA's regular chief operator was Burton Miller, a doctoral student, who won the job after Ray failed to return to campus that fall.[81] For a while Miller served simultaneously as the operator for WEBW, the station at Beloit College. This was feasible because the Beloit station operated only on Sundays, the "off" day for WHA. Like Hanson, Miller had a close call with high voltage. In December 1924 defective insulation on some of the Beloit equipment gave him two 2,000-volt shocks. Commenting on the event, a Beloit professor said: "Anyone with a weak heart would have been instantly killed by the shock Mr. Miller took last night."[82]

One other important event occurred during the summer: WHA's license expired and the government deleted the call letters. WHA had been operating under the authority of the Class C limited commercial license dated April 3, 1924, which like all licenses of the period was in effect for three months. It expired on July 6, 1924, but WHA programming continued for another twenty-two days. On the face of the April 3 license is a penciled notation: "Delete per LSR Chicago 9/8/24."[83]

A new Class A limited commercial license was issued to the University of

The WHA staff and the station's directional antenna atop Sterling Hall, 1924
Terry (left) and radio operators Malcolm Hanson (center) and Burton Miller (right) on the roof of Sterling Hall near an experimental directional antenna. (University of Wisconsin Archives series 23/24/3)

Wisconsin on October 4, 1924. In the section "report and recommendation" is the notation "forwarded and recommending that class 'A' license for 275 meters be issued and that former call WHA be re-assigned."[84] Although the program lists for WHA indicate the station resumed scheduling guests for evening broadcasts beginning Monday, October 13, some sources say delays in station repairs and modifications pushed the first day of the fall broadcasting to October 25.[85]

It may have been that some lag in the paperwork associated with a change in frequency resulted in the brief period with no license. It may also have been that since the license would expire at about the time that WHA shut down for summer vacation, the staff thought it unimportant to apply for a new license until it was ready to resume broadcasting in the fall.

With the new license WHA now found itself temporarily on the new 275 meter wavelength (1090 kHz). The Department of Commerce had finally realized that three radio frequencies for the entire country were not enough. In the spring of 1923 the department had held the Second Radio Conference, which recommended that 545 to 222 meters (550 to 1350 kHz) be used for broadcasting. After Congress failed to act, Commerce Secretary Herbert Hoover assumed responsibility for assigning wavelengths to stations and classifying them. The new bandwidth allowed for stations to be assigned to individual wavelengths. In the fall of 1924, WHA forwarded an application to the Department of Commerce requesting a new classification and frequency assignment, but word had not been received by the end of the year.[86]

The popularity of music programs among the WHA listeners led to regular programs under the auspices of a committee from the School of Music, beginning in the fall of 1924. Gordon helped establish the committee, which was originally responsible for a Monday evening offering and soon expanded to Wednesday evenings as well. The format called for a fifteen-minute faculty talk bracketed by live music performances by faculty members, student musicians, and student ensembles. On occasion there would be two faculty lectures, or the entire program could be devoted to a musical concert.

However, the music faculty insisted that its performances be broadcast from Music Hall, because of the poor quality of the piano in the WHA studio. This was less efficient on two fronts: remote broadcasts were more complicated and resulted in poorer sound quality than a broadcast from the new studio. Finally, in December 1925 the studio got a better piano and the School of Music faculty agreed to move back to the Sterling Hall studio for performances. Having a piano available also figured in a fondly remembered musical offering. Without telling Terry, one WHA operator invited a popular pianist from

Madison commercial station WIBA to Sterling Hall for an unannounced performance. Terry arrived the next morning and was surprised to find four sacks
of cards addressed to the station demanding more "jazz."[87]

WHA resumed broadcasts on January 7, 1925. By early February the radio
inspector in Chicago had informed the station that it had been assigned to
535.4 meters (560 kHz). The broadcast schedule continued with three evenings
a week, but now the Monday and Friday programs began at 7:45 p.m. and
the Wednesday evening concert at 9 p.m.[88] Also early in the year, the university administration funded the conversion of a room in Music Hall for a new
"radio broadcasting chamber." This addition improved remote music broadcasts.[89] In March the station broadcast an intercollegiate debate, and the radio
audience was allowed to pick the winner by mailing in votes on postcards.[90]

WHA's new frequency was not its alone. Westinghouse station KYW in Chicago was on the same frequency, and WHA had to adjust its program hours to
accommodate them. When Illinois went to Daylight Saving Time, the change
forced WHA to move the start of its Wednesday evening program to 8 from 9
p.m.[91]

In early 1925, a recommendation came down to radio stations from officials
at the Department of Commerce. It read in part: "According to reports received
by the bureau the announcers of some of the broadcasting stations continue
programs for long periods without announcing the call letters of the station
and as some of the call letters are not readily understood, suggestion has been
made that some other method be adopted which will make identification more
positive. It will probably be helpful if when making an announcement the call
letters of a station are followed by the name of the city in which the broadcasting station is situated and it would no doubt be appreciated by the audience
if the announcers would announce distinctly the call letters and name of the
city at somewhat regular intervals."[92] This is in essence the same rule stations
follow today: the legal hourly station identification of call letters followed by
city of license. Given some of the complaints received at WHA over its first
few years, it was probably not one of the offending operations.

Lighty continued his efforts to promote the station, and he responded to
numerous requests from papers near and far for WHA program schedules that
they could print in their radio columns. The distribution list included the wire
services as well as the *Wisconsin Farmer, Radio Digest, Christian Science Monitor,* and local papers in such places as Louisville, Brooklyn, Pittsburgh, and
Cincinnati.[93] However, except for a small program schedule, mentions of WHA
in the pages of the hometown *Capital Times* become scarce after 1925, when

the paper began operating its own radio station, WIBA (on its engineering staff was Lighty's son Russell, who had once worked at WHA).[94]

The summer of 1925 brought an interesting press report from a small town near Madison. In an interview with the *Stoughton Daily Courier-Hub* that ran on July 28, Hans Swan, a local merchant, complained that radio had shifted his customers' buying patterns. He said: "Now people don't buy pianos very much. All they want is radios. The stores here have almost quit selling pianos. Now I sell mostly small stuff in music. Ukeleles, and such things."

WHA maintained the thrice-weekly program schedule through the end of the summer session and then shut down after the evening broadcast of August 5. The station returned to the air on September 30 with a special remote broadcast. For the dedication of Madison's new Masonic Temple, C. H. Mills, director of the university's School of Music, presented an organ recital from the building. To get the signal back to WHA for broadcast, the station used ordinary telephone lines. The regular schedule continued with a two-hour block at 7 p.m. Mondays and Fridays and a one-hour timeslot at 8 p.m. Wednesdays.[95] By mid-October, the start time for the evening broadcasts was moved to 7:30 p.m. and in November to 7:45 p.m. The station shut down again early in December 1925, because its antenna tower had to be removed to allow construction of an addition to nearby Bascom Hall. The station received $1,601 from general university funds to move the tower. This was in addition to the $3,600 per year in radio operating funds from the physics department budget, for a total of $5,201 for the year. But even as WHA was getting by on $100 a week, other public universities were pouring substantial sums into their radio stations: the University of Illinois would soon budget $100,000 to improve the operation of its station.[96]

In 1925 WHA moved out of the basement of Sterling Hall, where it had been located since the wartime days of 9XM. It didn't move far, just to the first floor rooms 132 and 133, but the transmitter equipment remained in the basement in room 38. Before making the move, WHA staffers could apply more advance techniques in studio construction. The new WHA home was described as "a room 16 x 19 feet, sound proofed with balsam wool, window spaces draped and floors effectively covered." A Steinway piano sat in one corner of the room, and the operator occupied another corner at a control desk.[97] The proximity to laboratories continued to be a problem: the physics department used the studio's anteroom for its course on glassblowing, and some laboratory equipment occasionally caused electrical interference with the broadcast gear. In later years, room 132 was cut through to make a passageway to a building addition. The remaining outer sections of the room were divided and renumbered; 1500 and 1502 are offices for graduate students who work as teaching assistants in the physics department, while 1501 is a storage room. There is no clue that there was ever a radio operation located here, nor anywhere inside Sterling Hall. There are, however, some antenna mounts that remain on the roof of the building.[98]

WHA began its 1926 broadcasts on January 11. The Monday-Wednesday-Friday evening schedule continued, with basketball games and occasional specials on other evenings. These programs, however, required special arrangements with KYW in Chicago for use of the frequency. Operations continued until the end of the spring semester. Terry's pioneer status in educational broadcasting was recognized, as he began serving as vice president of the Association of College and University Broadcasting Stations. The group had been formed the previous November and in 1934 would be reconstituted as the National Association of Educational Broadcasters.[99]

The university's College of Agriculture had been providing speakers each week on a variety of topics of interest to the state's farmers since 1923. The college had created a faculty committee, chaired by Hopkins, to oversee this part of the WHA operation. This committee also scheduled speakers from the home economics department, and by the spring of 1926 they were appearing almost weekly. This was the beginning of what in 1929 would become the separate *Homemakers' Program,* a long-running feature of WHA (see chapter 20). The College of Agriculture also budgeted money for an assistantship. The person assigned was responsible for the radio program. This was the first time a department other than the physics department had allocated money for broadcasting.[100]

The station was off the air for the week of June 21–25, 1926, an intersession break. The station returned to the air on June 28 and continued in operation until the end of the summer session on August 11.[101] During the summer of 1926 WHA used the remote lines to Music Hall to broadcast something new: community songfests. These events were a regular part of the summer session at the university, and the broadcasts generated excitement among the participating students. With the cessation of broadcasting in August, Burton Miller rebuilt the transmitter, increasing its power from 625 to 750 watts and adding a new "crystal control frequency stabilizer," built in the university laboratories. According to the *Press Bulletin* of October 6, the new stabilizer was supposed to reduce fading in reception.

The fall season of broadcasts began on Monday, October 25, with an 8:15 to 9 p.m. program, a new regular feature from the School of Music, under the direction of E. W. Morphy.[102]

Sharing a frequency with a big-city commercial station like KYW became increasingly problematic for WHA. When the station resumed operation in the fall, the *Daily Cardinal* reported on September 29 that WHA would not be able to broadcast Wisconsin football contests, because KYW was carrying the University of Chicago games at the same time and on the same frequency. WHA's sharing arrangement with KYW was further complicated when the Chicago station joined the NBC Blue network. KYW now wanted WHA's Monday-Wednesday-Friday evenings to accommodate network programs and began taking the time, in direct violation of its sharing agreement with WHA. Lighty tried to enlist the aid of Wisconsin alumni in the Chicago area to pressure KYW but to no avail. Lighty and Terry went to Chicago in early 1927 to try to reach some accord with KYW officials, also without success.[103]

WHA had scheduled a music program one night, an educational lecture on another evening, and a farm and home broadcast on a third. However, the ongoing conflict with KYW prompted the Madison staff to combine all the features into a single two-hour program on Monday evenings only, starting at 7:15 p.m. This once-a-week schedule would be the low point in WHA's program history. The staff also arranged for special broadcasts of events like debates and university banquets as well as basketball games.[104]

Terry and Lighty believed they could use the popularity of Wisconsin basketball broadcasts to build support among listeners. While in Chicago for the meeting at KYW, they had also conferred with the district radio inspector, and they were granted special permission to use 509 meters (590 kHz) on Tuesday nights for basketball broadcasts.[105] WHA used the new frequency throughout the spring of 1927 for basketball games and received permission to use it on Thursday, March 10, for the broadcast of an intercollegiate debate between Wisconsin and Northwestern University. At other times WHA operated at 560 kHz, with its signal encountering constant interference from KYW in the evening, and with its daytime broadcasting limited to times when operations wouldn't interfere with activities of the physics department. The reduced service did not go unnoticed by professors. Many now turned down the opportunity to appear on air, as they felt the station's reduced range and correspondingly smaller audience made it not worth their trouble.[106]

On May 31 WHA's managers received some good news. The new Federal Radio Commission had issued an order that reassigned the stations throughout the country. WHA was moved to 940 kHz and ordered to share time with WLBL–Stevens Point, the station owned by the Wisconsin Department of Markets. Having to share time with another non-commercial, state-owned station was a hopeful development. Lighty was pleased, optimistic that negotiations for sharing the frequency would be satisfactory. The fact that both stations were owned by the State of Wisconsin prompted the idea that they could somehow be linked to form a network. The College of Agriculture's radio committee discussed the idea, and a trial broadcast was proposed. Terry looked into the cost of a land line to connect the two stations and found that the telephone company would only consider an annual contract costing $5,000.[107] Once the stations were formally allied with each other beginning in 1933, the high cost of the line would always be an issue.

Having a usable frequency helped to inspire considerable enthusiasm for WHA on the Wisconsin campus. Early in 1927, Glenn Frank, the new university president, had been urged by Lighty to form a large University Radio Committee to secure campus-wide assistance for the development of the radio operation while the Agricultural Radio Committee held a meeting to plan the expansion of its broadcast offerings.[108] One proposal was for an independent series of home economics programs. This series was the responsibility of a graduate student, May Reynolds. The station also added a new program director. Lighty managed to get funding from the Extension Division to hire E. Ray Skinner, a graduate student in the speech department. He had big plans: after the station resumed broadcasting, he wanted to increase its hours, retaining the three evenings a week and adding 1 to 6 p.m. each afternoon.[109]

After the usual summer break WHA resumed its schedule. The fall broadcasts began on Saturday, October 1, with a live broadcast of a football between Wisconsin and Cornell. The broadcast featured "Red" Mich, a *Wisconsin State Journal* sportswriter, at the field calling the game, with Burton Miller back at the transmitter in Sterling Hall. The WHA transmitter log for this particular day was saved in the WHA files. It shows that the station signed on the air at 2 p.m. for the beginning of the game and signed off at 4:25 p.m. immediately after its conclusion. Operator Miller also jotted down the halftime and final scores of the game on the log itself.[110]

The regular weekday evening schedule began on Monday, October 3. Four speakers were scheduled for that evening, beginning at 7:30 p.m. The schedule for the first evening has segments for both farmers and homemakers:

"Serving 71 Wisconsin Counties"—Glenn Frank/President of the University of Wisconsin

"What Lies Right Ahead in Farming"—K. L. Hatch/assistant director of agricultural extension

"Winter Compensations"—Nellie Kedzie Jones/state leader of home demonstration agents

"The Athletic Outlook for the Coming Year at the University of Wisconsin"— George Little/director of athletics[111]

Broadcasters around the country were dissatisfied with the new frequencies they'd been assigned earlier in the year and applied to the radio commission for changes. As a result the 940 kHz spot on the dial began to fill up with additional stations. The WHA staff was beginning to think that 940 kHz would not be usable. Terry met with the managers of commercial station WRRS in Racine and officials from WLBL in Stevens Point. The three stations agreed to share time at 900 kHz. Terry forwarded a request for the change to the radio commission, which granted its approval on November 9, 1927. The cascade of requests for channel changes continued, and the 900 kHz frequency began to get crowded as well, with ten other stations assigned to it and other powerful stations on adjacent frequencies.[112]

Beginning on November 30, 1927, WHA's two evening programs began to follow a set format. The regular Monday evening program, airing from 7:30 to 9:30 p.m., consisted of music and discussions of agricultural and home economics topics. The new Wednesday evening program offered music and educational features. It too aired for two hours at 7:30 p.m.

The next day WHA unveiled its first professionally printed monthly program guide: the *University Antenna*. WHA may have gotten the idea from educational station WEAO at Ohio State, which had been producing a program guide since November 1926[113]; some early examples of the Ohio guide are in the WHA files at the University of Wisconsin Archives. One feature of the WHA guide was two listener comment forms that could be clipped off the main schedule page. They had spaces for date, quality of reception, interference, compliments, and suggestions. The guide also carried the logo of the Extension Division on the cover. That month the station was on the air only eight evenings, two of which were devoted to basketball game broadcasts.[114]

Throughout the remainder of 1927, Terry tried for a better frequency. He asked that WHA be shifted to 640 kHz, but the radio commission turned down the request, saying that WHA would cause interference with other stations, including KFI in Los Angeles. On December 29, 1927, Terry tried again, this time suggesting six different frequencies he thought might be usable. The lowly status of educational stations during this era was evident in Terry's request: he was reduced to asking for only ninety minutes on two evenings per week.[115]

In January 1928 the station brought back a program from the 9XM days. A report on road conditions supplied by the Wisconsin Highway Commission would be broadcast at 6 p.m. Mondays through Saturdays.[116] New programs were added to the broadcast schedule: a member of the political science department appeared on WHA with a "political review of the month" and a similar "economic review of the month" was also offered with a professor from the Commerce School.[117]

WHA shut down for the summer in June 1928, a departure from previous years when broadcasting was maintained at least through the summer session. WHA staff members were discouraged by the endless interference on the 900 kHz frequency, which limited the broadcast range to only twenty-five miles. Terry thought it pointless to continue broadcasting under these circumstances, and the staff decided to use the summer to pursue a better frequency and rebuild the transmitter.[118]

With the station off the air Burton Miller dismantled the transmitter and spent the summer rebuilding it. Also during the summer the station made an unsuccessful attempt to move the transmitter from Sterling Hall. C. H. Mendenhall, chair of the physics department, had urged moving the entire radio operation to Camp Randall on the southwestern edge of the campus, and plans were made to put the station's towers near the new mechanical engineering building.[119] Camp Randall had been a military training facility during the Civil War, the university's football stadium had been built there in 1917, and a new fieldhouse would open in 1930. Both remain to this day along with numerous later engineering buildings.

In September 1928 WHA was assigned to another frequency, 570 kHz, to be shared with *Milwaukee Journal*–owned commercial station, WTMJ, as well as with WLBL in Stevens Point, although there is no evidence that WLBL ever moved to the frequency before additional shifts were announced. Also, WHA appointed a new program director, Louis Mallory, another graduate student in speech.

In later years Mallory said he wasn't sure who appointed him to the job, except that all his negotiations were with the speech department, and he believed his salary came from its budget.[120] By late February 1929 WHA would have more participation from this department after Henry L. Ewbank, a speech professor, was appointed to chair the University Radio Committee.[121]

Mallory had time to plan new programs, because negotiating with the other Wisconsin stations for sharing time on the new frequency meant the start of the fall season would be delayed until November 19. Once the station was back on the air, Mallory debuted a new program called *Know Wisconsin,* which was designed to present information about the state, including science, history, music, literature, and drama.[122] The first guest on the new program was state geologist E. F. Bean, who spoke on the geologic history of Wisconsin.[123] Mallory said he planned to comb the entire university for material and talent and have every department represented. Another new program was *Wisconsin*

Interviews, an early attempt at an interview format rather than the simple "talks" that had been aired up to that time. The *Daily Cardinal* reported on October 30 that "pertinent discussions by members of the university community will be presented to radio fans by the Socratic dialogue method of questions and answers."[124] Also, a mail-in question service was begun, with faculty members from various departments answering questions sent in by listeners.[125] The Agricultural Radio Committee introduced a new program feature too: a community calendar listing events of interest to Wisconsin farm families.

The new frequency, along with a usable agreement for sharing it, meant a clear signal over a large area. The *Daily Cardinal* reported that "points in a 150-mile radius are now hearing the university station with little of the interference of past years."[126] With a good signal restored, Terry hoped the endless shifting of frequencies and battles with other stations for division of time were over and that the station would be able to keep its frequency for a while. However, on October 28, 1928, it was announced that WTMJ-Milwaukee would be moved to another channel and that WRM at the University of Illinois at Urbana and WPCC at Chicago's North Shore Congregational Church would be joining WHA on 570 kHz. WHA staff members were cautiously optimistic about this change, no doubt since one of the other stations (WRM) was also a non-commercial educational outlet at a major university and would likely be more flexible with regard to time-sharing than would a commercial station.

Hopes were dashed when WHA received news that three other stations had applied for 570 kHz: WIBO-Chicago, WHT-Chicago, and WNAX-Yankton, South Dakota. The Federal Radio Commission notified WHA that a hearing on the issue would be held in Washington, D.C. Despite the importance of the hearing, university president Glenn Frank did not grant Terry's request to attend in person. Frank had recently reprimanded Terry over unfavorable publicity stemming from WHA operations. One critical newspaper item (later retracted) had been the result of a misunderstanding about WHA's basketball broadcasts and the other was an editorial in the *Capital Times* attacking the university for operating a radio station, which the newspaper felt was competing with their own radio operation.[127] This lack of support brought Terry to the brink of abandoning the university radio operation altogether.[128] Terry did submit a long brief to be presented at the radio commission hearing, and he relied on Professor J. R. Wright of the University of Illinois, who attended and looked out for the interests of both his station and WHA. Terry wrote: "The University of Wisconsin insists that, because of its long record in broadcasting work, it is entitled to a desirable channel. It desires to point out to the

Commission that it has been a pioneer in the broadcasting field. Of the broad-casting stations now in operation in the United States, KDKA alone anidates [*sic*] WHA, and that by a few months only."[129] He also pointed to WHA's three years of successful operation at 560 kHz and asked that WHT in Chicago be assigned to 570 kHz with WHA.

The commission decided that WHA would have to share time with both WIBO in Chicago and WNAX in Yankton. With no alternative WHA nego-tiated with the two stations for airtime and ended up with noon to 12:45 p.m. daily and 7 to 8 p.m. on Mondays, Wednesdays, and Fridays. Programs began on November 19, 1928.

During the winter Terry and Hopkins got the idea that if the university had a fully equipped high-power broadcast facility, the Federal Radio Commission might be persuaded to award WHA a clear channel. They approached the alumni association with the suggestion of finding a wealthy donor willing to fund the construction. Judge Evan A. Evans, the alumni association president, expressed a strong interest. He started to canvass for donors, while Terry calcu-lated what such a facility might cost and came back with a figure of $200,000.[130] This was more than Evans had anticipated, and he said raising such a sum was impossible.

Like KYW, WIBO in Chicago soon disregarded its agreement for sharing time with WHA and began operating during WHA's scheduled evening hours. This caused so much interference that WHA stopped trying to broadcast in the evening, and by January 9, 1929, the station had moved the evening pro-grams to noon to 12:45 pm on Mondays and Wednesdays.[131] WIBO officials were emboldened by their success at getting WHA's evening hours and started to play Victrola records during the noon hours belonging to WHA. Terry lodged a complaint with the Federal Radio Commission, which responded that it would not take action, because the agreement for time sharing was a private one between WHA and WIBO. Terry was equally unsuccessful in getting WIBO to give WHA its allotted time back, and he relayed his experience to the com-mission in a letter of March 18, 1929. He said WIBO's argument was that all the hours between 9 a.m. and 1 p.m. had been contracted with advertisers, and should WIBO give up any of its time, it would be a breach of its contract with its clients. Terry pointed out to the commission that if the government were to force WIBO off the noon hours, WIBO would not be in breach of its contracts as they were drawn subject to the rules and regulations of the com-mission. He asked that the commission order WIBO off the noon time period and added that the request was not to be construed to mean WHA was relin-quishing its claim to other time on air.[132] The interference from WIBO made attempts at broadcasting from Madison so difficult that WHA shut down in late March 1929.

In an attempt to find a solution the Federal Radio Commission sent a telegram to Terry, offering temporary use of 940 kHz again during daylight hours. The commission said that if the station encountered no interference, it could apply for permanent assignment to that frequency. To get back on the air, Terry accepted the new frequency and reluctantly gave up the station's right to broadcast in the evening.

WHA programs resumed at 940 kHz on April 2, 1929. At the same time program director Louis Mallory decided to split the noonday farm and home show into two separate programs. The new homemaker program was moved to late morning, so its audience might be better able to tune in. Its inception also marked the first regular morning programming on the WHA schedule. For the first month the show was on two mornings a week, but by May 1 it aired each weekday. For the first week back on the air, the agricultural program was a Monday-Wednesday-Friday offering at noon, followed at 12:30 p.m. by educational broadcasts. Thursdays were reserved for the School of Music and Tuesdays for presentations by faculty and university groups. The first day back on the air, the School of Music program had selections from the musical *Hi-Jack,* a burlesque of Chicago's gangland that was performed by the Haresfoot Club, the university's musical theater troupe. Along with this was a presentation by a regular WHA guest, meteorologist Eric Miller.[133] By the end of the month, he was appearing on the program several times a week.[134]

Also, on its first day as a separate offering, WHA's *Farm Program* was heard in Milwaukee. Commercial station WTMJ began simulcasting the program on a Monday-Wednesday-Friday basis, receiving it over long-distance telephone lines. The arrangement marked the first regular rebroadcast of a WHA program by another station.[135] Even though WHA expanded the *Farm Program* to a Monday through Saturday schedule the next week, WTMJ continued to carry it only tri-weekly. The Milwaukee station aired the *Farm Program* through mid-August.

For the first time in several years the station could again be heard at long distances and with little interference. On April 30, 1929, Terry forwarded an application to the radio commission to make the assignment to 940 kHz permanent. In it he said WHA understood that it was restricted to daytime hours but that during the daytime, the hours were unlimited.[136] However, this move eliminated one popular program offering: with no broadcasting allowed after sundown, the station could no longer carry University of Wisconsin basketball games.

The application was Terry's last act on behalf of the station he had founded. Early the next morning he died at his home of a heart attack at age fifty. He had been employed by the University of Wisconsin for nineteen years and had become a full professor only the previous year. Also, on the day before he died, he had completed the final page of the revision of his well-known laboratory manual of electrical measurements.[137]

More than anything else Terry accomplished, WHA would be his legacy. His obituary said: "He had charge of WHA, University of Wisconsin radio station, a pioneer station among American universities and did much work in the radio field. . . . In 1919, when wireless was shifting from the laboratory to the industrial stage, Prof. Terry and his associates succeeded in establishing a wireless telephony set, which permitted broadcasting of university events."[138] Terry's funeral was held from the home of physics department chair C. E. Mendenhall. University president Glenn Frank, a sometime guest on WHA, but at times ambivalent about the station and its leader, was quoted as saying: "Mr. Terry served the institution with a singlemindedness that knew no distractions. In almost four years I have worked with Mr. Terry, my regard for him has steadily risen. I feel his loss very keenly."[139]

Two years later Hanson closed a letter to Hopkins by saying, "I have not touched on the struggle which it often was for Professor Terry to keep up this early work and to obtain the backing of the faculty or funds from the regents. If this work has come to mean anything to the people of the state, it is chiefly because of the foresight, quiet enthusiasm, and devotion which was given it by Professor Terry. I would therefore like to suggest, if the opportunity should present itself, that the broadcasting station at the University of Wisconsin be named the Earle M. Terry Memorial Station."[140]

CHAPTER 7

WHA Comes into Its Own

1929–30

It would seem desirable to be on the air more hours per day.

With the death of Earl Terry, Edward Bennett of the electrical engineering department found himself assigned to take Terry's place as WHA's manager. Fourteen years earlier Bennett had allowed Terry to "borrow" his experimental radio license 9XM for the physics department's wireless operation. Bennett, along with speech professor H. L. Ewbank of the University Radio Committee and Hopkins of the Agricultural Radio Committee, would lead the station through the next few tumultuous years.

Ewbank recalled that he, Hopkins, and Bennett went to see university president Glenn Frank and told him that unless the institution wanted to "do something" about radio, they might as well stop right then. Glenn rejected the idea of discontinuing the radio operation.[1] During the summer of 1929 the new leaders of WHA looked at the prevailing environment for radio broadcasting and concluded that it was important to extend the activities of the station, improve the facilities, use more state agencies for programming, and broaden its scope. There was an urgency to their efforts. The value of radio stations was rapidly increasing, and the federal government continued its frustrating practice of renewing licenses every few months. In a letter to the dean of the College of Agriculture, Andrew Hopkins stated, "It would seem desirable to be on the air more hours per day if the station is to win favorable standing before the Federal Radio Commission."[2] Hopkins, Bennett, and Ewbank began exploring the possibility of merging their operation with that of WLBL (see chapter 8), the station owned by the Wisconsin Department of Agriculture and Markets in Stevens Point, but they also began improving the WHA operation.

More frequency changes were threatened. Although the station had been on

WHA's Bennett, Hopkins, and Ewbank
Edward Bennett (left to right), Andrew W. Hopkins, and Henry L. Ewbank guided
WHA after Terry died. (University of Wisconsin Archives series 23/24/5)

940 kHz only since April, the Federal Radio Commission wrote WHA during the summer asking if the station would switch to 1280 kHz and share time with WEBC in Superior, Wisconsin. The northern station was currently on the air half-time but had applied for full-time hours.[3] Fully remembering attempts at securing equitable division of airtime with commercial broadcasters, the University Radio Committee declined the recommendation and refiled to remain at 940 kHz.

In the late spring Harold B. McCarty, a graduate student in theater from Illinois, was asked if he'd like to take over as announcer of the one-hour noon program at WHA. His only prior experience with WHA was that he had once played his violin over the air as part of a trio.[4] He was told that the current announcer, Louis Mallory, was going to devote the coming semester to his studies and would be unable to continue his radio work. McCarty had a brief stint as an announcer at WIBA in Madison, and then began his work at WHA in October 1929 at twenty-five dollars a month. It marked the beginning of McCarty's decades-long association with WHA.[5] He would soon be named chief announcer, then program director, and later still, manager. He would be involved with the station and the one-day network for more than thirty-five years.

Over the summer WHA lost another of its long-time student staff members. Chief operator Burton Miller received his doctoral degree and departed for a position with the Wired Radio Company in New York.[6] Taking over the technical duties was Glenn Koehler, an instructor in the electrical engineering department; he was given the title assistant technical director.[7]

The WHA's fall season began on October 9, 1929. The schedule included the *Homemakers' Program* from 10:15 to 10:45 a.m., the *Farm Program* from

Harold B. McCarty, Sterling Hall studios, 1931 (University of Wisconsin Archives series 23/24/5)

noon to 12:30 p.m., and the *School of Music Hour* from 12:30 to 1 p.m.[8] The
first day Ewbank was a guest, titling his lecture "The Radio in Education"; he
was followed by Lighty, whose talk was entitled "The Uses of Leisure."[9] By
December the station had added a half-hour broadcast timeslot at 4 p.m., the
first regular use of afternoon hours. It was extended to two hours several days
a week in May. It was discontinued at the end of the semester in June, replaced
by a Saturday program from 1 to 2 p.m., which remained throughout the summer session.[10] The contributions by faculty now were arranged so that they
appeared as series, rather than at random. On October 11, 1929, the political
science department began its Friday series, *What's Back of the News,* one of the
earliest examples of a news analysis program.[11] The first installment featured
Professor J. M. Gaus, an authority on British politics. He analyzed that week's
visit to the United States by British Prime Minister Ramsay MacDonald.[12] A
few weeks later, on November 1, Professor W. A. Morton of the economics
department had an especially timely lecture: "The Wall Street Crash."[13] Other
series were begun as well: the Bureau of Municipal Information presented a
series about problems facing local government, and the chemistry department
offered a regular Tuesday program called *The Mysteries of Chemistry.*[14] Coinci-
dent with the start of the broadcast season, Ewbank, Bennett, and Hopkins
requested the radio committee be enlarged with wider representation from
campus, the idea being to secure more participation from various departments.
Representatives from the Extension Division as well as from law, medicine,
home economics, music, and education were added as were representatives of
the registrar and the university's business manager.[15]

Other state agencies began contributing to WHA. Among the new features
in the fall of 1929 was a program by the Wisconsin Conservation Commission about wildlife and the state laws governing natural resources. Another
series came from the Department of Public Instruction, which looked at the
educational problems facing the state. The State Board of Health began a regular series under Dr. C. A. Harper, the state health officer, and it was scheduled to follow the *Homemakers' Hour.*[16]

New program director George Gerling got more students involved in the
station by arranging with the *Daily Cardinal* to produce an all-student hour
three times a week, beginning in December. By the spring of 1930 the program
featured a student-written one-act play. The paper boasted that the Cardinal
Radio Players were "the only student-directed, student-acted radio dramatic
group in the world presenting original student-written plays."[17] The *Cardinal*
also ran large announcements about the program in the paper, and they often
included the rest of the day's program schedule.

Radio schedule logo in the Daily Cardinal
In the early 1930s the *Daily Cardinal*
used this illustration over the WHA
broadcast schedule that appeared in
each issue. (The Daily Cardinal/
University of Wisconsin Archives)

The School of Music continued to offer musical ensembles to WHA, and in February 1930 Major E. W. Morphy organized a twenty-piece radio orchestra made up of players he selected from the main university orchestra. The smaller group often served as a studio orchestra for WHA and "achieved a large following for its 'tired business men's program' of lighter classics."[18]

While these programming innovations continued, maneuvering was underway to combine the operations of WHA with those of WLBL. The debate about this proposal occupied the WHA managers for all of 1930 and part of 1931 and served to illustrate the struggles being faced by educational radio stations.

CHAPTER 8

The WHA–WLBL Merger

1930–31

There is 1931 seen thru medieval spectacles!

Throughout the mid-1920s WHA in Madison and WLBL in Stevens Point operated independently and paid little attention to each other. On May 31, 1927, General Order #11 of the Federal Radio Commission reallocated radio station frequencies, and WHA found itself assigned to 940 kHz and ordered to share time on the frequency with WLBL. Sharing time with another non-commercial station was a happy development and was met with great enthusiasm by the WHA staff. They were sure that an equitable arrangement for sharing time could be worked out. Even though both stations changed frequencies during the next couple of years, the idea of combining the two state-owned stations to form a network, or "chain," was now firmly established.

By the fall of 1929 the pressures of commercial broadcasters were a direct threat to both state-owned stations. WHA was still operating at 940 kHz and 750 watts, while WLBL was at 900 kHz and 2,000 watts. Both stations were daytime only and both had small budgets and limited studio facilities. Professors Bennett, Ewbank, and Hopkins made a careful investigation of the possibility of merging the two stations.

Educational broadcasters continued to be under pressure from commercial stations, who coveted their frequencies (unlike the situation with FM radio after World War II, the AM band has no frequencies reserved for non-commercial, educational use). The federal supervisor of radio suggested to WIBU in Poynette, Wisconsin (about twenty miles north of Madison) that they and WHA consolidate into one facility. The move indicates that the radio commission was bowing to the demands of commercial broadcasters at the expense of educational stations.[1]

The Radio Act of 1927 had included a provision that seemed to encourage the merger of WHA and WLBL: it set forth a system whereby clear-channel stations would be allocated among the states based on their population. Clear-channel stations in the early days of radio had exclusive use of their frequencies between sunset and sunrise, and since they often used high transmitter powers, could be heard over most of the country at night. Under this system Wisconsin was allotted 0.88 clear channels but did not have any. Illinois, on the other hand was allocated 2.21 clear channel stations, yet Chicago alone had 4.57.[2] The Madison staff thought that this imbalance would make it difficult for the Federal Radio Commission to deny an application from Wisconsin for a clear channel, since it followed the guidelines of this allocation system.

The idea was discussed with WLBL's owners and other state agencies, and all agreed that Wisconsin should apply for one strong station and, further, that the various state agencies would share the costs of this proposed station. The University Radio Committee conferred with Captain Guy Hill of the Federal Radio Commission, who recommended that the state submit an application for 5,000 watts at 900 kHz.

This application was sent to the Federal Radio Commission on January 8, 1930. It called for establishment of the main studio on the University of Wisconsin campus with a branch studio in the State Capitol. The transmitter itself would be moved to a rural location to avoid interference with any center of population; the site chosen was in Morrisonville, about twenty miles north of Madison. Also, once the new station was established, the state would relinquish the frequency assignments for WHA and WLBL.[3] In a move that demonstrated a bit of style, the applicants also asked for new call letters, WIS, although they were already in use at a station in Columbia, South Carolina. That station had been granted the designation in early 1929, and Bennett had even appealed to its owners to relinquish their call sign so Wisconsin could use it. The South Carolina station wired back its refusal, and those call letters today remain in use by a television station in the South Carolina capital.[4]

The application was specific about the programming planned for the new station. The categories included information about agriculture, health, and conservation, the *Homemakers' Hour,* adult education, supplementary instruction for rural schools, discussion of public issues, and experiments in education.

A week after the application was filed, the university's Board of Regents authorized spending $20,200 to build the new station and an additional $10,000 for operation during the 1930–31 school year. Other state agencies pledged operating funds as well, reflecting the anticipated programming. The participating agencies included the Department of Agriculture and Markets

($7,000), the Highway Commission, ($2,000), the Conservation Commission ($1,900), the Board of Health ($1,000), and the Department of Public Instruction ($900), for a total operating budget of $22,800.[5]

The applicants hoped that the commission would grant a construction permit for the new station without a formal hearing, but opposition to the plan surfaced almost immediately in Stevens Point. Residents there understandably felt slighted because no one had consulted them. Their concern was that the new station in Morrisonville would be too far away for people in the northern part of the state to hear it clearly. They also actively supported and participated in their station. J. W. Dunegan of the First National Bank of Stevens Point organized a citizens' group. He had been a booster of WLBL for years and had helped raise money for a new radio room on the roof of the Hotel Whiting back in 1927 (see chapter 18).[6] The group enlisted the aid of the area's state legislators, as well as that of Republican U.S. Representative Edward Browne of Waupaca. The *Stevens Point Daily Journal* editorialized that the local interests were in an uphill fight to prevent the loss of their radio station, "which is coveted by the University of Wisconsin." The paper noted that the university had an advantage with regard to influence: "It is near the seat of government. It knows the men who make decisions and is able to approach them socially and politically. The university has been working on the quiet."[7]

Wisconsin governor Walter J. Kohler Sr. attempted to mollify the Stevens Point group, directing the Department of Markets to hold a public hearing in the city. Charles Hill, the head of the agency, forwarded a report on the March 14 hearing to the governor. Hill said those attending gave three reasons for wanting the station to remain in Stevens Point: a sense of loyalty; a fear that they would not be able to receive a station located farther south; and the difficulty that central Wisconsin residents would face in traveling more than one hundred miles to Madison to participate in local programs. Hill told the governor that he had presented the arguments for the joint station, adding that reception of the new station would be at least equal to WHA's and WLBL's signals and that service would be improved.[8]

After the hearing Kohler met with Hill and the University Radio Committee to see if they could alter the proposal to satisfy the northern interests. Bennett suggested changing the location of the station to Hancock, which was less than thirty miles from Stevens Point (and sixty-eight miles north of Madison). Bennett said the plan was acceptable, so long as the state could come up with additional money to pay for the additional line rental costs. The governor consulted with the various state agencies involved and budgeted an additional $5,800 per year for the station. The radio committee forwarded a new application to Washington on April 28, 1930, specifying a 5,000-watt station in Hancock at 900 kHz.[9] The hope was that the commission would grant the permit without a hearing, but the Stevens Point interests continued to oppose the plan and were joined by William T. Evjue, editor of the *Capital Times* of Madison, which was part owner of the Madison commercial station WIBA. Evjue had also enlisted the aid of Wisconsin's congressional delegation to oppose the consolidation.

Evjue charged that partisan politics was behind the consolidation efforts. In a front-page editorial he strongly attacked the plan and said it was going ahead despite the protests of farmers in the northern part of the state. In his *Capital Times* piece of May 26, he wrote: "Service is not the answer. The answer lies in a new Madison Ring that desires to use this new radio station to perpetuate itself. We predict that with a new station controlled by the Kohler administration and its followers that the crop and market reports will be saturated with plenty of propaganda. The whole deal is a fraud on the people of northern Wisconsin."[10] Evjue must have been chagrined when his candidate for governor, Philip La Follette, won the 1930 election, for La Follette strongly supported the WHA–WLBL consolidation plan.

A WHA ally was closely monitoring events in Washington. C. M. Jansky Jr. had been a member of the "wireless squad" as a University of Wisconsin student during the early 9XM days, and he had become a broadcast engineering consultant. As early as February 1930 he had been writing to Bennett with advice about how to proceed with the application. After this latest round of opposition Jansky recommended that Bennett go to Washington to exert influence with the members of Wisconsin's congressional delegation. Hill and Bennett met in conference with the entire delegation to push for the new station. Banker Dunegan and Congressman Browne argued against it.[11]

To the disappointment of the Wisconsin applicants, the commission announced in June that it would hold a hearing on the matter in November 1930. In a final attempt to placate the opposition, the applicants used the delay to modify their application once again. This time they recommended moving the transmitter even closer to Stevens Point, to a spot about eight miles from the city. The University Radio Committee sent an amendment to the application to the commission and notified the Stevens Point group. The move had the desired effect: Dunegan wired Hill to say that the Stevens Point group would now support the consolidation.[12]

The hearing was held in Washington, D.C., on November 19 to 21, 1930. Appearing in favor of the consolidation were university president Glenn Frank, Bennett, Hill, Jansky, and recent convert Dunegan. Joining them in the fight was Armstrong Perry, the chairman of a new national group, the Committee on Education by Radio. Opposing the action were two radio stations: commercial station WEBN of Buffalo, New York, and WHAD at Marquette University in Milwaukee. The Buffalo station was operating at 900 kHz with unlimited time on the air and was concerned about possible interference from what would be a more powerful operation in Wisconsin. The Milwaukee outlet's participation stemmed from frequency changes going back two years. Back on October 15, 1928, the Marquette University station had been moved to the 900 kHz frequency and ordered to share time with WLBL. The move was short-lived: fifteen days later they were moved to 1120 kHz, told to reduce power, and ordered to share time with commercial station WISN in Milwaukee. WHAD had twice reapplied for 900 kHz and had been turned down both times, most recently because of the pending WHA–WLBL discussions.[13] Because of their station's interest in the 900 kHz frequency, officials from Marquette University were allowed to participate in the hearing.

In arguing for their position the Wisconsin applicants said the State of Wisconsin had a right to use radio as part of its educational system and that educational broadcasting should have assured standing and adequate facilities. Further, sufficient talent and funding were available to provide satisfactory programs. In referencing the quota system for clear channels, they pointed out that Wisconsin was under quota and that even if the application were to be granted, it would not place the state over its quota for powerful stations. From a technical perspective they said that the station location would provide maximum service to those state residents who needed the service the most; that the merger would not require any other station to change its time, frequency, or power; that the number of stations would actually decrease; and that the new facility would not interfere with any existing station "in areas where they can legitimately be expected to deliver broadcast service."[14] This last point addressed the concerns of WEBN, the Buffalo station. Having respected engineers like Jansky and Bennett available to speak to this issue was valuable, and some testimony involved how far the Wisconsin station's signal might reach over Michigan's Lower Peninsula and Lake Huron. The commission also questioned Hill about the nature of WLBL programming and at what distance the station was being heard.

Hearing examiner Elmer W. Pratt took the case under advisement. On April 9, 1931, he submitted a report to the commission that recommended denial of the application. He said he had been involved in a number of cases involving educational stations where the applicants had asked for more in the way of facilities than they were willing to use. He said that if an applicant proposes a service that justifies granting its demands, the commission could make the facilities available.[15]

La Follette met with Hill and the University Radio Committee about the report, and on May 2, 1931, the governor sent a telegram to the chair of the Federal Radio Commission, taking exception to the examiner's report and requesting oral argument before the commission. The commission granted a hearing on June 3, 1931, and gave the Wisconsin applicants one hour to present their case. The governor directed state attorney general John Reynolds to help prepare their argument, and a member of Reynolds's staff assisted the University Radio Committee's lawyer, H. L. Lohnes, before the commission.

On June 27, 1931, the commission filed its final order of denial. Part of it reads: "While the Commission consistently has been of the opinion that the devotion of radio facilities to work in education is important in a consideration of the public interest, nevertheless it has never held that a state has a fundamental right to use radio in connection with its educational system. Radio is not essential in the dissemination of education. It has been and may be used as an efficient supplemental means thereof when employment of a particular facility to that end is consistent with the public interest, convenience or necessity. Radio is not education itself, or the means of its dissemination, but at best education is only one use to which radio may be put. And the power to regulate radio communication as an instrument of commerce has been delegated to the Federal Government."

From the perspective of educational broadcasters, the commission's statement only validated their experience, that the Federal Radio Commission was biased against educational radio stations. Still, the disparaging tone of the order was shocking. The publication *Education by Radio* wrote: "There is 1931 seen thru medieval spectacles! There is an answer which should silence forever those who contend that the methods of educators are backward. Certainly radio is not essential in the dissemination of education. Neither is printing; neither are books; neither is paper and pencil." It went on to say that "Wisconsin has asked no great favor. Unlike the mighty broadcasting chains, it sought no great amount of power, nor did it seek to acquire other stations to form a gigantic system of monopolistic proportions. It might have been better if Wisconsin had wanted those things because the Commission normally favors such applications. Wisconsin asked for a single station with sufficient power to permit programs sponsored by agencies of the state government to reach citizens in all parts of the commonwealth."[16]

The only recourse left to the Wisconsin group was to appeal the commission's decision to the federal courts. La Follette told his attorney general to do so, and on July 14, 1931, the appeal was filed with the U.S. Court of Appeals of the District of Columbia. However, upon reflection the University Radio Committee decided that an appeal would be futile and recommended to the governor that it not be pursued.

With the defeat the radio committee recommended that the only way to keep and safeguard the radio rights of WHA and WLBL was to make maximum use of the licenses. That meant affiliating the two stations in order to share programming.[17] WHA had improved its facilities and programming in the previous two years, but WLBL's operation had not improved much since the mid-1920s. The Stevens Point station was still broadcasting hourly farm market information, along with home-talent music programs, some local sports, and other miscellaneous spoken-word offerings. Moreover, the WLBL transmitter was putting out a full 2,000 watts but was doing so inefficiently, so its power was equal to that of only a 500-watt station. The Federal Radio Commission had warned WLBL about its power output, and the state agency and university officials feared that if the station did not use more of the broadcast day, it would lose some of its allotted airtime.

All agencies agreed to improve the operation of WLBL and to find a way to link the two stations to share programming. The project was delayed by lack of funds—the state legislature had not provided funding during the long merger battle. The improvements recommended for the WLBL operation included a new studio location in the Fox Theatre building in Stevens Point and a new transmitting facility in Ellis, about seven miles northeast of the city; both changes were accomplished in the spring of 1932.

After the Federal Radio Commission denied the consolidation plan, Edward Bennett of WHA began corresponding with officials at the Wisconsin Telephone Company about the costs associated with broadcast telephone lines and telegraph "order" or control circuits between WHA and WLBL. Bennett asked for cost estimates for using the lines for a half-hour or hour every evening between 7 and 10 p.m., and for six or seven evenings per week. He also asked for the costs of similar lines to the studio of commercial station WEBC in Superior and the transmitter of WTMJ in the Milwaukee suburb of Brookfield. Bennett sought two separate quotes for the WEBC connection: one directly from WHA and one with an intermediate "tap" into the WLBL studio in Stevens Point.[18] The request may indicate that WHA and/or WLBL planned to provide program materials to the two commercial outlets, both of which were in areas that had only fair to poor reception of the state stations. The request for evening hours on the lines is intriguing, since WHA and WLBL were limited to daytime operation. It could be that programs would be produced in Madison or Stevens Point specifically for WTMJ and WEBC and would not be heard over WHA or WLBL.

The full-time broadcast line between WHA in Madison and WLBL in Stevens Point went into effect January 2, 1933; their first "network" broadcast was of the inauguration of Governor Albert Schmedeman. Regular daily use of the circuit began on February 6. The bidirectional line allowed either station to provide programming for both. WHA began airing WLBL's regular markets programs in southern Wisconsin, and WLBL started carrying the *Farm Program*, the *Homemakers' Program*, and the Wisconsin School of the Air series of programs for use in public school classrooms (see chapter 21).[19]

Sadly, the high cost of the broadcast line ($1,000 per month in 1933) made it a tempting target during tight budgets. The line was eliminated on July 1, 1933, when the new fiscal year began. To allow joint programming to continue, an off-the-air system was installed at WLBL, with a ground antenna more than one thousand feet long put into operation near WLBL's transmitter site. This system had two shortcomings: the quality of the WHA signal was now partially a function of favorable atmospheric conditions, and it was one way only, so WHA no longer broadcast WLBL programs. One bright spot for WLBL was that the availability of the radio receiver and antenna probably played a part in its decision to air Green Bay Packers games from 1933 to 1938. The broadcast line was reinstalled in the fall of 1935 and then abandoned again on May 1, 1938, after the Department of Agriculture and Markets found that it could no longer afford the connection. The off-air relay was used at WLBL again, but it was found to be unsatisfactory, so the Board of Regents appropriated money in October 1938 to reestablish the line through February 1, 1939. The line was discontinued again and the off-air system used until 1942, when the line was restored for the final time.[20] It remained in use until 1949, when new state-run FM stations went on the air and WLBL could use their signals for the program feed.

CHAPTER 9

~

More Hours on the Air

1930–33

Peculiarly adapted to the radio

While the debate about consolidating WHA and WLBL was underway, improvements and innovations continued at WHA in Madison. In late August 1930 WHA managers received a letter from WIBA in Madison. The commercial outlet wanted to install a line between the stations to allow WIBA to carry some WHA programs. It was especially interested in the *Homemakers' Hour,* perhaps getting the idea for the rebroadcast from WTMJ, which had simulcast the WHA *Farm Program* the previous year. WHA agreed, specifying conditions for rebroadcasters that would remain in effect for years to come. The agreements stated that the program would have to be carried on a noncommercial basis, its source would have to be identified, and the commercial station would have to pay the line charge to WHA.[1] WIBA program listings described the program as being from "the University of Wisconsin" and did not list the WHA call letters. By December the connection was also being used for the student-produced *Cardinal Hour,* which originated at WHA and was carried over WIBA.[2] In the years ahead these arrangements would be used for everything from the weather to the Wisconsin School of the Air offerings. Similar connections would be installed to Madison stations WISC and WKOW, as well as to WIBU in Poynette. WHA later entered into a courtesy arrangement with WIBA that gave the university station access to WIBA's NBC network feed for programs like presidential addresses and other non-commercial specials. WIBA had joined NBC as an associate member on July 18, 1931.[3]

During the summer of 1930 WHA joined some other educational radio stations in attempting to develop an early non-commercial network. Programs from WEAO at Ohio State University in Columbus (now WOSU) would be picked up by commercial station WLW in Cincinnati and rebroadcast by WXAL, a 10,000-watt shortwave station there. WHA would receive the shortwave signal and rebroadcast it. Other stations agreeing to participate were KOB at the New Mexico State College of Agriculture and Mechanical Arts, WCAJ at Nebraska Wesleyan College, WTAW at the Agricultural and Mechanical College of Texas, and WAPI in Birmingham, Alabama, an educational station that had several owners. (Alabama Polytechnic Institute developed the station and by this time was sharing ownership with the University of Alabama and the Alabama College for Women).[4] Eventually, phone lines were to be installed from participating stations to the Cincinnati shortwave station, so the stations could feed programs for rebroadcast.[5] The original plan was for WHA to carry an hour of Ohio-originated educational programs at 1 p.m., immediately after the *Farm Program* on Mondays, Tuesdays, and Fridays.[6] The series was to begin September 29, but WHA didn't have the receiving equipment in place in time.

The first educational network broadcast over WHA was not made until October 14, 1930, when three twenty-minute Ohio School of the Air programs aired from Columbus at 2 p.m. These were *Nature and Man in New England* and *Nature and Man in the British Isles,* both geography programs. They were followed by *The Flute Which Blew from Fairyland,* a story program for young children.[7] Unfortunately, the crude transmitting and receiving equipment of the era was not up to the task, and the shortwave signal was deemed too poor for rebroadcast on a regular basis. WHA carried Ohio School of the Air programs on Tuesdays and Fridays through October 24, only four one-hour broadcasts in all.[8] Of the stations involved in this experiment, only WHA and the Ohio State station have survived to the present day as non-commercial broadcasters.

In September 1930 more competition developed for WHA when the *Wisconsin State Journal* began operating its station, WISJ. Over the summer the paper had purchased WEBW from Beloit College in order to enter the broadcasting field.[9] One of the WISJ engineers was former WHA staff member Russell Lighty, who had been at WIBA for its debut five years earlier.[10] He also had worked for WHAD at Marquette University, WTMJ in Milwaukee, and WEBW at Beloit.

On October 8, 1930, U.S. Secretary of the Interior Ray Lyman Wilbur spoke on campus, and WHA originated the broadcast of the speech for national distribution by NBC.[11] It was the first time the station supplied a program feed for a national network. In future years WHA would provide program series for the Mutual Broadcasting System, National Association of Educational Broadcasters, National Educational Radio Network, and, much later, National Public Radio and Public Radio International.

In mid-February 1931 the University Radio Committee had promoted Harold McCarty from his position as chief announcer to the official post of program director on a part-time basis. With the promotion came a raise (he augmented his salary by teaching a course on business letter writing in the economics department).[12] By September he was the full-time program director, and continued to work as an announcer on various programs.

Almost immediately, McCarty began work to expand the program schedule. He cajoled friends and students to get involved in the radio station and by March had issued the first open invitation to students to audition. A graduate student in economics named Harold Engel took him up on his offer in the spring of 1931. In the late 1920s Engel had been a junior high school teacher in Flint, Michigan. While there, he had been involved with a safety project for children and asked McCarty if WHA was doing anything along these lines. McCarty said no, so Engel developed the *Badger Radio Safety Club.* This program for school-age children aired on WHA on Saturday mornings and was produced in cooperation with the Wisconsin health and highway departments.[13] It featured characters like Sergeant Safety, Aunty Dote, and the Accident Creatures. By the end of the year more than eight thousand children had pledged to "play safe always," and the program continued through March 1935.[14] Various other programs especially for children were added to WHA's Saturday lineup during this period, including *Tiny Tots Tunes, Tiny Troubadours*

Harold Engel in the Sterling Hall studios, ca. 1932 (University of Wisconsin Archives series 23/24/1)

Time, Wendy's Make-Believe Land, and *Adventures in Puppet Land.*[15] By Decem-ber Engel had joined the staff as McCarty's part-time assistant at the rate of ten dollars per week, and by the fall of 1932, he was named to the job on a full-time basis, the station's second full-time employee. He remained at WHA through his retirement in 1968 as assistant manager and publicity director. Engel served as de facto legislative liaison in addition to developing the Wis-consin College of the Air. He also served as a consultant in the 1930s to the New Mexico Radio Service and the Rocky Mountain Public Radio Council.

In the spring of 1931 the state also added an educational series, a noncredit course in Spanish presented by the department of Spanish and Portuguese on Mondays and Wednesdays at 5 p.m.[16] It was repeated in the fall, joined by a regular twice-weekly course in music appreciation taught by Dr. Charles H. Mills from Music Hall.[17] It was the station's first regular broadcast from a Uni-versity of Wisconsin classroom.

That fall WHA again presented University of Wisconsin home football games, beginning with a contest against North Dakota on October 3, 1931. The games were called by McCarty himself, joined by what today would be called a color commentator: J. Russell Lane. At the University of Illinois, Lane had been one of Red Grange's teammates.[18]

Starting January 1, 1932, WHA staffers began making up a typewritten pro-gram schedule on WHA letterhead for each day's broadcasts. Often, they in-clude handwritten notes indicating last-minute deviations from the schedule. One copy from each day was saved in the files, either the original or one of the many carbon copies. The university archives hold a mostly complete set of these documents through 1964.

The summer of 1932 brought a major improvement to the WHA opera-tion. Having the transmitter and antenna at Sterling Hall had hampered the development of the station for years. Terry had tried several times without suc-cess to find the money to move the transmitter and antenna to a new site. In 1927 the state legislature even appropriated $5,000 for new towers, which were never put up because of opposition to the proposed locations and the ongoing uncertainty about WHA's frequency. In 1930 the Board of Regents allocated $19,000 for a new studio and transmitting facilities, but the money was never used because of the long delay caused by the debate about consolidating WHA and WLBL.

It was a merger of commercial stations that provided a solution for WHA. The two commercial operations in Madison, WISJ and WIBA, consolidated their operations on June 14, 1931, and decided to dispose of the WISJ trans-mitter site and towers two miles south of Madison on Silver Spring Farm. The

towers had little residual value, and the University Radio Committee figured
WHA could acquire them at low cost. In July 1931 it recommended the purchase of the site, building, and towers, and the request was presented to the
Board of Regents in October. Because of the Depression the regents sought
special funding from the State Emergency Board. On March 23, 1932, the
board approved $2,000 for the purchase, and the university bought the tow-
ers and leased the building and land from the Badger Broadcasting Company.
The State Emergency Board also granted the station $7,300 to reconstruct
the transmitter, which was accomplished by Koehler and chief operator Orrin
Buchanan. On July 20, 1932, WHA began broadcasts from the new site.[19]

Another classroom broadcast began the same week, as WHA carried the
political science course American Government and Politics, taught by Ford
MacGregor, direct from his classroom in South Hall. The course, was thought
to be of general interest and aired Wednesdays and Fridays at 8:30 a.m.[20] About
the same time, a change came to WHA's afternoon classical music program.
Early in the year it had been given the title *Music of the Masters,* and the name
would remain in the schedule until 1974. By August 1932 the regular host of
the program was Carmelita Benson, one of the first women outside the *Homemakers' Program* or the Wisconsin School of the Air to hold a regular on-air
announcing position at WHA.[21]

The early months of 1933 saw a burst of interest in old-time fiddle music
over WHA. Wednesday editions of the *Farm Program* began featuring Grover
Kingsley and the Old Timers playing "old favorites." By February the live fiddle
offerings had a regular fifteen-minute slot at 1 p.m. Tuesdays and Thursdays,
and on Saturday, February 25, 1933, WHA broadcast the All-Wisconsin Old-
Time Fiddlers Contest. It was such a success that the station planned a regular
series of noncompetitive fiddlefests featuring old-time music on Saturday afternoons,[22] and it ran through the end of May. WHA rang out 1933 with the
Old Year Fiddle Fest on December 30.[23] The fiddler Grover Kingsley would
make occasional appearances on WHA for the next several years.[24]

By mid-1933 WHA's program schedule had grown to fifty-three hours a
week. It also remained on the air throughout the entire summer for the first
time in its history. During the summer months WHA offered another innovation in education by radio: a course in touch typewriting. Ann Orr, a teacher
at the Madison Vocational School, came up with the idea, formulated the
course, and broadcast the lessons herself. The fifteen-minute course aired at
9:15 a.m. each weekday for six weeks. Based on her experience teaching summer typing courses in the classroom, Orr predicted that students completing
the course would be typing at a rate more than twenty words a minute. They

WHA's 1932 transmitter towers
WHA acquired these towers from commercial station WISJ in 1932 and continues
to use the site for its transmitter and tower today. (University of Wisconsin Archives
series 23/24/4)

also would learn about the keyboard, the essential parts of the machine, and spacing requirements for punctuation. She believed that by the end of the course, students would reach the point where practicing would be the main factor in their improvement. She encouraged students to practice what they learned immediately after each broadcast.

Orr had two helpers in the studio during the program. One was an experienced typist who used a typewriter to provide the sound effects and set the cadence. The other was a beginner whose role was to react to the instructor so she would have some idea about the pace of the lessons and how well students might be comprehending her directions, as well as to set the pace for the students listening to the broadcast.

The program was a success, and Orr explained that typewriting is a subject "peculiarly adapted to the radio." She said that when typing is taught in the classroom, the teacher calls out the letters but it not essential that the teacher see the students type the keys—or that the students see the teacher, for that

WHA typing class in the Sterling Hall studio
WHA managers believed that their 1933 experiment in teaching typewriting over the radio had never been attempted before. Instructor Ann Orr is at the center desk. (University of Wisconsin Archives series 23/24/5)

matter. WHA's Harold Engel wrote an article about the course and noted that all kinds of people want to learn to type. He said that Orr's students included teachers, social workers, clerks, businessmen, students, housewives, radio operators, salesmen, and many unemployed people who "hoped to fit themselves better to obtain employment." Engel said that the students ranged from high schoolers to those who "bordered on old age" and the program offered them tangible and lasting value. He said those taking the course "added something to their 'stock in trade' which will always be of value to them." He gave much credit to Orr, whom he called a superb teacher, with the "voice quality, manner and attitude which combine to make a most pleasing radio personality."[25] She repeated the program the following summer, scheduled from 7 to 7:15 p.m. to reach a different audience.[26] Orr later taught a course in business letter writing over WHA.

Starting on November 1, 1933, WHA moved *Band Wagon,* a program of marching music, to the sign-on slot weekday mornings, and it became an early-morning fixture over WHA and the state stations for many years.[27] It had debuted as a midmorning program the previous August.[28] For a time its host was Willard Waterman, a University of Wisconsin student from Madison who later achieved fame in numerous network radio programs. In 1949 he took over the role of the Great Gildersleeve from Hal Peary and reprised the role of America's most beloved civil servant on television.[29]

By the end of 1933 the daily programming lineup included *Band Wagon* in the morning, morning and afternoon Wisconsin School of the Air programs, the afternoon Wisconsin College of the Air offerings (added that fall, see chapter 22), the midmorning *Homemakers' Program,* the noontime *Farm Program* and *State Capitol Program,* and the classical music program *Music of the Masters.* This schedule framework would remain in effect for a generation.

CHAPTER 10

❧

More Challenges from Commercial Stations

Future generations will consider our times as simply crazy, insane with
commercialism when they view such proceedings.

From radio's earliest days through the early 1930s, educational stations were
at a disadvantage in the broadcast marketplace. With no channels reserved for
educational broadcasting, commercial broadcasters coveted their frequencies
and argued before the Federal Radio Commission that the educational stations
were not making full use of their spots on the dial. During the Depression
cash-strapped colleges and universities found that their radio frequencies were
an asset that they could easily sell to commercial interests, and dozens did.

Armstrong Perry, director of the Service Bureau of the National Committee on Education by Radio, contacted WHA whenever any action was being
considered that concerned the 940 kHz frequency. Stations on both coasts and
in Kentucky, Michigan, North Dakota, and Oklahoma were among those
applying for more power and would therefore have the potential of interfering with the Wisconsin station's signal in fringe areas. WHA had endured
numerous conflicts with commercial stations over the years, but the managers
of the university station were unprepared for what transpired in the summer
of 1933, when two of the state's large commercial stations petitioned the Federal Radio Commission to eliminate both WHA and WLBL.

The first threat came from the owners of WIBA-Madison, the Badger Broadcasting Company; 67 percent of the stock in this company was held by Madison's *Capital Times*. The company applied to the Federal Radio Commission
on June 16, 1933, to increase the station's power to 25,000 watts and for half-
time rights on 720 kHz, the clear-channel station operated by WGN-Chicago.
Part of the application requested the discontinuance of both WHA and WLBL.
WHA had filed a routine application to renew its license, and the commission

120

wrote back to inform WHA managers of the challenge and designate the matter for a hearing. Part of the hearing was devoted to determining whether the continued operation of WHA would serve the public interest, convenience, and necessity.[1]

In its application WIBA claimed that it could provide "radio listeners in Wisconsin in particular and surrounding areas in general unique programs which will originate at the seat of government of Wisconsin, and the seat of the University of said state, such as educational, governmental, and agricultural information and instruction; athletic and other University and State events; that the service to the State and the University will be far superior to similar service now rendered by any existing station."[2] The proposed programming was much like that already being offered by WHA.

This application may have been a strategic move to eliminate competition from WHA and thereby increase the profitability of WIBA. To add to the uncertainty at the time of the application, the state legislature was nearing adjournment and had not yet taken up the appropriation request of $18,000 for WHA. Fortunately, Wisconsin governor Albert Schmedeman supported the station and secured its funding for the next two years from the state's Emergency Board.

While WIBA was challenging WHA, WTMJ in Milwaukee, owned by the *Milwaukee Journal,* opened an attack on both WHA and WLBL. On June 27, 1933, the Journal Company filed an application to operate a station of 2,500 watts at 900 mHz, WLBL's frequency. The filing also called for the facilities of WHA and WLBL to be consolidated into one station located in Madison, which was similar to the original 1930 merger plan. However, two weeks later WTMJ submitted a new application for 5,000 watts at 670 mHz, the frequency at the time held by NBC-owned WMAQ in Chicago. The application called for the elimination of not only the Chicago station but also WHA and WLBL.

In an interesting twist WTMJ proposed to build its new station near Stevens Point and offered to provide the university with free airtime. McCarty pointed out that this was a renewal of a proposition from two years earlier and would offer the state and the university only two hours of airtime a week.[3]

Adding to the uncertainty that summer, Schmedeman signed a measure sought by a legislator from central Wisconsin to protect the state's ownership of WLBL. The plan called for the state to lease WLBL to another operator for two years until the state could provide sufficient funds to resume its operation. The state would retain the license throughout the period.[4] Not surprisingly, one of those applying to operate the station was Milwaukee station WTMJ.[5] By October the state had scrapped the plan because savings from discontinuing the broadcast line to WHA allowed WLBL to continue to operate independently (see chapter 18).[6]

In response to WTMJ and WIBA the State of Wisconsin filed a joint application with the Federal Radio Commission, once again seeking to consolidate WHA and WLBL. This time the state stations requested half-time authority at 670 kHz at 5,000 watts, sharing time with WMAQ in Chicago. Remembering the concerns of Stevens Point listeners during the earlier consolidation battle, the application called for the studio to be in Madison and the transmitter and tower at Stevens Point. The application was filed on November 20, 1933, and was signed by both the governor and the president of the university.[7] Hill, of the Department of Markets, pointed out that the state was in a good position to meet the challenge, what with all departments of state government behind the consolidation plan. Further, the state was providing financial and legal support for the effort.[8]

The hearing before the Federal Radio Commission was postponed to January 8, 1934, and in the meantime the agency received many complaints from Wisconsin residents who were opposed to the elimination of the state stations.[9] Much support no doubt came from people who listened to Wisconsin School of the Air and Wisconsin College of the Air programs, which had not been part of the station schedule during the earlier battles in 1930–31. Editorials sympathetic to WHA also appeared. On November 24 the *Cambridge News* had written that the commercial broadcasters were not satisfied with their wavelengths, and "if progress is to be made in the use of radio in educational work, if new ideas are to be built into radio, it will not be a commercial station which sells its time that will lead the way. If need be, cut the commercial stations and give these two stations a chance to broaden their field."

This sentiment was echoed by Dean C. J. Anderson of the university's School of Education. He said, "Our experiences with commercial stations in broadcasting educational programs has been that they will throw out our programs if they can sell the time."[10]

More support for WHA and WLBL came from E. A. Ross, the chairman of the sociology department at University of Wisconsin. The *Daily Cardinal* interviewed him, and the story was reprinted on the editorial page of the *Stevens Point Daily Journal*. The article took pains to point out that this "internationally famous sociologist" was not speaking in an official capacity as someone with a direct connection with the stations but rather as "one intensely interested in the question and amply competent to comment upon the effect of such an abandonment." Ross said: "I think the effort of these commercial stations to snuff out these public stations is abominable." He said from the standpoint of long time results, "The commercial stations have no such sense of responsibility and no such purpose as public stations. Future generations will consider our times as simply crazy, insane with commercialism when they view such proceedings."[11]

The commission never did rule on the case as both WIBA and WTMJ withdrew their applications. Joseph Hirschberg of the Wisconsin Attorney General's office entered into negotiations with the two commercial operators and agreed to simultaneously withdraw the state's competing application, without prejudice.[12] Henry L. Ewbank, who now chaired the University Radio Committee, believed that the commercial stations canceled their plans because of "unfriendly public sentiment."[13]

In 1934 the Federal Radio Commission took on the title it has today: the Federal Communications Commission. In October 1934 the agency held public hearings about the non-commercial uses of radio, and the University of Wisconsin was invited to represent the National Association of Educational Broadcasters. Ewbank prepared testimony, which was later distributed as a booklet entitled *Conservation of Radio Resources.* It outlined Wisconsin's experience with regard to the functions and service of public and educational radio. It also offered recommendations to the commission. It urged the commission to develop an integrated plan of frequency assignment, to reserve a sufficient number of channels for non-commercial purposes, and to allot the reserved channels to governmental and educational agencies. Further, he suggested that commercial operators could use the frequencies temporarily, until they could be assigned to government agencies. He also recommended that channels be allotted for longer periods of time and that commercial stations pay rent for the privilege of using their assigned channels.[14] In the years ahead the FCC would reserve FM channels for non-commercial use and allocate television channels for educational broadcasting.

For educational AM radio, however, pressure from commercial interests and the financial difficulties of the early 1930s had taken a heavy toll. Of the 430 AM stations operating in the United States in the fall of 1933, only twenty-six were non-commercial educational outlets.[15]

CHAPTER 11

◠

The Political Education Forum

The success of a democracy depends upon an informed
and enlightened citizenry.

Early in the history of WHA, the staff wanted to present political material over
the air. The university leadership was nervous about this and delayed imple-
mentation of the ideas for many years. Still, WHA and WLBL were pioneers
in developing radio as a tool to keep the electorate informed about the work-
ings of government, and innovators in using radio during election campaigns.
As early as 1928 members of the university's political science department were
appearing over WHA with a "political review of the month."[1] Local election
results were broadcast over WLBL that fall, in cooperation with the *Stevens
Point Daily Journal.*[2]

One of the earliest attempts at regular programming of political material
was the news analysis program *What's Back of the News,* which debuted in 1929.
In 1930 University of Wisconsin president Glenn Frank envisioned using radio
"to revive the town meeting in this machine age." In a statement to the Federal
Radio Commission Frank said: "Through an adequate broadcasting service,
such as the station has sought, the town meeting similar to that held in New
England in the Puritan days, could be revived. Debates over political issues
could be revived so that an interest similar to that which greeted the Lincoln–
Douglas engagement could be aroused."[3] More political programming came
to WHA in March 1931, with the debut of the weekly *Radio Forum* hour. In
it, numerous controversial issues were discussed and different views argued for
by those who held the position.[4]

In October 1931 a permanent broadcast line was installed between WHA
and the State Capitol, and elected officials and other government employees
occasionally used it for speeches. Its existence led to the development of the

regular *State Capitol Program,* which debuted right after the *Homemakers' Program* at 10:45 a.m. on March 21, 1932.⁵ Initially, the program featured government officials such as the highway and insurance commissioners.

All these efforts led to a series of broadcasts collectively known as the *Political Education Forum.* During the primary and general election campaigns of 1932, the stations offered half-hour time slots to all state parties and all statewide candidates at no cost. Managers from WHA and WLBL met with representatives of the five major political parties in Wisconsin on August 12, 1932, to draw up an agreement, which the parties signed. It outlined their hope for the series:

> We, the representatives of stations WHA and WLBL and of the various political parties and groups, heartily endorse the use of Wisconsin's state-owned radio stations for political campaigns.
>
> We believe that one of our truest platitudes is that the success of a democracy depends on an informed and enlightened citizenry. At present, many of our voters get only one point of view; they read only one newspaper; and they attend, when they go at all, only the meetings of one political party. But if each party or group is allowed an equal opportunity to present its case over the state stations, the voter can get a much more adequate understanding of the issues and can cast a much more intelligent ballot.
>
> Another consideration touches the use of money in political campaigns. The state sets limits to the amount that can properly be spent. The charge is often made that parties without large financial resources are handicapped because they cannot get their argument before the voters. If the state places its radio facilities without charge at the disposal of each party or group, a step will be taken towards meeting both of these situations.
>
> We are aware that, unless political uses of the radio are properly safeguarded, unpleasant situations may arise. Some feel the danger of friction is so great that the attempts to use the radio in political campaigns should not be made. However, we do not take this position. The process of avoiding danger often results in avoiding programs of any sort. Wisconsin has a real opportunity to lead the way in taking problems of government to the people by radio.⁶

Members of the Democratic, Prohibition, Republican, Progressive Republican, and Socialist parties agreed to the proposal and were assigned their time periods by lot, with a half-hour each weekday and an hour late each afternoon beginning August 22 and running through September 21, 1932. WHA managers said that if they could find the money to pay for a broadcast line, WHA and WLBL would operate as a "chain"; otherwise, the stations would operate independently, and each would allot time for candidates. It appears that WLBL tried to carry the WHA feed on August 22, likely off-air, but by September politicians were appearing at both WHA and WLBL.[7] The political parties would select the speakers and apportion the time. Candidates in local elections could appear but only to discuss party issues. Also, the stations agreed they would not censor the material in any way, warning that the speakers would be held responsible for any libelous statement.

WHA manager McCarty stayed in touch with WLBL manager Frank Calvert by mail and, after the series was underway, asked about local response to the program. McCarty said that WHA had received a number of letters and a few calls for copies of talks, "but the general excitement which we had hoped for has not arisen."[8] Gradually, however, listeners grew to appreciate the service. Early in 1933 Henry Ewbank of the University Radio Committee told a state representative: "The response to these broadcasts was large and favorable. Many requests have been received from other states for information concerning our plan and its operation."[9]

Even if the initial reaction of the public was lukewarm, the politicians welcomed the opportunity to use the stations to get their message out. The even-handed way that time was allotted and the carefully crafted ground rules won friends for WHA and WLBL among members of all parties. These allies would prove valuable in the future when the stations were accused of bias or otherwise threatened. At McCarty's request the Wisconsin Democratic State Central Committee made a formal appeal to the Federal Radio Commission to allow WHA to remain on the air until 6 p.m. on November 3, 1932. The committee gave the station a copy of the telegram it sent to Washington, which read, "We have arranged for a forum with other political parties over radio station WHA on November third wish you would extend broadcast to six p m which will give all parties a chance to be heard."[10] It's unknown if permission was granted, but the request was an indication of how politicians had come to value this service.

Following the success of the *Political Education Forum,* WHA gradually changed the *State Capitol Program.* Originally, this program had featured officials from government departments, but by February 1933 it had been moved to a different time slot and modified to include various members of the state senate and assembly speaking about pending legislation. The first was Assembly Speaker Cornelius Young, a Milwaukee Democrat, with his address titled "What the Legislature Is Doing."[11] The *State Capitol Program* began as a fifteen-minute offering but was later expanded to a half-hour and would on occasion feature two speakers. These programs were rebroadcast by commercial stations WIBU in Poynette and WTAQ in Eau Claire.[12] The rules governing the speakers were the same as those outlined for the *Political Education Forum*. WHA's Harold Engel emphasized that "each speaker is allowed free rein; no censorship is suggested. Even in the most controversial of problems, there have been no cases of indiscretions or ungentlemanly conduct."[13] As the station's political liaison, Engel regularly invited legislators to appear on the program. Even those who did not accept would remember that they had been offered the opportunity, would have a positive impression of the station, and might be called upon to support WHA in the future.

After the FM network was in place, the program, now called the *Wisconsin Legislative Forum*, was recorded so it could be played again during evening hours. WHA also offered training to make the legislators' radio appearances more effective. The free evening classes in radio speaking included the opportunity to have a recording made of a test speech, so the lawmakers could hear their own voice. Participation was high: in 1965, 105 lawmakers took part in the broadcasts, a full 79 percent of the legislature.[14]

The political broadcasts of the 1930s continue today: all candidates appearing on the statewide ballot are offered time on Wisconsin Public Radio's call-in programs.

CHAPTER 12

❧

A New Home

1933–36

We are on the air, call back later.

By the early 1930s the WHA schedule had grown to the point that the Sterling Hall studio was no longer efficient. Proposals to move to Music Hall and to a site near Camp Randall had not worked out, and the radio station and the physics department were finding it increasingly difficult to coexist. The anteroom of the WHA facility was still being used to teach a physics course in glassblowing, and station manager Harold McCarty noted that when twenty students all had their Bunsen burners operating along with compressed air tubes, the room turned into a "roaring furnace," frightening to anyone entering the studio.[1] Things got so bad that McCarty moved his desk, files, phone, and other items into the WHA studio proper and attempted to work there while programs were underway. Proximity to working laboratories caused other problems as well. On October 21, 1932 the *Daily Cardinal* reported: "Sophomore physicists did impromptu broadcasting last week. Every time they ran the gravity acceleration apparatus its sparking mechanism let off a motor boat put-put that penetrated the studio amplifier board and went out on WHAves all over the state with the rest of the program. Rather to the exclusion of the program." Staff members from the era recalled that people came and went from the single WHA room continuously, records were piled on the windowsills, and the telephone was smothered with a pillow. If it rang during a program, it was answered in a whisper: "We are on the air, call back later."[2] Finding a new home for the station was imperative. One possibility was an 1882 building on campus that was sitting vacant.

The building, which had originally been the university's heating plant, had most recently served as the Mining and Metallurgy Laboratory, and it was right

behind Science Hall, the original pre–World War I home of 9XM. The mining building's chimney had even supported one end of the 9XM wire antenna
in the early years. The mining and metallurgy department had moved to new
quarters on University Avenue, and the old building had been vacant for two
years, since its interior was thought to be unsuitable for other purposes.

However, when funding became available through the New Deal's Civil
Works Administration in 1933, it was thought that it might be possible to
renovate the building for WHA. In November, the Board of Regents approved
a request for $7,000, which would be matched by $2,700 in university funds.
The CWA requested an additional $1,000, which was granted by the regents
in January 1934. Work started immediately and much of the interior was completed when President Roosevelt cancelled all CWA projects in March. Work
resumed in September under the auspices of a new agency, the Federal Emergency Relief Administration.[3] While the CWA project was idle, the Federal
Communications Commission granted WHA a power increase from 1,000
watts to 2,500 watts.[4]

Despite the delay in the remodeling project, one construction effort continued to move ahead. WHA's new music director H. Frederick Fuller labored
through the spring to rebuild an organ for the station and install it in the new
building. The Barton organ, made in Oshkosh, Wisconsin, originally had been
installed in the Madison Theatre on State Street but for the past fifteen years
had been languishing in storage in a tobacco barn in nearby Stoughton. Fuller
was able to acquire it for WHA by paying $250 in overdue storage charges.[5]
Buying and reconditioning the instrument cost less than $1,000. He had it
installed and working by April 1934 and gave a daily organ recital over WHA
in the unfinished building amid piles of construction materials.[6] Fuller's long-
running late afternoon program, *Cathedral Echoes,* became such a favorite of
listeners that WHA produced postcards featuring Fuller's picture to satisfy
numerous requests. One version included a testimonial from a fan letter: "These
organ reveries are the finest entertainment on the air. As an organist, Mr. Fuller
has no peer."[7]

Although the FERA reconstruction project was not completed until May
1935, the station and staff moved into the building and began broadcasts from
what was now called Radio Hall on December 3, 1934. The total cost of the
remodeling was $18,232, of which the University of Wisconsin paid only
$4,200.[8]

The new facility contained a control room and three studios, five offices, and
a large reception room that featured a glass window so spectators could see
into the main studio. The reception room and its furniture were done in a

WHA music director H. Frederick Fuller
Fuller (right) during the installation of the organ in Radio Hall in 1934. Fuller was
the performer on WHA's *Cathedral Echoes*, a popular late-afternoon organ recital.
He provided music for numerous WHA programs. (University of Wisconsin
Archives series 23/24/1)

Native American motif, celebrating early forms of communication. The uphol-
stery was produced by Navajos in New Mexico, as cloth weaving is not a craft
typically practiced by tribes in Wisconsin. Art professor Wayne Claxton, host of
the Wisconsin School of the Air's *Creative Art* program, did much of the design
work on the interior, assisted by C. E. Brown, director of the State Historical
Museum. The Native American theme included a petroglyph frieze done by a
student in the style of native carvings found on cave walls along the Wisconsin
and Mississippi rivers. The early communication theme included the light fix-
tures that looked like native drums. Some student work was paid for by a
National Youth Administration program.[9] Another student project created a
modernistic mural to conceal the organ pipes. Its six motifs represented a keyboard, piano, organ pipes, microphone, sound waves, and vertical lines of music.
The cost of the mural's frame, canvas, paints, and stencils came to $7.20.[10]

WHA continued to use grants from New Deal programs to further improve
the building. In 1936 the station applied to the Works Progress Administration

Radio Hall
WHA used grants from various federal agencies to turn an abandoned heating plant
and laboratory building into a state-of-the-art broadcast facility. It was home to
WHA from 1934 to 1972. (University of Wisconsin Archives series 23/24/4)

for funding to remodel its south end. When this project was completed, WHA
had an additional studio and control room as well as four more offices.[11]

Coinciding with the move to Radio Hall, WHA released a new program
guide, covering the period through May 1935. The attractive twelve-page booklet gave the daily schedules, program descriptions, and other useful information.

In 1935 a major equipment purchase changed WHA operations. The station
acquired its first transcription disc recorder, the then-standard technology for
making audio recordings. Now the station could prerecord programs for airing at a later date and could air popular programs multiple times. This also
allowed the station to offer its recordings elsewhere or enter noteworthy ones
in competition for awards. The standard format was a sixteen-inch disc of glass
or aluminum with an acetate coating. Many of these discs remain in the
archives of the University of Wisconsin, and others are in the collections of the

RADIO
PROGRAMS

*America's Oldest
Educational Radio Station*

NOV.
1934 to MAY
1935

WISCONSIN
STATE–OWNED STATION
MADISON

WHA program guide, 1934–35 (WHA Radio and Television
Records/University of Wisconsin Archives)

WHA transcription recorder
In 1935 WHA acquired its first lathe for making transcription recordings. The technology was supplanted by tape recording after World War II. (University of Wisconsin Archives series 23/24/5)

University of Wisconsin School of Music and the Wisconsin Historical Society Archives. The earliest recordings in the collection are some Wisconsin School of the Air programs from the 1935–36 school year. The format remained popular even after the advent of reliable tape recorders: WHA was still using it as late as the fall of 1959.

In 1936 a new transmitter was put into operation for WHA to accommodate an increase in power to 5,000 watts. Rather than purchase a new factory-built model, station engineers designed and built the unit at a substantial savings. It was rebuilt several times and remained in use until October 1951. Its efficient and economical design was copied in 1937 for use at WLBL's new transmitter facility in Auburndale.[12]

CHAPTER 13

Budget Woes and New Programs

1935–41

It's that weather man of yours who beats everything. . . .
I get a great bang out of listening to him.

Throughout the early 1930s WHA never appeared in the university budget; its funding came directly from state government through its Emergency Board. Some observers have maintained that this was an asset, because it focused attention on the radio operation. University president Glenn Frank assumed this situation would continue: the Emergency Board had provided funds for the 1931–33 biennium and the first year of the 1933–35 biennium. In June 1934, at the request of the University Radio Committee, he asked Governor Albert Schmedeman to fund the balance of the biennium. The Emergency Board designated $16,623 for the next fiscal year.[1]

In 1935 the university again omitted WHA from its appropriation request. Frank appeared before the legislature's Joint Finance Committee and said he felt the radio station should not be part of the university budget. In part, the university was feeling the financial pressures of the Depression, but Frank also believed that many of WHA's functions were "not closely connected" with the university and were instead serving schools, farmers, homemakers, and other groups.[2] John Stanley Penn points out in his dissertation that this view was at odds with the Wisconsin Idea and could just as easily be applied to the Extension Division and many functions of the College of Agriculture.[3]

In response, Governor Philip LaFollette included WHA in his budget request for the only other state agency that had any radio function, the Department of Agriculture and Markets. When the legislature approved the request, it transferred control of WHA to the agency. The governor did not intend that the transfer would change or interfere with WHA's operation. Rather, the move was designed only to ensure the station's continuance.[4] The responsibility for the operation and administration of WHA remained with the University Radio Committee. La Follette's appropriation provided $20,000 for each year of the biennium, a substantial increase. The legislature appropriated $12,550 more for a new 5,000-watt transmitter. For 1937–38 the station's budget increased to $24,000 and for 1938–39 to $27,000.

The FCC had recently rejected a power increase for WLBL and the Washington officials stated that the station was not in the optimum location to take advantage of the requested change. Some state lawmakers felt that reviving the legislation to transmit programs over the ten commercial stations might be preferable to appropriating more funds for WLBL. The thought was that the savings arising from discontinuing the Stevens Point station could be applied to the cost of the ten-station hookup. In reaction to the criticism from the FCC, officials with the Department of Markets worked to improve conditions at WLBL so they could make a new request for a power increase.[5]

In January 1938 a new remote broadcast line was installed between Radio Hall and the weather bureau office in North Hall, the oldest building on campus. The bureau was still staffed by Eric Miller, a participant in the station since the days of the 9XM telegraphic weather broadcasts. Having the broadcast line to his office allowed Miller to present the forecast himself beginning on February 7; within a week, commercial station WCLO in Janesville began rebroadcasting the feature.

Miller's informal and unpretentious style immediately charmed his listeners. Some said he was the most unintentionally funny person on radio. On one occasion a phone call was routed to his office during his broadcast, and the telephone rang continuously in the background until he finally said, "Hang on while I answer that blasted telephone, will you?" With the microphone still live, the radio audience heard him answer "Weather bureau" and give the caller the current temperature before continuing his broadcast. On another occasion he had just finished giving the forecast when listeners heard a long pause, after which Miller said, "Now what on earth am I thinking about? That was yesterday's forecast. I really must straighten up this desk." In commenting on crop conditions Miller once said, "Farmers are planting sweet potatoes in Georgia. They're coming up in Florida." Then, realizing how that sounded, he said: "Uh, well now, how about that for a long root system!" One radio listener encountered Miller on the street one day and found the forecaster was wearing a raincoat and carrying an umbrella. The listener pointed out that Miller's radio forecast had said nothing about rain, and Miller replied: "Yes, I know, but you see my wife doesn't listen to my broadcasts."[6]

Miller had a famous fan, the poet Carl Sandburg. In 1941 Sandburg met

McCarty at a teachers' conference and said he regularly tuned in the Madison station from his home in Harbert, Michigan. Sandburg told McCarty that WHA was his favorite station and had the best music on the air. But, Sandburg said, "It's that weather man of yours who beats everything. He beats anything I ever heard for being natural. I get a great bang out of listening to him."[7]

McCarty, who was always looking for promotional opportunities, maintained in later years that Miller was the nation's first broadcast weatherman. Miller, however, did not make the claim. He noted that while he did appear over WHA in the early days talking about weather topics, station announcers gave the forecast itself. He said he did not become the "regular commentator" until after broadcast trials by a weatherman in Norfolk, Virginia, had found "an enthusiastic audience among the fisher and sailor folk of lower Chesapeake Bay." He lamented that he had not taken advantage of the opportunity to be the first in the field.[8] Miller remained in charge of the Madison weather bureau until his retirement on August 31, 1944.

By the spring of 1938 WHA was airing some syndicated music programs, the station's first regular offering of programs produced by others. These fifteen-minute programs were delivered by transcription records. Ensembles like the

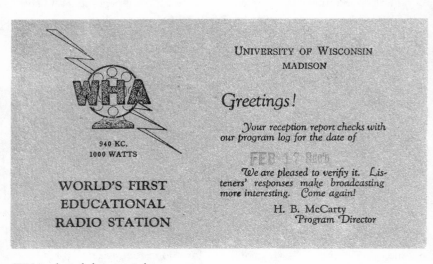

WHA acknowledgment card
Tuning in distant stations continued to interest radio listeners in the 1930s. Those asking for verification of their reception of WHA received this "QSL" card; this one was sent to a Jersey City listener in 1934. The promotional skills of McCarty and Engel are evident in the slogan, which now proclaims WHA as the "World's First Educational Radio Station." (Collection of Norman Gilliland)

Federal Music Group, Los Angeles Federal Symphony Orchestra, and Southern California Federal Choir were regular weekly features through early 1940.[9] The summer of 1940 featured programs from the New York City Federal Orchestra and the U.S. Marine Band. Locally produced music included studio performances by a fifteen-piece student band called the Radio Hall Firemen. Music director H. Frederick Fuller assembled the group to perform each Saturday morning on *Band Wagon*.[10] A weekly spoken-word series also began airing in late 1939. *Lest We Forget* examined American history and government. It was produced by the Institute of Oral and Visual Education in cooperation with the Boston University Radio Institute.[11]

In the spring of 1938 Ralph Ammon, director of the Department of Agriculture and Markets, suggested the creation of a radio council to set policy for

The Radio Hall Firemen
This musical ensemble, made up of University of Wisconsin students, performed live each Saturday morning over WHA in the early 1940s. This photo was taken at the Madison fire station on West Dayton Street, near the entrance to Camp Randall. (University of Wisconsin Archives series 23/24/5, negative 16070-C)

both WHA and WLBL.[12] The University of Wisconsin Board of Regents created what would be the first State Radio Council on June 17, 1938.[13] The council's statement of policy reiterated the belief in non-commercial broadcasting and said, "The aim always should be to give the news of interesting projects and developments, to give factual information from which listeners may draw their own conclusions, to give programs that stay well within the limits of what is generally understood by the terms 'education' as opposed to 'propaganda,' or 'news' and 'information' as opposed to 'promotion.'"[14]

Also in 1938 the Committee for Reorganization of the state government recommended to La Follette that WHA and WLBL both be transferred to the control of the university, and an executive order by the governor made the change effective as of September 1, 1938. WLBL's managers submitted the paperwork required to reassign their station's license to the university.

While the reorganization struggles were underway, WHA made one more attempt at a better channel assignment. The expanded programming schedule was proving popular with listeners, and the station enjoyed good support from the university administration and the governor's office. Moreover, the FCC would be reallocating frequencies soon, and WHA wanted to ensure increased power and post-sundown rights.

The WHA staff met with the president of the university and the governor, then submitted an application to the FCC on July 16, 1938, for a new frequency and higher power. In a move that McCarty himself would later say was audacious, WHA asked for a 50,000-watt station at 670 kHz. At the time the frequency was held by WMAQ-Chicago, a station owned by NBC. In late 1933 WHA had applied to share time on the frequency to face the challenge posed by WTMJ. The 1938 application called for the transmitter to be twenty to forty miles north of Madison in Columbia County. Like the applications of the past, it pointed out to the FCC that Wisconsin had no clear-channel stations, whereas Illinois had four, and that granting the application would "bring about a more equitable distribution of radio facilities between states."[15] The FCC scheduled a hearing for February 21, 1939.

During his discussions with WHA La Follette said he would seek money for the new station from the 1939 legislature, providing he was reelected in November 1938. The governor laid the groundwork for the next legislative session and called a conference for September 1, 1938, in Madison. The meeting was chaired by the state attorney general and included representatives of many state agencies, educational groups, and civic organizations. All agreed to make a full effort to support the WHA application before the FCC. La Follette contacted the five members of the Wisconsin congressional delegation who were members of the governor's Progressive Party as well as U.S. Representative Raymond Cannon, a Democrat. All wrote letters to the FCC in support of the application.[16]

The Wisconsin efforts did not go unnoticed in Chicago. The *Chicago Tribune* blasted the application in an editorial on October 2 headlined "Piracy on the Air Waves." The paper charged that the La Follette administration was behind the move and that WHA "is dedicated exclusively to the advancement of the political fortunes of the La Follette machine." The editorial claimed that "state owned radio does not mean freedom of expression for the citizens. It means a monopoly of this form of communication by the political group in power. This has been demonstrated in Germany, Italy, and Russia, and it is such a monopoly that politicians of the La Follette stripe are seeking in the United States." The *Tribune* made a bizarre argument in support of WMAQ's right to the frequency: "The wave band assigned to the original operators of WMAQ was of no value until they spent many thousands of dollars building a broadcast station to use the band. The station itself was useless until they had spent hundreds of thousands more to employ talent and provide programs which attracted listeners."[17] Engel's dual role as publicity director and legislative liaison for WHA was put to good use in this instance. He collected letters of support from legislators and candidates of all parties who had appeared on regular broadcasts from the State Capitol and on the *Political Education Forum*. He used their comments to refute the editorial in letters to individuals and media outlets.

In November 1938, La Follette lost his bid for reelection. With the start of the new year the Wisconsin Senate rescinded La Follette's executive orders. This included all the reorganization orders of his administration, including the authorization of the State Radio Council and the order transferring both WHA and WLBL to the university's Board of Regents. With the move, this radio council went out of existence. Although the Wisconsin Assembly sought to return administration and control of the stations to the regents, the state senate killed the bill. WLBL managers now had to submit even more paperwork to Washington to restore their license to the Department of Agriculture and Markets.

The WHA plan for more power and a different frequency also suffered when new governor Julius Heil called a meeting on February 15, 1939, to find out more about the pending FCC application. The governor invited members of the University Radio Committee, the new attorney general, representatives of Wisconsin's commercial broadcasters, and executives from NBC. Not present were the numerous groups from the September 1938 meeting who were all staunch supporters of the WHA application. According to McCarty, members of the NBC delegation were incensed by the nerve of WHA and even pounded on the governor's desk in frustration at one point.[18] The state's commercial broadcasters were equally opposed to the application and proposed an alternative. They would provide an unspecified number of evening hours as a state network if the state would assume the cost of line rentals. Heil asked for a written proposal, but none was ever submitted, despite repeated requests from the University Radio Committee.[19]

The FCC postponed its hearing on the matter until November 10, 1939. The delay allowed for legislative action. The state assembly approved a bill to provide financial support for the new station, but the senate tabled it, and it died with the adjournment of the legislature on October 8.[20] The University Radio Committee recommended to the university president that the application be withdrawn, which it was.

Despite the turmoil WHA continued to thrive. In February 1939 the University Radio Committee issued its first annual report, which outlined the station's activities during 1938. As it was the first such report, it included a history of the station to that point, and improvements in transmitter output, hours on air per week, and budget appropriations over the years in addition to program advances.[21]

WHA made a rare Sunday broadcast on February 19, 1939, beginning at 2 p.m. with chamber music, followed by a 2:30 p.m. varsity concert. However, the main reason for the special schedule began at 3 p.m.: the Wisconsin Hoofers Seventh Annual Ski Meet from Muir Knoll. The broadcast featured a ski jump competition, followed by interviews and an announcement of the final standings.[22]

On May 21, 1940, Madison's *Capital Times* printed another criticism of WHA. The paper ran a short item headlined "Communist Fronts Here in Madison" and listed five organizations "seeking support under false pretenses." The paper made a point of saying that two of them, the Workers Alliance and the Wisconsin Conference for Social Legislation, were both "now being given time over the university radio station WHA."

Late in 1940 budget negotiations were underway to fund the various operations of the Wisconsin Department of Agriculture ("and Markets" had been dropped from the agency's name the previous year, but its duties remained unchanged). During the process Heil indicated a desire to reduce the budget for WHA and WLBL. Department director Ralph Ammon suggested instead that the governor first consider separating the two stations, since WHA was really run by the University of Wisconsin, despite being part of the budget of the agriculture department. The governor agreed.[23]

The federal census of 1940 showed that the prediction Earle Terry had made twenty years earlier had come to pass: 83 percent of U.S. homes now had a radio, whereas only 55 percent had bathtubs.[24]

On March 29, 1941, in accordance with the North American Radio Broadcasting Agreement, all but 91 of the 893 AM stations then operating shifted to new frequencies at 3 a.m. Eastern Time. At the same time the AM band was expanded to 1600 kHz. One reason for the treaty was to create clear-channel frequencies for Canadian and Mexican stations. All AM stations between 880 and 970 moved up 30 kHz to between 910 and 1000 on the dial. In what would be the last of many moves on the AM dial, WHA shifted from 940 to its current frequency, 970 kHz. Despite the move, the station was still limited to daytime operation.

After years as part of the Department of Agriculture budget, WHA returned to the university's budget under a 1941 act of the Wisconsin Legislature transferring "management, control and operation of station WHA from the Department of Agriculture to the Board of Regents of the University." The transfer became effective July 1, and the measure appropriated and transferred $47,640 per year to operate WHA.[25]

With the transfer of station management and operation, the Board of Regents created a Division of Radio Education, at the recommendation of the University Radio Committee and with the approval of university president Clarence Dykstra. In the belief that education by radio should be an "all-University function, utilizing every resource of the University as a whole . . . but being subordinate to no single administrative division of instruction," the committee recommended:

· that the Board of Regents create a Division of Radio Education as an all-University service to the people of Wisconsin, this Division to be responsible directly to the President of the University.

that the authority for the control and the administration of radio education, and the operation of Station WHA, be vested in a faculty committee to be known as the Radio Committee of the University of Wisconsin.

that the Radio Committee be charged with the responsibility of forming the policies and directing the activities of Station WHA. It shall submit to the Board of Regents an annual budget and recommend appointments and promotions within the Division.[26]

Now fully returned to the university, WHA was about to face the challenges of broadcasting during the war years.

CHAPTER 14

⌒

The War Years and After

1942–47

A good step in the direction of improved international
understanding through radio.

The entry of the United States into World War II changed the programming
on WHA, with about a fifth of its airtime devoted to various governmental
agencies and the war effort. The station also aired more than sixty spot announcements a week about salvage, rationing, recruiting, price controls, and
other issues related to the home front. Some programs done locally with members of the armed services were recorded and sent to radio stations in the home
states of the participants.

The war also decimated the WHA staff roster. McCarty was on loan for ten
months to the Office of War Information for work related to psychological
warfare through shortwave broadcasts, Engel entered U.S. Army service as a
first lieutenant, and production manager Gerald Bartell entered navy service.
The following year *Farm Program* host Milton Bliss also left for the U.S. Army.
In 1944 music director H. Frederick Fuller joined the Coast Guard and
scriptwriter Helen Frey joined the Women's Army Air Corps. WHA also lost
six student operators in 1942 who resigned to accept assignments directly
related to the war effort, and fourteen announcers left as well. For the first
time WHA trained women students to work as operators and announcers.[1]

Despite the shortage of personnel, WHA added regular Sunday broadcasts
beginning in February 1942, bringing the station to seven-day service. From
this point forward, the station would be on every day, except for major holidays. One program added to the new Sunday schedule was *University Roundtable,* patterned after the *University of Chicago Round Table* and Northwestern
University's *Reviewing Stand.* A special faculty forum committee was formed
to help select topics and suggest participants.[2]

One Sunday afternoon series was *Civilians in Service*. One 1942 episode written by Romance Koopman and James Terzian and performed by the WHA Players was called "The Strong Black Hand." It called for equality for African Americans in the war effort. The episode won an Ohio State Award that year for outstanding cultural program. Another Ohio State honor came for the School of the Air social studies program *Let's Find Out*, named the finest program for primary grades, and *Afield with Ranger Mac* received a Peabody Award that year as the outstanding educational radio program in the country.[3]

During the late spring of 1942 WHA appealed to the Board of Regents for money to subscribe to the new Associated Press broadcast wire service for radio stations. The regents asked McCarty why the station simply couldn't use the AP wire already in place for use by the journalism department, which had been alternating between AP and United Press service on a yearly basis since its first Morkrum Teletype printer was installed in 1927.[4] McCarty explained that the journalism department was using the newspaper wire, and was paying for only the school year, whereas WHA needed the new broadcast circuit and year-round service. On May 30 the regents voted to approve the contract for the 1942–43 fiscal year: twenty-five dollars per week for the first six months and thirty-five dollars per week for the second six months.

The wire service Teletype was installed in Radio Hall and began operation on July 18, 1942. McCarty saved a scrap of that first day's wire copy, which included a message welcoming WHA and commercial station WCKY-Cincinnati to the service.[5] WHA wasted no time in promoting the addition of the news wire. The promotional slogan "All the News—and the News Only" was in use by that autumn. In print materials accompanying the slogan, WHA managers hinted that they realized the station had been at a competitive disadvantage without a wire service and that some listeners were perhaps turning to other stations for news updates. They wrote: "That slogan typifies the several news periods on WHA each day! Your state station is in constant touch with the news centers of the world through the wires of the Press Association, the radio service of the Associated Press. WHA gives a sane presentation of the news and reports all the important happenings. It will interrupt programs when flashes of transcendent importance come in. Listeners are telling their friends that they can now stay tuned to WHA and be sure that in addition to a good program fare they will get 'All the News—and the News Only.'"[6]

During 1943 WHA programming continued to reflect the nation's involvement in the war. That year's annual report by the University Radio Committee noted that the station's offerings were geared to the winning of the war and the peace. WHA designed the schedule to "stimulate action on the home front, to promote understanding of the basic issues of the war, to further knowledge and appreciation of other peoples, and to give guidance to planning for the future." The report also listed the schedule from a single day (November 10), showing the extent of "war programs" on the station:

7:45—War News Summary

8:30—University Forum: "Can Strikes in Wartime Be Justified?"

9:15—War Headlines and Background Analysis

10:00—Homemakers' Rationing and Shopping Guide (*Homemakers' Program*)

10:15—Effect of War on the Minds of Children (*Homemakers' Program*)

10:45—How Planes Fly (science lesson for the intermediate grades) (*School of the Air*)

11:00—Backgrounds of World War II (University Course) (*College of the Air*)

12:20—War News Summary

12:30—Food for Freedom: Milk (*Farm Program*)

1:00—Reading of "Reprisal," a novel of the French underground (*Chapter A Day*)

2:00—Stephens Family Dramatization: "To Buy or Not to Buy" (*College of the Air*)

3:30—Reading for Wartime

4:15—Voice of the Army

4:30—Lest We Forget: "Our Nation's Shrines"

4:55—War News Summary

In addition, weekly programs were presented in cooperation with the armed services, including *These Are the WAVES* and *Hello from the U.S.O.* The station also carried the Army Air Corps graduation ceremonies at Madison's Truax Field and on campus at the Naval Training School.[7] The debut episode of a Saturday series called *This Is Truax Field* on March 27, 1943, appealed to listeners to donate their old radios and radio parts to the base's Truax Training School. The announcer said: "Turn in your old radio . . . the one that hasn't worked for years now. . . . Keep the cabinet if you can find a use for it . . . but turn the rest over to the Truax Training School." He told listeners to "drop a card to your station . . . tell them you have vital radio equipment for Truax Field."[8] The campaign was a huge success: listeners donated more than 350 old or inoperative radio sets that would be taken apart and built into models of military radio equipment for training purposes.[9]

In 1943 the station also began the regular broadcast of programs from the British Broadcasting Corporation that were delivered on transcription records.

The University Radio Committee's annual report said the WHA was "privileged" to present the series *Answering You,* described as "a transatlantic conversation which answers many questions arising in the minds of British and Americans about each other," and said that the program "seems a good step in the direction of improved international understanding through radio." WHA also was airing the BBC program *Freedom Forum.* Another program series, called *Beyond Victory,* offered opinions about postwar planning and was made available from the World Wide Broadcasting Company in cooperation with the Carnegie Foundation.[10]

The BBC transcriptions would be a programming staple for the station for years and offered an unintended benefit. Because many transcription records were recorded on only one side, the thrifty staffers at WHA used the blank "B side" to preserve their own programs. The university archives today hold many WHA programs from the 1940s and 1950s that were cut into the reverse side of BBC transcriptions.

Also in 1943 Radio Hall received an addition to its decor that remains today. Student John Stella completed a six-by-eighteen-foot mural depicting the early history of WHA.[11]

Late in 1943 WHA began publishing a separate monthly classical music

Radio Hall mural
When someone depicted in the mural stopped by for a visit at WHA, he was often asked to pose in front of his likeness for a photograph. The mural remains in Radio Hall to this day. From the left are glassblower James B. Davis, student operator Ross Herrick (who had the run-in with Pablo Casals in 1923), student operator Burton Miller, student operator C. M. Jansky Jr., physics department "mechanician" J. P. Foerst, extension professor/program director William H. Lighty, student operator Malcolm Hanson, agriculture professor Andrew H. Hopkins, engineering professor Edward Bennett, station founder Earle M. Terry, speech professor Henry L. Ewbank, musician Waldemar Geltch, music educator Edgar B. Gordon, and musician Paul Sanders. (University of Wisconsin Archives series 23/24/4)

guide for mailing to interested music fans. The flier listed the featured recordings for *Music You Want* (8 to 8:30 a.m. weekdays), *Music of the Masters* (2:30 to 3:30 p.m. Monday through Saturday), and *Masterworks of Music* (5 to 5:30 p.m. weekdays).[12] Interestingly, the May 1944 guide indicates that music selection was driven in part by record label, with *Music You Want* relying on Victor albums and *Masterworks of Music* using Columbia recordings.[13] During periods when the station published a full program guide, the listings of selections would be incorporated in it; at other times, the music listings remained a separate document. It was discontinued as a mailing in 2003, but the Wisconsin Public Radio Web site continues to provide music listings.

In 1944 WHA switched its news wire service to United Press. The station forwarded wire service bulletins to the *Daily Cardinal* and placed them on a bulletin board in the university's Memorial Union for the benefit of students and faculty.[14] (Wisconsin Public Radio stayed with UP's successor, United Press International, until the 1980s, when it moved back to service from the Associated Press.) During 1944 WHA also originated four "coast-to-coast" broadcasts of classical music by the Pro Arte Quartet for the Mutual Broadcasting System.[15] Another addition to the station that year was a weekly program called *Dear Sirs*. This fifteen-minute program featured the reading of letters from listeners, with questions fielded by WHA managers. It typically would air on Friday morning and would be repeated on Saturday morning. It remained in the schedule for more than twenty-five years.

In 1944 WHA managers also took the first step in planning a postwar network of FM stations. On September 30 the university's Board of Regents authorized the formation of another State Radio Council (see chapter 15 for more information about the council and the development of the FM network).

In January 1945 WHA began producing a monthly printed program guide for distribution to listeners that retained the same format, either monthly or six times a year, through January 1968. In addition to the program grid, it usually included a detailed description of the scheduled guests for the *Homemakers' Program*.

Beginning in late August 1945 and continuing through the end of October, WHA carried several programs from the Mutual Broadcasting System.[16] Throughout September the station aired a weekday program of music from Mutual called *Summertime Melodies* at 3:30 p.m., with *Music for Half an Hour* in the same time slot on Saturday. Also, a Mutual music series by various military bands aired each weekday morning, and a program called *Alfred Wallenstein's Sinfonietta* aired weekdays at 6:30 p.m.[17] In September and October a fifteen-minute talk/interview program hosted by Jane Cowl was broadcast weekdays at 4:45 p.m. Cowl was an actor and playwright who during the war was codirector of the Stage Door Canteen in New York[18]; her Mutual program featured interviews with people in the performing arts. Some of these programs could be heard locally over WIBU in nearby Poynette or over WGN-Chicago, both Mutual affiliates.

Later in the year WHA provided a series for the Mutual network. On December 9, 1945, the station began offering a weekly half-hour program featuring the music of the Pro Arte Quartet.[19] The acclaimed European ensemble had been on tour when World War II began, and the musicians were stranded in the United States. They accepted a residency at the University of Wisconsin. The half-year series continued to be produced for Mutual through mid-1948.[20] It is believed that the series was recorded in Madison on transcription records and sent to the network, partly because the WHA annual reports list "rebroadcasts" of the series, and by the fact that at least one transcription recording from the 1945–46 series exists in the hands of a private collector.[21]

The precise nature of the relationship between WHA and Mutual is not known. The September 1945 program guide said only that the programs on WHA were presented "in cooperation with the Mutual Broadcasting System." WHA may have had a program line from the network, used the existing line between WHA and Mutual affiliate WIBU in Poynette, or used a telephone feed. WHA has some transcription records of programs that originated at Mutual Broadcasting but that were recorded at WHA. The Saturday program *Music for Half an Hour* aired at the same time that WIBU carried it, but WHA delayed the Jane Cowl program (which was not carried by WIBU) from its live airtime of 1:15 p.m. The Mutual programs that WHA carried in 1945 may have been experiments, perhaps offered in exchange for WHA's producing the Pro Arte series for the network. All these Mutual programs are believed to have been "sustaining" ones, meaning they contained no network commercials. They would therefore be legal for broadcast over a non-commercial station like WHA.

One other event passed unnoticed during the final days of 1945. As had always been the case, WHA did not sign on for Christmas Day. It would be the last time the station would be off the air for the holiday.

In the weeks before the first of the FM stations went on the air, WHA came up with a way to generate some extra revenue. It offered high schools the opportunity to receive a telephone feed from the state high school basketball tournament with customized play-by-play reports. Some schools had asked WHA to provide this service in previous years but often called too late for arrangements to be made. For 1947 McCarty sent a letter to the principals of schools participating in district tournaments. For a small fee WHA would provide a customized "broadcast" of the game by phone line direct to the school's auditorium, where it could be played for the student body and "hometown folks." WHA charged fifteen dollars for equipment, engineering services, and announcer at the University of Wisconsin Fieldhouse in Madison. An additional charge of $21.50 covered installation of a local phone line loop between Madison and the local high school. The only other cost was for use of the line itself, estimated at ten cents per hour for each mile of distance between Madison and the participating school. University student Lou Landman would call the games. WHA described him as "a sports enthusiast with a good deal of broadcasting experience," and the station promised that he would include "any hometown players, principal, coach or students who wish to participate in order to give a colorful, personalized description of the activities."[22]

The proposal caught the interest of some people in Neenah, about one hundred miles northeast of Madison. Neenah's high school is a regular participant in the state basketball tournament with more than twenty appearances since the team's first trip to "state" in 1920.[23] In March 1947 Neenah's local AM station, WNAM, was still under construction and about two months from its first broadcast. The managers there contacted WHA, offering to pay for the service as a promotion for their station. They would cover the cost of the line from Madison to the control board at WNAM and would relay it from there via phone line to the high school's assembly hall. In a letter to WHA's Bill Harley, WNAM vice president Don C. Wirth said: "Also, WNAM isn't on the air as yet and all this is WNAM promotion. Therefore, I would appreciate it if you would have your man there give us a little plug now and then calling the broadcast a 'public service feature of WNAM in cooperation with Wisconsin's State Station WHA-Madison.' Would you do that for me? Thanks pal."[24]

After the successful "broadcast," Wirth wrote to thank Harley. WHA had evidently included a program guide in the mailing to WNAM, and the Neenah station wanted to be on the regular mailing list for the WHA program guide as well as on the list for WHA-FM, which had gone on the air only two days earlier. Moreover, Wirth said WNAM wished to carry some WHA programs and wanted a list of series available on transcription recordings. The state network was particularly interested in the *University Band* and *Outdoor Wisconsin* series.[25] Harley responded in an informal, jovial style:

> You have been placed on our mailing list, and henceforth, lucky fellow, you will receive the same practically each month. If you will cast your jaundiced eye over the bulletin again you will perceive that we have managed by a clever feat of devilish ingenuity to include the FM schedule along with the AM.

Unfortunately, the Out Door Wisconsin series is off at present; however, the Conservation Commission, which sponsored the series, is willing to resume the shows as soon as we can dig us [*sic*] the right man to do them. Art Lewis graduated and returned to WOWO, Fort Wayne. If the series is resumed, I'll let you know.

The U.W. Band series is all handled by Bob Foss, University Press Bureau; we don't have nothin' to do with it. I'm sure he'll be glad to add your station to his transcription circuit.

We don't have any other scintillating transcribed stuff available now. Next fall though—lookout! We'll try to talk you into carrying a flock of Wisconsin School of the Air programs for the schools in your area. WEAU is doing five a week for us now.[26]

The letter had the desired effect: by the fall of 1947 WNAM in Neenah was indeed carrying a daily offering of the Wisconsin School of the Air by transcription records, joining WEAU in Eau Claire and WLCX in La Crosse in doing so.[27]

CHAPTER 15

ᕼ

The FM Network

*To make application for such facilities as may be needed
to provide satisfactory coverage*

Through the 1930s and the war years, WHA and WLBL faced two problems, both peculiar to AM broadcasting. One was their daytime-only authorization. Staff members at WHA truly wanted to provide more adult education but were unable to broadcast in the evening when working people would be able to listen. The other problem was finding a way to efficiently get the broadcast signal to all parts of the state. The line connecting WHA and WLBL was frightfully expensive, and the coverage of the two stations, despite both being at 5,000 watts, still didn't provide a clear signal in many parts of the state.

Reception in eastern Wisconsin from Kenosha to Manitowoc, including Milwaukee, was described as "wholly inadequate," as was reception in the far north, the far northwest, and heavily populated northeastern parts of the state. Reception became more of an issue as the postwar years saw an explosion in the number of AM stations. Many of those in Wisconsin and nearby states were on frequencies adjacent to those of WHA and WLBL and further limited the listening range of the two state stations.

The stations tried other ways to extend the reach of their programs. Some School of the Air programs were recorded on transcription discs and shipped to commercial stations for airing. However, for this to be a reliable service, it required the continuing cooperation of commercial broadcasters. Moreover, it was awkward, because a local station might air a program weeks after it first aired over WHA and WLBL. With the availability of FM broadcasting, WHA managers realized they might have a solution to all their transmission problems.

FM broadcasting had been available in the years before World War II but operated on a different area of the broadcast spectrum than today's FM broadcast band. The prewar FM band consisted of forty channels between 42.1 and 49.9 mHz. In 1940, the FCC reserved the first five channels (42.1 to 42.9 mHz) for educational use, a departure from earlier years when non-commercial AM stations had to compete with commercial broadcasters for frequencies. Some FM broadcasters (including some educational ones) who had entered the field before the war put broadcast expansion on hold. FM's inventor, Edwin Armstrong, had even put together a network of commercial FM stations in New England called the Yankee Network that had managed to amass an audience of a half-million listeners. With the end of the war concern over interference issues and successful lobbying by some in the radio industry resulted in a shift of the FM band in 1945 to 88–106 mHz (with 106–108 mHz added later). The several dozen prewar FM broadcasters found themselves with useless frequencies and the hundreds of thousands of consumers who owned prewar FM receivers were equally out of luck. The one positive aspect of the switch was that a larger percentage of the new band had been reserved for non-commercial broadcasting: 88.1 to 91.9 mHz, twenty full channels. Many commercial radio operators shied away from the "new" FM system, unsure if it would be permanent or whether the "once-fooled" public would buy new receivers. This era of uncertainty would turn out to be a boon for non-commercial broadcasters. They would enter the field in force and would learn to use the new medium with minimal pressure from commercial competitors.

For WHA, the possibilities of FM were all they could hope for. Here was a transmission system unhampered by daytime restrictions. Also, its signal was unaffected by electrical interference. Glenn Koehler of the WHA engineering staff had the idea to build a statewide network of seven (later eight) FM stations. These were not to provide additional programming staff nor to generate their own programming but rather would serve as a way to efficiently get the signal of WHA in Madison to the entire state. The design proposed was simplicity itself: carefully placed FM transmitters that would pick up a clear, static-free signal off the air on one frequency and rebroadcast it on another. The stations would be located so that the Madison station would be picked up off the air and rebroadcast by a station near Milwaukee. Its signal would be picked up and rebroadcast by a station in northeastern Wisconsin, whose signal would feed a station in central Wisconsin, and so forth.

WHA management reported that the Board of Regents took the first step in setting up the network on September 30, 1944, when it authorized the formation of another State Radio Council. Sitting on the council were the governor, the president of the University of Wisconsin, the state superintendent of public instruction, the secretary of the Board of Normal School Regents, the director of the Department of Vocational and Adult Education, the director of the Department of Agriculture, the dean of the School of Education, the associate director of agricultural extension, the director of the Extension Division, the director of the Division of Public Services, and the chair of the University Radio Committee.

McCarty served as executive secretary of the council. During the council's first meeting on January 5, 1945, the group voted to recommend to the regents that "the State Radio Council be authorized to register with the Federal Communications Commission its plan for a coordinated State FM Radio System and to make application for such facilities as may be needed to provide satisfactory coverage of the State." Four days later the Board of Regents passed such a motion.[1]

Before the year was out the state legislature passed Act 631A "relating to the creation of a state radio council, the establishment of a state broadcasting system for educational purposes and making an appropriation." By statute the State Radio Council was to "plan, construct, and develop a state system of radio broadcasting for the presentation of educational, informational, and public service programming," to "formulate policies regulating the operation of such a state system," and "to coordinate the radio activities of the various educational and informational agencies, civic groups, and citizens having contributions to make to the public interest and welfare." With the legislation came funding: $60,595 for constructing and equipping the "initial units" of the system, $11,000 for operations, and $1,000 for maintenance. Added to this was $32,250 originally appropriated by the 1941 legislature for modernization of WHA's facilities. It had never been used because of wartime materiel shortages. Wisconsin's attorney general ruled that these funds could now be applied to the FM project. The act stated that all funds would be administered through the University of Wisconsin business office.[2]

While planning was underway in the summer of 1945, WHA held an event in cooperation with the U.S. Office of Education called the FM Radio Education Institute. About one hundred program planners, technicians, and administrators who were to be responsible for the development of educational FM broadcasting around the United States were invited to the three-week event. Attendees included FCC member C. J. Durr, FCC chief engineer George P. Adair, and Edwin Armstrong, the inventor of FM.[3]

In October 1945 the council filed applications with the Federal Communications Commission to build the first two stations in the network. A 3-kilowatt transmitter would be located on the Madison campus "where research and experimentation in technical operation, programming, and reception can be advantageously carried on." Also, a 10-kilowatt transmitter would be built near Delafield, west of Milwaukee, to serve the state's largest city and the lakeshore region.[4] Construction permits for the stations were granted on February 13, 1946. The original call letters planned for the stations were WIUN in Madison and WIUV in Delafield.[5]

By the spring of 1947 the Madison FM station, now WHA-FM (at 91.5 mHz) was ready to begin operation. McCarty chose his birthday, March 30, for the first day on the air. The ceremonial first broadcast included messages from the governor and from the state agencies represented on the State Radio Council. Part of the broadcast was a dramatic reenactment of the early days of 9XM. Emeritus professor William H. Lighty was on hand and hailed the new FM development as a step forward in achieving the goals he helped to set in 1921–22 while serving as the first WHA program director. WHA also held an open house that day, and a throng of more than 2,500 people came to Radio Hall to watch the broadcast, see the new transmitter, and hear the quality of the FM transmission over the numerous FM radios on display.[6] When station identification was made that day, the message for WHA-AM continued to include the slogan "the oldest station in the nation," while WHA-FM dubbed itself "the newest station in the nation."[7]

At first WHA-FM did not come on the air until 4 p.m., then WHA-AM and WHA-FM broadcast programs simultaneously until sunset, when WHA-AM was required to sign off. The FM station continued through 10 p.m., airing a variety of "adult features," including the rebroadcast of certain College of the Air programs. The WHA staff finally realized its dream of presenting adult education programs on a schedule when working people could listen to them. WHA-FM gradually expanded its hours of operation until it was on thirteen hours a day. During the first year the evening hours featured a wide range of programs, including college debates, the state high school music festival, classical music performances, addresses by President Truman, and college basketball contests. Listeners reported regular reception within sixty miles, and the most distant report came from 128 miles away.[8] WHA announcer DeAlton Neher ran a promotion for FM called "the first thousand club," recognizing the first households to acquire new FM receivers. Evening broadcasts that first year generated scores of eloquent testimonials about the value of FM.[9]

The plan for FM was to build two stations at a time, with each successive legislature appropriating the money for two more until the entire network was in place. By early 1948 the legislature had appropriated funds to build the first four stations: WHA-FM in Madison, the station near Milwaukee in Delafield,

3:30	Afternoon News	Afternoon News	Afternoon News	Afternoon News	Afternoon News	Afternoon News
3:45	Editor's Desk	Editor's Desk	Editor's Desk	Editor's Desk	Editor's Desk	Treasury Salute
4:00	Musical Varieties	Musical Varieties	Musical Varieties	Musical Varieties	Musical Varieties	Alpine Melodies
4:30	University Forum	New World A'Coming	U.W. Concert Band	Beyond Victory	Voice of the Army	Wake Up, America
4:45	University Forum	New World A'Coming	U.W. Concert Band	Eyes on Future	London Letter	Wake Up, America
5:00	University Forum	Masterworks	Masterworks	Masterworks	Masterworks	Cleveland Symphony
5:30	Masterworks	Advents. Our Town	Book Trails	Let's Find Out	Ranger Mac	Cleveland Symphony
		—(Rebroadcasts)	—(Rebroadcasts)	—(Rebroadcasts)	—(Rebroadcasts)	
6:00	News	News	News	News	News	News
6:15	Dinner Musicale	Dinner Musicale	Dinner Musicale	Dinner Musicale	Dinner Musicale	Dinner Musicale
91.5 Megacycles	**WHA-FM PROGRAM SCHEDULE**					**#218**
6:45	Salon Music	Salon Music	Salon Music	Salon Music	Salon Music	Salon Music
7:00	Concert Hour	Concert Hour	Concert Hour	Concert Hour	Concert Hour	Concert Hour
7:30	College of the Air	College of the Air	College of the Air	College of the Air	College of the Air	College of the Air
8:20	News	News	News	News	News	News
8:30	Music of Masters	Music of Masters	Music of Masters	Music of Masters	Music of Masters	Music of Masters
9:30	Editor's Desk	Editor's Desk	Editor's Desk	Editor's Desk	Editor's Desk	Editor's Desk
9:45	News	News	News	News	News	News

1947 WHA-FM program schedule
Initially, the broadcast day for WHA-FM began at 4 p.m. For the first year, it operated at 91.5 mHz, and moved to 88.7 mHz in May 1948, where it remains today as WERN-Madison. (WHA Radio and Television Records/University of Wisconsin Archives)

one in Calumet County in east-central Wisconsin, and one in the center of the state at Rib Mountain, near Wausau. Future appropriations would allow for a station in the Ashland–Superior region of northwestern Wisconsin, one in Dunn County in west-central Wisconsin, one near La Crosse, and one in southwestern Wisconsin near Blue Mounds.

The second station in the network went on the air on June 30, 1948, at 90.7 mHz. Originally planned to be WUIV, the call letters ultimately selected were WHAD, for WHA and Delafield, where the transmitter was located. The addition of WHAD to the state FM network provided a strong signal to the Milwaukee area. (By selecting these call letters, the station ended up with a historic designation. Marquette University in Milwaukee had operated an AM station with the WHAD call sign from 1922 to 1934.) Six weeks before the debut of the Delafield station, WHA-FM in Madison changed frequencies from the original 91.5 mHz to 88.7 mHz, evidently to provide the necessary channel separation between the Madison station and the FM station planned for southwestern Wisconsin, which would operate on 91.3 mHz. In 1974, the call letters of the Madison station were changed to WERN, which remain in use today.

The third of the FM stations went on the air on January 1, 1949. WHKW was located in Chilton, about thirty-five miles south of Green Bay, and operated at 89.3 mHz. Like its sister station in Delafield, this outlet provided a clear FM signal to a large population area that had previously had only spotty reception of WHA and WLBL. The pattern for call letters was now established as well: the network would attempt to have all call letters begin with *WH*.

The last of the original four FM stations covered by the first two appropriations was located on Rib Mountain, the second-highest point in the state. WHSF went on the air on June 10, 1949, at 91.9 mHz. At the request of the State Radio Council, the FCC agreed to change the call letters to WHRM— *RM* for Rib Mountain.[10] The station later changed its official community of license from Rib Mountain to Wausau, and in October 1975 its frequency was changed to 90.9 mHz.

The actual division of programming was that the daytime programming on the FM station was "taken from WHA," with the after-sunset hours programmed "by Radio Council personnel." An added benefit of the new stations in Chilton and Rib Mountain was that they could be used to provide the program feed for WLBL in Auburndale, twenty-five miles west of Stevens Point, thereby retiring the expensive phone line system in use on and off since 1933.

By late 1948 the dual nature of the network led to some adjustment in how budgets and personnel were handled. The State Radio Council budget paid for the technical operation of the FM stations and program expenses after WHA signed off at sundown. The University of Wisconsin continued to pay for WHA-AM and its programs, including the Wisconsin School of the Air, the Wisconsin College of the Air, the *Farm Program,* and the *Homemakers' Program.* Many WHA staff members now held joint appointments to the State Radio Council and the university's Division of Radio Education. McCarty, Engel, and engineer John Stiehl all had these dual appointments, with "each budget carrying a proper proportion of the salary."[11]

Two more stations were added to the network in 1950, both paid by 1949 legislative appropriations. On June 28 WHWC began operating at 88.3 mHz in the west-central Wisconsin community of Colfax. On November 21 WHLA– West Salem began operation near La Crosse at 90.3 mHz. In 1950 nearly all local programs on WLBL ended in Auburndale, which was now receiving its network programming from the FM station on Rib Mountain. In 1951 the legislature modified the duties of the State Radio Council to add the management, operation, and maintenance of WLBL. The license for the station was transferred from the Wisconsin Department of Agriculture to the State Radio Council on July 1, 1951.[12]

A commercial network much like the Wisconsin system began in the summer of 1950 in New York State. The owner of early FM broadcaster WFMZ in Allentown, Pennsylvania, had approached the *New York Times*–owned commercial classical station WQXR-FM to ask whether his station might rebroadcast some of the New York station's programming. Unable to afford program lines, the manager of the Pennsylvania outlet found that he could get a clear signal over the air at most times. WQXR agreed to the affiliation, provided that WFMZ carry the *New York Times* newscasts. Then a group of twelve new FM stations called the Rural Radio Network, begun by the Grange League Federation to transmit farm programming to its members, approached WQXR. The Rural Radio Network wanted its station in Poughkeepsie to pick up the WQXR feed and rebroadcast it over a line of stations north to Troy (near Albany) and then west to Niagara Falls, with "branches" to Utica, Watertown, Ogdensburg, and Hornell. A station in New Haven, Connecticut, had been added as a rebroadcaster by the time the network got underway in July.[13]

The staff in Madison was watching the WQXR developments with interest and noted a *New York Times* editorial of July 22, 1950, that reported that the availability of WQXR programming was stimulating sales of FM receivers in New York State.[14]

WQXR eventually added stations north to Providence, Rhode Island, and Boston and south to Philadelphia, Baltimore, and Washington, D.C., but partially through the use of land lines. Its network remained in operation through late 1963. One major problem was that these stations all did local programming, so that if, say, Poughkeepsie wanted to air a local program in place of WQXR programs, all the stations down the line were deprived of the WQXR feed. Wisconsin got around this problem by making the FM stations only repeaters without the ability to originate programs.

In December 1951 a letter from a listener in Rockford, Illinois, arrived at Radio Hall. It said in part: "Last spring when I was considering purchasing high-fidelity equipment, I was doubtful about the wisdom of investing in an AM-FM tuner. Fortunately, I decided to go ahead. Since I am not a Wisconsin resident I have had no opportunity to help defray the cost of your broadcasts and for that reason I am enclosing a check to be used in any way you desire. The amount of the check is small when compared with the pleasure my family has received from your broadcasts." With the letter was a check for five dollars.[15] The staff seemed more interested in this unsolicited gift as a validation of the value of the FM service than in recognizing that such donations might be a source of operating income, which would be the case in the future with the advent of the pledge drive.

The last two of the eight original FM transmitters in the Wisconsin network went on the air the same day, September 14, 1952; both were paid for by 1951 appropriations. WHHI in the southwestern Wisconsin community of Highland operated at 91.3 mHz. WHSA served northwestern Wisconsin from a location in the Brule River State Forest; its call letters stood for Superior and Ashland. It was put on the air at reduced cost since the transmitter was originally installed in 1949 at WHRM on Rib Mountain. WHRM had installed a new unit, making its original transmitter available for the new facility in Brule.[16] The remoteness of the Brule station earned it the nickname "loneliest station in the state."[17] The state conservation department built a road from the transmitter site to the highway in exchange for being allowed to mount its own antenna on the tower, part of the communications system for forestry stations.[18]

The day after the Brule and Highland FM stations went on the air, *Newsweek* ran a profile of the state network, featuring a photo of a smiling Harold McCarty in front of a large Wisconsin map showing the location of the stations. The article quoted McCarty as saying that the annual cost of operating the network was ten cents—the price of a bag of popcorn—for every Wisconsin resident. The article also praised the Wisconsin School of the Air, Wisconsin College of the Air, and programs serving farmers and homemakers. It concluded with a mention of McCarty's plans to ask for an appropriation for a state-owned television station during the next legislative session.[19]

Two full-time State Radio Council engineers staffed each FM station. They shared the duties of signing the equipment on and off, taking transmitter readings, and monitoring the broadcast. The engineers split the duties to their mutual satisfaction. They also were in charge of activating the local station identification at certain times, alerted by a series of chimes played at the studio in Madison.

The solitary nature of being a State Radio Council engineer was dramatically illustrated in January 1952. At 2:30 p.m. one afternoon WLBL operator Bob Hanson played his local station identification, and while it aired, he listened to the network signal coming from WHRM on Rib Mountain, thirty miles away. He was supposed to hear its station identification coming down the line. Instead, he heard the identification from WHKW in Chilton, which the Rib Mountain operator was supposed to cover up. After Hanson heard the Chilton identification again at 3 p.m., he called the transmitter at Rib Mountain and got no answer, then called Radio Hall in Madison to say that something was amiss. Finally, a breathless Hilding Foreen, the WHRM operator, answered the phone at the Rib Mountain transmitter site. Foreen had climbed up on the roof to clear a coating of sleet off an antenna, and the wind blew his ladder over. The bitter cold got to him before the next operator arrived, so he risked a jump from the roof and fortunately was not injured.[20] Operators in remote locations also had to contend with wildlife. Ken Bastian of WHKW once had to chase away a deer that stuck its head through the open door of the transmitter building. Operators at WHSA found that bears had ruined their weather measurements by drinking from the station's rain gauge and that porcupines would chew through the rubber hoses on their cars.[21] The WHSA staff even topped the WHKW deer story, when a doe gave birth in the building's garage.[22]

Despite advances, FM remained a novelty for some years to come. Oscar Rennebohm, who served as Wisconsin governor during the early years of the development of the state FM network, once asked at a press conference: "What is this FM, anyway? Any of you reporters got it?" Seven or eight of the assembled dozen reporters raised their hands. When the governor asked why, one reporter replied: "To listen to WHA of course."[23] Still, others saw no future for the new technology. WGN in Chicago had run a prewar FM station (W59C, later WGNB at 45.9 mHz) and in postwar years acquired a license for a station in the new FM band. Seeing no value in it, WGN returned it to the FCC in 1954. The move allowed commercial classical station WFMT to move to 98.7 mHz from 105.9 mHz, and eventually WFMT tripled both its power and antenna height.[24] A commercial FM frequency in Chicago is now worth millions of dollars. Similarly, the lack of interest in FM during this period meant some early non-commercial community radio stations were able to get now-valuable frequencies in the commercial part of the band in places like Berkeley, California (KPFA), and some smaller communities. Some public broadcasters were also able to acquire frequencies in the commercial part of the band.

Managers at WHA constantly promoted the value of their FM service, recommending in program guides the purchase of an FM receiver as a gift for Christmas or other occasions. In early 1952 the owner of a Madison hardware store forwarded to Radio Hall a list of the names and addresses of 180 people who had recently purchased FM receivers. At his suggestion the station staff sent a program guide to each one. About the same time the station mailed leaflets promoting the FM service to the three thousand radio dealers in the state.[25] The staff even developed a small program to provide hospitals with FM radios so patients could request them for the rooms. The case of each radio carried a printed promotional message for the state stations and was a way to introduce more people to the FM service. A citizens' group called State Radio Listeners, Inc., paid for the hospital program and also provided FM receivers to some libraries, where patrons could check one out just like a book.[26]

Once the entire eight-station network was in place, the retransmission of the signal from Madison went up both sides of the state. The far northwestern station in Brule had the option of tuning in the Madison signal via Delafield–Chilton–Rib Mountain or via Highland–West Salem–Colfax. This was useful when a station in one of the "links" had to be off the air for maintenance.

Engineering studies showed that despite the numerous "jumps" of rebroadcasting, the signal at the end of the line in Brule was of high quality and any loss in fidelity was so minor that it was imperceptible to the ear.

In late 1952, the state FM network took advantage of its round-robin nature to provide an innovative feature. On December 1 the state stations instituted the *Weather Roundup.* Twice each weekday and once on Saturday and Sunday, the engineers at each transmitter would take turns describing the local weather conditions at their locations, including cloud cover, visibility, precipitation,

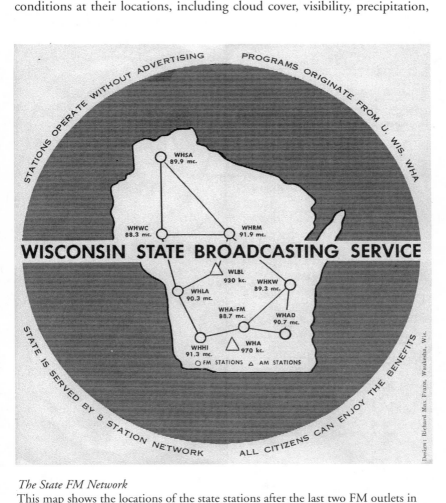

The State FM Network
This map shows the locations of the state stations after the last two FM outlets in the original plan went on the air in September 1952. This illustration was featured on a promotional pamphlet from the late 1950s. (Wisconsin Public Radio Collection)

winter road conditions, and occasional humidity and barometric pressure readings. Over time, some even added comments about how the fish were biting in the area or how local crops were doing.[27] They would close with the local temperature, which was the cue for the next engineer down the line to begin his report. None of the engineers gave the forecast, as none was a trained meteorologist, but for a time the last voice on the roundup was that of a U.S. Weather Bureau forecaster at Truax Field in Madison who presented the statewide forecast. In later years the engineer at Wisconsin Public Television transmitter WLEF in Park Falls was added to the lineup, and staffers at the Wisconsin State Patrol offices in Dodgeville and Waukesha participated as the Highland and Delafield FM transmitters became remote-controlled sites handled by the staff in Madison.

The engineers sometimes provided dramatic descriptions of local conditions. George Davenport of WHHI gave this account of the Wisconsin spring day he was experiencing on March 26, 1959: "The weather here in southwestern

The Weather Roundup
Wisconsin Public Radio graphic designer John Ribble captured the charm of the *Weather Roundup* with this illustration. It graced the cover of WPR's December 1980 Radio Guide. (Wisconsin Public Radio Collection)

Wisconsin today has not been fit for either man or beast. So far today, we have had wind, rain, an ice storm, hail and snow, also once the sun shone for a few minutes. There will be no temperature report from this station, a hail stone broke our thermometer. We have been operating on emergency power here since 12:30 this afternoon due to the fact that ice damaged the power line. At the present time, visibility is very poor on account of blowing and drifting snow. The road here by the station is already drifted shut. There's a strong gusty wind blowing from the northeast. Next we transfer to the United States Weather Bureau at Truax Field in Madison in hopes our weather girl, Ethel Christianson, will have some better news for us."[28]

The *Roundup* was one item that commercial stations were eager to rebroadcast. Joe Rigny, a meteorologist at the weather bureau at Truax Field, determined that the thirty commercial stations rebroadcasting the roundup in 1961, along with the ten state stations, constituted the largest radio "network" in the country that was served by one weather bureau office.[29]

Throughout the years, the engineers genuinely enjoyed their participation in the *Roundup*. George Caspers at the Brule transmitter considered it "one of the finest contacts with the public—people use the reports to make their plans

Presenting the Weather Roundup
WHRM engineer Hilding Foreen is seen at the simple announcing set-up provided at transmitter facilities for participating in the *Weather Roundup*. (Wisconsin Historical Society Archives image WHi-23540)

about business and recreational travel." Jim Molledahl of La Crosse thought listeners enjoyed the segment "because they like to hear laymen like themselves describe the day." Vacationers would often seek out the remote locations of the transmitters to meet the engineers.[30]

Improvements were made to individual stations. WHRM at Rib Mountain expanded its coverage area by 30 percent when the antenna was moved to an adjacent television tower in 1958. That same year WHWC and WHLA had emergency generators installed, the final two stations in the network to be so equipped. The emergency power equipment was surplus material from the state Department of Public Instruction, purchased for the stations at a fraction of its original cost.[31] The value of having a backup system was demonstrated in November 1958, when power to WHSA in Brule was interrupted for thirty-two hours, yet the station was able to remain on the air with its generator. The engineers were kept busy shuttling back and forth to a gas station in Brule to keep the generator fueled.[32] Their generator also powered the communication service of the state conservation department. This was another economical installation, being a war-surplus unit renovated by station engineers.[33]

In the mid-1950s, "end-of-the-line" WHSA in Brule had some problems receiving its network signal, which was coming primarily from WHWC near Eau Claire. This was in part due to geography, but a television station in Duluth on channel 6 was also causing interference with the signal from WHWC. To alleviate the problem a studio-transmitter link was installed near Hayward, where the WHWC signal could be received clearly, and it was rebroadcast at 945 mHz for reception at WHSA.[34] Other improvements continued: in 1963 WHAD in Delafield got a new tower, which was actually used equipment, formerly owned by the Madison commercial television station WMTV. It had installed a new tower and donated its old one to the University of Wisconsin.[35] Other modifications were made to several transmitter sites in 1965, "hardening" them as fallout shelters and laying in emergency supplies of food and water.[36]

Stereo broadcasting came to the state stations on January 13, 1963, when WHA-FM began limited stereo transmissions. The technology was extended to WHAD in Delafield on January 19, 1964, and in May 1966 the remaining FM stations in the state began broadcasting in stereo.[37]

Far northeastern Wisconsin still had inadequate reception, which prompted the addition of a ninth FM station in 1965. WHMD carried the letters *M* for the city of Marinette on the Michigan border and *D* for Door County, the peninsula of Wisconsin that juts into Lake Michigan. The plan was for the station to rebroadcast the signal from WHKW in Chilton. To build the new station at low cost, the state used items that other stations in the network had replaced. WHMD initially used for its transmitter a 1-kilowatt exciter unit formerly in use at WHAD-Delafield and an antenna previously used elsewhere. Unlike the other FM stations, WHMD was not staffed by State Radio Council personnel. It shared space with commercial station WMAM-Marinette, and its engineers took the meter readings and monitored the transmitter under contract for a "nominal service fee."[38] Because these engineers did not play the station identification, a recording for WHMD was triggered by the operator at WHKW.[39] Shortly after the station began operating, plans were made to move the transmitter thirty-five miles west to the community of Suring, where it would share space on the tower of commercial station WRVM. The move was made in 1968, and eventually the station's power was increased to 37,000 watts. It provided a clear signal to the northeastern corner of the state and extended the network's offerings to the Michigan cities of Menominee, Escanaba, and Iron Mountain.

In the summer of 1966 the state FM stations inaugurated their subsidiary communications authorization, or SCA service. SCA is an electronic method that permits the transmission of additional signals in piggyback fashion over an existing FM signal; a special radio receiver picks up the additional signals. Originally, the technology was limited to commercial operators, who often used the service to provide background music for a fee to stores, restaurants, and offices. This revenue allowed many commercial FM stations to remain

The Wisconsin State Broadcasting Service
This map from the April 1968 program guide shows the radio network after the addition of the ninth FM outlet in northeastern Wisconsin. (Wisconsin Public Radio Collection)

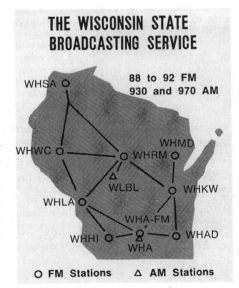

financially viable in the 1950s. In 1961 the FCC allowed educational FM stations to use the technology, provided that they did so in a manner compatible with their non-commercial status. WHA-FM began using SCA in the
summer of 1966 with the transmission of a French-language program to Lincoln High School in Wisconsin Rapids for use during that school year.

The university's Extension Division allocated money for SCA transmitting
equipment for the FM stations in the state network, and by the next year SCA
receivers had been installed in eighty locations. An experimental monthly program on gardening tips was sent out over the system and recorded at the offices
of county extension agents. They then took the tapes to local commercial
stations for broadcast. The University News Service and the State Historical
Society also provided programs to commercial stations through this method.[40]
Later the service would be used for reading services for the visually impaired,
medical instruction, and the classroom broadcasts of the Wisconsin School of
the Air.

The addition of the sister network of educational television stations around
the state between 1954 and 1977 resulted in the relocation of some radio
transmitters in the interest of greater efficiency. In 1963 WHA-FM moved its
antenna to the new WHA-TV tower. A consultant's report in 1968 recommended more of these moves and that WHA-FM's frequency be changed to
88.9 mHz. This would allow an increase in power to 100 kilowatts and an
increase in antenna height to 1,150 feet (this change was never made). The
report also recommended moving WHKW in Chilton to DePere to share space
with WPNE-TV south of Green Bay. This move occurred in early 1973, and
the FM outlet changed its call letters to WPNE-FM and its city of license to
Green Bay. The consultants also called for moving WHMD from Suring to
Lakewood, Wisconsin, but with the move of WHKW north to Green Bay, it
was felt that WHMD was no longer serving a purpose, so on January 6, 1973,
it went off the air. The report also suggested moving WHHI in Highland to a
location in Platteville to share space with a proposed UHF television outlet.[41]
Moving radio transmitters to share space with television facilities continued.
In February 1974 WHLA near La Crosse and WHWC near Menomonie also
moved their transmitters to television tower sites.

After more than twenty years without a new FM outlet, Wisconsin Public
Radio put WHBM on the air in Park Falls in northwestern Wisconsin in
November 1988. The call letters adhered to the *WH* pattern for most stations
and honored former manager Harold B. McCarty, who had recently died.

∾

CHAPTER 16

From Educational Radio to Public Radio

1947–70

This is the Midwestern Educational Radio Network.

As the state network of stations grew, so did the staff and number of programming innovations. In the fall of 1947 a new position was added to the station staff as Roy Vogelman became WHA's first news director. He had been a student announcer since the late 1930s and a staff member since 1943, serving as chief announcer and later news editor. On October 1 he submitted his "Memorandum on WHA News Policy," which offered his vision of how the news should be handled by a station that was in part a state enterprise as well as part of the university. He outlined not only what to include in the newscasts but also things like presentation style.[1] Many of his policies remain in effect at Wisconsin Public Radio today. Vogelman served as news director until shortly before his death in 1978.

In January 1948 WHA management was happy to announce the return of college basketball to the station for the first time since the 1920s. The daytime-only limitation had kept basketball off WHA-AM, but the addition of WHA-FM meant the games could again be offered. The station provided the on-air talent for the home contests and carried the road games "through a courtesy arrangement with station WIBA."[2] In May the stations began carrying home contests of University of Wisconsin baseball games, opening with a game against Indiana.[3]

On February 3, 1949, the network broadcast a speech given in the Wisconsin Union Theater; it was one of the events of the university's Farm and Home Week. Dr. John A. Schindler of the Monroe Clinic in Green County, Wisconsin, gave a talk on psychosomatic illness entitled "How to Live a Hundred Years Happily." WHA replayed it three days later as the "encore of the week," a timeslot when notable programs received a second airing. It was played yet again in place of *Freshman Forum* of the Wisconsin College of the Air, which had been canceled that week because of exams. Listener interest prompted McCarty to offer recordings of the speech to other non-commercial stations, and before the year was out, fifteen stations in the United States and one in Canada had aired it. The speech was condensed for print in five national magazines, including *Reader's Digest.* More than twenty thousand printed copies of the speech were distributed, and an industrial corporation planned to print 130,000 for its employees. Schindler himself wrote a book on the topic based on the public interest, and it was published in numerous languages.[4] Listeners continued to write to WHA for copies of the speech through the early 1960s. Interestingly, in 1998, Schindler's granddaughter Catherine Brand was hired as a WPR announcer: she was at the time a graduate music student at UW–Madison.

Roy Vogelman, WHA's first news director
A one-time student announcer, Roy Vogelman was named WHA's first news director in 1947 and held the job longer than anyone else. In addition to his radio duties, he also hosted programs on WHA-TV. He is shown here near the United Press Teletype in Radio Hall. (University of Wisconsin Archives series 23/24/1, negative 88638-C)

In the years after the war it became obvious to WHA management that Radio Hall, which had seemed so roomy in 1934, was rapidly running out of space for the radio operation, let alone the planned expansion into the world of television. While pondering how to deal with the problem, a letter came in from William Tamminga, an architecture student at the Massachusetts Institute of Technology. He proposed to design a radio arts building for WHA as his graduate project. His plan called for a multilevel building to be built immediately behind Radio Hall. The WHA staff was impressed with his initial design and asked him to modify it so that it could be built as an extension of Radio Hall. Tamminga responded that to research this adjustment would require a trip to Madison, which he could not afford. Engel advanced $150 of his own money to pay for Tamminga's airline ticket from Boston. The building was never built, but Tamminga did submit the design for his master's degree in architecture on October 1, 1949.[5]

Late in 1949 WHA received some revenue from an unexpected source. Audio Devices of New York City was offering fifteen cents for each sixteen-inch aluminum transcription record in order to reclaim the aluminum. McCarty wrote back to say WHA had one thousand to sell and asked for a dozen shipping labels.[6]

Because the FM network and several Madison commercial stations were broadcasting University of Wisconsin football games in the fall of 1949, the WHA staff figured that also carrying them on WHA-AM was needless duplication, so WHA maintained its regular program schedule during the football games that year. It was the first time that two programs were offered simultaneously and was a glimpse into the future, when the radio service would offer two distinct simultaneous program services. Also in the fall of 1949, a new organ from the Wicks Organ Company was installed in Radio Hall to replace the one that H. Frederick Fuller had rescued from a tobacco barn sixteen years earlier.[7]

One new development in 1950 was the beginning of what was informally known as "the bicycle network." Twenty-nine educational radio stations cooperated to establish and maintain a transcription network under the auspices of the National Association of Educational Broadcasters (NAEB). The idea was to provide a way to share distinctive programs produced at various radio operations. It had begun the previous year when WNYC–New York made five sets of recordings of the *Herald-Tribune Forum* and distributed them to twenty-two NAEB stations.[8] In 1950 WHA was airing the series *A Long Life,* which was produced by the Lowell Institute Cooperative Broadcast Council in Boston (later to form WGBH), and *Music for the Connoisseur* from WNYC. Plans were in the works to get the Canadian Broadcasting Corporation involved in the exchange, and WHA was looking forward to carrying its theater and concert series.[9] A five-year grant in 1951 helped expand and improve the NAEB system and made more programs available, including *The Cooper Union Forum, Chicago Round Table, The People Act,* and offerings from the BBC.[10] A central recording and distribution center for the programs was set up at the University of Illinois. In February 1952 the stations formed the Network Acceptance Committee to oversee the audio quality of the programs. Ray Stanley, a WHA producer, served on the committee, which held its first meeting at Purdue University.[11] The exchange later was known as the NAEB Tape Network and, much later, as the National Educational Radio Network.

Also in the fall of 1950, the state FM stations were again involved in the transmission of University of Wisconsin football games. A group called the League of Wisconsin Radio Stations originated the broadcasts and fed them to the state FM network without charge. Any commercial station within range of the then-six state FM stations could rebroadcast the games. Home games were free if stations carried them on a non-commercial basis and twenty-five dollars if broadcast with local sponsors. Similarly, they could carry away games for twenty-five dollars if the games were aired without commercials and fifty dollars if commercially sponsored. The state FM stations received no income and incurred no expenses. The State Radio Council touted the arrangement as "a vivid example of the many ways in which the state stations and commercial broadcasters can work together cooperatively to their mutual advantage."[12]

However, the Madison managers were vigilant when it came to the use of their signal. They asked transmitter operators around the state to listen to the games on commercial stations in their areas to ensure that they were following the rebroadcasting rules. In 1962 WHKW operator Ken Bastian taped one football game during which the commercial station violated every point of the broadcast agreement. He sent the tape to Harold Engel at WHA in Madison, who immediately rescinded the offending station's rebroadcast authorization. By the following Friday the commercial station was asking to be reinstated, with a promise to adhere to the rules. It resumed the football broadcasts and WHKW operator Fritz Hervey's tape that Saturday confirmed the commercial operation had indeed cleaned up its act.[13] Hervey had also caught a commercial broadcaster carrying the *Weather Roundup* and representing it as being sponsored by an advertiser.[14] Harold Engel himself would sometimes monitor commercial stations in the Madison area and would ask the Radio Hall production staff to make recordings of WHA programs that were being rebroadcast on nearby stations.

In 1951, a bill was introduced in the state legislature that would alter the membership of the State Radio Council. The council had earlier favored a wider base of representation, and University of Wisconsin vice president Ira Baldwin, representing president Edward Broun Fred on the council, had moved for the appointment of a committee to recommend changes to the makeup of the council. The bill, sponsored by state Senator Melvin Laird, Jr., a Republican from Marshfield, would remove from membership "the administrative head of the University of Wisconsin Extension Division; the administrative head of the University of Wisconsin Agricultural extension; the Dean of the School of Education, University of Wisconsin" and "the director of the Department of Public Service, University of Wisconsin" (this latter position no longer existed in university administration). The bill called for the addition of "the state health officer; the conservation director; the director of the department of public welfare; and the chairman of the legislative council." In April the Wisconsin Broadcasters' Association had requested representation on the council and an amendment to Laird's bill would have added "one member who is either a commercial station licensee or an employee or agent of such licensee to be appointed by the governor for a four-year term." This amendment became a focus for controversy when the bill came up for a vote in the state Senate, and both the bill and the amendment were killed.[15]

That year also brought more rebroadcasting of WHA programs by commercial stations. WTCH-Shawano, WRCO–Richland Center, and WLDY-Ladysmith carried the entire School of the Air series, several others were carrying the *Farm Program* and the highway and weather reports, and forty-one stations were airing *Civilian Defense Reports* from WHA. College basketball contests continued to be popular among commercial stations, with twenty-three in Wisconsin, two in Illinois, and one in Iowa carrying some or all of the schedule. The rules covering rebroadcast of the basketball games had been formalized, with the university reserving the right to accept or reject any sponsor, the product advertised, and the length and content of commercial announcements carried by the rebroadcasters. The state Department of Agriculture was involved as well, covering the charges for line costs and expenses of the athletic department in return for stations' airing announcements during the game that promoted dairy products.[16]

The NAEB tape exchange service continued to improve. WHA carried a variety of NAEB cultural, educational, and public affairs programs, such as *BBC World Theatre, New York Herald-Tribune Forum,* and the *Cooper Union Forum.* WHA was also contributing to the network, providing recordings of Professor Gunnar Johansen's thirteen-week series of Bach commemorative recitals.[17]

The Ford Foundation's fund for Adult Education made a grant of $300,000 to the NAEB that year for production and distribution of programs about "international understanding, American heritage, the nature of man, and public affairs." WHA's program director Bill Harley was selected by the NAEB to be program coordinator for the project and was granted a year's leave of absence through June 1, 1952.[18]

In October 1951, the network launched a quality control effort called Operation Penetration to "achieve maximum penetration of the sound we transmit." The effort enlisted the help of all staff members to monitor broadcast levels, distortion, muddiness, and anything else that compromised the sound of the programming, with special attention paid to studio acoustics, microphones, equipment maintenance, and quality control of syndicated programs.[19]

That same month, the homebuilt WHA-AM transmitter from 1936 was replaced with a new 5,000-watt Westinghouse unit, the station's first factory-built transmitter. The old transmitter had operated more than fifty-two thousand hours and had been rebuilt several times.[20]

The WHA staff continued to be interested in audience research. The Madison managers wanted to know who was listening, how many, why people were not listening, the effectiveness of educational offerings, and the relative effectiveness of different types of programs. Three doctoral candidates conducted an interview survey of listeners and nonlisteners in Rock and Green counties in southern Wisconsin. The statistical laboratory at Iowa State College assisted in preparing the survey, and the costs of the project were shared by the University of Wisconsin Graduate School and the Division of Radio Education. On a more basic level WHA managers once again conducted a random telephone survey in the Madison area to determine the percentage of homes with an FM radio. In July 1949 only 18.4 percent of Madisonians had FM radios, but by April 1951, the number had increased to 36 percent. The survey also noted that sixteen commercial FM stations were operating in the state, but seven others had suspended operation.[21]

As the original FM network was nearing completion, attention turned to television. McCarty was anxious to use the new medium for the same kind of educational broadcasting offered through radio, and a television laboratory went into service on the Madison campus in 1953 to allow for training and experience in television techniques. Broadcasting began on May 3, 1954, when WHA-TV went on the air on channel 21, becoming the nation's fourth educational television station. The original program schedule was two and a half hours a day. The operation was based in the former chemical engineering building across from Radio Hall and shared space with the psychology department and the alumni Addressograph office. Although the location was convenient, the ancient building (two years older than Radio Hall) was ill suited for television, with creaking floors and obtrusive pillars in the studios. Its address, 600 N. Park Street, provided it with a nickname. Because the *6* on the front of the building looked like a *G,* staffers took to calling it "Goon Park." The radio staff also served the television operation in the first years with WHA radio program director Bill Harley named WHA-TV's first station manager.[22]

Many radio programs were adapted for the new medium, with television versions of the *Farm Program* and *Homemakers' Program.* The Wisconsin School of the Air had a television versions of its courses as well, with WSA regulars Fannie Steve and James Schwalbach appearing on air, as did radio news director Roy Vogelman and music director Don Voegeli. By 1963 more than twenty thousand students in south-central Wisconsin were enrolled in the WSA television courses, and copies were used by school systems in Milwaukee, Chicago, Indianapolis, and Minneapolis.[23]

The television station's first hit was a fifteen-minute children's program called *The Friendly Giant,* with WHA radio announcer Bob Homme in the title role and WHA chief announcer Ken Ohst as the voices of Rusty the Rooster and Jerome the Giraffe. The program aired nationally, and in 1958 Homme was lured away to Toronto to reprise the role for the Canadian Broadcasting Corporation.

The WHA tradition of making do with less carried over to the television operation. In 1961 the television engineers converted a surplus X-ray van from the State Board of Health into the station's first remote broadcast unit.[24] In 1964 the television operation rented a former state highway commission building west of campus and remained there until Vilas Hall opened in 1972.[25] Innovation continued: in 1965, WHA-TV station manager (and future Wisconsin governor) Lee Dreyfus hosted an experimental video hookup between a high school French class in Wisconsin and an English class at a high school in France.[26]

The same month that WHA-TV went on the air in 1954, the state FM radio stations made their first offering of jazz programming, with several series airing on Monday evenings. The first series was from WFMT in Chicago, hosted by S. I. Hayakawa, a University of Chicago professor and jazz aficionado. Hayakawa had been born in Canada to Japanese immigrants and was well known for his book on semantics. He also had a Wisconsin connection: he received his doctoral degree in English and American literature from the University of Wisconsin–Madison in 1935 and taught there through 1939.[27] For the jazz series Hayakawa outlined the history and development of jazz and used records from his own collection.[28] Hayakawa later was president of San Francisco State College (now San Francisco State University) and served in the U.S. Senate from California from 1976 to 1983. After the Hayakawa series had concluded, the state stations presented another jazz offering called *Mr. Jelly Roll,* featuring the recordings of jazz pianist Jelly Roll Morton. The series was distributed by the Library of Congress and produced by folklorist Alan Lomax. It was drawn from interviews that Lomax had conducted with Morton in 1938 for the Library of Congress's Archive of Folk Song. The Wisconsin stations were the first in the country to broadcast this series.[29]

In 1955, state budget cuts affected the radio operation. The ambitious proposal to build a statewide network of educational television stations ran into formalized opposition, and funding for the radio network got caught up in the debate. The legislature decided to cut the budget for WHA-AM by 3 percent, with the budget for the State Radio Council being reduced by more than 12 percent. While WHA-AM was able to absorb the smaller reduction, the cut to the FM network was so great the service had to be reduced. Some money was saved by having the FM network sign off an hour earlier each day, but McCarty concluded the network would have to be off the air one day a week. The original plan was for the network to go silent on Sundays, but the staff found listeners liked the Sunday offerings, so the decision was made to have the FM network (and WLBL-AM) not operate on Saturdays.[30] Effective October 1, 1955, WHA-AM would be the sole station on the air on Saturdays, since its budget was not part of the State Radio Council appropriation. Even so, the FM network had to remain on for a few hours on Saturdays through the end of the football season to accommodate the transmission of Wisconsin games, which had already been offered to commercial stations. Additional Saturday operation came in 1963, when some of the FM stations would sign on for the live Metropolitan Opera broadcasts. During the winter months, these FM stations stayed on after the opera until 5 p.m. (even though WHA-AM had signed off at sundown); host Jack Marlowe filled the post-opera slot with a jazz program. By September 1965, the Saturday operation of the FM network had been increased to ten hours (noon to 10 p.m), but full service on Saturdays was not restored until January 1974. For much of the time that the network stations were silent on Saturdays, the transmitter operators would take the opportunity to hold an annual get-together and cookout, later dubbed the "FM Operators' Conference."

The first hint of organized public support for the state FM stations appeared in 1955 as well. A nonprofit group called State Radio Listeners was formed to support the radio service. The organization helped publicize the stations and was active in touting the service to elected officials. It even paid for some brochures that promoted the network. Because the group was not a state agency, they did not have to be quite so rigid with regard to commercial alliances. One brochure from 1956 had one page given over to a paid advertisement for Zenith FM radios. The ad revenue covered the cost of producing thirty thousand brochures.

On November 30, 1955, Lawrence College in Appleton was granted a construction permit for its new FM station, prompted by the donation of a used FM transmitter from the *Green Bay Press-Gazette*.[31] Although the college originally wanted the call letter WLCA, the station went on the air in March 1956 as WLFM. State Radio Council engineer (and Appleton native) Frederick "Fritz" Hervey from nearby WHKW provided technical assistance for this project,[32] as did Donal Sieb, a former Lawrence student who would later be a Wisconsin Public Radio engineer. The original plan was for the station to be on the air Saturdays only, the day the state FM network was silent. As the station expanded its schedule, its staff planned to counterprogram it relative to the state network: WLFM would play music when WHKW was presenting spoken word programming and vice versa.[33] In December 1957 the Lawrence College Choir performed *The Messiah* over WLFM and the program was picked up at WHKW for statewide broadcast. Engineer Hervey had assisted in the production, coaching the announcers, checking copy, and even arranging for a special microphone to be sent air express from Germany.[34]

In 1956 the state stations presented the first in their series of "Stereophonic Concerts." These were special stereo broadcasts that involved the transmission of two separate signals and required listeners to tune in over two separate receivers in the home, each tuned to a different station. This predates the first "multiplex" broadcasts, where a single signal can carry the two audio channels. The pilot of the series of eight broadcasts began June 10 over WHA-AM and WHA-FM. Listeners were asked to set up two radios eight to fifteen feet apart, one tuned to WHA-AM and the other tuned to WHA-FM. Requests from Milwaukee listeners resulted in the extension of the experiment to WHAD. The initial series used special high-fidelity tape recordings that featured the Chicago Symphony Orchestra, led by Fritz Reiner.[35] The public response was enthusiastic, and on October 7 a new thirteen-week series of stereophonic concerts was begun over WHA, WLBL, the eight State Radio Council stations, and commercial stations WWCF-Baraboo and WFMR-Milwaukee.[36] The eight state FM stations would provide one channel, called the "blue channel," with WHA, WLBL, and the two commercial FM stations airing the other, the "green channel."[37] WHA managers touted it as the first stereophonic network in existence. WHA-TV's transmitter sent out the green channel signal, which was received at WWCF, and its signal in turn was fed to both WLBL and WFMR. The Baraboo station's prior commitment to carry baseball broadcasts forced a change in start time for the feature in the spring of 1957.[38] The Hi-Fi Center in Milwaukee reported crowds of more than two hundred people in its listening room during the first season of broadcasts.[39] A similar effort had been attempted in New York as early as 1952 with live performances over WQXR-AM and -FM. In 1958 WOR in New York used recordings in a similar effort, with one channel going out over WOR-AM and the other over WOR-TV.[40] Commercial classical station WFMT in Chicago also made an attempt at two-channel broadcasting. In that case the program had its right channel carried over the radio station and the left channel carried over Chicago educational television station WTTW.[41]

In October 1956 the state stations began airing the syndicated *Gilbert Highet Program*. Highet was head of the classics department at Columbia University, chief literary critic for *Harper's Magazine,* and a member of the board of judges for the Book-of-the-Month Club. The weekly program featured Highet's discussion of literature, language, and the arts.[42] By the time the program ceased production in 1959, it was being heard on more than three hundred stations in the United States and Canada as well as on the BBC and Voice of America. Highet later revised many of the radio talks for Oxford University Press, which published five volumes of his radio essays.[43]

During the summer of 1956 work began on a thirteen-part series called *Scrolls from the Dead Sea,* to be aired over the state FM stations and distributed by the NAEB Tape Network. Menahem Mansoor, a professor in the University of Wisconsin's Department of Hebrew Studies, traveled to Jerusalem to interview archaeologists, biblical scholars, and others studying the scrolls. The trip included an interview at the Vatican, for the official view of Catholicism on the significance of the discovery. Program supervisor Cliff Eblen and production manager Karl Schmidt developed the idea for the series, which was funded in part by an NAEB grant.[44] By the time the final segment was completed in the spring of 1957, forty-three other stations around the United States were airing the series.[45] In response to numerous requests the network made the tapes available for rental by clergy, religious study groups, theological seminaries, and teachers. (The charge was $1.50 for a single program or $15 for the entire series.)[46] Stations remained interested in broadcasting the program for years thereafter, with requests coming in as late as 1965. The continuing use of the tapes qualified them as "consumer durables," a term one-time WHA program director Bill Harley used to indicate the desirability of producing programs with lasting value.[47]

WHA continued to offer the *Band Wagon* program of marches in the early morning. It had been the sign-on program since 1933 after its debut the previous year. Over the years the program added humorous sketches. In later years these Friday segments featured host Bob Homme, who interviewed faculty members from the campus of the fictional Band Wagon Correspondence School (BWCS). Ken Ohst played all of the parts, including head weatherman J. Winston Vane, chief of the department of meteorology; birdwatcher Russell Grouse, head of the BWCS Bureau of Ornithological Research; football coach Rocky Adamant, leader of the Fighting Pale Grey and Beige Hoard ("eleven of the best"); Old Doc Glockenspiel, leader of the Band Wagon Marching and Concert Band; Dr. Coreopsis La Fleur, director of the BWCS formal gardens; and La Fleur's assistant, Grover Earwig. (There was one role not played by Ohst: a fondly remembered instance where WHA news director Roy Vogelman played on-the-scene reporter Stark Raving, who ostensibly was broadcasting live from the last rapidly melting ice floe on Madison's Lake Mendota.) Tapes of these live programs exist mostly because the State Radio Council engineers working the morning shift at the transmitters would record the program to share with their afternoon colleagues. The *Band Wagon* humor segments continued through mid-1958. Letters from listeners show that they either loved or hated the segments. This difference of opinion about the program extended into McCarty's home. He was at best lukewarm about the segments, whereas his wife was a fan of the Friday morning antics.[48]

In March 1958 the state stations again originated the broadcasts for the state high school basketball tournament for what would be the last time before commercial operators took over the broadcast. Twelve commercial stations carried the feed from the state FM network. The complete package of nine games was made available to commercial stations for less than fifty dollars each, paid to the University of Wisconsin Athletic Department. From this account the athletic department paid the costs of the operation, including $300 for operation of the network on Saturday.[49]

One program addition in May 1958 reflected the change in landscape of commercial radio. In its earliest days WHA had avoided playing jazz, because it was regarded as a "commercial" format. While the stations had carried some educational series on jazz in 1954, they did not offer locally produced programs. Chief announcer Ken Ohst and WHA music librarian Elizabeth Monschein were finally able to convince McCarty that jazz was an appropriate musical genre for the state stations. Ohst had done some jazz programming in late 1957, offering two weekly half-hour jazz sequences as part of the *Dinner Musicale* program. In May 1958 Ohst began early evening programs called *Jazz*

Musicale and *Jazz Interlude.* In March 1959 he debuted *Jazz Impressions,* a half-hour show that aired at 4:30 p.m. three times a week. Monday's program would feature traditional jazz, Friday would be progressive jazz, and Wednesday would be a potpourri.[50] By 1963 the Friday program was being transmitted in stereo and had been changed to specifically air new releases. Ohst continued to host jazz programs over the state network until his retirement in November 1984, and his expertise was honored with an Ohio State Award for a 1977 program he produced on the early recordings of Duke Ellington.

In November 1958 another regular program of humor was begun to fill the void left by the demise of the *Bandwagon Correspondence School.* The new late afternoon offering, *Etcetera,* was described as a "collection of odds and ends from here and there." It featured everything from the reading of humorous essays by people like Robert Benchley or James Thurber to contemporary comedy albums by monologists like Bob Newhart, Andy Griffith, Woody Allen, and Jonathan Winters. It too had a cast of regular characters, including Maestro Manfredini Badoglio, Henry Wadsworth Shortshanks, Sandra Pholicle, and Monica Gonigle. The charm of the program was recognized outside the state: Boston University station WBUR aired tapes of the program in the mid-1960s.[51] Beginning in 1973, the program relinquished its Monday and Friday 5 p.m. time slot to allow the full ninety minutes of National Public Radio's *All Things Considered* to air on those days. *Etcetera* continued as a weekly offering through March 1984,[52] and included fictional underwriters such as Weyauwega Airlines, named for a small town in central Wisconsin.[53]

On February 26, 1960, the University of Wisconsin tried one last time to get the Federal Communications Commission to grant a better frequency and more power for WHA. The application was for 10,000 watts of daytime power at 750 kHz. The plan was to locate the tower on a new site east of Madison between Cottage Grove and Deerfield, and the purpose was to provide a stronger AM signal to the populous counties of southeastern Wisconsin.[54] The FCC denied the application on July 29, 1964, after earlier announcing it would be making no additional daytime assignments on clear-channel frequencies.[55]

On March 3, 1960, although no one knew it at the time, the state FM stations broadcast their last Wisconsin basketball game, a home contest against Purdue. Commercial operators became the sole providers of the game broadcasts the following year.

In August 1960 the National Association of Educational Broadcasters held a seminar in Madison on live radio networking, with discussions about developing a live nationwide educational radio network to supplement the existing NAEB tape service. WHA staff members attended along with fifty representatives of

WHA chief announcer Ken Ohst
Ohst's voice defined the WHA "sound" from the 1950s until his retirement in 1984. A jack-of-all-trades, he trained scores of announcers, was the voice of football play-by-play, brought locally hosted jazz to the network, was a coconspirator in the humor of the *Band Wagon Correspondence School*, and read for *Chapter a Day*. (Wisconsin Historical Society Archives image WHi-23541)

educational stations around the country. Wisconsin managers were particularly interested in the experiences of the Eastern Public Radio network, then in the planning stages. It would connect stations from Montreal to Chapel Hill, North Carolina.[56]

By the end of 1960 the program schedule was such that the Radio Hall pipe organ was getting little use, so the decision was made to sell the unit. McCarty wrote to former WHA organist H. Frederick Fuller for his opinion on what the market might be for the instrument. The organ had cost $13,500 in 1949 and had been well maintained, so McCarty thought it would probably be worth about $10,000, and he hoped to find a church in the market for a slightly used instrument. In addition to a possible monetary windfall, the sale would also open up space in Radio Hall: the plan was to convert the organ pipe alcove into two offices.[57] Music director Don Voegeli made up a sales flier that was distributed to churches in Wisconsin,[58] but customers were scarce. It wasn't until April 1965 that WHA finally accepted an offer of $3,500 for the organ from Madison's Good Shepherd Lutheran Church.[59] The congregation got their money's worth from the instrument: it remained in use until 1996.[60] The alcove that had held the organ pipes found new use as a home for the SCA equipment.

In the spring of 1961 a special six-part series from the BBC was aired over the state FM stations. The Reith Lectures on contemporary thought were named for Sir John Reith, the first general manager of the BBC. The series had aired in Britain the previous year and was called *Art and Anarchy*. It featured Dr. Edgar Wind, an art history professor at Oxford University and a Fellow at Trinity College.[61] Reith Lectures continued to be aired over the state stations for several years. One radio producer commenting on the series said the programs "set a standard for broadcasting that most of us tried to emulate . . . and could never quite succeed in doing."[62] The BBC continues to produce the annual series, which airs on BBC Radio 4. A similar series from the Canadian Broadcasting Corporation, called *The Massey Lectures,* was also carried by the state stations.

In 1961 Wisconsin governor Gaylord Nelson's budget bill recommended that the legislature provide funding to restore Saturday service on the FM network ($28,500 for the biennium), a remote-controlled transmitter for the Marinette–Door County areas of far northeastern Wisconsin ($13,500), improvements to WHAD-Delafield to extend coverage in the southeastern part of the state ($30,000), and a capital appropriation of $14,000 to replace the 1937-era transmitter at WLBL-Auburndale. By a one-vote margin the Joint Finance Committee eliminated all the funding except the money for the new WLBL transmitter. The move came as a shock to the radio station managers, because

McCarty said the public hearing a few weeks earlier had an attitude of "friendly interest" and that many people had turned out to support the radio network. These included representatives of State Radio Listeners, Inc., the Warning and Communications section of the State Bureau of Civil Defense, the Wisconsin Education Association, the Milwaukee Public Schools, as well as members of the general public. Opposition had come from two representatives of taxpayer groups. One acknowledged that the State Radio Council programs were "quite popular" in his community but questioned the worth of the service since "no examinations are given to measure how much education the people are getting."[63]

The staff of the radio network continued to come up with innovative ideas. For the fall 1962 election the engineers at Rib Mountain planned to enlist the aid of the state's amateur radio operators to gather vote totals. Volunteers would send the information to the engineers at WHRM, where it would be collected and then sent out via radio and television.[64]

In late 1962, WHA program supervisor Cliff Eblen went to Ann Arbor to confer with officials of the University of Michigan radio operation WUOM about a schedule for experimental transmissions and pickups of its programs. Less then a year earlier, WUOM had added a high-power FM repeater station in Grand Rapids (WVGR) and the staff in Madison thought that either WHKW in Chilton or WHAD in Delafield could pick up the signal for rebroadcast, so the Wisconsin network could carry some of the Michigan programs.[65] In January 1963 Eblen traveled to Chicago for a meeting of the Council on Institutional Cooperation of the Big Ten and the University of Chicago. The committee had been meeting for a couple of years to develop a live radio network for the stations at Big Ten schools. Carl Menzer, director of the station at the University of Iowa, estimated that the network would cost $120,000 per year for line rental and network staff. The committee recommended pursuing foundation support for the initial operation of the network.[66]

With the first reports of the assassination of President Kennedy, WHA and the state network joined the NBC Radio Network and carried their continuous coverage. WHA's courtesy arrangement with WIBA in Madison for use of their NBC feed proved especially valuable in this case. The NBC feed was used from 1 p.m. until 4:30 p.m. The state network then resumed local origination, but abandoned the regular program schedule in favor of appropriate music, with breaks for news updates. Someone at WHA—most likely news director Roy Vogelman—had the presence of mind to record all the state network's coverage that weekend, thirty-six hours in all (the tapes remain on file in the Wisconsin Public Radio newsroom). The stations also aired a memorial service from the Madison campus.[67] WLBL transmitter operator Joe Selner made this brief notation in his station's operating log: "1230 President Kennedy assassinated in Dallas, Texas. NBC news coverage carried until sign off."[68]

Two weeks later the state stations added a new feature: live broadcasts by the Metropolitan Opera. The first carried was *Aida,* featuring soprano Leontyne Price. The series appears to have been added on short notice, as the November–December 1963 program guide does not mention it. The opera broadcasts had been on the commercial networks for years: on both NBC networks from 1931 to 1940, on NBC-Blue (later ABC) through 1958, and on CBS 1958–59. In 1960, the opera's media department began direct distribution of the broadcasts. The sponsor, however, remained the same, Texaco, which had sponsored the broadcasts since December 7, 1940, and would continue to do so (as Chevron-Texaco) through the 2003–4 season, one of the longest continuous sponsorships in broadcasting history. In 1963, Milton Cross was the national host for the series. He had been on the program since the first broadcast on Christmas Day 1931 and would remain the voice of the program until his death in 1975.[69] Because the Wisconsin FM network was still silent on Saturdays, airing the opera meant additional costs for transmitter operators. It was announced that to carry the full season would cost $200 per station. A group of listeners to WHWC in the Eau Claire area and from as far away as Rochester, Minnesota, raised money to keep the opera broadcasts on the air.[70]

Not all the stations carried the opera broadcasts in the 1960s. For the 1964–65 season the only FM stations signing on to join WHA-AM in airing the operas were WHA-FM in Madison, WHKW in Chilton, WHRM at Rib Mountain, WHWC near Eau Claire, and WHLA near La Crosse. The La Crosse station was not originally included in the lineup but was added in midseason after WHLA operator Charlie Ferris offered to staff the transmitter without pay during the opera broadcasts.[71]

Throughout the early 1960s, State Radio Council engineers assisted Wisconsin educational institutions with the planning and application process for their FM stations. Platteville State College (now the University of Wisconsin–Platteville) received help with its planned broadcast outlet, which was to provide "facilities for student training and serving local and sectional needs." The station, WSUP, went on the air on February 25, 1964. The engineering staff also helped the University of Wisconsin–Milwaukee with the application for its FM station, WUWM, which went on the air on September 24, 1964. The Madison staff had high hopes for this operation, saying that "it will make possible the origination of programs for the State FM Network by direct pickup at WHAD," the idea being that some WUWM local programs would air statewide.[72] Similar assistance was provided to Wisconsin State University–Whitewater (now the University of Wisconsin–Whitewater) for its 10-watt station WSUW. It went on the air on January 10, 1965.[73]

In January 1964 the state stations offered a thirteen-week series of folk music called *As I Roved Out.* The series was hosted by folklorist and folk musician Jean Ritchie and aired on Sundays.[74] It was produced by WRVR, a station run by the Riverside Church in New York City. The station is notable in that many future National Public Radio staff members worked or interned there, including *Talk of the Nation* host Neal Conan and *All Things Considered* host Robert Siegel, who served as the WRVR news director for a time.[75] In May 1964 the network began airing a series of concert performances by the Cincinnati Symphony Orchestra.[76] The taped series from the National Educational Radio Network aired on Sundays and returned the following year in a Saturday time slot. The program listings made no mention of the fact that the ensemble had first appeared on 9XM in November 1921 in the first live concert broadcast of a symphony orchestra.

Two major program changes occurred in 1966. On May 1 the *Homemakers' Program* took on a new name, *Accent on Living,* and widened its scope to cover all sorts of lifestyle and social issues in addition to its traditional programming for homemakers. The other change came on November 19, when the state FM stations aired their last University of Wisconsin football game, with the Badgers hosting Minnesota. Ohst did the play-by-play, Karl Schmidt handled the color commentary, and WHA music director Don Voegeli was technical director. Ohst had a fond memory of working the football games with Voegeli. One night before a Wisconsin–Purdue contest, Ohst and Voegeli attended a press banquet with coaches and media representatives from both teams. It was a dull occasion until Voegeli began playing a piano in the banquet hall, and the group sang songs into the night. One Purdue coach who had been singing along took Ohst aside and said, "We'll trade you right now: a linebacker and a defensive end for that piano player."[77]

In July 1967, at the end of a live radio lecture broadcast from the University of Wisconsin campus, chief announcer Ken Ohst said: "This is the Midwestern Educational Radio Network." A network of about twenty educational radio stations in Wisconsin, Illinois, Ohio, Michigan, and Minnesota had carried the lecture live, completely by over-the-air rebroadcasting. The network spanned more than six hundred miles and featured the longest air-to-air relay ever attempted in the United States, stretching from Collegeville, Minnesota, to Bowling Green, Ohio. It was designed to demonstrate that a large part of the country could be served without the expense of land lines, as well as to

hint at the possibility for future interstate coverage of "events of regional inter-
est." Donald McNeil, the first chancellor of the University of Wisconsin–
Extension, and Edwin Burrows, chair of the Board of Directors of the National
Association of Educational Broadcasters, planned to highlight the MERN ex-
periment in their testimony before the House Interstate and Foreign Commerce
Committee in relation to a pending educational broadcasting bill.[78]

During the year the state legislature adopted the Kellett Plan, which allowed
it to reorganize the executive branch of state government. As a result the State
Radio Council became the Educational Broadcasting Board, and the legislature
created the Educational Broadcasting Division, which it placed under the board's
supervision. Both were attached to the Coordinating Council for Higher Education (CCHE). CCHE had formerly been responsible for extending educational
television services in the state.[79] It became the Educational Communications

WHA music director Don Voegeli
A graduate of the University of Wisconsin School of Music, Voegeli used his
keyboard and composing skills at WHA for decades. He wrote themes for
numerous WHA programs and was an early experimenter with electronic music.
He also wrote the distinctive theme song for NPR's *All Things Considered*.
(Wisconsin Historical Society Archives image WHi-23544)

Board and a separate state agency in 1971. The Educational Communications Board continues to hold the licenses for the original state FM stations and WLBL-Auburndale.[80]

The Vietnam-era unrest on college campuses around the country turned violent in Madison on October 18, 1967, when city police were called to break up a student protest prompted by the presence of recruiters from Dow Chemical. Sixty-three students and thirteen police officers were injured in the confrontation.[81] With many WHA staff members either on vacation or working on productions outside of Madison, news director Roy Vogelman enlisted the aid of host Jack Marlowe and other staff members who happened to be in Radio Hall at the time to cover the event. They managed to pull together a forty-five-minute documentary in less than three hours and had it on the air that evening.[82]

Jazz hosts Ken Ohst and Jack Marlowe
In the late 1950s Ohst (left) and other staff members finally convinced McCarty to allow jazz programming on the state stations. Several years later Marlowe (right) expanded the jazz offerings on the network with his modern jazz program *The Other World of Jazz*. This picture was taken in Radio Hall in February 1968. (University of Wisconsin Archives series 23/24/2, negative 3030-J-1)

Also in 1967 McCarty stepped down as director of radio and television. He had asked to be relieved of administrative duties to pursue several special projects. The new manager was James Robertson, who was chosen after a nationwide search from a roster of more than fifty candidates. Robertson had substantial experience in educational television, serving at WTTW-Chicago and KCET–Los Angeles, which was one of three television stations that he had helped put on the air. He also had radio experience, beginning at WHA in 1935. While Robertson was still in high school, McCarty had invited him to join the announcing staff.[83]

In 1968 WHA Radio, WHA-TV, and the state FM stations set aside the week of April 29 to May 3 to present programming that focused on the inner city of Milwaukee. The umbrella name for the special effort was *The Inner Core.* Beginning in September 1967, producer Ralph Johnson and other WHA staff members interviewed dozens of people, including teachers, students, home-makers, and representatives from some of the social agencies operating in Milwaukee's inner city. These conversations were originally broadcast over the radio network in October 1967 and were incorporated into the special programs the next year. Other scheduled programs during the week, such as *Accent on Living* and *Etcetera,* featured material related to the specials, and *Chapter a Day* that week featured a reading of Dick Gregory's book *The Shadow That Scares Me.* WHA-TV aired evening documentaries, followed by a live panel discussion moderated by UW–Extension chancellor Donald McNeil. These live programs also aired over the radio network and educational television station WMVS in Milwaukee.[84] The program series generated favorable press coverage and won the stations both an Ohio State Award and a Major Armstrong Award. WHA-TV's participation earned it the first Emmy ever awarded to a public television station.[85]

Television and radio teamed up again in December 1968 for the sixth annual Work Week of Health, in cooperation with the State Medical Society of Wisconsin. The title of the series was *Youth on a 4-Day Trip* and offered eight different programs over WHA-TV on alcohol and drug abuse among young people as well as other issues affecting teens. Five programs also aired on the state radio network. A grant from Wisconsin Physicians Service Blue Shield helped pay for broadcasting the series, one of the earliest known examples of underwriting for either WHA radio or television.[86]

One other change came in September 1968. The *Farm Program* took on a new title, *The Midday Report.* It was now a one-hour program, "with a variety of news features, including a ten-minute news summary, background to news developments, a report on agricultural markets, interviews and features with agricultural experts and detailed weather information from the U.S. Department of Commerce Weather Bureau, Truax Field."[87] The fall election season also brought some innovations, including an early attempt at call-in programming. For *Politics '68* state candidates could make a five-minute presentation, then members of the public could call collect to ask questions. The series was simulcast over the state FM stations and WHA-TV. WHA-AM and the state stations also acquired a network affiliation, subscribing to United Press International's audio service, not only for political coverage but also for general news. It was believed that there was only one other non-commercial subscriber to UPI Radio at the time.[88]

One change in personnel occurred in 1968 as well when Harold Engel retired. He had been associated with WHA since 1931. One Engel creation was reissued at about the time of his retirement. A new edition of his booklet, *Wisconsin Place Names,* was produced. First issued in February 1938, this "pronouncing gazetteer" collected the local pronunciations of Wisconsin place names from "extension workers, sheriffs, teachers, local historians, students and recognized 'old timers' in various communities." It was offered for sale at the nominal fee of one dollar to "radio and television announcers, speakers, politicians, businessmen, teachers and others concerned with statewide references."[89]

In February 1969 the radio network rebroadcast the popular presentation by Dr. John Schindler, "How to Live a Hundred Years Happily," in celebration of the twentieth anniversary of its original airing. The station again offered a printed booklet with a synopsis of the speech for twenty-five cents.[90] It had also been broadcast on its tenth anniversary in 1959 and, despite no prior publicity, generated more than thirteen hundred requests for printed copies.[91]

Station management picked 1969 to celebrate WHA's fiftieth anniversary. A special commemorative booklet and long-playing record marked the occasion. Publicity surrounding the event prompted both KDKA in Pittsburgh and WWJ in Detroit to send materials to WHA in support of their claims as America's oldest radio station.

During the year the Educational Communications Board received a grant of $30,350 from the U.S. Department of Health, Education and Welfare to upgrade the network's SCA service. The addition of more FM stations in Wisconsin was causing such interference to the subsidiary service that in some areas of the state it was almost unusable. The improvement plan called for eliminating the off-air pickup of the FM network and replacing it with the voice communications network of the Wisconsin Department of Motor Vehicles.[92] WHA also received a grant to establish the National Center for Audio Experimentation.[93] Long-time music director Don Voegeli headed up the center, which worked with early music synthesizers and developed electronic music segments for use in broadcast productions. The center distributed more than two dozen collections on long-playing records to non-commercial stations around the country. One outgrowth of this project was the Voegeli-composed theme music for NPR's *All Things Considered.* Yet another grant was awarded to establish a regional radio network for Wisconsin, Michigan, and Minnesota, similar to the MERN experiment of 1967.[94]

Toward the end of 1969 the state legislature changed the representation on the Educational Communications Board. The membership would now also include one representative each from public school professional staffs, public school boards of education, private higher education, private elementary and secondary education, and citizens at large. In addition, the four-year terms of the members were staggered to "ensure against 'packing' of the Board by any state administration and to maintain continuity." The board now numbered thirteen: four citizen members, four members representing higher education, four representing elementary and secondary education, and the governor or his representative.[95]

In the summer of 1970 the sound of the state network changed. Manager Ralph Johnson decided the network would eliminate the chimes used to alert the operators to play a station identification. It was felt the chimes gave the network an undesirable old-fashioned feel. A standard verbal phrase would be the new identification cue.[96]

In November 1970 a new experimental program was unveiled with the provocative title *This Program Is Out of Context.* It ran weeknights from 10:45 p.m. until midnight on WHA-FM only, following the sign-off of the remainder of the stations. It was billed as a departure from the network's usual programming and was targeted at young listeners in south-central Wisconsin. The program included drama, poetry, sound sculpture, environmental portraits, and live interviews, both in studio and by phone. Music on the program was primarily progressive rock, but any genre might air if appropriate to the mood.[97]

CHAPTER 17

❧

The Era of Public Radio

1971–78

This is the Wisconsin Educational Radio Network.

In 1971 WHA and the state FM stations signed up for a new program service called National Public Radio. Since the 1930s the educational stations in the United States had hoped for some sort of network like those enjoyed by their commercial counterparts. NPR began its live programming service on May 3, with a ninety-minute afternoon newsmagazine called *All Things Considered.* The Wisconsin network was there for the debut broadcast, which was hosted by Robert Conley and had as its producer Jack Mitchell, a former WHA public affairs director and future director of Wisconsin Public Radio. The program was delivered by a medium-fidelity telephone line, which would remain the transmission method until 1979. The new NPR offering was initially heard on all of the eleven state stations and continues to air over WPR to this day.

In the fall of 1971 the Corporation for Public Broadcasting provided a grant to the University of Wisconsin Board of Regents for a project called *Earplay.* The program series was intended to resurrect radio drama, with original scripts solicited from authors around the world. Karl Schmidt headed up the project, which began by contacting literary agents, writers' organizations, and literary journals and by placing ads in various publications. By the end of the first three months of the operation, it had purchased twenty-one scripts from the 327 submitted. Producers were happy to see that literary quality could be high even in shorter (five- to ten-minute) works, so the plan was to purchase perhaps one hundred scripts rather than the sixty originally envisioned. The series was produced in Madison for the first few years, and it later included recordings made in other cities, with postproduction remaining at WHA. The series was distributed to non-commercial stations around the country by long-playing record and also through National Public Radio.[1]

During its decade-long run *Earplay* featured a wide range of works, from *Anythynge You Want* by Firesign Theatre to *Statements after an Arrest under the Immorality Act,* a play about apartheid by Athold Fugard, South Africa's leading playwright. Established writers like Archibald MacLeish and Edward Albee were contributors as were new writers like David Mamet. Mamet eventually had three works accepted for the series and said writing for radio taught him a lot about the art of writing drama. He later wrote: "Working for radio, I learned the way all great drama works: by leaving the endowment of characters, place, and especially action up to the audience."[2] In an interesting twist, Edward Albee's *Earplay* work, *Listening,* was later performed on the stage, a rare instance of a play's first performances being on the radio. The BBC purchased the *Earplay* production of Anne Leaton's *My Name Is Bird McKai.* The *London Times* called it one of the three best radio dramas of the year.[3] The series attracted numerous well-known actors, including Meryl Streep, Jeff Goldblum, Jean Marsh, Tony Roberts, Bruno Kirby, Howard da Silva, Judd Hirsch, Nancy Marchand, and Charles Durning, as well as performers with no previous acting experience.[4] The series was showered with honors, including a Peabody Award, two Major Armstrong awards, two Ohio State awards, and three Prix Italia awards, the most prestigious international honor for radio production. In later years the program became a cooperative effort of WHA and Minnesota Public Radio, and it continued until 1981.

Also in 1971 the composition of the Educational Communications Board was altered to also include a member of each political party represented in the state senate and assembly, appointed the same way that members are appointed to standing committees of those bodies. Former manager Harold McCarty strongly opposed the move, because he believed that the board's original composition of professional educators and government officials directly associated with the programming was preferable.[5]

In October 1972 the radio and television operations achieved a long-time goal and moved into their present home, Vilas Communications Hall, about two blocks south of Radio Hall. The first official attempt to gain a unified facility and more space had come in 1957. At one time the new building was planned for the same site as the WHA-TV facility in the old Chemical Engineering building at 600 N. Park Street. Representatives of the radio and television operations met with their counterparts in the departments of communications arts, journalism, and drama to prepare a building request for the university administration. Various studies were presented beginning in 1958, the new building became number 41 on a list of buildings for the 1961–63 biennium, and it received funding by 1965–67. Space requirements, funding complications, and inflation resulted in numerous modifications, but the result was a seven-story, 240,000-square-foot building that cost just over $13.8 million, with a bit more than $1 million of the total provided by the William F. Vilas Trust Estate.[6] Vilas (1840–1908) was a Civil War officer, UW law professor, member of the Board of Regents, and member of the Wisconsin Assembly. He later served as Postmaster General and Interior Secretary, and later still, became a U.S. Senator from Wisconsin. He bequeathed his estate to the University of Wisconsin and revenue from it continues to generate millions of dollars each year for use as scholarships, endowments, and university projects. Radio Hall remained a University of Wisconsin–Extension facility, continuing to house the SCA services as well as the educational telephone network, another distance-learning technology. Various other UW–Extension broadcast and distance-learning operations continue to occupy the historic building today. The original interior decor remains, including the mural and much of the Native American motif, although the spacious lobby area now contains office cubicles.

On October 6, 1972, the Educational Communications Board changed the official title of the FM network to the Wisconsin Educational Radio Network. This gave the title of the service wording similar to that of the television service and replaced the various names in use up to that time for sign-on, sign-off, and network cues.[7]

Shortly after the move to Vilas Hall, the state stations presented a special election night broadcast. The program originated at UW–Milwaukee's WUWM, where a sixty-two person news team had been assembled to add up the vote.[8]

In late 1972 the concept of the FM stations' being only repeaters of the broadcast from Madison was modified a bit. WHAD began airing a local Milwaukee program to serve the Spanish-speaking audience in southeastern Wisconsin. The program concept was developed in November 1971 and began to take shape with grants from the Wisconsin Department of Industry, Labor and Human Relations, and the Allen Bradley Company of Milwaukee. The money paid for remodeling and equipping a small studio in downtown Milwaukee in space provided by United Migrant Opportunity Services. A phone line provided the hookup to the Delafield transmitter, and the program, *Programa Cultural en Español,* aired from 6:15 to 7 p.m. weekdays beginning December 8, 1972. The project also provided members of the Hispanic community with the opportunity to attend classes in radio announcing, operations, and programming. The classes prepared students to take the FCC exam for a third-class operator's license, then a requirement for anyone seeking employment as a radio announcer.[9]

In 1973 the state FM stations participated in special coverage that helped make a name for National Public Radio. The new network was offering live coverage of the Watergate hearings from Washington, D.C., and the state stations carried much of the proceedings. It disrupted some of the schedule and forced the rescheduling of some *Chapter a Day* offerings.[10]

In late 1974, WHA began offering a program schedule that was separate from the rest of the state network, something that had been contemplated for several years. This had been tried on Saturdays during football broadcasts, and during the final months in Radio Hall a WHA-only public affairs program had aired at 6 a.m. weekdays, an hour before the rest of the network signed on.[11] Now separate programming for WHA would be the pattern each day. To reinforce the division between WHA and the FM network, the Educational Communications Board had applied to the Federal Communications Commission to change the call letters of WHA-FM. The new identification was WERN, identifying the station as the flagship of the Wisconsin Educational Radio Network. Since programming on the network was no longer coming from WHA, the Educational Communications Board found itself in the new role of program origination. An office, studio, and master control room were outfitted for the Educational Communications Board in Vilas Hall. Remote control operation of monitoring of the transmitters for WHAD-Delafield and WHHI-Highland would also be done from the Madison facility, in place of on-site transmitter engineers.[12]

With WHA a separate operation, the station began printing its own program guide, called *Nine Seventy.* The separation also marked the first time since the early 1930s that classroom instruction would not be part of the station's programming.[13] The same year the WHA Radio Association was formed. It was established as an independent, nonprofit listener organization committed to enhancing and supporting public radio in south-central Wisconsin. Memberships began at ten dollars, and members were invited to "spend a day at WHA," take a station tour, meet the staff, learn about radio production, and get together with other WHA listeners. The group later became the Wisconsin Public Radio Association.[14] One of its early board members was a former University of Wisconsin graduate student named David Giovannoni.[15] He later formed a company called Audience Research Analysis, which has contracts with the Corporation for Public Broadcasting, National Public Radio, Public Radio International, and many public radio stations around the country. The firm provides statistical analysis of public radio's audience, and Giovannoni has been named one of the most influential figures in shaping the sound of public radio today, garnering praise for national audience growth and criticism for undermining local (usually music) programming in favor of NPR fare.[16] The wide acceptance of this research is one reason that most public radio stations around the country are carrying a similar lineup of national programs.

Being separate from the rest of the network also gave WHA the freedom to experiment with a new type of radio programming: the on-air pledge drive. The Educational Communications Board was reluctant to try this new method of fund-raising (as were some of the on-air staff), so the first one was a WHA-only effort, held over the weekend of April 1–2, 1978. The Saturday drive was held at an area shopping mall and dubbed the Second Annual Warhorse Day, reprising a special broadcast day from the previous year when listeners could request the playing of a classical music "warhorse." For the fund-raising version a pledge of at least ten dollars had to accompany the request. The second day of the drive was held from the Philo Buck studio in Vilas Hall and called Desperation Sunday, with the theme "We'll Do Almost Anything for Money." This included live jazz and folk music as well as a variety of performances by WHA staff members.[17] Network-wide pledge drives came the following year, with a five-day marathon held September 27 to October 1. It raised $43,000 from more than fifteen hundred new members.[18] The network now does three drives a year, and the proceeds are an important part of the operation's finances.

CHAPTER 18

❧

WPAH/WLBL, the Other State Station
1923–51

The Chautauqua of the Air

The Wisconsin Department of Markets got involved in radio when it began providing market information to 9XM in Madison on September 19, 1921. Agency personnel were enthusiastic about the potential use of the medium in delivering market information. Staff members reported that more than twelve hundred "stations" (radio receivers) were using the daily Madison market broadcasts by early 1922. They said that these stations were located not only on farms but also in banks, at radio dealers, in schools, and at newspapers and other locations. They also reported that recipients of the market reports would often post them on bulletin boards in public places, as had been the tradition with the original 9XM weather forecasts. In some cases rural telephone companies would receive the market reports and then verbally retransmit the material to farmers on the line. The agency said that recipients found the reports to be "very valuable" and had reported many instances when having the market reports had "made money for the growers and shippers of farm products."[1]

The department wanted WHA to broadcast its information several times each day and wrote to Earle Terry to ask what the charge would be. Terry responded that the substantial increase in service requested would mean greater costs; he quoted $200 per month, which he said would cover half the station's additional expenses.[2] Department officials decided that having their own station would be a way to give unlimited service at minimum cost, and they anticipated that the radio reports would eventually replace the distribution of market bulletins through the mail. They also could eliminate the $2,000 yearly cost of having the leased wires for market reports in Madison.[3] Moreover, department officials were dissatisfied with WHA's poor reception in northern Wisconsin.

Edward Nordman, the commissioner of the Department of Markets, believed that the station could serve rural residents of Wisconsin, and his agency made plans to locate it in the central part of the state. Officials from the Civic and Commerce Association of Waupaca lobbied successfully for the station, citing the city's central location and the concentration of the potato industry in the region. The city agreed to provide office and studio facilities. Some city officials had already expressed an interest in radio, and in 1922 the Civic and Commerce Association was even issued a license for a station on 360 meters (833 kHz) with the call letters WIAA, which was never built.[4]

Waupaca is the county seat of Waupaca County, an agricultural region about one hundred miles north of Madison and Milwaukee, and in 1920 the city boasted a population of 2,839. In addition to potato farming, which was even then on the decline, dairy farming was (and is) a major component of the local agricultural economy.

The Department of Markets began construction of the station in November 1922. Anticipating the start-up of the Waupaca station, the department discontinued its market reporting from its Madison office on November 1, 1922, and concentrated all activities at the new facility in Waupaca the following week.[5] The department at the time was employing a "radio specialist" who would give assistance to anyone who was thinking about buying radio equipment in order to receive the market reports. This person probably was Max Littleton, who had been involved with the market reports from 9XM/WHA in Madison since September 1921. He would later install the equipment for the Waupaca station and act as its first operator and manager.

The location provided for the studios and offices was a storefront at 100 North Main Street in Waupaca. The building was owned by A. J. Holly and Sons, a family in the furniture and undertaking business. The radio operation would be in the building's mezzanine. (The building is still standing and is now an office supply and stationery store.) Two 110-foot towers with twenty-two-foot-square bases arrived unassembled from the factory in Freeport, Illinois, and were installed 210 feet apart on a site on Jefferson Street in the city. The antenna was 140 feet long between the towers, and instead of using a ground, "the station uses a series of wires 18 feet above the ground directly under the antenna." It was known as counterpoise and was said to be superior to the regular ground system.[6] The representative from the factory said the Waupaca towers were the finest he'd installed.[7]

While construction of the towers was underway, several members of the city council came up with the idea of putting a high-powered light atop of each tower, which the council approved. However, the lights were not intended to act as a warning to aircraft but rather as a publicity vehicle for the city. It was thought "having such a light, that Waupaca at night will be visible quite a distance in the country."[8]

On December 12, 1922, the U.S. Department of Commerce authorized the station and assigned it the call letters WPAH. The call letters had no meaning; they were simply the next ones in sequence. Other stations authorized the same month were given calls in the series from WPAJ to WPAX.[9]

The new transmitting equipment was fully installed by mid-January 1923. At least one local business hoped to capitalize on the start-up of the new station. The Waupaca Radio Sales Company ran an advertisement in the *Waupaca County Post* on January 18. Under the heading "Broadcasting the Markets," the copy read, "Weather forecasts and other valuable information from the Waupaca station, WPAH, will soon begin on their regular schedule. Are You Equipped to Receive Them? $12.50 will buy you a complete receiving outfit that will make this valuable information available to you 365 days of the year. Can you afford to be without this service at such a small cost? See us about your outfit."

After some initial testing during the previous weekend, WPAH officially went on the air at 8:30 a.m. on Monday, February 5, 1923, broadcasting at 485 meters (618 kHz). The *Waupaca County News* reported the first broadcast with the headline "Waupaca on the Air—Radio Station Sending." The article listed the broadcast schedule of the six original market programs:

8:30—Estimated receipts of livestock for the more important markets. Carload shipments for United States of the more important fruits and vegetables, especially potatoes and cabbage, with special reference to Wisconsin.

9:30—Daily weather forecast and weekly forecast every Monday. Also repeating livestock receipts for Chicago and St. Paul, together with shipping point information on potatoes and cabbage for Wisconsin and competing states.

10:30—The butter and egg markets from Chicago and New York, also cheese markets from Fond du Lac and Chicago, together with the Chicago market on potatoes and cabbage.

11:30—Complete livestock markets from Chicago, which includes cattle, hogs, sheep and live dressed poultry.

3:00—Hay, feed and other related markets.

5:00—Special announcements together with extracts from the daily marketgram and crop news of interest to the Wisconsin producers.

Press accounts indicate that each of these programs was fifteen minutes long and all were telephonic[10]; there is no record that WPAH ever broadcast any regular programs by Morse code. This is understandable, because the station's programs were directed to farmers rather than code-savvy radio amateurs. The programs consisted primarily of the market quotations, but may have included additional items. The February 5 *Waupaca County News* article provides this hint: "In order that the material broadcasted may not become monotonous to the listeners the programs are generally interspersed with musical selections." It appears that the station was not broadcasting continuously during the day. Instead, the transmitter was probably turned on for each program and then turned off until the next one. Still, the schedule was even more extensive that what the department had been requesting of WHA the previous summer.

The WPAH transmitter was said to be one of the most powerful in the nation at the time, perhaps second in power only to WGY, the General Electric station in Schenectady, New York.[11] The *Waupaca County Post* of February 8 reported that WPAH received more than two hundred letters and telegrams from listeners who had heard the first test broadcasts the previous weekend. One of the first was from a former Waupaca resident who lived in New Leipzig, North Dakota, about nine hundred miles away. Other reports came in from places as far away as Brooklyn, New York; Washington, D.C.; Montgomery, Alabama; Waco, Texas; Walla Walla, Washington; and Regina, Saskatchewan.[12] The evening programs in late 1923 brought reception reports from nearly every state, much of Canada, and even Puerto Rico and England.

Initial reception reports from these listeners prompted Littleton to draft an acknowledgment letter, dated February 6, 1923, the second day of station operation. In it he described the transmitter equipment and its regular output. He also apologized for occasional distortion and "raspy" sound, which he blamed on inconsistent voltage from the commercial power line. This problem would later figure in the future of the station. Also in the letter was the schedule of programs and a note: "At present we have no night programs arranged, but will in the near future start on a small nightly program, and will notify you when we do." The letter closed with a thank you for the report because "this is about the only way we can gauge our power and modulation."[13]

WPAH experimented with evening programs during its first month on the air. On the evening of February 22 it aired a special program for the Wautoma Commercial Club banquet in nearby Waushara County. The program consisted of musical selections and greetings for attendees at the banquet, where a borrowed "radio outfit" had been installed for the event.[14]

Regular evening programming debuted that summer. WPAH broadcast the

Thursday evening concerts from the bandstand in front of the courthouse in downtown Waupaca.[15] The concerts were such a popular entertainment in the area that area merchants would close their doors on Thursday evenings. As remote broadcasts go, these band concerts would have been comparatively easy to do because the bandstand was across the street from the WPAH studio.

The station operated through midsummer and then shut down for repairs and maintenance for nearly all of August. When it returned to the air on September 4, the schedule had been slightly modified, and the frequency had been changed to 360 meters (833 kHz). This was evidently done because of interference with other stations on the 485-meter wavelength.[16] The frequency change is puzzling. Market reports were typically considered "government" broadcasting, so WPAH should have been required to remain on 485 meters. The expanded broadcast schedule had been fine-tuned:

> 8:45 a.m.—Estimated receipts on live stock for South St. Paul and Chicago markets. Carlot shipments, potatoes, apples and cabbage.
>
> 9:45 a.m.—Weather forecasts for Wisconsin. Opening markets on rye, wheat, corn and barley from Chicago. Repeating all of the material broadcast on the 8:45 a.m. schedule.
>
> 10:45 a.m.—Chicago, New York and Milwaukee butter and egg markets. Chicago and Wisconsin cheese markets, wholesale basis on all days except Tuesday; Tuesday the Plymouth market is given. Chicago potato and cabbage markets.
>
> 11:45 a.m.—Complete live stock markets from Chicago.
>
> 12:30 p.m.—Complete summary of ALL the above-listed markets with additional information as follows: Chicago and New York butter and egg futures; Pittsburgh, Cincinnati, Kansas City and St. Louis potato markets. Other miscellaneous crop and market information.
>
> 1:45 p.m.—Chicago grain closes on rye, oats, barley, wheat and corn. Poultry markets from Chicago (live poultry). Hay markets from Chicago.
>
> 4:30 p.m.—Market reviews, weather summaries and general reports on marketing matters.[17]

In addition to the daytime farm market programs, WPAH began offering evening entertainment programs that were the responsibility of the city, sort of an early example of community radio. The regular evening programs featured a mixture of live music performances and spoken-word presentations. The usual arrangement was to spotlight a particular community, with local talent from that area along with boosters promoting their town. The broadcasts were often made under the auspices of a local paper or chamber of commerce, and they occasionally featured short remarks from the community's mayor. Some of the evening programs featured dance bands that had performed on other radio stations.

WPAH's management liked to repeat a comment contained in a letter from a Madison listener. In complimenting the station on an evening program, he referred to the station as the "chautauqua of the air," and the phrase was appropriated as the station's slogan.[18] The station's managers were proud of the evening offerings and felt they were the equal of any "lyceum course or entertainment that could be provided."[19] One regular feature scheduled for the Monday evening programs was a talk about health presented by a physician from the State Medical Society of Wisconsin, assisted by local Waupaca doctors. Station officials thought the health talks were especially valuable and felt "fortunate in securing this really worth while material."[20] Evening programs were offered on Mondays, Wednesdays, and Saturdays, starting variously at 7 p.m., 7:30 p.m., or 8 p.m. Sundays were added for religious broadcasts beginning November 11; these programs went on the air at 6 p.m. A complete list of the evening programs does not exist, but newspaper accounts show these programs from 1923–24:

September 26: Rena Bauer and Florence Baldwin: music instructors from nearby Weyauwega with a program of fifteen classical music selections[21]

October 19: Arthur Cole and his Recordograph Orchestra from Milwaukee[22]

October 22: Stevens Point Chamber of Commerce program, featuring the Wolverine Orchestra, the Florida Five Orchestra, the Majestic Orchestra, the Whiting Syncopators Orchestra, the Kiwanis Club male quartet, the Orion Male Quartet and other vocal solos, as well as humor talks, a business talk and a health talk by Dr. J. W. Coon of the River Pine Sanitorium[23]

October 26: *Clintonville Tribune* program, with classical solos, duos and trios, an address about Clintonville, xylophone solos and concertina solos of "old-time airs"[24]

November 5: Wisconsin Rapids Chamber of Commerce program with addresses from the city's Mayor, the county agricultural agent and local businessmen, and humor monologue. Music from the Rotary Glee Club, Arthur Kohl and his Recordograph Orchestra, and semi-classical vocal solos[25]

November 11: religious program with a sermon from Reverend J. W. Clevenger of Waupaca's First Baptist Church[26]

November 18: Baptist Church services[27]

November 19: Oshkosh Normal School program with members of the Oshkosh Normal School Orchestra, a male vocal quartet, vocal and

instrumental solos, and a speech about the value of music instruction in
elementary grades[28]

November 22: American Legion Vaudeville Show[29]

November 24: A dance orchestra from Appleton "under the direction of Mr.
Harriman"[30]

November 26: Fond du Lac Commercial Club program featuring Si Melberg
and his Dance Orchestra, talks on dairying and the veterans compensation
bill, readings, vocal solos and other addresses: the group also offered prizes
for distant listeners[31]

November 28: Wausau Chamber of Commerce program with 18 classical
music selections, literature readings, a talk about Wausau and an
announcement of the details of a missing persons case from the city: also,
four pairs of shoes were offered as prizes for most distant responses from
the north, south, east and west[32]

December 3: *Appleton Post-Crescent* program featuring the faculty of the
Lawrence Conservatoire of Music with classical and semi-classical music[33]

December 10: Ripon program with the Zobel Concert Orchestra, readings
and talks about both Ripon and Ripon College[34]

December 17: Program under the auspices of the Pettibone-Peabody Company
of Appleton (a department store) featuring the Lawrence College of Music
with classical music, the Lawrence College Methodist Choir and the Green
Bay High School Saxoband[35]

December 19: Sankey's Radio Syncopators (from Minneapolis, often heard on
station WLAG) "under the direction of Mr. C. H. Sayles of the Winter
Garden," plus a health talk by Dr. Sleyster of Wauwatosa, president-elect of
the State Medical Society[36]

February 3: Sermon by Reverend W. P. Leek, superintendent of the Fond du
Lac district of the Methodist Church and former Fond du Lac pastor[37]

The addition of the religious programs led the Ministerial Association of
Waupaca County to form a radio committee by December 1923 to "handle
all radio dealing with the churches, especially regards the Sunday services to be
given out by radio." Plans were made to install direct lines to some Waupaca
churches for live broadcasts of services, and an ambitious schedule of several
Christmas Eve remote broadcasts was in the works, including a live broadcast
of the midnight mass from the Episcopal church in Waupaca.[38]

The Holly family, which owned the building that housed WPAH, installed a
high-quality receiving set and invited members of the public into the store to
listen to distant broadcasts when WPAH was not broadcasting. Of particular

interest was the reception of college football scores on Saturday, October 20, 1923, as well as a play-by-play broadcast of that day's game between Northwestern University and the University of Chicago. The *Waupaca County News* reported that "so clear was the material coming in that the college cheers could be heard, together with the blasts from the referees [*sic*] whistle. To one who understood the game it was almost as good as a seat in the grandstand."[39]

As was the case for 9XM/WHA and other stations during this period, one intriguing aspect of radio was that the local programs were heard at great distances; newspaper reviews of evening programs included reception reports for WPAH. The November 26, 1923, program by the Fond du Lac Commercial Club was the first to capitalize on this interest by offering prizes to distant listeners. The major prize for the most-distant reply was a "cross-tight top for an automobile," with a radio receiving set and men's and ladies' footwear going

The WPAH office in Waupaca
Two unidentified men inspect a vacuum tube in front of the WPAH office in early 1924. (Courtesy of the Waupaca Historical Society, Waupaca, Wisconsin)

to runners up. The club also offered a box of candy to the first listener from each state who contacted the program. During the show more than 150 telegrams came in from Maine to California, and many were read on the air during the broadcast. In anticipation of the Fond du Lac program, that city's Postal Telegraph office took out a newspaper ad, saying they would remain open during the evening of the broadcast so local residents could send messages to Waupaca.[40] The broadcast received reports from forty-three states, four Canadian provinces, and a wire from England.[41] The Clintonville broadcast received positive responses as well, with listeners particularly enjoying the "old time airs" on concertina performed by Arthur Schoenike, a former Waupaca resident.[42] A late-arriving report indicated the Clintonville broadcast was also heard in Puerto Rico.[43] Waupaca was so caught up in the mania for radio that one of the local papers ran an illustration in December showing Santa Claus "taking orders." The engraving shows St. Nick at his receiving set, complete with headset and carbon microphones.[44]

Fluctuations in the commercial electric power available in Waupaca caused constant problems for the Department of Markets. The agency brought in radio experts who recommended the use of batteries to help stabilize the station's power. The agency approached the city with plans for correcting the problem and also requested better studio facilities and additional financial support. The city council passed a resolution, agreeing to furnish up to $600 worth of free electric power per year as inducement to keep the station in the city. The council's action prompted a local citizen to hire an attorney, who won an injunction ordering the mayor, city clerk, city treasurer, and Board of Public Works to pay out no money and to do no further work as a municipality to keep the station. The injunction stated that the plaintiff was a taxpayer and that he brought the action on behalf of himself and all other taxpayers in the city. It further stated that the city's resolution was illegal, "inasmuch as the municipality does not own the station, is not buying it, or does not contemplate buying it."[45]

The injunction caused a flurry of activity. The Department of Markets rapidly released information to the newspapers that spelled out in detail what the agency expected from its host city in terms of support. Waupaca boosters found themselves defending efforts to keep the station in their city, and they seemed to feel betrayed because the Department of Markets was not more interested in staying put. They suspected that the agency had structured the demands in such a way that Waupaca would be unable to satisfy them.[46] Sensing an opportunity, others began lobbying to have the station moved to their cities. Among the cities mentioned in press reports were Appleton, Antigo, Fond du Lac,

Green Bay, Marshfield, Oshkosh, Rhinelander, Wausau, and Wisconsin Rapids. Many communities made offers, and it was pointed out that in the interest of economy the city chosen would be on the line of the markets telegraph wire, which ran parallel to the Soo Line Railroad across the middle of the state. "Drops" to cities not on this line would increase the cost of the operation. Also, the Department of Markets wanted the station as close to the center of the state as possible to serve the maximum area.[47] Despite their efforts, Waupaca officials believed the decision had already been made. Officials from the Department of Markets had considered all the offers and selected Stevens Point to be the station's new home. Waupacans believed that they were the victims of double-dealing and made their displeasure known in the pages of the local papers.

In February 1924, WPAH played an important role during a snowstorm that affected the eastern part of Wisconsin. On the one-year anniversary of the first scheduled broadcast in Waupaca, WPAH helped relay messages for railroads whose telephone and telegraph lines had been knocked out by the snowstorm. WPAH relayed train-dispatching messages between radio stations and to amateurs who were able to contact the railroads by local telephone.[48] Other stations participating in the relays included KYW-Chicago, WLAG-Minneapolis, and WOAW-Omaha.[49]

On February 26, 1924, the WPAH equipment was dismantled. Evidently somewhat soured on the business of broadcasting, the Waupaca Chamber of Commerce offered the now-abandoned radio towers for sale to the highest bidder. The Stevens Point Ski Club prevailed with a high bid of $100. Its intention was to have the nearly new towers dismantled and then reuse the structural steel to build a ski jump in nearby Plover Hills.[50] The same crew that dismantled the station equipment was enlisted to take down the towers for the ski club.[51]

The station transmitter and studio equipment were reused in Stevens Point and installed at the station's new rent-free facility at the Hotel Whiting, which now sported two hundred-foot towers on its roof for the antenna, paid for by the citizens of Stevens Point. The transmitter was located in a room on the roof, and the studio was located in the basement of the building. The Stevens Point Chamber of Commerce formed a radio policy and program committee, an indication that the city anticipated that it would be able to exert a good deal of control over the evening programming on the new station, with the Department of Markets continuing to manage the daytime markets broadcast. By February 1924 the committee had adopted a guide to radio policy, calling for high standards from potential performers. The station outlined a policy that "expressly eliminates party politics, religious controversial questions, personal advertising or that which may be construed as intended for personal aggrandizement or preferment, and unreasonable requests." One other policy was a premonition of things to come: "Possibilities for educational extension are unlimited."[52]

The committee also said that although most broadcasts would originate in the studio at the Hotel Whiting, several churches and other institutions were planning to install lines to allow for remote broadcasts. Some musical groups that wanted to appear on the station had already approached the Chamber of Commerce. Officials welcomed the offers but were careful to point out that "all of the talent must be given gratis and no organizations or individuals will receive pay for their part in the programs."[53] The radio committee said that all programs would originate in the Hotel Whiting studio unless they used permanent remote transmitting devices, which would include "microphones installed in several churches and both theatres as well as possible installation at the Normal and High schools." The committee also said the dining room at the Hotel Whiting would be equipped with a microphone.[54]

The first test broadcast from Stevens Point was made in the early morning hours of Sunday, March 9, 1924, and featured live music from the Majestic Theatre's orchestral trio and a group called Lutz's Original Florida Entertainers. The next night's broadcast featured a local group called Lutz's Virginians. These two groups were under the direction of local bandleader Irv F. Lutz, who had brought music groups to Waupaca to perform on WPAH the previous autumn. Morgan Chase of the Stevens Point Chamber of Commerce was the announcer for both broadcasts that weekend. In charge of the programs was the chair of the radio committee, Raymond M. Rightsell, a member of the faculty at Stevens Point State Normal School. During the tests, the station operated on its original wavelength of 485 meters (618 kHz).[55]

Before on-air testing began in Stevens Point, press accounts continued to refer to the station as WPAH, even though the Department of Commerce had deleted the call letters on February 28, 1924. However, once the testing period was underway, the station was granted temporary permission to use the call letters WCP and applied to the Department of Commerce to make these call letters permanent. The call letters stood for "Wisconsin, the Country's Playground." The *Stevens Point Daily Journal* of March 10, 1924, reported that the first test broadcast generated responses from thirty states. Listeners were asked to make recommendations for other slogans to accompany the WCP call letters. Among the suggestions: "Wisconsin Cheese Pays," "We Can Progress," "Wisconsin, the Camper's Paradise," "Wisconsin Convinces People," "Wisconsin

Cows Produce," "Wisconsin Chemically Pure," "Wisconsin, Classiest Programs," and "Wisconsin Certified Potatoes."

Postmidnight tests continued for several weeks, offering a mix of live music performances and short addresses, as well as abbreviated market reports. The new WCP was now operating at 536 meters (probably 535.4 meters, or 560 kHz). By mid-March 1924 the local Jacobs Novelty Company had begun a sale on radios, urging people in newspaper ads to tune in "hometown" station WCP. A set, "complete with phones," sold for twelve dollars.[56] The ads were reminiscent of those that ran in the Waupaca paper before WPAH went on the air the previous year.

A plan to offer broadcasts earlier in the evening was postponed because of a delay in replacing what was a temporary cable between the basement studio and rooftop transmitter. The new permanent cable was mistakenly sent by ordinary freight rather than express and was lost in transit. It finally arrived on April 3, 1924, twenty-six days after it was shipped from Boston.[57]

Once the new cable was installed, the station was inspected for its license on April 15, 1924. Representatives of the radio committee assured the inspector that WCP would at all times "put on concert programs of high quality." The station passed its inspection and began a regular schedule on April 22, 1924, that featured seven daily market updates, Monday through Saturday, during daytime hours (similar to the WPAH schedule), plus a regular weekly concert put on by the Chamber of Commerce radio committee every Wednesday evening. By September the evening programs had moved to Tuesdays, with occasional specials on other evenings as well. The station continued to use the WCP call letters during this early period, but an application was made for the call letters WLOL, which would stand for "Wisconsin, Land O' Lakes."[58] This was more than just a clever slogan: in early March, Stevens Point had been competing with other communities in northern Wisconsin to be the headquarters for the Wisconsin Land O'Lakes Association, a group that promoted northern Wisconsin as a tourist destination.[59]

Shortly after regular daytime broadcasting got underway, the *Daily Journal* began producing a daily news program for the station, the first of many partnerships between the paper and the broadcaster. The thirty-minute program was called the *Badger State Crier* and was assembled by two members of the newspaper's editorial staff. The program featured "a summary of the important news events of the day," and, the paper said: "Wisconsin news will be featured in concise form, but brief summaries of important world-wide developments will also be flashed out to radio listeners."[60] The news program originally aired at 4 p.m., just as the paper was going to press, but was soon moved to 2 p.m., immediately after the 1:45 p.m. market report. Shortly thereafter the newspaper announced the suspension of the news program to allow for some modifications at the station but promised the interruption would be temporary.[61] Although the article said the paper would print a notice when the program returned, no such item appeared. In all likelihood the newspaper staff quietly abandoned the idea, perhaps overwhelmed by the effort required to produce a half hour of live radio news on a daily basis.

On May 12, 1924, word was received that the station was given a class A license for unlimited broadcast on 278 meters (actually 277.6 meters, or 1080 kHz) instead of the 536 meters it had been using. Press reports said the change was advantageous, as only four other stations in the Midwest were using the frequency: a station in Valparaiso, Indiana, that operated only on Sundays; a station in Tuscalo, Illinois; and two stations in Omaha, one that broadcast only in the daytime and the other low power. With the change came a new set of call letters, WLBL for "Wisconsin, Land of Beautiful Lakes." The originally requested WLOL was not available because the federal government then required that all four-letter call signs have a *B* as their third letter. After all such call letter combinations were exhausted, *C* could be the third letter, and so on. Stevens Point officials were satisfied with the WLBL call letters and felt that "they form a good descriptive slogan for state publicity."[62]

With the beginning of the regular schedule in 1924, WLBL began sending out a cleverly designed penny postcard that efficiently served as a reception acknowledgment, a thank-you letter from the station's owner, and a program guide. It also gave a technical description of the transmitter and antenna and had a small picture of the Hotel Whiting with the towers on the roof. The card predates the first professionally printed WHA program guide by about three years.

During the first few weeks of full operation, WLBL helped police several times. In late May WLBL broadcast the description of a missing fifteen-year-old Stevens Point youth, and in June it broadcast hourly bulletins about the "honeymoon slayer," a man who was suspected of murdering his wife a week after their wedding. WLBL broadcast the suspect's description as well as that of his automobile and its license plate number.[63]

During the first summer of operation in Stevens Point, WLBL was the subject of an article in *See America First,* a national tourism magazine, published in Sheboygan, Wisconsin. WLBL announcer Morgan Chase wrote the article, which featured photos of the Hotel Whiting and its radio towers, a picture of the tower crew, and photos of Chase, who listed himself as announcer, and Raymond Rightsell, whose title was given as "Chief Program Maker and Studio

Director WLBL." In flowery language the article focuses on the evening programs under the auspices of the city. Chase made only passing mention of the daytime farm market offerings and no mention at all of Max Littleton (who left WLBL shortly after the move to Stevens Point) or the other Department of Markets personnel.

Chase said radio was the modern equivalent of native smoke signals from the "days of Nicollet" and recounted how one of the station's first programs featured the opera singer and Indian princess Tsianina Redfeather, in full native garb, who presented a story of early Indian life and folklore. He wrote: "Surely communication has traveled apace since the days of her father's father!"[64] Redfeather had appeared on the station the evening of April 30, 1924, with soprano solos as part of a program assembled for the annual convention of the Wisconsin Music Teachers' Association, held in Stevens Point.[65]

Chase described what happened as the "period for radiocast" arrived. He wrote: "the engineer throws the switch and the powerful motor-generators in a compartment below the floor send up a contented hum of action. The remaining switches go into a place with regularity and the engineer watches the dials above. Then the signal is flashed to begin the program in the studio at some distance in the same building. The announcer goes into action and the outside world hears 'Well, well, well, well! Good Evening, Everyone. You are listening to WLBL, Wisconsin Land of Beautiful Lakes.'"

Chase described the studio, which had a grand piano: "The walls and ceiling are draped to eliminate echoes. The floor is padded and carpeted. A signal box is placed in easy sight of the artists who watch it for information relating to the intensity of their rendition. The room is artificially lighted and the drapes are drawn over the door. An air of seclusion and quiet is impressed on those who enter. The faintest sound is easily picked up by the innocent looking little box suspended from a metal standard in one corner of the room. This is the microphone which performs the same duty for the station that the transmitter performs for the telephone, only in a much greater way owing to its super-sensitive construction."

As had been the case in Waupaca, listeners were encouraged to contact the station during the live performances: "Phones in an adjoining room begin to ring almost as quickly as the program starts. Someone and everyone desire to complement the artist now at the microphone and hope that she will later sing an encore which is named. There is hardly a dull moment on the phone lines thereafter, for persons at points of great distance are eager to express their delight with one feature or another."

He also touted the daily market programs and said that "a rapidly growing clientele of farmers, dairymen, cheese makers, produce buyers and many others are on the 'listening end' during the six periods that this information is sent out daily." Chase mentioned the *Badger Town Crier* news program and told of plans for a weekly "midnite frolic" with the intriguing title *Enemies of Sleep.* He concluded by inviting readers to visit the station, which he called "one of the many show points of the great state of Wisconsin."[66]

In November 1924 WLBL outfitted a booth with a large American flag and a loudspeaker-equipped radio receiver for the Stevens Point Fair. A hand-lettered poster that promoted the station and its services read, "The Progressive Farmer and Merchant Receives Market News the 20th Century Way via Radio." During the fair fifteen-minute programs of markets, weather, and musical numbers were offered for the benefit of fairgoers. A picture of the exhibit in the *Stevens Point Daily Journal* of November 11 shows Frank R. Calvert,

WLBL towers atop the Hotel Whiting in Stevens Point, 1924 (See American First magazine)

who had taken over as manager that summer and would serve in that role for the rest of WLBL's existence as an independent station. Its caption also identifies WLBL staff member Guy Hernis and says that station engineer H. O. Brickson was not pictured, "inasmuch as his was the pleasant voice heard issuing from the loudspeaker."

Some evening broadcasts during this period were similar to those done in Waupaca, and some of the same towns sent delegations to Stevens Point to perform on the radio. Clintonville talent, which had appeared on WPAH to great acclaim, did a four-hour broadcast on Friday, November 14, 1924. The group presented a program of mostly classical selections performed by thirty-five townspeople, including the Clintonville High School Orchestra. As was the case in Waupaca the previous October, the concert aired under the auspices of the *Clintonville Tribune*. Because the "old time airs" performed on concertina by Arthur Schoenike had generated such positive response during the Waupaca broadcast, he was asked to perform during this one as well. He had two sections of the broadcast, one a duet with violin, and the final section of the evening, listed as "old time dance numbers with official caller," evidently in square-dance style.[67] During the broadcast the station received twenty-six long-distance telephone calls and twenty-one telegrams from distant listeners. The Clintonville group had put up prizes of candy, cigars, a speedometer, and a five-pound cheese for responses from the greatest distances.[68]

WLBL reached a milestone in late January 1925, when it received a reception report from a listener in Ogden, Utah, the last of the forty-eight states to contact the station. WLBL was in fact being swamped with such reports, to the point that station management considered abandoning the courtesy of mailing out acknowledgments. WLBL managers reported receiving as many as five hundred letters after a single evening's program and said WLBL had been heard in all Canadian provinces, Puerto Rico, and a city in Mexico.[69] A Canadian railway also contacted the station to say that WLBL was received aboard a passenger train that was traveling through Ontario (by this time a radio receiver was a luxury feature in the lounge cars of long-distance passenger trains in the United States and Canada). Letters arrived in response to the regular Tuesday evening entertainments, and listeners especially enjoyed the *Enemies of Sleep*, which began at midnight on Saturdays. This was an entertainment offering of Stevens Point talent with "instrumental and vocal numbers as well as talks." The idea of having a midnight program dated to the earliest weeks of WCP's testing broadcasts the previous year, and station officials solicited requests from the public for an appropriate name for this "night radio club." The first outing was Saturday morning, March 24, 1924, when the Ripon

College Glee Club put on a one-hour recital.[70] The following week, the still-unnamed program was moved to Sunday mornings.[71] The program developed a club of sorts for its regular listeners. Those sending in a dime would get a lapel button and were granted "all the privileges of the organization." By March 1925 more than one thousand listeners "who keep late hours" had joined the club.[72] How far into Sunday morning this "late late show" aired is not known, although some early episodes were either an hour or ninety minutes long.

Also in January 1925 the station announced that it would be installing broadcast lines between WLBL's studio and both the Lyric and Majestic theaters in Stevens Point. The plan was to broadcast certain concerts and "other entertainments." As had been the case in Waupaca, the station operators had found their Whiting Hotel studio space inadequate to accommodate local musical groups. The estimated thirty dollar cost for installing the lines was to be met through subscriptions, with Stevens Point mayor J. N. Welsby starting the fundraising campaign with a five dollar donation.[73] Fund-raising through subscriptions had also been used the previous year, when the station collected $500 to cover the cost of moving the equipment from Waupaca.[74] A pattern was developing: when a program idea was proposed to WLBL, the station's management would respond with a request for money to fund the project. Although these subscription efforts were probably not mentioned on air, the appeal to listeners for direct financial support of the station employs the same logic as a modern-day pledge drive.

By late 1925 the station's evening schedule included a 6 p.m. program on Mondays and Fridays that featured market summaries and news items, "followed by dinner hour program." On Tuesdays and Saturdays the station aired an 8 p.m. musical program, and *Enemies of Sleep* came on at 11:59 p.m. on Saturdays.[75] A contest held late in the year offered cash prizes for letters promoting the value of the station. Hundreds of entries arrived from many states, with the first cash award given to a resident of Sherwood, Wisconsin, whose topic was "Object and benefits Derived from the Broadcasting of Market and Weather Reports, Frost and Storm Warnings, Cattle Flashes, etc."[76]

Early in 1927 the station needed a new room on the roof of the hotel for its radio equipment. This would allow the station to move the transmitter out of the elevator penthouse and away from the elevator motor, which was interfering with the broadcast signal. Stevens Point officials offered $1,000 to pay for building the new room. As in Waupaca three years earlier, a local resident filed an injunction against the city to prevent it from spending any money on the project and, for good measure, prevented the city from paying the five dollars it had promised to cover the cost of tuning the piano in the WLBL studio. City officials said they could legally use tax money to pay for public concerts to entertain city residents and thought the evening music broadcasts on WLBL met this definition. The sticking point seemed to be whether the broadcasts could be heard by a large enough percentage of the city for the programs to qualify as being "public."[77] A judge upheld the injunction, and city officials briefly pondered a challenge to the ruling but in the end agreed to abide by the restriction. The money for the station was again raised through subscriptions, and station manager Calvert, although disappointed, promised the station would continue as best it could under the circumstances.[78] A new transmitter was installed in the rooftop radio room, which also had office space. The old office space in the basement of the Hotel Whiting was remodeled into a studio.[79]

In March 1927 the Stevens Point Lions Club approached local school officials and requested permission for WLBL to air the regional finals of the state high school basketball contest from nearby Marshfield.[80] Because of a miscommunication the Lions dropped their plans to pay for the broadcast, but the Marshfield Rotary Club stepped in to cover WLBL's costs. This sponsorship may have been acknowledged on air, which could qualify as WLBL's first

(Wisconsin Land of Beautiful Lakes) Station W L B L

Stevens Point, Wisconsin.

Dear Radio Friend:
We acknowledge with thanks your report on our broadcast. Letters, cards, telegrams and telephone calls are always greatly appreciated.
Very truly yours,
Wisconsin Department of Markets.

DESCRIPTION OF W-L-B-L

The 500 watt transmitter is located on Hotel Whiting, and comprises four 250 watt tubes; two as oscillators, and two as modulators, with a 50 watt tube as speech amplifier. The power is furnished by a motor generator unit. The antenna is a T type extending between two steel towers 100 feet in height mounted on the hotel. Located directly under the antenna is a sixteen wire fan shape counterpoise. Musical programs are broadcast from a specially constructed studio located in the hotel.

BROADCAST SCHEDULE ON 278 METERS
—CENTRAL STANDARD TIME.
Market reports are received over the leased wire of the United States Department of Agriculture.
8:45 A. M.—Carlot shipments and Wisconsin Shipping Point information on Fruits and Vegetables. Early Chicago hog flash. Estimated livestock receipts.
9:45 A. M.—Weather forecast. Repetition of 8:45 A. M. Schedule. Late Chicago hog flash.
10:45 A. M.—Weather forecast. Milwaukee, Chicago, and New York butter and egg markets. Chicago potato market. St. Paul hog flash.
11:45 A. M.—Weather forecast. Wisconsin Primary Cheese Market. Wisconsin Cheese Exchange and Farmers' Call Board prices Saturdays only. Chicago livestock market.
12:30 P. M.—Weather forecast. Complete summary of the day's markets. Late news items. Feed quotations Wednesdays and Saturdays only.
1:45 P. M.—Weather forecast. Chicago live poultry. Chicago hay market. Farm news items Mondays only.
3:00 P. M.—Each Tuesday and Saturday, musical programs.
6:00 P. M. Each Monday and Friday, market summary and news items followed by dinner hour program.
11:59 P. M.—Each Saturday, "Enemies of Sleep" program.

WLBL program schedule postcard
WLBL had been mailing out program guide/reception report postcards since its earliest days in Stevens Point. This version was mailed to a listener in Neillsville, Wisconsin, in January 1926 and shows the program schedule in effect at the time, including *Enemies of Sleep*. (Wisconsin Public Radio Collection)

underwriter.[81] More high school basketball was broadcast the following year, but only the Stevens Point–Wisconsin Rapids game and the March tournament were offered because of the costs associated with the broadcasts.[82]

In April 1927 the station was authorized to increase its power to 750 watts, and a new transmitter was put in operation on April 19, still on 1080 kHz.[83] In May the station changed frequencies, to 940 kHz.[84] On October 31 the station changed frequencies again, this time to 900 kHz, authorized for 2,000 watts during the day and 1,000 watts at night.[85]

In the spring of 1927 state senator Herman J. Severson of Iola sponsored a bill to appropriate $12,000 for WLBL, both for operations and for additional equipment. The measure passed the Senate and in July the Assembly concurred. Severson had proposed to make the station "a clearing point not only for market reports but for broadcasting road and weather bulletins and favorable publicity on varied state activities and facilities."[86] The *Stevens Point Daily Journal* called it "one of the distinctly forward services provided at this session" and hoped the bill would receive the signature of Governor Fred Zimmerman. The paper noted that the governor had once been a guest on WLBL.[87]

One item of new equipment contemplated for the station was something called a "general selector transmitter" to be installed at WLBL, with "selector receivers" installed at police departments. In the event of a bank robbery or other crime, WLBL would be notified by wire and sound a general alarm on air. This would set off a "gong" at those locations with the special receivers set for a specific wavelength, which would then be ready to receive the bulletin.[88] The curious setup seems to have aspects of the Cold War–era Conelrad emergency broadcast system, the self-activating weather radios of today, and the recent use of Emergency Alert System (EAS) equipment at broadcast stations for transmitting "Amber Alerts" when a child is abducted.

While awaiting the governor's decision on the measure, WLBL presented a blow-by-blow description of the Jack Dempsey–Jack Sharkey boxing match from Yankee Stadium. For the special event, WLBL manager Calvert sat at a remote microphone in the offices of the *Stevens Point Daily Journal* and relayed details of the fight over the air as they came in on the newspaper's United Press Teletype. Updates were also announced to fight fans gathered outside the newspaper office.[89]

Although both houses of the legislature supported the WLBL appropriation bill, Zimmerman vetoed it on July 23, 1927. He said that if the station's equipment was unsatisfactory, an additional $12,000 "will hardly make it a strong enough station to compete with others now on the air." He further said that WLBL "cannot be spoken of as a competitor to these large stations."[90] Scheduled maintenance continued despite this setback. The station shut down after the last broadcast that day and did not return to the air until Monday, August 15. During the downtime the fourteen antenna wires between the two rooftop towers were replaced.[91]

In late November 1927 WLBL's management ran a contest to collect information about the extent of the station's audience. People who were regular listeners to the market reports were invited to send a letter or card to the station to be included in the station's "roll call," which would also make them eligible to win a prize. To induce people to participate thirty local merchants had contributed prizes, and winners of the drawings were announced on the air Christmas Eve. More than 2,500 listeners were logged from all parts of the state, an impressive number considering that the station had changed frequencies twice since May. The station also asked for suggestions about improving the programming. Many asked for more complete weather reports and information about road conditions.[92]

In early 1928 WLBL was able to take part in a special rail tour. A train was chartered to make a fifteen-day tour of twelve southern states to promote the importance of Wisconsin as a dairying and agricultural state. The trip would start from Madison and travel through San Antonio to New Orleans, returning north through Mobile and St. Louis. On the trip from Stevens Point would be Assemblyman M. J. Mersch and county agent H. R. Noble, representing Portage County. A delegation from Wausau was also making the trip, and the organizers hoped that the two communities would send enough people to fill one of the ten Pullman sleeping cars on the train (a standard Pullman of the era had space for twenty-seven passengers). A committee that included Calvert was formed to plan the station's activities during the tour and to raise money to send the station's representative. Mersch hoped that WLBL would send someone to represent not only the station but the city of Stevens Point. WLBL planned to offer live broadcasts from the trip via phone lines three times a day. The station's management hoped that people in southern cities who saw the live broadcast would tune in to WLBL and thereby have a lasting reminder of Stevens Point. Back home in Wisconsin, schoolchildren were asked to tune in to the special "booster" radio broadcasts and participate in a statewide essay contest. Officials in New Orleans said the train's arrival would be part of the opening day ceremonies for Mardi Gras.[93]

Newspaperman James W. Hull of the *Stevens Point Daily Journal* was chosen to be WLBL's representative on the trip, with daily broadcasts scheduled each day at 8:30 a.m. and between 5 and 6 p.m., with an update during the noon newscast. However, the first scheduled live broadcast on February 8 did not air: a snowstorm moved through Stevens Point the night before, bringing down tree limbs and power lines as well as the fourteen wires of the WLBL antenna on the hotel roof. The WLBL staff thought it could get the station back on the air by noon and certainly by the early evening broadcast.[94] Although WLBL did not request reception reports for these special broadcasts, the station received letters from Brownwood, Texas; Concord, New Hampshire; and Detroit, as well as from points in Pennsylvania and Ontario.[95]

In early 1928 WLBL was off the air for a few days for repairs, and the station's silence prompted a frantic letter from one listener. Station management forwarded it to the *Stevens Point Daily Journal,* which wrote a February 4 story about it headlined "He's Happy Only When WLBL's On." It showed how the rural listeners of central Wisconsin had come to rely on the station and would search the dial for it if it were off the air, figuring it had moved yet again:

> The days are just about ruined for J. J. Horn, Boyd, Wis., if he doesn't get WLBL, state broadcasting station here when he tunes in, according to a letter he has written to the station management. WLBL is now back on its regular schedule after having been down for a number of days while adjustments were being made and a new water cooled tube installed. "We have nearly twisted the dial out by the roots in our radio trying to find WLBL," writes Horn. He says further: "Are you, or are you not in, or on the air? If you are, where? I am afraid my wife will wear that darn machine out if she soon doesn't find WLBL. Would you please answer soon and save wear and tear on our radio? My wife has had some telephone calls asking: 'Can you get WLBL? I can't.' I work six miles from Boyd in Cadott and we watch the weather as I use a car to go down and back and every evening I get the WLBL weather and news from my wife, and now I only hear what babies were born, if any, and who was drunk, or who was sober, if any, and who won the card party prize. If it ain't too much trouble let us know where the trouble is and thank you."

Live broadcasts of local talent continued to be part of the station's offerings. In early July 1928 the small community of Pittsville came to call and offered a Native American powwow as a segment.[96]

WLBL and the staff of the *Stevens Point Daily Journal* collaborated to produce a special broadcast for the state's primary election on September 4. The newspaper staff would collect returns from county precincts, and the Associated Press would compile the statewide numbers.[97]

That same month WLBL announced its plan to move to 570 kHz and share time with WHA in Madison and the *Milwaukee Journal*–owned WTMJ.

However, there is no evidence that WLBL operated on the new frequency before another assignment was made. On October 15 a new arrangement was announced: station WHAD at Milwaukee's Marquette University would shift to the 900 kHz frequency and would share time with WLBL. Fifteen days later, WHAD was moved to 1120 kHz, ordered to reduce power, and forced to share time with Milwaukee commercial station WISN.[98] On November 1, it was announced that WLBL would be reduced to daytime service only. This was in response to General Order 40 of the Federal Radio Commission, issued two days earlier, which reallocated radio frequencies to reduce interference. Different frequencies were designated for local, regional, or clear channel use. WLBL's frequency of 900 kHz was one designated for regional use. However, there was some good news: WLBL would not be required to share time with other stations. As sort of a "last hurrah" for nighttime programming, Calvert himself hosted a four-hour special on the evening of the general election. As had been the case with the earlier election special, the *Stevens Point Daily Journal* teamed up with WLBL for the broadcast.[99]

Although the station was restricted to daytime broadcasting, the program schedule gradually expanded. In February 1930 WLBL planned to begin airing a live concert every Tuesday morning by the Stevens Point High School Band. The concerts aired from 8:15 to 9 a.m. and were scheduled to continue through the rest of the spring semester. The operation was sponsored by the Citizens National Bank, which paid for the installation of the broadcast lines to the high school and assumed their ongoing costs. Bank officials believed the broadcasts would promote interest in the band.[100] The sponsorship of the broadcast was possibly mentioned on air and if so, it might qualify as WLBL's earliest underwriter for regularly scheduled programming. The first concert was broadcast on February 25.[101]

Music programs from community groups continued to be a part of the late afternoon offerings by the station. In the first two months of 1930 groups came to WLBL from Granton, Wausau (twice), Manawa, Fremont, Marathon City, Blenker, Curtis, Larsen, Spencer, and Marshfield. The Wausau YMCA sent a group to perform, as did the Boy Scouts. Also on the station during this period were what Calvert called "educational talks." These were called *U.S. Public Service Health Talks* and *U.S. Radio Service Home Economic Talks*. The health talks aired Wednesdays at 1 p.m. in cooperation with the city's health department.[102] These were probably radio scripts provided by government agencies. In February these were augmented by "several talks furnished by professors of the College of Agriculture of the University of Wisconsin." The station also broadcast two afternoon sessions of the Portage County Farmers' Institute, held in the Fox Theatre and evidently transmitted from that site using remote lines.[103]

Starting March 19, 1930, WLBL and the *Daily Journal* began collaborating to provide a new service. The radio station agreed to broadcast the paper's lost-and-found ads during the noon hour; ads placed by 10:30 a.m. would air that day.[104] A few weeks later the paper reported that a lost dog was returned to its owner because a radio listener had heard the announcement.[105] This down-home program feature continued through much of the 1930s. In the fall of 1930 the station did some more sports broadcasting, airing a high school football game between Stevens Point and Wausau on October 10 and a college football contest between Central State Teachers College and Oshkosh Normal on October 11.[106] (See chapter 8 for the 1930–31 efforts to combine WLBL with WHA in Madison to form a single high-powered station.)

In 1931 WLBL was still on a six-day schedule and broadcast fixed market information at the top of the hour between 8 a.m. and 1 p.m. The station also offered "weather forecasts, frost and storm warnings, forest fire forecasts and police information."[107] The staff assembled a collection of compliments from "fan letters" that demonstrated the station's value to farmers:

> From a listener in Brussels, Wisconsin: "The market reports are of great value to country stores, and farmers. We are posted on egg prices, for when the egg buyers come in, we get top price of the market, and the farmers get the full value of it."
>
> From Rosholt: "It is a saving to all the shippers in this state as well as those states it reaches. The reports save me monthly at least $5.00 in telephone expense."
>
> From Merrill: "Pork took a jump here a while ago and we gained a lot on our hogs by waiting till the broadcast came in. The market broadcast has added plenty of extra dollars to our account."
>
> From Auburndale: "We live on a farm and have no telephone, so we benefit greatly by the market reports, especially poultry, eggs and sheep. I sincerely hope we continue to get them as they mean dollars and cents for us."
>
> From Wisconsin Rapids: "This year before buying our winter supply of potatoes, we listened to the market reports and were rewarded for this precaution."
>
> From Dorchester: "I am a cheese manufacturer and interested mainly in the cheese and butter report which has been beneficial to me. I know I have made money for my patrons by following the daily market outlook."

One Wisconsin Rapids listener said the reports were even benefiting those farmers without radios, because she was transcribing the information for them. The thin profit margin of farming was evident in a letter from a listener in Arpin who wrote: "Words cannot express what a good you are doing over your broadcasting station; your market reports have more than three times paid for the cost of operating this electric radio." A listener in Kaukauna wrote that he'd harvested his cabbages earlier than he'd planned because of a frost warning over WLBL that saved his crop. He said the market reports also made him money. He wrote: "Some weeks ago I took some geese and 50 leghorns to a poultry buyer in Kaukauna. He said he was paying market price at 6¢ and 8¢, so I did not sell as I had listened to your reports and heard they were two cents higher. I took them home and took them to a poultry fair later, and I received above market price. Your reports earned for me the difference of $18.10. So I am surely well pleased with your station."

However, not everyone was happy with the market reports. A Stevens Point listener wrote: "An official of a certain concern that buys farm produce made this remark, 'We could pay the farmers less if it were not for WLBL giving market reports so often.' When I heard that I said to myself, more power and more time to WLBL."[108]

After the consolidation plan with WHA was denied, both state AM stations turned their attention to improving their existing facilities. By this time federal requirements forced WLBL to remove its transmitter from the city of Stevens Point to avoid "blanketing" the broadcast band. The interference from the WLBL transmitter in the center of the city was preventing Stevens Point residents from tuning in to distant stations. Also, a plan was in the works to add stories to the Hotel Whiting, which would require moving the rooftop towers in any event.[109] In response WLBL shut down on Saturday, March 5, 1932, to move to a new location. The new six-acre tower site was in Ellis, about seven miles northeast of the city. A new building to house the 2,000-watt transmitter was built on the site, along with two 150-foot towers. The studios moved from the Hotel Whiting to new facilities in the Midwesco Theatre building, home of the Fox Theatre. Like its space in the Hotel Whiting, WLBL's new home was offered rent-free.[110]

The station signed back on the air at 11:45 a.m. on Monday, May 2, 1932, with a special dedication program featuring broadcasts from WHA. Among the speakers were Harold B. McCarty of WHA; University of Wisconsin president Glenn Frank; Commissioner William F. Renk and Chairman Charles Hill, both of the Department of Agriculture and Markets; O. H. Plenzke of the Department of Public Instruction; and Chris Christiansen, dean of the University of Wisconsin College of Agriculture. The dedication broadcast was also carried over commercial station WIBA in Madison. The debut program continued into the afternoon hours and featured musical acts, including a male chorus from the nearby village of Rosholt and the Stevens Point High School Band.[111]

With the construction of the new transmitter facility in Ellis, it occurred to someone at WLBL that perhaps the towers should be painted bright colors. Correspondence in the WLBL files indicates that the staff decided to check with the federal government on the off chance that it had a standard for tower marking. The government responded with the very specific rules that were then in effect. Unlike today's regulations, which call for alternating bands of white and a particular shade of reddish orange, the 1932 standard specified equal-width bands of yellow and white, separated by black bands half as wide.[112]

The WLBL transmitter facility in Ellis, Wisconsin, ca. 1936
WLBL maintained its transmitter and broadcast towers at this location from May 1932 to June 1937. The towers have been removed, but their concrete footings remain. The transmitter building is now a private home. (Wisconsin Educational Communications Board Archives)

Purely local broadcasting on WLBL ended in 1932. It was already airing some WHA-originated programs that year: in August the Stevens Point station retransmitted WHA's candidate broadcasts on *Political Education Forum* and was "protecting" time slots from 12:30 to 1 p.m. and 6 to 7 p.m. to accommodate them. A letter from Calvert, in response to a letter from WHA's McCarty, indicates that personnel at the Madison station had only a vague notion of the nature of WLBL's program schedule. Calvert outlined a largely indecipherable program lineup, but it included:

> 8 a.m. to 8:15 a.m.—markets and agricultural talks
> 8:15 a.m. to 9 a.m.—music of various kinds
> 9 a.m. to 9:15 a.m.—markets, weather and talks
> 9:15 a.m. to 9:45 a.m.—music and talks
>
> 10 a.m. to 10:15 a.m.—markets (plus home economics talks Mon/Wed/Sat)
> 10:15 a.m. to 10:57 a.m.—organ recital
> 10:57 a.m. to 11 a.m.—Naval Observatory time signals
> 11 a.m. to 11:15 a.m.—markets
>
> noon to 12:45 p.m.—markets, weather, agricultural talks and news items
> 12:45 p.m. to 1 p.m.—Noonday Devotionals
> 1 p.m. to 1:15 p.m.—markets, special announcements and agricultural talks
> 1:15 p.m. to 3 p.m.—various types of music
> 3 p.m. to 4 p.m.—musical and educational talk from State Teachers College
>   (winter)
> 3 p.m. to 3:30 p.m.—various types of music (Wed/Fri)
> 3 p.m. to 4:30 p.m.—various types of music (Thu)[113]

The morning organ recital originated in the Fox Theatre, the same building where the WLBL studios and offices were located. The noonday devotionals featured a variety of area clergy from a wide spectrum of faiths. A regular schedule for the devotionals was for a particular speaker to broadcast three days in a row. One would be on Monday, Tuesday, and Wednesday and the next one on Thursday, Friday, and Saturday.

In early 1933 a broadcast telephone line was leased to connect WHA and WLBL. The handful of previous WLBL rebroadcasts of WHA programs used the signal off-air from Madison. The new line was bidirectional, allowing either station to originate programming for the other. The substantial expense for the telephone line meant it was often a victim of tight budgets: it was removed and restored several times before finally being made permanent in 1942, and it remained in use until 1949. During other times the station reverted to getting the WHA signal off the air and experimented with various antennas and receivers. The experiments were underway by mid-September 1933. The first arrangement was a directional ground antenna consisting of two wires strung two feet above the ground. The antenna was 1,050 feet long and connected to a Brunswick radio receiver. A short broadcast telephone line connected the antenna to the WLBL transmitter about five miles away.[114] The system was devised by radio engineer George Brown. The La Crosse native had recently received his doctoral degree from the University of Wisconsin and was continuing to do research on campus. The total cost for the setup was ninety-five dollars.[115] One shortcoming of this arrangement was that it was only one way. It did not allow for the possibility that WHA would carry any WLBL programs, although it was reported that a similar installation could be made in Madison if the experiment was successful.[116]

In practical terms, during the first months of the shared program schedule, many WHA programs were heard on WLBL and few WLBL-originated programs were rebroadcast by WHA, other than farm market information. A WHA announcer schedule from early 1933 shows that WHA was on the air from 8 a.m. to 5 p.m., Monday through Saturday. WLBL provided WHA programming from 8 a.m. to 9:15 a.m., 10:57 a.m. to 11:15 a.m., and noon to 12:30 p.m. During other times WLBL either carried WHA programs or aired local fare (interestingly, the WHA student announcer assigned to 4 to 5 p.m. on Tuesdays was Willard Waterman, later to be the Great Gildersleeve on radio and TV).[117] In WHA's November 1934 program guide, the Madison station promoted WLBL's carrying of much of the WHA schedule, taking care to mention that both stations were "state-owned." The WHA programs that WLBL added immediately included the *Homemakers' Program* and the *Farm Program,* as well as the Wisconsin School of the Air offerings. During this time WLBL began using a new slogan, calling itself "The Official Agricultural Voice of Wisconsin."[118]

The effects of the Great Depression were being felt in the summer of 1933, and federal officials announced an economy move that would result in WLBL losing access to the federal markets wire service. Some juggling of funds in Washington allowed for restoration of the service to Stevens Point by mid-August.[119]

WLBL's operation also came in for scrutiny from state legislators interested in saving scarce budget dollars. In July Governor Albert Schmedeman signed a bill authorizing a two-year lease of WLBL to interested parties through July 1, 1935. The bill was sponsored by state senator Herman J. Severson of Iola to prevent the sale or shutdown of the station until the state could provide sufficient funds for operation. Offers came in from business interests in Stevens Point and Appleton,[120] as well as from Milwaukee station WTMJ, which at the time had an application before the federal government that called for the elimination of both WLBL and WHA. Another station was also interested in the WLBL frequency: WHBY in Green Bay–DePere.[121] The station was a commercial outlet that had been a non-commercial station until January 29, 1932. It was originally licensed to St. Norbert College and continued to operate as a subsidiary of that institution, offering non-commercial educational programs from area colleges and schools.[122] In mid-November the Portage County Board passed a resolution protesting the attempts by other groups to lease WLBL.[123] In the end the new ground antenna system for receiving WHA programs was what saved the station from being leased to other interests. The broadcast line that had been in use since the beginning of the year had been costing $1,000 per month. The savings from using the ground antenna system allowed WLBL to remain independent, with additional funds from the Department of Agriculture and Markets and the state's Emergency Board. State officials also said that none of the offers for leasing WLBL was satisfactory.[124]

Starting on December 6, 1933, the *Stevens Point Daily Journal,* always a booster of WLBL, began printing a detailed listing of the next day's programs in each issue, usually on page four, the editorial page. Until then the only program material in the paper on a regular basis was a list of the clergy who were presenting the WLBL noonday devotionals for the coming week. Although the full WLBL listing would be dropped for space reasons on occasion, it remained a regular part of the paper until most local programming ended in 1950.

WLBL's new alliance with WHA was not without friction. Calvert mentioned some disagreements in a letter to O. J. Thompson, the secretary of the Department of Agriculture and Markets. Calvert had a complaint about the WHA managers and expressed confusion about who spoke for WLBL. The controversy involved a small point: what could be said over the air during the morning organ recital from the Fox Theatre. The local theater manager had asked Calvert if he could mention on the air which films were playing that evening in the theater. Calvert had said no, but during a visit to Stevens Point in the summer of 1933, WHA's Harold McCarty had given his permission to the theater manager. Calvert told McCarty he was overstepping his authority "as he had nothing whatsoever to do with the operation of this station because of the hookup, and that my instructions were to the contrary." However, the question of the announcements had come up again, because the Fox Theatre staff had cited several instances when they heard WHA announcers (over WLBL) make announcements similar to the ones they were requesting. An exasperated Calvert said he now wanted a ruling on the matter: "So much stress has been laid on the fact that we are non-commercial of late, that I feel both stations should refrain from anything commercial."

Other actions by WHA staff members also bothered Calvert: "Another point raised last summer by Mr. Engel and again referred to in a recent letter from him is the location of the studio here. He suggested, and may have made inquiry of some member of the faculty while here last fall, that we locate in the Teachers College. I explained to him at the time how inconvenient it would be for us due to getting our mail, some reports coming from Chicago through the mail which we broadcast, and also getting bulletins we issue to the post office. So long as we have free space near the postoffice [sic] I feel that we should stay where we are, and will thank you to fully explain the situation to the Commissioners so that they will not fall in line with such a suggestion without having full information and giving the matter consideration from all angles. Also, Dr. Hyer of the Teachers College here, tells me he has recently had two letters from the staff of WHA suggesting they make use of time over this station. He informs me that he replied to the effect that the College was presenting a thirty-minute program each week which was all they cared for." The Teachers College was Central State Teachers College, now the University of Wisconsin–Stevens Point. Indeed, college president Frank Hyer had received a letter from WHA's Harold Engel dated December 14, 1933, urging the college to more fully use the radio facilities at WLBL or WHA.[125]

Calvert summed up his feelings and made suggestions for dealing with the situation: "Doesn't it seem to you that such matters as filling our time would best be left to us, and that some one in WHA is taking too much for granted on programs over this station? These are things I feel that should be ironed out right now before something goes wrong and there is hard feeling. It is my understanding that it was Mr. Hill's intention that we fill time between market schedules with WHA programs, retaining operating policies as in the past, turning over technical supervision of the transmitter to Prof. Koehler. However, if I am wrong on the matter I will appreciate being advised and at the same time, if I am right, I feel that the WHA staff should be instructed to take up through proper channels, either through your office or through this one, such matters as presentation of local programs, and studio location. We are here to cooperate fully on all matters and feel that we should receive the same consideration from the WHA staff."[126]

Thompson passed the letter to Charles L. Hill, chairman of the Department of Agriculture and Markets. Hill went right to the top of the Madison radio operation, writing to Professor Edward Bennett about what he said were "some very delicate matters." With regard to Engel's contacting the college for a new studio location, Hill said: "I can not see what possible business it is of his." He withheld judgment with regard to the matter of McCarty's involvement with the theater announcements and wondered whether it was accurate. Hill said that if it was, "I do not think they should have told the theater that, because I have always said that it was decidedly objectionable." He went on to lament that the connection between the two stations was now only one way and said he was disappointed that "it is not possible for WHA to pick up the markets from Stevens Point and broadcast them, so the whole state can see how mutual the hook-up is."[127]

Calvert received a copy of Hill's letter and wrote back thanking him for the effort. In closing he said: "I hope Prof. Bennett handles the Koehler-Engel-McCarty matters in such a way as not to cause any feeling. They are a fine bunch of fellows and I like them, one and all, personally. They were just a little over-ambitious and meant nothing I am sure."[128] It's interesting to note that Harold McCarty somehow acquired copies of all this correspondence and these items are included in his personal papers.

Still, while this correspondence was underway, McCarty sent a memo to Bennett regarding WLBL. Dated January 8, 1934, it reads: "Perhaps you saw the operating and program logs which Mr. Engel brought from WLBL at the time of his trip to DePere, or no doubt Mr. Koehler has told you of numerous irregularities and interruptions." He added: "Undoubtedly improvements are being made right along, but I still feel that an important change is needed to remedy the situation completely."[129] The log sheets told of numerous failures of the pick-up system used by WLBL to receive WHA programs. McCarty seemed frustrated that he had no way of knowing whether WLBL was pre-empting WHA material for local programs. In a letter to Bennett in February 1934, McCarty wrote: "We never know whether or not WLBL is taking our programs. Some arrangements ought to be made so that we can have a weekly report giving their schedule and the WHA features which they omitted and why. We are working pretty much in the dark here so far as that end of the line is concerned."[130] Clearly, McCarty would have preferred that the Stevens Point station carry WHA material full time.

Harold Engel's "trip to DePere," when he received the WLBL logs, was on December 11, 1933, and Calvert was there as well. Both had traveled to DePere because of a request from St. Norbert College for a power increase and change in frequency for its station, WHBY. It was operating at 100 watts and 1200 kHz but wanted an increase to 1,000 watts and a change to 1360 kHz. To save the expense of having all the interested parties travel to Washington, D.C., for a hearing, a court commissioner took depositions in DePere and forwarded them to the Federal Radio Commission. Both Engel and Calvert testified in opposition, because it was claimed that the approval of the changes to WHBY would result in the elimination of both WLBL and commercial station WGES in Chicago.[131] Ultimately, WHBY remained at 1200 kHz but was eventually granted the right to operate at 250 watts during daytime hours and 100 watts at night.[132]

WLBL began offering a new feature in the early 1930s: live broadcasts of Green Bay Packers football games. The Department of Agriculture and Markets entered into an agreement with station WTMJ in Milwaukee to carry the games, and the decision appears to have been made without consulting WHA's managers.[133] This also marked the first regular Sunday operation of the station since the mid-1920s. The WLBL cooperation with WTMJ in carrying these productions is all the more remarkable given that WTMJ then had an application before the Federal Radio Commission that called for the elimination of WLBL.

WLBL carried at least some games in 1933: a newspaper ad in mid-November lists WLBL as one of four stations carrying the games. Also, a WLBL operating log from that year shows Sunday operation on November 26 and December 3 with the notations "WTMJ pickup, intermittent interference" and "WTMJ very low volume, set not tuned."[134] Both indicate WLBL was receiving the WTMJ signal at a time when the Milwaukee broadcaster was indeed carrying the games, and WLBL probably was using the same radio receiver that it used to pick up WHA at other times. Having the receiver available (and idle on Sundays) may have given WLBL managers the idea of carrying the football broadcasts. The station also carried WTMJ-originated broadcasts of University of Wisconsin football games that fall.[135] These were also carried by WHA in Madison, but WLBL officials might have found the more powerful WTMJ signal of superior quality and preferred it to the usual WHA transmission.

WLBL also carried the NFL games in 1934 but apparently was not ready in time for the season opener against the New York Giants on September 30. The station did air the October 7 game between the Packers and the Detroit Lions.[136] The Packers broadcasts continued on WLBL through the end of the 1938 season, the last one on November 20, 1938, between the Packers and the Giants.[137]

Milwaukee Journal–owned WTMJ had broadcast Packers games as early as November 1929. That first year, announcer Russ Winnie had reconstructed the game in the studio from wire reports, using sound-effects records for the broadcast. By the time WLBL began carrying the games, they were being done in the normal manner, with Winnie calling the game from the site. For at least the 1933 and 1936 seasons the games aired on only four stations: originating station WTMJ in Milwaukee, WLBL, and commercial stations WTAQ in Green Bay and WKBH in La Crosse.[138] WSAU in Wausau and WJMS in Ironwood, Michigan, were added for 1937.[139] Ironwood is so far from Milwaukee (about three hundred miles) that unless the station took the WTMJ feed by telephone line (as WHA in Madison did for the University of Wisconsin's away games),[140] it may have had to rely on the WLBL (or WSAU) broadcast to get the signal. The limited interest in broadcasting the games reflects the place that professional football then occupied in the public consciousness. In the 1930s the big professional sport was baseball, with college football and college basketball also of more interest than the contests of the young National Football League. In the earliest years of Packers broadcasts, WTMJ did not even enjoy exclusive rights: WHBY in Green Bay–DePere also broadcast the games and provided its own announcer.

Neither the Packers nor WTMJ have any records relating to the broadcasts from this early period, but it is known that WTMJ did not begin paying the Packers for broadcast rights until the 1943 season. That year, WTMJ paid the team $7,500 to carry the games. WTMJ continues to produce and distribute the Packers radio broadcasts.[141]

Throughout much of this early period Wadhams Oil Company sponsored the Packers broadcasts. The firm franchised hundreds of Mobil gas service stations in Wisconsin and Upper Michigan, many of which featured pagoda-style architecture with a red tile roof. Wadhams had been involved with radio sports programming since 1929, sponsoring not only the Packers but also college sports broadcasts. The newspaper ads promoting the football series said that on WLBL the broadcasts would be on a "sustaining, non-commercial basis." This was the same arrangement that allowed WHA in Madison to carry WTMJ-originated commercial broadcasts of University of Wisconsin football games during this period.[142] It may have been that this required the WLBL operator to fade down the feed during commercials and substitute local content, like a musical interlude or perhaps an informational segment such as weather or announcements of the next day's programs.

The usual WLBL Sunday operation involved signing the station on at the beginning of the football broadcast and signing off immediately after its completion. However, there is evidence of experimentation with other Sunday programming. On Sunday, November 24, 1935, WLBL went on the air for two hours before the 1 p.m. start of the Green Bay Packers–Pittsburgh Pirates game to present a program from the Veterans of Foreign Wars.[143] This may have been a one-time special, perhaps associated with the Thanksgiving holiday, or it might have been a "make-good" if the program had been preempted previously. Once WLBL stopped carrying the games, the station was silent on Sundays and would remain so until 1956, even though WHA had begun operating on Sundays in 1942.

About the same time that professional football made its debut on WLBL, a local musical ensemble called the Northerners began regular Tuesday afternoon appearances on the station.[144] By late 1937 the group had become known as the WLBL Northerners, promoting the connection with its radio home.[145] Local organizations throughout central Wisconsin would hire the group for dances, and the notation "music by the WLBL Northerners" appeared in newspaper ads during this era. The ensemble continued to enjoy a weekly place in the WLBL broadcast schedule for a number of years.

On June 3, 1935, Calvert submitted the May activity report for the station to his superiors at the Department of Agriculture. It gives a detailed account of the regular operation of the Stevens Point facility, now with the WHA connection in place. He reported that the station was on the air a total of 202 hours and 19 minutes. Locally presented agricultural and market information accounted for 35 hours and 56 minutes. The remainder (166 hours, 23 minutes) was occupied by "educational features and entertainment originating in both the Stevens Point and Madison studios." He reported that about half this time was taken up by programming that originated at WHA via "the Madison pickup," the off-site radio receiver that WLBL used to receive the WHA programs. Twice during the month the pickup arrangement failed, once because a storage battery inexplicably lost its charge and another time because of problems with commercial electric power. On both occasions, Calvert said, the Madison signal became unusable, and the Stevens Point studio aired music from phonograph records.

Calvert said only one speaker from Stevens Point appeared on air during the month, Postmaster F. A. Hirzy, on May 1 to tout U.S. government bonds. In addition to Stevens Point, talent or speakers for WLBL programs during the month came from Tigerton, Waupaca, Knowlton, Galloway, Sherwood, Antigo, Wausau, Necedah, Arkdale, Weyauwega, Edgar, Fremont, Crandon, Mosinee, Marshfield, Nekoosa, Dancy, and Riplinger. He noted that "many of these points were represented by rural school organizations." A planned May 11 remote broadcast of the State High School Band Tournament parade in Wausau was canceled because of rain. Calvert said the $18.50 cost incurred in setting up the wire for the broadcast would be paid by the Junior Chamber of Commerce of Wausau.

The report also shows that the WLBL staff had duties other than broad-, casting: Calvert reported that the staff mailed out market newsletters six days a week throughout the month, in rough batches of 1,025 or 1,490. He said a 30,990 newsletters were issued in all. Regular station correspondence about matters other than music programs totaled sixty-four letters during the month, thirty-one incoming and thirty-three outgoing. The station also received 483 cards and letters, as well as eight telephone calls, about the music programs. Calvert explained that all the calls were long distance as WLBL had adopted a policy of not taking local telephone requests.

Although no new equipment was installed at WLBL during the month, the report notes that a regular monthly frequency test was conducted with the Federal Radio Commission between 4:10 and 4:30 a.m. on May 1. After finishing the test the engineer overslept at the transmitter and as a result the station was ten minutes late getting on the air that morning. The final entry in the report is a note that Calvert had forwarded an application to Washington to increase the station's power to 5,000 watts. He sent application on May 21 and received an acknowledgement of receipt two days later.[146]

Despite Calvert's opposition to moving the WLBL studio to the teachers' college, the campus did become a remote broadcast location. In 1935, the school paper, the *Pointer*, reported that broadcast lines had been installed at two campus locations. The story said: "Wires have been run from the transmitter at Ellis to the auditorium and to the training school in which our main studio is to be located. Plans call for the soundproofing of this room and the broadcasts will be run on a daily basis with several hours each day devoted to the broadcasting of college activities."[147] Having lines direct to the transmitter seems an unwieldy and unnecessarily expensive arrangement. It is more likely that the lines went to the studio at the Fox Theatre so that the WLBL staff could retain control of the signal.

The college presented the weekly *College Radio Hour* with student talent, including a "play of the week" presented in cooperation with the speech classes. Applications to take part in the broadcasts that autumn came in so rapidly that it was impossible to give everyone a proper audition. So the producers decided to devote the last part of the program to "a good old fashioned 'Amateur Contest,'" with "gong n' everything." The judges were selected from the faculty.[148]

Listeners requested so many dedications that WLBL management had to put a rule into effect in March 1936 that limited dedications to one half-hour program each weekday. Broadcast messages for birthdays, anniversaries, and shut-ins would be made only between 8:15 and 8:45 a.m., and the request had to come in by mail over the signature of the sender. The station announced that it would no longer take telephone dedications and that it would not give them on the air during other times.[149] Also, the station was participating with the *Stevens Point Daily Journal* in another endeavor, called *Play Safe*. This feature on safety ran on the editorial page of the paper near the WLBL program listings and was prepared in cooperation with the Safety Bureau of the Stevens Point Police Department. The material in each column was also broadcast over WLBL.[150]

In 1937 the station moved its transmitter site again, prompted by a power increase to 5,000 watts that the Ellis tower location could not accommodate. A consulting engineer recommended two new locations, one in Marathon County north of Marshfield in McMillan Township, and the other in the Wood County community of Auburndale (1930 population: 294). The latter site was chosen primarily because it had better highway access.[151] The decision was not without controversy. When it was announced, long-time WLBL supporter J. W. Dunegan complained, worried that the move would deprive the city of Stevens Point of its radio station. He maintained that the city had sites that offered similar physical characteristics and a move out of the county was unnecessary. The newspaper article about his opposition recounted his earlier successful attempts at blocking station moves and consolidations, and it noted that he had personally offered acreage on his farm in the town of Stockton for WLBL's use.[152]

On June 18, 1937, the transmitter site in Auburndale went into service. The new transmitter, designed by UW professor Glenn Koehler, was built in the university's machine shop, just like the low-cost unit installed at WHA the previous year. A two-story brick building housed the transmitter and other equipment. The total cost of the new plant was $75,000.[153] The new 450-foot tower was said to be the tallest manmade structure in the state at the time.[154] On June 21 the station offered a special program to celebrate the new facility. It included addresses from elected officials and various musical performances, including Evelyn Jansen's Accordioneers, a fourteen-piece accordion band from Antigo.[155] The WLBL building is the oldest structure still in use by Wisconsin Public Radio, and access to the site is via Mill Creek Drive, an unpaved rural township road.

Ten days after WLBL signed on at the new location, the federal government ordered it off the air because of a discrepancy in the station's license application regarding the exact location of the tower. WLBL was off the air for only a day and a half, during which manager Frank Calvert was in contact with Washington to wade through what he said was "yards of red tape."[156]

A few days later, a live afternoon broadcast gave an indication of the continuing importance of farm market reporting over WLBL. At 3:45 p.m. on

July 3, the Liahona Singers of Salt Lake City were in the WLBL studio for a live performance. Their concert had a two-minute "intermission" at 4 p.m. so the station could present the closing prices from the Plymouth Cheese Board, as scheduled.[157]

Also beginning in 1937, visitors to WLBL were asked to sign a guest register. The first signature, on April 22, 1937, is Koehler's, and nearly nine hundred people had signed by the end of the year. The register has more than two thousand names, with the last visitor signing in on October 14, 1972, although the book has no entries between July 29, 1950, and August 17, 1958.[158]

In early 1938 the agricultural cooperative movement got a boost as the Department of Agriculture and Markets participated in Wisconsin Co-operative Week. WHA, WLBL, and fifteen commercial stations in the region, including WLS-Chicago and WCCO-Minneapolis, aired seventy-five special broadcasts.[159]

On Labor Day 1938, WLBL moved its studios from the Fox Theatre to new quarters in the Training School Building of Central State Teachers' College. The college president provided space for two studios, a control room, a reception room, and two offices, with the remodeling expense borne jointly by the Wisconsin Department of Agriculture and the Works Progress Administration.[160] Broadcast telephone lines connected the new studio with the transmitter at Auburndale. Once again WLBL had rent-free studio and office space, but it was responsible for maintenance, repairs, electricity, and the salary of a janitor. WLBL was also required to excavate and build a basement under its portion of the building. This was to include the construction of a ten-by-fourteen-foot room for the station's use, with the balance of the new basement area going to the college.[161]

The office and studio spaces that WLBL abandoned at the Fox Theatre were eventually taken over by WFHR, a commercial broadcaster licensed to Wisconsin Rapids. The towers and transmitter building at the Ellis site caught the interest of a coalition of ten central Wisconsin counties seeking to jointly establish a shortwave police radio facility. The towers are now gone, although their footings remain. The 1932-era transmitter building also survives as a private home and is notable for its unusually thick walls.[162]

The move to the campus seemed to invigorate the radio operation. The result was more inventive local programs along with a new source of radio talent and ideas. During the next few years WLBL developed a wide array of local programs to complement its farm market offerings and the material rebroadcast from WHA. Some of these local efforts were done in cooperation with the college, and many local offerings emulated those produced by WHA.

One innovative local program actually introduced before the move to the college was a weekly fifteen-minute interview with area farmers, conducted in cooperation with county agents and county agricultural committees. Its purpose was "to give Wisconsin farmers, their wives and children an opportunity to present their views and 'swap' experiences over the air, and acquaint the people of this state with a faithful picturization of Wisconsin farm life." The first program in the series debuted November 12, 1937, and featured Peter Van der Ploeg, a farmer from nearby Arpin. He was interviewed by L. G. Kuening, a dairy marketing specialist with the state Department of Agriculture and Markets. Kuening was to "appear in each of these entertainments as an inquiring farm reporter." The series was to include farm families from every county in the state.[163] The letterhead for the station during this era carried a new slogan: "Wisconsin's Pioneer Agricultural Broadcasting Station."[164]

Studio A at WLBL
WLBL's new facilities on the campus of Central State Teachers College in Stevens Point included this large studio. The space was later home to WWSP, the college broadcaster at the University of Wisconsin–Stevens Point. (Wisconsin Educational Communications Board Archives)

Having the station on the campus allowed for involvement by students, who could try out for positions as radio control operators, work with the local college radio programs, and help with recordings. The National Youth Administration paid for some student announcing and clerk positions.[165] One role filled by students was engineering and announcing for the Saturday broadcasts of the college's football games, which were reinstituted in 1939.[166] If no local game was scheduled, WLBL could carry University of Wisconsin football contests from WHA.

The college also developed some programs, which were similar to those from the Wisconsin School of the Air and Wisconsin College of the Air from WHA. One series from 1939 was *This Land of Ours,* which was carried by WHA (and WLBL) as a Wisconsin School of the Air offering.[167] In 1940 the program series *Seeing the Americas* was a travelogue suitable for use by grades seven and eight, and another series, *The Speech Forum,* was also broadcast locally for use in schools.[168]

WLBL lobby, ca. 1938
WLBL's new space on the Central State campus included this lobby/reception area.
(Wisconsin Educational Communications Board Archives)

In late 1938 came the state's decision to transfer WLBL to the University of Wisconsin, as detailed in chapter 13. An executive order to that effect was issued in September, and WLBL's January 1939 application for license renewal named the University of Wisconsin as the new licensee. The reorganization order was voided by the legislature in June 1939, after La Follette lost his bid for reelection. The next month, paperwork was completed to have the FCC reassign the station to the original licensee.[169]

Starting in October 1939, WLBL added two daily newscasts using material from the Associated Press. A program of overnight news aired from 8:05 to 8:45 a.m., and a fifteen-minute afternoon newscast ran at 4 p.m.[170] At that time the Associated Press did not have a radio wire, with broadcast-length stories designed to be read on air. Indeed, until 1941 the AP would supply only written material to radio stations that were owned by AP-member newspapers and then only when the news was of "transcendent importance."[171] WLBL may have convinced the wire service to sell its material to the station, and its noncommercial status may have made such a deal possible. Another possibility is that the station's close working relationship with the *Stevens Point Daily Journal* made the difference. The *Journal* had by this time been an AP affiliate for more than ten years and regularly ran promotional ads for the wire service, touting AP's worldwide reporting staff and national wire network. If the *Journal* did not object to the agreement (or perhaps even advocated it), the AP may have been less reluctant to affiliate with WLBL. It may even have been the case that WLBL staff members simply picked up wire copy at the newspaper (perhaps material the paper had decided not to publish) and that there was no separate Teletype equipment at WLBL.

In late 1940 WLBL and the state Department of Agriculture instituted a clever on-air giveaway to measure the station's coverage area. The contest was an outgrowth of an agriculture department promotion of Wisconsin cheese as a holiday gift idea. For twenty days the on-air contest offered a free package of cheese to the most distant listener who identified the name of the feature: "Cheese for Christmas." WLBL found it had listeners not only in distant parts of the state but also in Michigan, Iowa, Minnesota, Illinois, North Dakota, and Nebraska.[172] The event was reminiscent of the 1923 evening broadcasts on WPAH with prizes for faraway listeners.

During its years on the college campus, the station also offered numerous music programs. *Music You Want,* a local midafternoon offering in the schedule for years, featured "light classical and symphonic music."[173] However, WLBL featured other musical forms and had such programs on the schedule as *American-Scandinavian Music, Rhumba Time, Tea-Time Dancing Party, Gospel*

Singers, South Sea Serenade, Operetta Favorites, Hawaiian Melodies, Polka Time, and *Hillbilly Selections.* A Saturday afternoon program called *Music of Poland* eventually became the responsibility of a group of Polish clergy from area parishes. They would take turns hosting on a rotating schedule and most likely did their announcing in Polish. Local talent programs of all sorts were regularly offered under the umbrella title *Our Neighbors on the Air.*

Other programs with intriguing titles show up in the schedule. A fifteen-minute program called *Postal Oddities* was a late afternoon offering in 1939.[174] For part of 1943 the 9:30 a.m. Saturday program was *Bicycle Traffic Court,*[175] and an early morning program called the *Drink More Milk Club* promoted dairy products.[176] A fifteen-minute afternoon program was featured in 1947 with the curious title of *Rent Control on the Air,* possibly a broadcast of available rental properties.[177] WLBL also had the Stevens Point city nurse on the air with *Wisconsin's Health,* Reverend John T. Kendall as the *Religious News Reporter,* and a program called *The Women's Corner.*[178] The wide variety of locally produced niche programs and the volunteer involvement of area residents gave the WLBL operation the feel of a modern-day community radio station.

In 1941 WLBL began offering its daily 11 a.m. market report to commercial stations. The fifteen-minute program was rebroadcast on WFHR–Wisconsin Rapids, WSAU-Wausau, KFIZ–Fond du Lac, WCLO-Janesville,

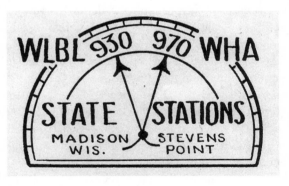

New frequencies for the state stations
WHA was happy to promote WLBL when the Stevens Point station was carrying Madison-originated programs. This graphic from the 1942–43 Wisconsin College of the Air bulletin shows the new frequencies assigned to WHA and WLBL in 1941. (WHA Radio and Television Records/University of Wisconsin Archives)

WIBU-Madison, and WRJN-Racine.[179] Whether this was by rebroadcast of the over-the-air signal or by some sort of telephone connection is not known.

On March 29, 1941, in accordance with the North American Radio Broadcasting Agreement, about 90 percent of the nearly nine hundred AM stations shifted frequency at 3 a.m. eastern time. At the same time the AM band expanded to 1600 kHz. WLBL's long-time frequency of 900 kHz was now reserved for Canadian clear-channel use, and all AM stations between 880 kHz and 970 kHz moved up 30 kHz to between 910 kHz and 1000 kHz on the dial. WLBL ended up at 930 kHz, where it remains to this day. WHA moved at the same time from 940 kHz to its current frequency of 970 kHz.

In 1942 WLBL's owner made the claim that the station was the first in Wisconsin to have a news wire service. The statement is not entirely accurate, because the United Press broadcast wire was available to Wisconsin commercial stations as early as 1936, and WLBL may have already been a subscriber to the AP newspaper wire. However, WLBL may be able to claim that it was the first Wisconsin station to sign up with the new Associated Press broadcast wire service. Beginning on April 15, 1942, the station leased an AP wire and used the material in its six daily newscasts. WHA was close behind in acquiring such service and had an AP Teletype in Radio Hall by mid-July. The Department of Agriculture reported that "the ever-changing world conditions and the necessity of keeping up morale of a well-informed public" prompted the addition of the wire service.[180] The previous year, despite nervousness on the part of member newspapers, the AP had developed its Circuit 7760, a wire service offering material specifically written for radio.[181]

Also in 1942 WLBL bought a transcription disc recorder, which it used at farm gatherings, meetings, and the Wisconsin State Fair, and then broadcast the transcriptions of speeches and interviews. The unit was moved to state Department of Agriculture offices in the State Capitol in 1943 to more easily allow for recordings of university experts, agency officials, and elected officials. WLBL also acquired weekly agricultural features, including *Voice of the Market* and the *Future Farmer Broadcast,* from other sources. These evidently were syndicated program offerings delivered on transcription records.[182]

WLBL played its part in the war effort by training radio operators. In 1941 the station had started a "civilian defense school" to teach local residents and prospective military candidates the fundamentals of radio and both code and voice transmissions. Eighty-five people took the preliminary course, and WLBL reported: "Many graduates of the school are now holding specialists and officers ratings in the United States Army, Navy and Air Force." With the U.S. entry into the war, the school developed into a radio code training school for

"Naval Aviation Cadets training such naval flying squadrons as the 'Fighting Foxes' and the 'Wisconsin Valley Thunderbirds.'"[183]

In April 1943 WLBL further aided the war effort by vacating its large studio A so the Ninety-seventh Air Corps Training Detachment could use it as a barracks. The agreement between the state agriculture department and the college said that if use of the studio as a barracks interfered with WLBL's ability to operate under its FCC permit, the college would provide the station with alternate facilities.[184] Calvert sent a memo to producers of ten local radio programs, with copies to the military unit and the college president, outlining how the change would affect programs, now that the station was limited to using only its smaller studio B. As of May 1, the station would curtail various live talent programs for the duration of the war. Bands would not be allowed, orchestras would be limited to six people, and choruses and dramatics groups could have ten people and an accompanist. For roundtable discussions ten people would be allowed "but all will be required to stand." Calvert said that because of insufficient ventilation in studio B, groups will "find it almost unbearable," but he asked their indulgence and cooperation "until such time as VICTORY is ours and studio 'A' can be made available for our use."[185]

In early 1944 the transcription recordings made by WLBL on agriculture topics caught the interest of WIBA in Madison, whose farm program director requested permission to include them as part of that station's broadcasts. An agreement was reached and WLBL was pleased that the programs would be heard in the southern part of the state, but made no mention of the fact that WHA was not carrying them.[186]

A mishap interrupted WLBL operations in early 1947. On the evening of February 12 the station's 450-foot tower collapsed. An investigation showed that crystallization of a porcelain insulator coupling in one guy wire had led to the failure.[187] Also, the collapse had so badly damaged the tower that it was not salvageable. City and state elected officials as well as representatives of Central State Teachers College and the Department of Agriculture met locally and in Madison to secure funds for a replacement tower. As a stopgap measure, two surplus towers available at Portage, Wisconsin, were brought to Auburndale and installed by workers from the Wisconsin Public Service Corporation. With the temporary towers in place the station returned to the air on March 3 at about 60 percent of its former coverage. Although the station had provided almost no notice that it would be returning to the air, the Department of Agriculture received more than seven hundred cards and letters from happy listeners in forty-four counties during the first week after broadcasting resumed.[188]

The state appropriated $19,500 to pay for a new tower, which was placed in operation on December 22.[189]

In June 1949 WHSF-FM at Rib Mountain (later WHRM) went on the air, and its clear FM signal from fewer than thirty miles away became the source of the WHA programs on WLBL, and the expensive phone line was finally retired. WLBL could also receive the WHA signal from WHKW in Chilton and, later, from WHLA near La Crosse.

In the early months of 1950, confusion surrounded the future of local programs on WLBL. A March 11 report in the *Stevens Point Daily Journal* said the station could "close" and that the WLBL staff members would lose their jobs as of July 1. The report was denied by both Donald Wilkinson, supervisor of radio for the Department of Agriculture, and Harold B. McCarty of the State Radio Council. Wilkinson gave a confusing explanation, saying that "WLBL will be on full instead of part-time on the state network," adding that local origination of programs would continue from the Central State Teachers College's "Radio Workshop," the group that was producing the campus offerings over WLBL.

The true nature of the change was revealed in an Associated Press report from Madison a few days later. The AP, acting at the behest of the *Stevens Point Daily Journal*, had urged Governor Oscar Rennebohm to provide details. He revealed that the plan was to "coordinate" WLBL with the state network. A member of the governor's research staff had worked out a plan with the approval of Donald N. McDowell, the director of the state Department of Agriculture, whose agency held the WLBL license. The plan was for WLBL to carry the FM network feed from Madison full-time, and this would now include the market news service from Madison, which WLBL had carried exclusively. The result was that local programs produced by WLBL personnel and area residents would end. One exception was that those programs produced by the Radio Workshop at Central State Teachers College could continue, and would be allowed to preempt the network feed. Except for two engineers who would remain at the Auburndale transmitter, the WLBL staff would be eliminated, and an attempt would be made to find other jobs for them in state service. The estimated annual savings was $20,000, largely from the personnel reductions and the elimination of wire services to WLBL.[190]

The explanations regarding WLBL's future aroused suspicion among Stevens Point residents. In an editorial, the *Daily Journal* questioned the real motives for the move, noting that if economy was the rationale, there was no reason for the original "evasive and distorted explanation." The paper pointed out that this economic move came at the same time that the state was spending money to expand is FM network. The editorial also predicted that the local programs from the college would be hamstrung once the station staff at WLBL was gone and the line to the transmitter eliminated. Although the college had been told it could still broadcast over WLBL, no one addressed who would pay for the line to the transmitter or for any personnel who might be needed on site in Stevens Point. The editorial also wondered whether agriculture department officials really were in favor of the consolidation or had caved in to pressure, and it asked why the public had had no opportunity to participate in the decision. The editorial ended with a tidbit of history, saying, "It must be remembered that a similar maneuver was attempted many years ago and that when it became known, the public blocked it."[191]

McDowell found himself on the defensive and issued a three-page statement in response to the editorial. He said that the reason for the station's existence was to provide market information and other agricultural information to Wisconsin's farmers, and that "all other programming at the station is incidental to this primary function." He said savings could be realized through the consolidation and that paid announcers often were on the air at the same time in Madison and Stevens Point, often offering identical programs and reading identical newscasts from wire services at each location. He did say that both the college and the city had been afforded opportunities to produce local programs but that he was disappointed by their response. He claimed that having a state radio station could not be justified unless it provided something not available on regular commercial outlets, and the popular music programs over WLBL put the state in the position of competing with commercial enterprises.

He dismissed the call for public participation, saying that personnel and programming decisions are "purely administrative problems." He noted that the number of local WLBL programs had been decreased gradually for the past two years in favor of more Madison-originated programming, and the station had received few complaints. He did say that six letters came in complaining about the dropping of the Naval Observatory Time Signals, but these "were all from jewelry people." A few letters had complained about the elimination of the 4 p.m. newscast, but McDowell noted that a new 5:45 p.m. newscast had been added. McDowell said that all the other letters that had come in expressed approval for the new programs over WLBL.

He promised that the change did not preclude local broadcasts, and he said the Department of Agriculture would continue to pay for the line to the college through the end of the biennium in July 1951. He said that the college could then request money from the legislature to continue the broadcast connection. He closed with a reassurance that the plan was not the work of the University of Wisconsin or the State Radio Council but rather was the work of his department in cooperation with the State Division of Departmental Research.[192]

Confusion about the station's future also reached officials at Central State Teachers College. The principal of an area school wrote college president William Hansen for "authentic information regarding WLBL." The principal said he valued the programs and wanted to work toward their continuance but needed information before proceeding.[193]

Hansen's response shows that the college had been out of the loop as well. Hansen said that Calvert had told him that the station staff would vacate its campus facilities around July 1, 1950. Hansen said that the cost of the broadcast line from the campus to the transmitter was $1,500 a year and that the college could not justify this expense for its two short daily programs. He guessed that the state wanted to do away with the connection completely, with all programming coming from the state FM network. In an unusually candid statement, he pointed out that "the network is under the State Radio Council's direction. The Radio Council is composed of eleven members and the Governor, and eight of the eleven are either members of the University staff or the University Board. This means the so called State Radio Council is really a University of Wisconsin Radio Council and nothing more." He suggested that the best approach was to complain directly to the Department of Agriculture in Madison.[194]

Local groups entered the fray, with the Stevens Point Chamber of Commerce issuing a statement in support of local WLBL programs. The chamber listed all the services that the plan would eliminate, including local programs for the 4-H and Future Farmers of America and the long-running *Morning Devotionals* "for shut-ins throughout central Wisconsin."[195] The chamber urged all residents in central and northern Wisconsin to oppose the proposed changes to WLBL.[196] Stevens Point mayor A. L. Jacoboski appointed a committee to fight the consolidation plan. On it were local aldermen and Frank S. Hyer, who had been president of Central State Teachers College when WLBL moved there in 1938. Hyer made an impassioned plea for action to prevent the station from becoming "WLBL at Auburndale."[197] The Portage County Republican Voluntary Organization also gave its support to WLBL. State senator Oscar W. Neale addressed the group and expressed the opinion that neither the governor nor the State Radio Council had the authority to abolish the local station, because it had been established by the state legislature.[198] The Young Republicans at Central State began circulating a petition to maintain WLBL and scoffed at the state's investment in FM, noting that many commercial stations were discontinuing their FM operations. The editors of the *Stevens Point Daily Journal* also criticized FM as a failure.[199]

In Madison, McCarty was also under pressure and had to respond to Stevens Point assemblyman John Kostuck, who had mailed McCarty clippings from the Stevens Point paper. McCarty's response was that "any questions, doubts or misgivings that have been raised have been most unfortunate, for I can assure you that those in charge have been genuinely motivated by a real concern for the general welfare and nothing else. There is one thing of which you can be certain, and that is that neither the University nor the State Radio Council has made a single move to take over Station WLBL or sever the connection between the transmitter and the city of Stevens Point." He also said he favored retention of the Stevens Point campus studio and the local programs from the college, saying, "A truly representative state radio service should have its roots in all parts of the state."[200]

Hansen also heard from Eugene R. McPhee, the director of the Wisconsin Board of Regents of Normal Schools and a member of the State Radio Council. McPhee said that the transmitter line would remain in place, paid for by the state Department of Agriculture through the end of the biennium. He also said that programs from the college could continue—they would have to be coordinated with the State Radio Council, "but that should not be a problem." McPhee added that the college could offer its studio facilities to local groups, to maintain their "access to the air," and that at the end of the biennium "it will be decided if the Department of Agriculture is to continue the phone line or if new equipment should be installed to make the telephone line unnecessary, etc." McPhee sent a copy of the letter to Neale.[201]

Hansen himself was not sure exactly how long the line would remain in place, whether it would be disconnected at the end of the fiscal year, July 1, 1950, or the end of the biennium, July 1, 1951. He wrote to McDowell at the agriculture department and said that if the line was going to be in place for another year, the college would try to expand its broadcast offerings as much as possible. He invited McDowell to stop by the college at some point to discuss the matter.[202]

In May 1950 the Department of Agriculture and Central State Teachers College reached an agreement to transfer a department employee to the college to serve as program director for the local offerings. Vern Varney Jr. began work at the college on May 29. His plan was to increase the local programming to one and a half, perhaps two, hours per day. The college had won a promise from the state to maintain the line to Auburndale until July 1, 1951, when, the college assumed, it "may be provided a special appropriation to continue the line." In a press release the college said it would continue as much current local programming as possible and add new shows "as rapidly as can be." Furthermore, it was planning to run tests to determine whether the WLBL signal could be picked up by WHRM at Rib Mountain for rebroadcast to the entire state; this would allow a local WLBL program to be heard statewide.[203]

Despite the addition of the new program director, local programs not produced by the college ended the next month. On Saturday, June 17, the Twilight Music Club presented its last broadcast. The local paper said that after the broadcast, the station identification would change from WLBL–Stevens Point to WLBL-Auburndale.[204] Calvert ended his WLBL service on July 1. He had been with the station since June 1924, serving all but three months of its time in Stevens Point. Although he initially planned to retire, he remained with the Department of Agriculture for another year with its markets service.

Because turntables and tape machines had not yet been installed at the Auburndale transmitter, Varney agreed in the interim to have the campus studio provide "fill" around the few remaining local programs from the college. In a memo he noted that when a local twenty-minute program was preempting a thirty-minute WHA offering, the college would program ten minutes of music fill, rather than cut back to the network for a program in progress.[205]

On July 12, Hansen presented a resolution to a meeting of the Board of Regents of the State Normal Schools. He asked authority to split the costs of Varney's salary and the line to the transmitter between the college and the state Department of Agriculture. The request was granted with the board appropriating $2,460. Hansen thought the college could transfer the amount to the Department of Agriculture and it could make all the payments, the college could agree to pay Varney's salary up to that amount, or the agriculture department could pay all but that amount of Varney's salary, at which time he would be transferred to the college. Hansen said that any method that met the approval of the State Auditing Department and Bureau of Personnel would be acceptable.[206] By October, the Department of Agriculture said they would be able to take care of Varney's salary through June 1951.[207]

By early August 1950 Central State Teachers College had arranged to assume the cost of the broadcast line between the campus and the transmitter at Auburndale. The Wisconsin Telephone Company charged $124.50 per month for the line, or $1,494 for a year's service.[208] McPhee, a member of the State Radio Council, tried without success to get it to pay the costs of the college station; in a letter to Hansen, McPhee questioned the advisability of the college's spending $7,500 a year to continue its radio operation. He asked how discontinuing the line would affect the college, whether the people of Stevens Point were getting service equal to the cost of providing it, and whether the college could provide the same service by recording programs on tape and taking them to Auburndale for broadcast.[209] Hansen replied that he had no idea how to estimate the value of the local programs to listeners. While he thought tape recordings might work, he said the savings from doing that would be offset by the need for additional personnel on campus to produce two hours of programming per day. He did say that the college could provide a half-hour per day if "confined to the personnel we formerly used." He closed with a veiled threat: "Since you are a member of the Radio Council, I would like to advise you that the Council will, of course, have to be prepared to indicate that its service does not all stem from Madison. It may be forced in the next session of the legislature to establish its case as a State Radio Council. I am sure the Council is aware of this."[210]

With the broadcast line to the campus still in place, Central State Teachers College continued to produce some programs for WLBL through the first five months of 1951. Its programming aired from 1 to 1:30 p.m. and 3 to 4 p.m. weekdays, and noon to 12:20 p.m. Saturdays. A copy of the radio schedule for the week of January 15–20, 1951, shows the early afternoon program on Monday through Thursday was *Organ Melodies,* while Friday was given over to the *FFA and FHA Program.* The program of January 19 featured the Future Homemakers of America from Weyauwega, Wisconsin, so different chapters of the FHA and Future Farmers of America may have used the time slot. The mid-afternoon hour was made up mostly of programs and series from the college, but the station also aired *Adventures in Research,* a syndicated scientific program provided by the Westinghouse Electric Corporation. These transcription recordings were retained after broadcast and made available for classroom use. The college offerings included the series *Campus Echoes, The Book Corner, Conservation in Wisconsin, The Workshop Players, Education and the Child, Bob's Bandwagon, College Roundtable,* and *Music for You.* The twenty-minute Saturday time slot was held by the *Portage County Farm and Home Program,* hosted by county agent M. P. Pinkerton.[211] For *The Workshop Players* Vern Varney had secured radio plays from the National Scripting Service, and all students participating in the Radio Workshop received college credit.[212] Varney left the college in mid-March 1951 and was replaced by Maurice "Mo" Mead, a Rhinelander native. Mead and Radio Workshop director Gertie Hanson would oversee the final few weeks of local programming.[213]

The final program series produced by the college aired on Mondays and promoted the value of Central State Teachers College to area communities. Each program would feature a different topic presented by a member of the faculty or administration. Each episode would be dedicated to a county seat in the area, a bit reminiscent of the publicity value provided by the evening talent programs on WPAH in 1923. College president William Hansen was the speaker for the program's debut on April 16, 1951, dubbed Stevens Point Day. The series concluded June 4, 1951, with a program dedicated to Shawano that focused on the fine arts.[214]

The June 4, 1951, edition of the series is the last local WLBL program for which there is any record, although programs probably continued through June 8, when the FFA-FHA program would have aired. The line from the college to the transmitter was discontinued that day, even though the Saturday FFA-FHA programs had been scheduled through June 29. Hansen wrote to FFA-FHA representatives in Iola, Auburndale, and Waupaca, apologizing for the cancellation of their appearances. He did say that any future local programs would have to be "magnetic recordings" but that the Auburndale transmitter site was not yet prepared to receive them.[215]

With the discontinuance of the line from the college to the Auburndale transmitter, local programs ended completely. On July 1, 1951, the license for the station was transferred from the Wisconsin Department of Agriculture to the State Radio Council.

The WLBL studio space on the Stevens Point campus eventually became the home of student radio station WWSP, which went on the air in 1968 as WSUS. Ironically, it shared space for several years with Wisconsin Public Radio, when the state network established a news bureau on campus in 1986. The local WPR bureau reporter would use breaks in Madison-originated programs to read local weather and underwriting announcements over WLBL and WHRM-Wausau and for a time presented local newscasts tailored to a central Wisconsin audience. The bureau later moved to a new facility on the campus of the University of Wisconsin–Marathon County in Wausau.

A reminder of WLBL's tenure on the Stevens Point campus is located at the north end of what is now the Communication Arts Center, the building that housed the station from 1938 to 1951. In fading green paint on the stone trim under the first floor windows are three stenciled sets of the legend "WLBL Reserved," marking the station's spaces in a long-gone parking area.

WLBL generated a bit of programming beginning on December 1, 1952, when the *Weather Roundup* was instituted, featuring weather conditions around the state as reported by the engineers at each transmitter site (see chapter 15). WLBL operators contributed to the feature every day until August 20, 1973, and did three final reports in 1976.[216] In 1956 Norman Michie, program coordinator for the State Radio Council, asked the WLBL operators to occasionally use the phrase "located in Wisconsin's headwater country" as part of their morning weather scripts. He said he was passing along a request of the

Wisconsin Headwaters Association, and he asked the operators at WHRM on Rib Mountain to say the phrase during the afternoon *Weather Roundup*.[217] The hand-written weather scripts from October 1967 to July 1976 remain in the WLBL documents collection. They show that operators Joe Selner and Vern Alpine had resurrected the 1924-era slogan "Wisconsin, Land of Beautiful Lakes" for use as an identifier with the call letters.[218]

WLBL also broke away from the state network for a brief period each weekday morning in the mid-1950s, cutting away from the *Band Wagon* program for a short period of what was called *Morning Pops*. Selner suggested that this slot would be a good place to put the repeat of the network program *Dear Sirs*. Its usual Saturday time slot had been eliminated because the FM network and WLBL did not operate that day because of budget cuts.[219]

A new RCA transmitter was installed at WLBL in late 1961 and put on the air the last day of the year. It replaced "Old Betsy," the homemade university-built unit in use since 1937. Over its life, it had operated 71,451 hours, and during the final year of use had only been off the air for repairs and outages a mere four hours and twenty-one minutes. Just a few weeks before it was taken out of service, one of its tubes had been replaced after 19,803 hours of service.[220] The new RCA model BTA-5A transmitter was dubbed "Betty." Although it was superceded by a new solid-state transmitter in 1985, the 1961-vintage unit remains on site and functional as a backup unit. It is usually used during electrical storms, because its design makes it less susceptible to lightning damage.

In 1968 a consultant's report on the state FM network and proposed educational television network recommended the elimination of WLBL, perhaps by selling the facility to an educational institution, such as the college at Stevens Point. The consultants did not specify how much revenue this might generate.[221]

In late 1971, when a program schedule for WHA separate from the FM network was being contemplated, WLBL engineer Vern Alpine thought his station could be part of this idea, at least on an experimental basis, and it would provide central Wisconsin with a second program channel as well. However, not being able to rebroadcast the FM network signal meant the return of the thorny problem of how to get the WHA signal to WLBL. Alpine made the innovative and economical proposal to use the SCA channel to get the WHA programming to WLBL, either as a subcarrier over WHA-FM or having WHLA in La Crosse pick up the WHA-AM signal off air and send it via SCA from there.[222] However, there is no evidence this arrangement was ever put into effect.

Some local programs returned to WLBL in the 1990s. Gil Halsted, Wisconsin Public Radio's Wausau reporter, developed two weekly programs for central

Wisconsin that aired briefly on WLBL. One, *View from the Center,* featured Halsted and the editor of Wausau's weekly newspaper, *City Pages,* in an interview format covering local politics and public affairs, while the other, *It's Not Work, It's Fun,* was a call-in program about gardening. Starting in October 2004, WLBL again presented a local program, a weekly call-in show called *Route 51,* named for the north-south U.S. highway in Wisconsin that serves Madison, Stevens Point, and Wausau. In keeping with the tradition of the *Political Education Forum,* host Glen Moberg interviewed the candidates for U.S. Senate on the debut program, which was also carried on WHBM in Park Falls.

In the mid-1990s a commercial FM station in nearby Clintonville applied to change its frequency from 92.1 mHz to 92.3 mHz. The result of this move was that a low-power FM outlet would become available in the Wausau area at 91.9 mHz, the original frequency of WHSF, later WHRM. Wisconsin Public Radio wanted the frequency. By this time, the organization was offering two program services: one of classical music and NPR news programs and another of call-in programs. In central Wisconsin, WHRM carried the music/news service, while WLBL carried the talk programming. WPR preferred to have an FM outlet for the talk service, because the daytime-only restriction on WLBL meant it signed off as early as 4:15 p.m. in the winter. However, another broadcaster also wanted the frequency. Independent public radio station WXPR in Rhinelander had a 1-watt translator station in Wausau and wanted to replace it with the new station at 91.9 mHz to better serve that city. Management from the two organizations met and decided to jointly build the new station and share time on it, rather than compete for it. WPR's call letters for the station are WLBL-FM, and like its AM counterpart, its license is held by the Wisconsin Educational Communications Board. It carries WPR programming from 3 a.m. to 6 p.m. weekdays and from 5 p.m. to midnight on Sundays. For the balance of the weekend and during weekday evenings, programming on the station originates in Rhinelander with the call letters WXPW-FM.

Despite the addition of the new FM outlet, the daytime-only limitation on WLBL-AM continued to be awkward, with the station often signing off in the middle of a program. The Wisconsin Educational Communications Board applied to the FCC for postsunset broadcasting authority, and the request was granted. By early 2005 the station was allowed to remain on at night at reduced power, marking the first nighttime operation for the station since November 1928.

CHAPTER 19

෴

The Farm Program

A Half-hour of Useful Information

Since its first experimental broadcasts as 9XM, the staff at the University of Wisconsin station had sought to serve the state's rural residents with useful programming and live up to the spirit of the Wisconsin Idea. The earliest telegraphic transmissions from 9XM included the weather forecast (1916) and market reports (1919), both of which were designed to be of use to the state's farmers.

The debut of regular voice broadcasts in 1921 included the weather forecast, joined by the market reports later in the year. Malcolm Hanson approached Andrew Hopkins, a professor in the Department of Agricultural Journalism, to provide additional material about agriculture that farmers would find useful. Hopkins recognized that radio offered unique opportunities to present agricultural information. His department's first contributions consisted of material written specifically for broadcast, which Hanson read on the air during the noontime program, beginning in the spring of 1921.

When the noontime educational broadcasts began in May 1922, topics of interest to farmers sometimes were included, as were home economics topics. The farm programming became more formalized in the summer, when the markets reports were suspended. The university's *Press Bulletin* reported that in their place "a daily talk on agriculture and country life, prepared by the College of Agriculture, will be broadcasted at 12 noon." This would be followed by another half hour with music and the educational broadcast.[1] This move made the agricultural material a scheduled daily segment instead of the short remarks and bulletins presented up to that time. Hopkins and his staff were now responsible for a regular daily program. The summer schedule had the weather forecast at noon, followed by the new agricultural program through 12:15 p.m. After an intermission the regular educational offering began at 12:25 p.m. After the station changed wavelength from 360 to 485 meters, the weather forecast was repeated by both code and voice, and the time signal went out at 12:59.[2] In January 1923 the frequencies were reversed, beginning with the time signals at 11:59 a.m. on 485 meters, weather by code and voice at noon, followed at 12:07 p.m. by the agricultural program. At 12:20 p.m. the educational broadcast was sent at 360 meters.[3] Throughout the 1920s the offerings from WHA included agricultural material, even when the station was limited to one or two days of operation per week. In 1926 Monday evening programs were dedicated to farm and homemaker issues and included *Farm News of the Minute,* presented by F. B. Morrison, assistant director of the Agricultural Experiment Station.[4]

On September 20, 1927, the Agricultural Radio Committee held its first meeting. The group was formed to oversee the agricultural contributions to WHA's programs; its members included Hopkins as well as May Reynolds of the home economics department. At the second meeting the following day someone suggested a hookup with WLBL in Stevens Point and that the weekly program be arranged to have three ten-minute talks, one sponsored by the home economics department.[5] In 1927 the program was officially called the *Agricultural and Home Economics Program* and aired on Mondays from 7:30 to 8:15 p.m. It featured three or four speakers, including one from the home economics department.[6] By the following March the program was featuring area farmers giving first-person presentations on agricultural topics.[7]

In April 1929, when WHA returned to the air after being off for a few weeks, it had a new frequency (940 kHz), and program director Louis Mallory split the homemaker segments off from the agricultural offerings, making two separate programs. For the first week the farm segments aired on Mondays, Wednesdays, and Fridays, but the next week it began a Monday through Saturday schedule.[8] The *Farm Program* would remain a midday offering for nearly forty years.

In 1929 the agricultural program was initially hosted by whomever happened to be the announcer on duty during the noon to 1 p.m. time slot, which was given the umbrella title of *University Noon Hour Program.*[9] For the spring and summer Mallory himself was the host, and for several months the program also aired on Mondays, Wednesdays, and Fridays over WTMJ in Milwaukee, which received it over long-distance telephone lines.[10] In the fall Mallory said he wanted to give up his on-air duties to concentrate on his studies, and graduate student Harold McCarty was hired to be the announcer.[11]

To serve the audience of the program the staff prepared a weekly bulletin and offered it free to anyone who asked to be on the mailing list. By 1931 the station was sending out 1,250 bulletins each week.[12] In 1934 the publication became a monthly booklet. The station used the slogan "A Half-hour of Useful Information" to promote the program.

In 1930 graduate student Kenneth Gapen was assigned to be the program's regular host, and he held the title of radio editor for the University of Wisconsin College of Agriculture.[13] Gapen brought previous radio experience to the job, having presided over a similar program at the Kansas State station, KSAC, in the late 1920s.[14] His master's thesis for the University of Wisconsin was about the agricultural broadcasting being offered by commercial and non-commercial broadcasters. Part of it was a survey of regular listeners of the WHA *Farm Program* that not only asked them about reception but enlisted their assistance to judge a test week of programs. The test programs tried different styles of presentation, which were later incorporated into the program, replacing the standard "talk," which had been the format up to that point.[15] The topics were wide ranging, including land use, marketing, and, of course, the latest in farming techniques as presented by university and government experts. Once the broadcast line was installed between WHA and WLBL in 1933, the Stevens Point station immediately began airing the *Farm Program,* which nicely complemented its other agricultural offerings.

By the mid-1930s the format for the program was well established. It always began with the farm weather forecast, with farm news on Mondays, Wednesdays, Thursdays, and Saturdays. Poultry news was provided each Saturday, and a segment for dairy farmers called "Stretching the Feed Dollar" aired on Thursdays. William Canfield of the Wisconsin Press Association appeared several times a month with "Farm News from beneath the Capitol Dome," and various chapters of the Future Farmers of America would hold "radio rallies" on the program.[16]

Musical interludes were also part of the program, with recordings used in early years, "old-time" fiddlers on occasion, and WHA music director H. Frederick Fuller on hand from time to time with organ pieces. Gapen's listener survey showed nearly two-thirds of respondents preferred to have some music in the program.[17]

Gapen also was the first host to take the program to remote locations, and WHA claimed it was the first station to offer this feature in agricultural broadcasts. He took advantage of WHA's remote lines to many campus locations to offer the live broadcasts. These might include a visit to the university's dairy barn for a description of the correct way to clean milking equipment, a trip to the feed house for an explanation of mixing animal feeds for better results, or a discussion in the laboratory about the study of farm crops and ways to increase yields on Wisconsin farms.[18] In 1934 a jump in pork prices prompted a unique program. Gapen joined livestock man James Lacey in the swine barn to broadcast the actual butchering of a hog, the cutting of the carcass, and the canning of the meat. It was thought that the program would be useful to those who had never done it or had not done it for years and would be attempting it now to take advantage of the higher prices. The demonstration was carefully planned so that listeners would not object to any part of it. Farmers and agricultural workers familiar with the process praised the broadcast as "excellent from all points of view" and said the material was presented clearly and understandably.[19]

Gapen left the program in 1935 to join the U.S. Department of Agriculture. He initially worked for the agency's radio script service, was the principle spokesperson for the USDA from 1946 to 1954, and moved the department into television programming while continuing to be involved with USDA's numerous radio operations.[20]

Gapen was succeeded at WHA by Milton Bliss, a recent graduate of the University of Wisconsin. At times Bliss did double duty, hosting various agriculture series for the Wisconsin College of the Air. For the 1935–36 WCA course *Farming Tomorrow,* Bliss assembled a large group of presenters, scheduling two per program. One guest expert was Aldo Leopold, the chair of game management in the university's department of agricultural economics. For *Farming Tomorrow,* he gave three presentations about "game cropping" and the state's game supply;[21] he had presented short essays over WHA as early as 1929. In 1939, Leopold became the chair of the department of wildlife management, the first department of its kind in the nation. Leopold's posthumously released book of essays, *A Sand County Almanac and Sketches Here and There,* is regarded as a landmark in conservation science and he is considered the father of wildlife ecology. A later WCA agriculture course, *Soils and Men,* was timely, coming on the heels of the Dust Bowl years of the mid-1930s. Bliss hosted this course himself, presenting theories about soil conservation and the problems caused by soil mismanagement.[22] Bliss also was involved with other WCA courses, such as *Farm Science Spotlight, Backgrounds in Agriculture,* and *Agricultural Horizons.*

Research showed that the *Farm Program* was popular and reached its intended audience. By 1941 a survey done by Bliss found regular listeners to the *Farm Program* in sixty-five of the state's seventy-one counties and an analysis of letters to the program indicated that 95 percent of listeners were from rural areas.[23] Remote broadcasts continued from locations like the Wisconsin State Fair, Junior Livestock Exposition, and county dairy-testing laboratories.

Bliss left WHA for military service in 1943, serving in the infantry in France and Germany. Rupert H. Rasmussen filled in as host until Bliss returned in 1946. Rasmussen was familiar to listeners, as he had hosted a segment called "What Our Listeners Are Asking," a regular feature on the program since the 1930s.

When the technology became available, the program used a portable transcription recorder to record interviews and in 1945 used it to make twenty recordings in ten counties.[24] In 1947 the program switched to tape recording.[25]

New features were added to the program over the years. Representatives of nearly every state and national organization related to agriculture found a regular place in the schedule and in 1947 meteorologists at the weather bureau office at Truax Field in Madison began presenting the weather forecast during the program. With the addition of FM stations the reach of the program increased, and in 1948 commercial stations in Madison, Poynette, Beloit, and Neenah were carrying the program live off the air. Such rebroadcasting by commercial stations would continue through 1963. By 1949, the mailing list for the monthly program bulletin numbered over 7,500.[26]

Farm Program *on location*
WHA's *Farm Program* regularly went on location, either as a live program or to record segments for future use. This 1944 photo shows host Rupert Rasmussen visiting a wartime hemp mill. (University of Wisconsin Archives series 23/24/5)

In 1950 the Wisconsin Department of Agriculture began producing two programs to augment the *Farm Program* over the state stations. It added a half-hour program of markets, farm news, and agricultural features weekday mornings at 7 a.m., and a five-minute market report at 9:55 a.m.[27] Also in 1950, Bliss left the program, joining his predecessor Kenneth Gapen at the U.S. Department of Agriculture's Radio-TV Service. In 1952, Bliss became director of the agency's *National Farm and Home Hour,* which aired over the NBC Radio Network. He held that position until July 1960, when the program folded after Allis-Chalmers withdrew their sponsorship.[28] He next worked in agricultural broadcasting at WFIL radio and TV in Philadelphia, but soon returned to his home farm in Hartford, Wisconsin and a position with the Soil Conservation Service.[29] After retirement, Bliss returned to the University of Wisconsin as a student to attend classes as part of the "senior guest auditor" program, which allows Wisconsin residents over age 60 to sit in on UW

Farm Program *advertisement* This advertisement for the *Farm Program* was one of several that ran during 1946 in *Wisconsin Country Magazine,* a publication of the University of Wisconsin's Department of Agriculture and Home Economics. (Wisconsin Public Radio Collection)

classes at no charge. Beginning in 1981, Bliss would drive to Madison several times per week to attend lectures, and over the years attended more than 60 different courses in a multitude of disciplines. As of 2005, this one-time College of the Air host was, at age 95, the oldest of the 41,000 students on the UW campus: a true "life-long learner."

Replacing Bliss at WHA was Maury White. White had been born in Clam Falls, Wisconsin, and had been with the University of Wisconsin agriculture journalism department during the years 1947–49, following that with farm radio experience as a radio specialist with the Ohio extension service and Ohio State station WOSU.[30] White hosted the program through 1968, save for two leaves of absence. The first, in 1957, was to investigate agricultural extension services in other countries,[31] and the other in 1959–60 to finish his doctorate. For this absence, Lloyd Bostian and Harold Parker from the agriculture

Farm Program *host Maury White*
White (right) hosted WHA's *Farm Program* from the early 1950s through 1968. He continued the program's tradition of remote recordings and broadcasts. (Wisconsin Historical Society Archives image WHi-23543)

journalism department filled in during the summer months, and starting in September 1959, Harold King, a Farm and Home Development agent from Marinette County became temporary host.[32]

By the time White became host of the program, the format was well-known to the farm audience of Wisconsin: weather, two seven-minute talks, market quotations, and a weather summary. In 1953 the show aired six hundred studio interviews and 150 field recordings from forty-five Wisconsin counties.[33] By the early 1960s White had developed scheduled specialties each weekday: dairying on Monday, gardening on Tuesday, poultry or a 4-H presentation on Wednesday, "meat animals" on Thursday, and information from the state department of agriculture on Friday.[34]

In 1968, White was promoted to an assistant dean and left the program. Larry Meiller, a student of White's who had filled in for him on the air, was asked to take over temporarily. Meiller continued to host the program while pursuing his doctoral degree and became the permanent host. In September 1968, the program dropped the word "farm" from its title and became the *Midday Report*. It still featured agricultural topics but also included nonagricultural news and features. In 1978 the *Midday Report* merged with *Accent on Living* (formerly the *Homemakers' Program*) to form a new program, *Wisconsin Hear and Now,* the state network's first daily call-in program. Meiller remained a cohost of the new program, which continued to offer farm market reports, agricultural topics, and experts from the University of Wisconsin–Extension. Later still, the program became *Information Radio* and then simply *Conversations with Larry Meiller,* taking on a title similar to those of the other call-in programs on the network.

CHAPTER 20

∾

The Homemakers' Program

When We Talk Over New Ideas on Homemaking

WHA's service to rural Wisconsin was not limited to farmers. Service to home-makers was also a function of the university's Extension Division and was considered as a potential topic for the radio operation. In mid-1922 the new noontime educational broadcasts and those on Tuesday evenings began offering many topics, some of interest to homemakers. The second week of evening broadcasts included Miss A. L. Marlatt with a presentation called "The Profession of Homemaking."[1] In the spring of 1923 WHA began broadcasting six nights per week, and homemaker topics continued: "Food, Nutrition, Health," by Miss H. T. Parsons, assistant professor of home economics, on February 7, and "Making a Home Attractive and Comfortable," by Evelyn Jensen, assistant professor of home economics, on April 6.[2]

Throughout the 1920s WHA continued to offer items of interest to home-makers. On September 21, 1927, the university's new Agricultural Radio Committee suggested that the weekly *Agricultural and Home Economics Program* consist of three ten-minute presentations, one of which was to be from the home economics department.[3]

In April 1929, WHA program director Louis Mallory split the homemaker segments off the agricultural offerings, and the new separate *Homemakers' Program* aired from 10:30 to 11 a.m., the first time that WHA had ever used any hours before noon for regular broadcasting. Originally, the show was on just two days a week, but it then went to a six-day schedule before settling on week-days only and with a 10:15 to 10:45 a.m. time slot. The staff found that scheduling three guests per day was overwhelming for a daily program, so two guests became the norm.[4]

In the early years of the program, various titles were used, both formally and

251

informally. Before finally settling on *Homemakers' Program,* it was variously called *Homemakers' Half Hours, Homemakers' Radio Program, Homemakers' Hour, Wisconsin Homemakers' Hour,* and *Home Radio Program.* Sometimes two different names for the show would appear in the same program bulletin.

The *Homemakers' Program* was the subject of one of the earliest surveys for any WHA offering. On December 28, 1929, while students were home for the holidays, May Reynolds of the home economics department sent a letter to each student in the major. It included a survey form asking about WHA reception, the identity of any station that might be interfering with the signal, and comments about the program. It also included a form to fill out to receive for the weekly program bulletin.[5] As was the policy for the *Farm Program,* a weekly circular available on request listed the topics and guests for each week. By the end of 1929 the *Homemakers' Program* was using a slogan: "When We Talk Over New Ideas on Homemaking."

In the early days, Reynolds was in charge of the program. As it grew, she needed help, so Agatha Raisbeck of the agricultural journalism department added radio to her duties. Announcers for the program were students from various university departments. Raisbeck left the program in July 1930 to join the staff of the *Ladies' Home Journal* and was succeeded by another instructor from her department, Waida Gerhardt, who remained until October 1933. A home economics journalism major, Elsie Onsrud Larson, took over as producer and changed the program's guide from a weekly mailing to a monthly booklet in July 1934. She resigned in September. Sisters Mildred and Marion Anderson handled announcing chores in the early 1930s. After Mildred graduated, Marion continued with the program until June 1933.[6]

Marion Anderson's successor was a woman who would become the person most associated with the program for the next three decades, Aline Watson Hazard. She was a native of Iowa and had spent several years in China while her husband taught at a university there.[7] *Farm Program* host Kenneth Gapen had urged her to audition for the position as an announcer, and she began her long tenure with the program on June 20, 1933. The host had to have grown up on a farm (Hazard had) and had to be a home economics graduate. Hazard's bachelor's degree from Grinnell College was not in home economics, so she enrolled as a student at the University of Wisconsin to get her degree in the field, which was granted in 1940. Hazard served as host, with Gerhardt and later Larson as producers. In September 1934 Hazard and Ruth Milne, a graduate student in journalism, joined the agricultural journalism department as assistants in charge of home radio programs. They faced a heavy schedule of duties. In addition to preparing and presenting the daily radio program, they had to write press releases about home economics, establish a mailing list, answer listener letters, and, for several years, work on programs for the Wisconsin College of the Air.

The Wisconsin College of the Air had entered the home economics field during its first season, with *You and Your Home*. For 1934–35 Hazard and Milne produced a WCA series called *The Girl of Today* and followed it the next year with *Homemaking as a Hobby*. The dramatized series *Air Lanes to Homemaking* aired in 1936–37, and the following year the series *Over at Our House* used the experiences of the fictional Stevens family to illustrate home economics topics. Students in the home economics program participated in these WCA offerings and in writing scripts for the *Homemakers' Program* as well; they received college credit for their efforts.[8]

Throughout the 1930s new ideas were incorporated into the program. One favorite was the Homemakers' Radio Book Club, which grew out of the regular Friday book reviews begun in December 1934. The program often featured authors, particularly those from Wisconsin.[9] By 1948, the segment was called "Invitation to Reading," presented in cooperation with the state Library Commission.[10] In February 1935, the Tuesday version of the show always included a segment on gardening under the title "The Homemakers' Garden Club of the Air." This segment was in response to the popularity of earlier occasional shows on gardening. By the summer, these Tuesday programs often went on visits to area gardens. These remote broadcasts, called "Garden Journeys," used temporary broadcast lines for the "traveling microphone."[11] Starting in 1937, Wednesdays featured "Travel Talks," with discussions about foreign lands. This developed into "Folk Days," which for the first four months of 1938 invited different nationality groups from around the state to share their history, music, and native recipes.[12]

By 1939 the schedule for the *Homemakers' Program* was following a time-tested pattern:

10:00 to 10:05—Introduction of the morning's features and a suggestion for the day

10:05—Pause for WLBL to join program

10:05½ to 10:15—Speaker, forum or interview

10:15 to 10:20—Special announcements and special information period governed by the announcer Home Program Director

10:20 to 10:30—Featured musicale

10:30 to 10:40—Guest speaker, interview, forum, dramatic play or group

10:40 to 10:44½ —Information, future program, closing[13]

The music selections were more than just filler; they followed a definite educational plan. Monday was "Music of Nations"; Tuesday, "Songs That Live"; Wednesday, "This Month in Music"; Thursday, "Music of the Church"; Friday, "Ballroom Melodies"; and Saturday, "Music of the Home." The music was a mix of recordings and live performers.[14] Because the program featured musical selections in addition to the homemaking topics, it was important that its assistant announcers have some knowledge of music.

Also in 1939 special remote broadcasts began using a new technology: shortwave. WHA began operating a mobile shortwave transmitter with the call letters WDAC; its signal could be picked up by a receiver at WHA. This 30-watt unit operated on a frequency of 2790 kHz and was first used for a garden visit on August 15, 1939.[15]

In 1939, the program was honored by the American Association of Agricultural Editors. The group awarded its blue ribbon for the best scripts among the nation's homemakers' programs. In the 1940s two episodes won Ohio State Awards in the "women's program" category—"New Life for an Old Hat" took a first place in 1946 and "Let's Plan and Plant the Home Ground" received an honorable mention in 1947. (The Thanksgiving episode of the WCA home

Homemakers' Program *host Aline Watson Hazard, ca. 1939*
Like the *Farm Program,* the *Homemakers' Program* regularly went to remote locations. Here, Hazard is using a shortwave transmitter to get the program back to the WHA studio. (University of Wisconsin Archives series 23/24/1, negative 26420-C)

economics series *Over at Our House* took an Ohio State Award for educational dramatization in 1941.)[16]

The program's producers continued to be interested in the number and location of listeners. They tried different ways to get a sense of who was listening. In April 1941 the show offered free seeds and drew 700 requests from 255 communities; a ten-day poultry recipe contest the next month brought 1,600 responses.[17] In 1943, 20,000 listeners responded to an offer of a single informational leaflet. Like many WHA programs, the *Homemakers' Program* changed its content after the United States entered World War II, providing segments

Special Circular   January 1939

Homemakers' Hour

10 A.M. EVERY WEEK DAY

January — February
1939

WHA
MADISON____940K.C.
WLBL
STEVENS POINT____900K.C.

WISCONSIN STATE-OWNED STATIONS
EXTENSION SERVICE OF THE COLLEGE OF AGRICULTURE, UNIVERSITY OF WISCONSIN, MADISON.

Homemaker's Hour
program guide
The *Homemakers' Hour* also offered its listeners a free program guide through the mail. This edition from 1939 exhibits the artistic style of WHA publications of the era. (WHA Radio and Television Records/ University of Wisconsin Archives)

on rationing, victory gardens, and the role of women in industrial war work, which was presented in seven live broadcasts "direct from factory floors."[18]

Throughout the 1940s and 1950s the program tried more "traveling microphone" visits to sites around the state, including historic locations, places where some folk craft was performed, or where a Wisconsin industry was in operation. The program regularly used the new technology of tape recording in postwar years.

On September 11, 1951, the program recorded for broadcast a remarkable event near the community of Galloway, about 120 miles north of Madison. Wisconsin Good Neighbor Day was the brainchild of Dr. B. J. Przedpelski, the associate county agent for Marathon and Portage counties. He had come to the United States from Poland and received his doctoral degree from Columbia University. He hoped to use an "agricultural social" to improve a farm in the area. Local farmers selected the farm of Frank Fleece to receive a helping hand. Fleece, his young wife, and two small children lived in a one-room house,

Homemakers' Program *visits a sorghum mill*
Program host Aline Hazard visited this sorghum-processing facility in Prairie du Chien in the late 1950s as part of a series profiling unusual Wisconsin industries. (Wisconsin Historical Society Archives series PH3612, image WHi-23498)

and he had only a small barn as a farm building. With the assistance of Extension Division staff, the Farmers' Home Administration, and local government agencies, hundreds of neighbors descended on the farm to erect a house, large barn, garage, milk house, granary, and machine shed. The blueprints for the new two-story house were drawn by Margaret McCordic, an extension specialist in housing. It had seven rooms, a full basement, and a modern kitchen.

More assistance was provided to the Fleece family. George Ziegler, a horticulture professor, designed a U-shaped drive to circle past the buildings. The volunteers built a pond for the livestock that later became a swimming pool for neighborhood children. The local garden club built a circular stone wall, filled it with soil and seeded it, and then planted trees and flowers. Busloads of schoolchildren arrived to clear stones from the fields.

To serve the volunteers, the county health department set up a first aid station to deal with any minor injuries and the home agent for the county assembled a committee from the local Polish community to feed the more than one thousand people who showed up to help with the project. The county highway department even blacktopped the road leading to the farm to allow easier access to the site. In addition to helping the Fleece family, the event advertised to area farmers and homemakers the assistance available from the university's Extension Division, as well as that provided by local agencies and clubs.[19]

The *Homemakers' Program* continued mostly unchanged for the next fifteen years, remaining a reliable part of the WHA program schedule. Special segments were presented on occasion: in 1957 the program presented a series on weight control, which was recorded for use in schools and as an aid in teaching home economics. The State Board of Vocational and Adult Education helped launch the series in high schools around the state.[20]

As with most WHA programs, commercial stations could request permission to rebroadcast the *Homemakers' Program*. In 1930 WIBA in Madison was the first to retransmit the program. Five stations were still rebroadcasting the *Homemakers' Program* in 1961, which turned out to be the last year that any commercial operation carried the broadcast.[21]

In 1965 Hazard retired from WHA and the *Homemakers' Program*. Her last show was June 11, and she officially retired July 1. She estimated that she had been involved with more than ten thousand broadcasts in the thirty-two years she hosted the program. A grateful WHA management presented her with a tape recorder as a retirement gift, and she moved on to be director of the news bureau for the American Baptist Assembly.[22]

The week after Hazard retired, graduate student Jean Fewster took over as host. She had formerly been director of home economics for Dairy Farmers of Canada.[23] Fewster was later was joined by Norma Simpson. On May 1, 1966, the program took a new name, *Accent on Living*, which recognized that many topics appealed to a broader audience. The new name lasted until 1978, when the show was merged with the descendent of the *Farm Program* to become *Wisconsin Hear and Now,* the network's first daily call-in program.

CHAPTER 21

೧

The Wisconsin School of the Air

The benefits are not limited to the few but are available to all.

Early in the station's history WHA staff members had envisioned using radio to provide educational instruction to schools. Earle Terry had mentioned in correspondence plans to develop programs for schools, perhaps in association with local Parent-Teachers' Associations.

Other university-based radio stations had experimented with programs to be used in classroom instruction. Among the earliest was KSAC at Kansas State College of Agriculture and Applied Science in Manhattan, Kansas. The station went on the air December 1, 1924. By February 2, 1925, the station had added *Rural School Program,* which aired regularly from 9 to 9:25 a.m. weekdays. It consisted of "good" music and discussion of educational subjects to inspire students in rural schools. It also included short music lessons and a period for calisthenics.[1]

Commercial radio broadcasters had also entered the field. WJZ in Newark, New Jersey, had begun airing a weekday series from the New York Board of Education on March 3, 1924.[2] Dr. Walter Damrosch, the conductor of the New York Symphony Orchestra, was drawn to radio and praised it as a great instrument for "spreading the gospel of music." He would host the *Music Appreciation Hour* on the NBC Blue network from 1928 to 1942; at its peak it was being used in 150,000 schools nationwide.[3] Over at CBS the American School of the Air was offered for in-school use, and without commercial sponsorship, from 1930 to 1948. It had a different program each weekday, and the producers had free rein to use any network resources they wished. This led to one well-known incident: when troops from Nazi Germany marched into Austria in 1938, the network was temporarily short of news reporters because Edward

R. Murrow and William L. Shirer were at the time helping to set up a music broadcast for an American School of the Air program.[4]

Interest in using radio for classroom instruction was growing among Wisconsin teachers, but available information was sparse. The *Wisconsin Journal of Education* noted: "All progressive educators have been eager to use the radio as an additional tool for teaching, but the questions when, where and how have been hard to answer."[5] In 1929 WHA managers decided to conduct a formal test of how radio could be used in education. The station applied for a grant from the Payne Fund for $750 to teach music and current events to sixth-, seventh-, and eighth-grade students in rural schools in Dane County. Twenty-five schools would use the broadcasts as part of classroom instruction, and twenty-five would not use the radio offerings and would serve as a control group. The current events program was on Monday, Wednesday, and Friday, with the music program on Tuesday and Thursday. WHA stalwart Edgar Gordon taught the music class, reprising his role as host of a music education program. His Extension Division colleague Mary D. Webb taught the current events radio class.[6]

The ten-week series of programs began March 17, 1930. The experiment was deemed a success and generated considerable interest from around the country, including a mention in the *New York Times,* and the series helped frame the issue of public service broadcasting by state-owned stations and the opposition to monopolization of radio by commercial interests.[7] For the next year, the staff at WHA continued plans to make classroom instruction by radio a regular offering.

In the late summer of 1931 McCarty visited Chicago and met with Judith Waller, manager of WMAQ. The powerful NBC affiliate had been offering in-school programming for Chicago schools for some time. McCarty had also been following the success of the Ohio School of the Air, which debuted in January 1929 over Ohio State University station WEAO and was rebroadcast on some Ohio commercial stations. WHA had even aired some Ohio programs in late 1930 as part of the short-lived experiment in which Ohio programs were transmitted to other educational stations by shortwave. McCarty returned to Madison and boldly announced to the staff that WHA would begin offering a Wisconsin School of the Air beginning that fall.[8]

An article by McCarty in the *Wisconsin Journal of Education* outlined the hope for the series. He wrote: "Many prominent people contend that the real future of radio lies in the direction of its adaptation to educational projects. The radio carries a message instantly to the humblest one-room school house as well as to the palatial city institution. The benefits are not limited to the few

but are available to all. Barriers disappear. In the founding of the Wisconsin
School of the Air the aim was to make accessible to the schools of the state the
work of leading educators and government officials. It serves better to acquaint
the people of Wisconsin with their leaders in thought and shares with them
the benefits of their years of experience, study and research." The article also
took pains to draw the distinction between the WHA programs and educational programs on commercial stations: "Many educational radio programs
have been, and still are, sponsored by commercial enterprises and quite natu-
rally embody advertising. The National Education Association frowns upon
the use of programs which carry advertising into the school room and recently
went on record as opposing the practice. In keeping with the policy of the
state that education shall be free and independent of commercial influences
the Wisconsin School of the Air is unhampered. It is sponsored solely by the
state, county and municipal educational agencies."[9]

The Wisconsin School of the Air debuted the week of October 5, 1931, on
WHA in Madison. The original schedule had two fifteen-minute programs
each weekday, at 9:35 a.m. and 2:10 p.m. The schedule for that first week
demonstrates the wide range of offerings and the appealing way they were
described:

Monday, October 5
9:35 a.m.: You and Your Government (Grades 7, 8, 9)
    "The State Executive Department"
    Governor Philip La Follette (broadcast from the State Capitol)
2:10 p.m.: Counselling [sic] and Guidance (Grades 9, 10, 11, 12)
    "Three Questions of Importance to the Student in Grades or High School"
    F. O. Holt, Registrar, University of Wisconsin

Tuesday, October 6
9:35 a.m.: Dramatization and Stories for Children (Grades 1, 2, 3, 4)
    "Adventures of Mr. And Mrs. Rat and the Child Blackie"
    Miss Carrie Rasmussen, Auditorium teacher, Longfellow School
2:10 p.m.: Wisconsin History (Grades 7, 8)
    "Coming of the White Man"
    E. G. Doudna, Secretary, State Board of Normal School Regents

Wednesday, October 7
9:35 a.m.: Let's Sing (Grades 4, 5, 6, 7, 8)
    Professor E. B. Gordon, University of Wisconsin

2:10 p.m.: Art Appreciation (Grades 5, 6, 7, 8, 9)
"How Can the Study of Art Increase the Joy of Living"
Mr. Walter R. Agard, Vice-president, Madison Art Association

Thursday, October 8
9:35 a.m.: Birds in Autumn and Winter (Grades 3, 4, 5, 6)
Professor R. H. Denniston—University of Wisconsin
2:10 p.m.: What Makes a House a Home (Grades 7, 8, 9)
Miss Katherine Counsell—Home Economics Instructor, Lowell School

Friday, October 9
9:35 a.m.: Health and Safety (Grades 1, 2, 3, 4)
"Some Health and Safety Firsts"
Mrs. Fannie Steve, City Director of Health Education
2:10 p.m. Poetry Club (Grades 7, 8, 9)
Miss Charlotte Wood, Department of English, University of Wisconsin[10]

The first program was about government and featured Wisconsin lieutenant governor Henry A. Huber, who discussed the history and function of the office of governor.[11] Although Huber sat in for Governor La Follette, most WHA publicity materials and in-house legends continue to aver that the governor himself took part in this first broadcast, which used WHA's new studio at the State Capitol.

The WSA programs were developed with the assistance of the state Department of Public Instruction and teachers from the Madison Public Schools, and the service was heavily promoted in periodicals serving the education community in the state. It was thought the programs would be of particular value to Wisconsin's rural one-room schools. In the fall of 1931 more than 138,000 students were attending the state's 6,600 rural schools. More than 1,600 of these schools had fewer than a dozen students.[12] Rural teachers could offer the radio instruction to part of a class and use the time for more intensive instruction for the other students, or the entire class could listen to the radio lesson, giving the teacher a much appreciated break. School of the Air courses in music and art were thought to best augment rural school instruction.

Programs were designed for specific age groups, and at least one program was offered for every grade, with emphasis on kindergarten through eighth grade; more offerings for high school–age students were added late in the decade. Teachers who had experience with an education series on the commercial networks found the WSA programs of more value because they correlated well with what the teachers were doing in the classroom.[13]

Participation was not limited to rural schools: larger schools in cities and towns also used the programs. In 1937, classes in 407 one-room rural schools, 241 elementary schools outside cities, 83 city schools, and 21 special schools of various types heard *Journeys in Music Land*.[14] Many people who attended Wisconsin grade schools through the early 1980s can remember listening to one or more School of the Air programs.

For each program the School of the Air offered teachers study guides, and it encouraged schools to purchase better-quality radio receivers, which educational suppliers made available. In reality, budgets at rural schools during the Depression meant that classes had to rely on consumer-grade radios that sometimes had poor reception. During the early years teachers often brought their radio from home, and some schools held fund-raisers specifically to acquire better radio equipment. For schools without electricity battery-operated radios were the rule, with time rationed to two or three favorite programs to conserve the battery.[15]

WSA personnel made it a point to say that the radio offerings were in no way intended to replace the classroom teacher. Engel wrote: "Radio does, however, strive to place at the disposal of the teacher material which will help her with her work. The belief that an inanimate loudspeaker can substitute for the inspiration-giving personality of the teacher will be entertained only by those lacking in this attribute."[16]

One added benefit was that rural students who took part in the radio courses now felt less isolated and experienced the sense that they were part of a larger community of students. Evidence of this isolation came early in the series: Wayne Claxton was teaching his WSA program *Creative Art* and, as part of the instruction, casually mentioned a football game. In one remote school only one child in the classroom had ever seen a football game in person.[17]

Schools soon found that the WSA programs had additional value. McCarty attended a teachers' meeting in December 1937 and heard that the good listening habits fostered by the WSA offerings were carrying over to regular classroom instruction. Another teacher reported that voluntary outside reading among students had increased 30 to 40 percent because of the WSA programs. Yet another praised the conservation program *Afield with Ranger Mac* and built an entire nature study course around the radio program. Moreover, the students had insisted on starting a school museum because of the series.[18]

The *Ranger Mac* program in particular developed a devoted listenership.

One young girl confined to a wheelchair had collected specimens of nearly every variety of Wisconsin wildflower, which she mounted in a book and presented to Ranger Mac to show her appreciation for the program. In the early 1940s Ranger Mac asked his listeners to see how many bird and animal trails they could identify from his descriptions. Nearly a thousand replies came in, more than half signed by a dozen or more children. Among the replies was one in Braille from a fifth-grade class at the Wisconsin School for the Blind in Janesville.[19]

For the first semester WHA reported 10,850 regular listeners and 7,994 occasional listeners. By the end of the second year of the series, the regular audience had increased to 23,000 pupils. After WHA was connected to WLBL in Stevens Point in 1933, more of the state could hear the programs; 70,000 students used the radio courses in 1938. In the 1943–44 school year 4,613 classes in 2,818 schools were using the programs. The total number of course enrollments was 319,616. Because the average student was hearing more than one WSA program a week, it was estimated that 133,097 students were using the programs, or about 1 in 3 of the state's elementary school pupils. Only two counties in Wisconsin were not represented: Ashland (in the far north) and Pepin (in the far west).[20]

In the fall of 1937 the University of Wisconsin began the Wisconsin Research Project in School Broadcasting, an intensive two-year study of the value of radio as an aid to classroom instruction. The project was funded by a special grant of $41,725 from the General Education Board and was supported by the State Department of Public Instruction, the Wisconsin Education Association, and the State Board of Normal School Regents. The plan was for experimental techniques to be incorporated in regular WSA offerings, with results closely monitored by a research staff and any teachers who wished to participate. The programs selected included *Journeys in Music Land, Afield with Ranger Mac, Neighbors 'Round the World, Community Living, Good Books, English as You Like It,* and *Good Speech.* The final report was published by the University of Wisconsin Press in 1942 under the title *Radio in the Classroom.*[21]

Because the WSA program series were among the first to be prerecorded on transcription records, they could be played several times. In 1941 WHA presented Summer School of the Air weekdays at 5 p.m., with rebroadcasts of the WSA series *This Our Democracy* and the Wisconsin College of the Air series *Our Wisconsin.* Unlike the school-year broadcasts of one episode a week, the summer schedule played them in order Monday through Friday from August 11 through September 18, a schedule that prepared the listeners for the coming school year.[22]

Before the development of the statewide network of FM stations, some programs were offered on transcription records to commercial stations and, in at least one case, directly to a school for playing over its public address system. The first reported use of transcriptions was in 1938–39, when the high school–level program *Good Books* aired over WEBC in Superior. This series also aired over the public address system at Eau Claire High School. In both cases the cities were outside the areas where WHA and WLBL could be heard clearly. The *Good Books* series of recordings even aired in high schools in Evansville, Indiana, as part of the Wisconsin Research Project in School Broadcasting.[23] One transcription record from the 1940–41 WSA series *This Our Democracy* carries a penciled notation on its label of "WHBL 4/8/41," indicating it aired on that commercial station in Sheboygan; it had been broadcast over WHA and WLBL on March 31.[24] A group of school principals from areas that did not have clear reception of WHA or WLBL obtained a special grant from the State Emergency Board to pay for the transcriptions and then arranged to have them played over local commercial stations.[25]

In postwar years more stations signed on for transcription recordings, beginning with WEAU in Eau Claire in 1946. By the next year WLCX in La Crosse and WNAM in Neenah had been added, and WHA had received requests from five other stations.[26] During the next few years WJMC–Rice Lake, KFIZ–Fond du Lac, WRFW–Eau Claire, WLDY-Ladysmith, WMAM-Marinette, WATW-Ashland, and WSBR-Superior also carried WSA programs by transcription. After being returned to Madison, the recorded WSA programs were rebroadcast over WHA at 5:30 p.m. weekdays for a while in the late 1940s, allowing for home listening by schoolchildren.

There is some evidence of commercial stations rebroadcasting some WSA programs off-air before the advent of the FM network. It is known that both WIBA in Madison and WCLO in Janesville carried the year-end music festival of *Journeys in Music Land* in 1938, but this may have been because it was a special event and could be carried on a stand-alone basis.[27]

The development of the statewide network of FM stations between 1947 and 1952 further expanded listenership. Not only were more students able to clearly hear the WSA broadcasts over the new state FM stations, but commercial stations could now simulcast the WSA offerings and avoid using transcription records. In 1949 WATW-Ashland, WEAU–Eau Claire, WJMC–Rice Lake, WMAM-Marinette, WRFW–Eau Claire, and WSBR-Superior were carrying WSA programs by transcription, while WLIN-Merrill, WLDY-Ladysmith, WNAM-Neenah, and WTCH-Shawano were all rebroadcasting a signal from a new nearby state FM station.[28] In 1958, the owners of planned commercial FM station WBKV in West Bend asked WHA for permission to carry the WSA morning programs five days a week, along with other programs from the state network. The station's owners submitted the rebroadcasting authorization in support of their application before the FCC.[29] As with all rebroadcasts, the commercial stations had to identify the source of the program on air and carry it without commercial sponsorship or interruption. As the FM network grew and more schools acquired FM receivers, fewer commercial stations rebroadcast the WSA programs. Only one rebroadcaster remained by 1962, the last year that any commercial outlet participated in the program.[30] However, WYMS, a non-commercial station licensed to the Milwaukee Public Schools, rebroadcast WSA programs for several years beginning in 1978.[31]

One charming anecdote has become part of WHA and School of the Air lore. WHA received a letter from a teacher who found her classroom radio would not work as she warmed it up for *Journeys in Music Land*. Rather than miss the program, she had the children put on their coats and led them outside, where they flagged down a passing car. The teacher asked the driver if he would allow the class to use his car radio for the program. He agreed, the students gathered around his open car doors to sing along with the program, and the driver joined in.[32] Classes taught by Roland Krogstad at the rural Fairview School, east of Ellsworth in Pierce County, also listened to a car radio. As a returning veteran of World War II, he discovered he rated a top place on the postwar waiting lists of those wishing to purchase a new car, so he bought a 1946 Ford with a car radio. Because his school was too poor to buy a radio receiver, he would take his class out to his car every Monday morning to listen to *Afield with Ranger Mac*. He recalled that they "got a little cold sometimes, but we never missed a program."[33]

WHA regularly received letters of appreciation from teachers. This one came from a school that was using the geography program *Neighbors 'Round the World:* "This is just a note to tell you how much we are enjoying the programs which you have planned for our use. The period today ended with 'Is that the end?'— and that in a room with thirty seats occupied by about sixty seventh graders and two teachers. Variety in method of presentation—the various voices and music help to hold the attention of all the pupils. There is a possibility that the entire seventh grade of about one hundred and thirty may be listening next week if a radio can be placed in the auditorium. Other teachers join me in expressing the opinion that your program is very much worth while [*sic*] and most enjoyable. The discussion period after the broadcast revealed that the children had learned a great deal."[34]

Fieldwork to promote the broadcasts continued throughout the series. WHA conducted countywide workshops to develop better use of radio in the classroom. In 1950, 1,135 teachers attended workshops in nine counties.[35] Also, the producers sometimes would travel to a participating school to watch how the children reacted to a program. In this way, the WSA producers gained a sense of which techniques worked well and which ones did not.[36]

Once the companion series Wisconsin College of the Air began in 1933, some of its offerings were also advertised for use in schools, particularly in high school classes. Programs offered as part of both series included *Following Congress, Backgrounds in Agriculture, Contemporary World Affairs, American Life and Books,* and *Better Speech.*

Some of the best-remembered Wisconsin School of the Air programs include:

Journeys in Music Land/Let's Sing

Professor Edgar "Pop" Gordon presided over this program from 1931 to 1955; he had been involved with music programs over the air since the 9XM days. The show debuted as *Let's Sing* during the first week that the School of the Air was broadcast and continued for years on Wednesday afternoons. The title was changed to *Journeys in Music Land* the second week, and it changed often during the early years. Students around the state would sing along with the program, using songbooks that WHA mailed to the schools. For most of Gordon's time as host, his program was the most popular of the School of the Air offerings. After he retired in 1955, the program continued under its original title, *Let's Sing,* first with host Warren Wooldridge and later with hosts Norm Clayton and Lois Dick, joined by long-time WHA music director Don Voegeli at the keyboard. Under both titles the program would go on the road each year and would draw large crowds of local students. In addition to these regional festivals, the program held a "state festival" in Madison throughout much of its history. It was scheduled for the last broadcast of the school year so the children could sing the songs they had practiced since the previous fall. These festivals started out in the university's Music Hall but soon were so large that they had to be held in the campus Stock Pavilion, and ultimately in the Fieldhouse, where about five thousand children participated. It is estimated that more than 800,000 Wisconsin schoolchildren participated in *Journeys in Music Land* during the years 1931 to 1955 alone. As *Let's Sing,* the program aired though May 8, 1974.

Let's Draw

Begun in 1936 as a followup to *Creative Art,* which began in 1932, *Let's Draw* was written by James Schwalbach, but in the early years others would present the scripts he prepared. For much of the series students would select the best works from their class for submission to Madison. A panel would judge the works for inclusion in a traveling art exhibition. From 1946 to 1961 the program held its annual Gathering of the Clan, during which students who had contributed outstanding artwork would come to Madison with their parents and teachers for recognition of their work and a visit to arts facilities on the Madison campus such as the art education department, the Memorial Union Arts and Crafts Shops, and the Student Art Show.[37] Professors from the university and other institutions or teachers from the Madison Public Schools judged the student-submitted works.

The *Let's Draw* episode called "Mystic King of the North" won WHA its first Ohio State Award in 1937. After WHA-TV went on the air in 1954, a version of the program was tried there, and Schwalbach found the art done by radio students was superior to the art submitted by television viewers: the

Professor Edgar B. "Pop" Gordon, host of Journeys in Music Land *Gordon began hosting music programs in the early days of WHA and was there for the first week of Wisconsin School of the Air broadcasts in 1931. (University of Wisconsin Archives series 23/24/1, negative 26207-C)*

radio students used their imaginations, whereas the television viewers were more likely to copy what they saw on screen.[38] The program ran through May 5, 1970.

Afield with Ranger Mac

Wisconsin Dells native Wakelin McNeel was Ranger Mac for this program about nature and conservation topics that debuted on September 25, 1933. A former teacher and school administrator, McNeel was a professor of agriculture and an extension agent overseeing 4-H clubs in the state. He was familiar to WHA listeners, as he had made presentations about nature as early as 1926 on the *Farm and Homemaker* program. His WSA program had particular appeal for teachers and administrators because it allowed their schools to satisfy a 1935 state mandate to provide some sort of conservation education, and

A grade-school class singing along with Let's Sing
Wisconsin School of the Air offerings were used both in rural schools as well as in larger elementary schools. This photo from 1958–59 shows students at a parochial school participating in *Let's Sing*. (Wisconsin Historical Society Archives series PH3612, image WHi-23512)

McNeel adjusted the content of his program to follow the state guidelines. While most programs originated in the WHA studio, McNeel did host some from his garden or from places like a fish hatchery. McNeel appropriated one idea for the program from Australia, where children were planting trees in areas near their schoolyards. He thought it was a great idea for restoring the cutover timberlands of northern Wisconsin. By mid-1944 his schoolage listeners had planted more than seven million trees in 214 school forest plots on twelve thousand acres of the cutover. This number did not include the seedlings planted by children on their own farm woodlots. McNeel believed "a tree planter is a tree protector." In 1942 *Afield* won WHA its first Peabody Award as the finest educational radio program in the country.[39]

Rhythm and Games

Fannie Steve hosted this program of music and activities designed for use by the youngest schoolchildren. She had been on the first week of WSA programs

Let's Draw *host James Schwalbach with student artists in Radio Hall* (University of Wisconsin Archives series 23/24/1, negative 33658-C)

with a program called *Health and Safety* and had done some earlier programs over WIBA in Madison. The *Rhythm and Games* program was touted as "encouraging rhythmic activities in the classroom to develop poise, grace and muscular coordination in children." In 1953 she instituted the Careful Club as part of the program, promoting safety attitudes and habits for primary school children. More than seven thousand children in 211 schools qualified for and received membership badges the first year. Mrs. Steve was ninety years old when she hosted her final program on May 13, 1966.[40]

Story Time for Little Folks

Carrie Rasmussen, a teacher at Madison's Longfellow School, also was on the air during the first week of WSA offerings, and she was "the Story Lady" on *Story Time for Little Folks,* a series that ran through 1938. With her program listing in the first School of the Air bulletin from 1931 was this suggestion: "Miss Rasmussen has found that darkening the room and placing a candle on or near the radio loud-speaker helps greatly in focusing the attention of youngsters."[41]

A sixth-grade class participating in Let's Draw (Wisconsin Historical Society series PH3612, image WHi-23503)

Music Enjoyment

From 1936 to 1952 Elyda Morphy, host of *Music Enjoyment,* taught children to enjoy music in its many forms. Each program had a theme and purpose, and used memory games, music riddles, stories about composers, and demonstrations of different orchestra instruments. This WSA offering had no teacher's manual and did not require teachers to do advance preparation. A course outline was available that listed program themes and the recordings played.

Trailer Travels

Trailer Travels was designed to augment fifth-grade geography studies. It was presented by the WHA Players and dramatized the travels of the fictional Thomas family (which included twin fifth-grade children) as they traveled with a camping trailer around the United States.

Young Experimenters

Begun in 1943 as an attempt to improve science education in the elementary grades, for many years *Young Experimenters* was hosted by a husband-and-wife

Ranger Mac
Wakelin McNeel was Ranger Mac to thousands of schoolchildren. Many remember his program sign-off: "May the Great Spirit put sunshine in your heart today and forevermore. Heap much!" (University of Wisconsin Archives series 23/24/1, negative 47504-C)

team, Mr. and Mrs. Lloyd Liedtke. A classroom evaluation of the program in January 1945 found a shortcoming in the teacher's manual. For a lesson about pendulums, the manual told teachers to have their students bring a piece of string and a nut to class. In this case the nut was supposed to be a metal nut for a metal bolt, yet many children brought walnuts and struggled to tie strings around them.[42]

The fall semester for the 1939–40 school year had this lineup:

> Monday 9:30 a.m.—*Afield with Ranger Mac:* Wakelin MacNeel of the Junior Forest Rangers, explores the out-of-doors, giving lively lessons in Nature and Conservation (Grades 5–8)

A conservation corner
The Wisconsin School of the Air Program *Afield with Ranger Mac* urged students to set up "conservation corners" in their classroom, and the show awarded prizes for outstanding efforts. Here Ranger Mac is inspecting one school's entry in May 1952. (University of Wisconsin Archives series 23/24/3, negative 81668-C)

Monday 2 p.m.—*Living History:* Weekly news analysis—summarizing major state, national and world events, with background material for social studies. A new feature! (Grades 7–12)

Tuesday 9:30 a.m.—*Stories of Peggy and Paul:* Appealing stories of real children help the primary teacher with problems of health and safety education, citizenship, and holiday observances. (Grades 1–3)

Tuesday 1:30 p.m.—*Literature—Then and Now:* A variety of material— books, drama and poetry—is presented in this series. Writings of the past and present are seen in relation to the people who produced them and the times that fostered them. Parallels in literary characters, motives and themes are pointed out for comparison. Both English and American works are included. (Also offered as a course in the Wisconsin College of the Air series) (For high schools)

Rhythm and Games *host Fannie Steve*
Steve began as a Wisconsin School of the Air host in 1931 and remained with the series longer than anyone else. She is pictured here in Radio Hall in 1949. (University of Wisconsin Archives series 23/24/1, negative 51033-C)

Tuesday 2 p.m.—*Let's Draw:* Stimulation and guidance for creative art activities
   are provided in this spirited feature by James A. Schwalbach. (Grades 5–8)
Wednesday 9:30 a.m.—*Nature Tales:* Facts, secrets, and mysteries of nature
   are woven into stories which catch the interest of very young children.
   (Grades 1–4)
Wednesday 1:05 p.m.—*Journeys in Music Land* (Beginning): Professor
   Gordon offers a new singing course for classes which have had no previous
   training. (Grades 4–8)

The WHA Players in Radio Hall
The WHA Players voiced numerous WSA programs, including *Trailer Travels.* This
photo from the 1955–56 school year includes UW student Bill Siemering (behind
the microphone), a native of the nearby community of Sun Prairie, where his grade
school had used WSA programs. His high school speech teacher, Ruth McCarty,
wife of WHA manager Harold McCarty, had encouraged Siemering to apply for a
position at WHA. He went on to manage educational radio station WBFO in
Buffalo, New York, and in 1970 became the first program director for National
Public Radio. He wrote the organization's mission statement and developed the
afternoon newsmagazine *All Things Considered.* (University of Wisconsin Archives
series 23/24/3, negative 96226-C)

Wednesday 2 p.m.—*Journeys in Music Land* (Advanced): Advanced lessons by Professor Gordon in singing, ear training, sight reading, and rhythm. (Grades 4–8)

Thursday 9:30 a.m.—*Music Enjoyment:* Good music and interesting stories are combined to provide pleasurable listening and understanding for primary children. (Grades 2–4)

Thursday 2 p.m.—*This Land of Ours:* Visits in various sections of the United States reveal the geographical and historical influences governing the lives of our people. (Grades 5–7) (Produced by Central State Teachers College in Stevens Point at WLBL)

Friday 9:30 a.m.—*Rhythm and Games:* Directed play activities help children to develop imagination, poise, muscular coordination, and group spirit. (Kgn.—Gr. 3)

Friday 11:30 a.m.—*The French Program:* Sketches, stories, and songs with conversation by persons who speak French natively enrich the study of the language in high schools. (For high schools)

Friday 2 p.m.—*Radio Reading Club:* Vivid stories and dramatizations guide children in the choice and enjoyment of good books. (Grades 5–8)[43]

In 1947 a study was made of the effectiveness of one of the new School of the Air offerings. The series, *Adventures in Our Town* for grades five through eight, had begun in the 1946–47 school year. It provided dramatizations of problems in human relationships, especially in regard to differences in appearance, ability, race, religion, or culture. The National Conference of Christians and Jews financed the study of the show, and early results showed the program did alter attitudes. The organization expressed an interest in establishing a continuing, long-term study of attitudes and prejudices as influenced by radio.[44]

In 1949, in response to requests from mothers, WHA developed some radio programs for younger children based on the WSA model. A daily ten-minute offering called *The Nursery School of the Air* featured games, songs, poems, and stories for the preschool child. On Saturdays the program was twenty minutes long, and it welcomed young children to Radio Hall to participate in the show from the studio. During the summer months the station offered a series of supper-hour programs with stories and music for children.[45]

With the beginning of the fall semester in 1953, School of the Air added a five-minute newscast for use in schools. *News of the Day* was scheduled for 8:55 weekday mornings.[46] In the fall of 1954 WSA tried another experiment. Although some French language instruction had been offered for high school students in previous WSA seasons, a new offering called *Visitons Mimi* was added to provide French instruction for grades two to four.[47] Because repetition was considered important for language instruction, each of the fourteen programs was broadcast twice, on consecutive weeks.[48] A follow-up series called *Revoici Mimi* began the following year. In a rare move these programs were acquired from KSLH, a station operated by the St. Louis Board of Education.[49] For the 1960–61 school year KSLH also supplied WSA with the series *Let's Find Out.*[50] WHA cooperated with the St. Louis station in other ways. In 1962 the St. Louis Board of Education hired WHA to produce a School of the Air series for use in Missouri schools. The history series *Our Missouri Heritage* was

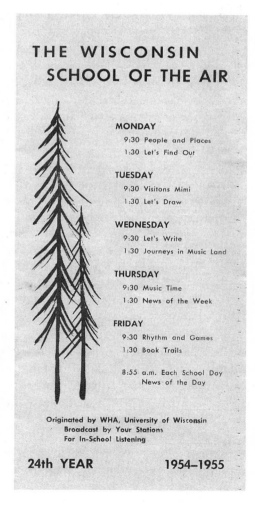

Wisconsin School of the Air bulletin Bulletins were mailed to schools promoting the Wisconsin School of the Air classes for the upcoming year. This one from 1954–55 was the first in more than two decades that did not include *Afield with Ranger Mac,* as Wakelin McNeel had retired that spring. It would also be the last to feature Edgar "Pop" Gordon at the helm of *Journeys in Music Land;* he retired from the program at the end of the school year. (Wisconsin Public Radio Collection)

THE WISCONSIN
SCHOOL OF THE AIR

MONDAY
9:30 People and Places
1:30 Let's Find Out

TUESDAY
9:30 Visitons Mimi
1:30 Let's Draw

WEDNESDAY
9:30 Let's Write
1:30 Journeys in Music Land

THURSDAY
9:30 Music Time
1:30 News of the Week

FRIDAY
9:30 Rhythm and Games
1:30 Book Trails

8:55 a.m. Each School Day
News of the Day

Originated by WHA, University of Wisconsin
Broadcast by Your Stations
For In-School Listening

24th YEAR   1954–1955

produced by WHA, and the only negative feedback involved the way the Wisconsin staff pronounced the word *Missouri*.[51]

As the FM network grew and more schools acquired FM receivers, enrollment in the WSA programs increased as well. From 335,700 course enrollments in 1945–46,[52] WSA had 639,864 enrollments in 1953–54. Again, since many of those participating were enrolled in more than one WSA course, it was estimated this amounted to over 213,000 individual students.[53] By the 1964–65 school year the numbers were 777,000 course enrollments among 311,040 students.[54]

In 1964 WSA began a program of health information for elementary grades. Called *Let's Ask Dr. Tenney*, it featured Dr. H. Kent Tenney, emeritus professor of clinical pediatrics at the University of Wisconsin School of Medicine, and cohost Karl Schmidt. The two had worked together on another medical program, *The March of Medicine*, for much of the decade. *March* was produced in cooperation with the State Medical Society of Wisconsin and offered tape recordings to commercial stations. In 1968 fifty-six commercial stations were carrying the program.[55] The State Medical Society had been involved with health programming over WHA since the 1930s.

In 1966 the U.S. State Department used WHA's expertise in educational radio for a special program series for use in Latin America. The Agency for International Development contracted with the regents of the University of Wisconsin to have WHA create and distribute audiovisual materials to combat the high rate of infant mortality in Latin America. The two-year project was dubbed Operation Niños, and its major thrust was the production of twenty-six fifteen-minute radio programs, called *La Familia Gomez*. The series was produced in Guatemala City and used the activities and experiences of the fictional Gomez family to explore topics, events, and places related to health and nutrition. The broadcasts were aimed at poor peasant farmers and their families, the people with the greatest need for health information. Despite their poverty, research had shown that most had acquired small transistor radios, so the State Department thought that radio was the ideal vehicle for presenting the information. The lead producer was Enrique Arce Behrens, a popular Guatemalan actor, master of ceremonies, and radio-television producer. He studied educational radio in Wisconsin during a visit in 1957 and had stayed in touch with WHA staff members over the years. Through his participation and leadership, the entire series was produced for only fifty-six dollars per program. By the end of the project in 1968, forty-six radio stations in five Central American countries were airing the series. The project also developed brochures, posters, charts, student books, and other instructional materials for direct distribution to children and their parents.[56]

Despite the publicized acclaim for the series, WHA staff members were concerned that the quality of the WSA presentations was slipping, and by 1967 the series was coming in for some criticism. That summer some WHA staff members analyzed the programs and solicited comments from the university's School of Education and the state Department of Public Instruction. Among the comments were "You've lost contact with your clientele" and "You don't really know their needs." WHA decided to make 1967–68 a rebuilding year to put the series back in the mainstream of elementary education in the state.[57]

WSA offered a special program for the 1969–70 school year. Building on the acclaim received for the previous year's *Inner Core* documentaries, WSA offered *The Darker Brother,* a series for grades five and six that focused on race relations in the United States. The course outline said: "These programs intend to sharpen perceptions, to awaken awareness, helping white youngsters become more conscious of their darker brothers and their relations with them. Forces in the past (slavery, primarily, but not only) that separated black and white left a residue in the minds of all Americans—black and white. We must be conscious of that before we can eradicate it. We must be conscious also of the shared humanity that can bring black and white together again."[58] This series was followed *We Are the Other People,* which examined the prejudice experienced by various ethnic groups in the United States.

A sampling of programs from 1968–70 shows these titles: *Reckoning with Boris* (a math program), *Exploring Science, Old Stories and New Ideas, Exploring the News, The Author Is You, Music Time, Worlds of Art, Book Trails, It Happened When, What Is Science? Let's Write, A World of Music, Footsteps of the Free, New World—New Lives, Our Living Language, When Men Are Free,* and *Wisconsin on the Move.* A 1969 survey of all elementary schools in Wisconsin showed that 80 percent were using at least one School of the Air program. Half were also using the School of the Air offerings from WHA-TV.[59]

Some WSA series were offered nationally through the tape service of the National Association of Educational Broadcasters, and later, via the tape service run by National Public Radio in its early years. Those offered by NPR included *The Way It Was, Reckoning with Boris,* and *Everywhere/Everything.*[60]

In later years WHA managers said that the WSA programs had an additional political value. On more than one occasion the series had saved the station from budget cuts. The value of WSA programs would be touted to politicians who questioned the tangible value of the state's radio stations. The programs also provided a practical value to WHA because without WSA programming the station would never have been able to justify such a large staff of producers and writers, who could also participate in other WHA productions.[61]

Despite these successes, the changing environment of public school education in the state led to the gradual discontinuance of the School of the Air. One factor was the wholesale disappearance of rural one-room schools. By the early 1960s the transition to "graded" elementary and junior high schools was nearly complete. By the end of the twentieth century few public schools in Wisconsin fit in the "rural" mold, with multiple ages in the same classroom under a single teacher. One of the last is located on Madeleine Island in Lake Superior, because of the peculiarity of geography. At the same time the new graded schools had more specialized teachers in music and art, reducing the need for radio to provide these services. Also, larger schools had greater access to educational television, films, audiotapes, and videotapes. As schools acquired tape-recording equipment, they could tape WSA programs for later use. Some series required their use within seven days, others within the current school year, while others could be taped and run anytime.

Finally, as the transition to public radio continued, these specialty classroom programs fit less well with the public radio fare. Many School of the Air programs migrated to the network's SCA service. This meant that parents would no longer be able to listen at home to the programs that their children were using in school. After the 1973–74 school year, flagship station WHA-AM ceased airing the WSA programs. By the time school resumed that fall, the Madison AM station was offering a program schedule different from that on the rest of the network, where new WSA programs continued to air. By the time the name Wisconsin Public Radio came into existence, the standard over-the-air broadcast of WSA programs on the network had been reduced substantially. By 1982, the network was airing only three programs: *Book Trails, The Author Is You,* and *Wonderful World of Nature.* The final season of over-the-air broadcasts was 1983–84, with the three remaining programs on Fridays only, running back-to-back in early afternoon.[62] Still, the SCA service offered more than forty other audio series.

When school resumed in the fall of 1984, the audio programs were available only over SCA receivers. The Educational Communications Board charged a subscription fee for the service: thirty dollars per year per school if the school was a member of a state regional service unit, and forty-eight dollars per year per school for nonmembers. Additional receivers could be leased for eighteen dollars a year.[63] The programs now were fed to the schools in the morning, in the belief that schools would be more likely to record the programs rather than use them when fed. Indeed, some series were sent out as a block feed to facilitate taping. Moreover, if a school missed recording a program for whatever reason, the staff could call Madison and request that it be fed again.

The number of programs fed over SCA also began to diminish. The final school year for the service was 1994–95. Among the twenty-four offerings that year were the long-running series *Book Trails* and *Wonderful World of Nature*.[64]

CHAPTER 22

⌘

The Wisconsin College of the Air

At their radios, notebooks in hand, storing up rich wisdom

From the earliest days, those involved with WHA had hoped the station could present the educational riches of the University of Wisconsin over the air. The first attempts were Edgar Gordon's music appreciation program in 1922 and the broadcast of various educational topics that began later that spring. However, as early as 1924 both Earle Terry and William H. Lighty were skeptical about presenting courses over the air for university credit, and Lighty was in no hurry to make an attempt. While he thought that sort of an announcement would make for "sensational headliner stuff," such efforts by others hadn't proved to have much value beyond that. He felt the possibilities for such work were in the future.[1] Some other university stations were experimenting with the concept of college instruction over the air. The University of Nebraska had even offered a two-credit course in business English and letter writing over its station, WFAV, starting in December 1924. Tuition for the course was $12.50.[2]

By the time Harold McCarty took over as WHA manager in 1931, he was concerned about the miscellaneous nature of the station's regular educational offerings. He felt that even a regular listener would have no sense of accomplishment because the programs were so wide ranging.[3] Coupled with this was a genuine concern raised by the Great Depression. Social scientists were growing increasingly alarmed about a generation of talented, able young people idled after high school because they couldn't afford to go on to college.

WHA made some attempts to provide adult education by radio in 1931. In the spring it offered a noncredit course in Spanish on Mondays and Wednesdays at 5 p.m., presented by the Department of Spanish and Portuguese and hosted by Guillermo Guevara, a native of Bolivia and a graduate student in the department. It was so successful that it was repeated in the fall. Also in the fall, a week before the debut of the Wisconsin School of the Air, WHA tried airing instruction direct from a University of Wisconsin classroom. Using the broadcast lines in place to Music Hall, WHA began broadcasting the music appreciation course taught by Dr. C. H. Mills. In the summer of 1932 WHA aired Ford MacGregor's course in American government and politics (see chapter 9).[4] Other offerings included a course in playwriting in the fall of 1932, lectures in aeronautics and in child study in the spring of 1933, and, over that summer, WHA presented the first of two seasons of touch typewriting courses.[5]

While the Wisconsin School of the Air was undeniably successful, its service to elementary school students wasn't really the university's function, whereas presenting university-level educational material to adult listeners was closer to the spirit of the Wisconsin Idea. Using the Wisconsin School of the Air programs as a model, the station decided to offer a similar series called the Wisconsin College of the Air, with formalized instruction during the school year. As much as the School of the Air had been Harold McCarty's operation, the College of the Air would be Harold Engel's. It began on October 2, 1933, offering five courses, each running thirty weeks. The half-hour courses would air at 1 p.m. weekdays over both WHA and WLBL. Each day would have a different course, "selected on the basis of general appeal and need." Here is the lineup for the first season:

Monday: *Farm Life and Living* (discussion of agricultural problems)
Tuesday: *Enjoying Your Leisure* (lessons for a better understanding of the arts)
Wednesday: *You and Your Home* (home economics)
Thursday: *The World about You* (lessons in science)
Friday: *Next Steps for America* (social problems of today)

Cooperating in the project were the State Board of Vocational Education, the State Department of Public Instruction, the State Board of Normal School Regents, the Wisconsin Teachers Association, the University of Wisconsin's Extension Division, the Wisconsin College of Agriculture, the University of Wisconsin School of Education, and the Wisconsin Press Association.

The courses were offered without any tuition or other fees. Those wishing to enroll simply wrote to WHA and requested a course outline. The instructors suggested optional texts for some courses, telling students they could buy the books or simply check their public library for a copy. While the university did not grant credit for these courses (and would not for more than thirty years), it awarded certificates of achievement to any student who took and passed an optional examination at the end of the course.

Although the primary audience was young people of college age, and specifically those who enrolled for the courses, others became regular listeners. Some high school classes used the programs to augment classwork and Wisconsin School of the Air offerings. Indeed, before the decade was out, some College of the Air offerings were "cross-listed" as School of the Air programs, especially for high school students. Also, casual adult listeners followed along, and some university students tuned in to hear professors whose classes they had been unable to take.[6]

One other notable effort in educational programming began in January 1934 as station WOSU at Ohio State University began its Radio Junior College. It started as an emergency project and the motivation for it was the same as the Wisconsin effort. Ohio used federal financing from the Civil Works Administration, the Federal Emergency Relief Administration, and the Works Progress Administration, with the federal agencies providing clerical assistance and fieldworkers from the ranks of the unemployed. In its first three years of existence, the Radio Junior College offered fifty-nine courses, six direct from the classroom. During that period more than 9,300 people enrolled for one or more classes.[7]

Beginning in the fall of 1934, WHA added a second half-hour series each weekday, bringing the total to ten courses. By the end of the year these radio courses were in use in an unexpected venue: prison. WHA's Harold Engel received a letter from John Faville Jr., director of education for the University of Wisconsin Extension Prisoner Education program. He gave Engel a summary of how the courses from the Wisconsin College of the Air (and the Wisconsin School of the Air) were being used at the Wisconsin State Prison in Waupun, about fifty-five miles northeast of Madison. Faville was using some offerings as instruction for the prison's teaching staff, while inmates themselves were taking some courses. During the previous week, prisoners had heard the WSA programs *Science News* and *Wisconsin Pioneer Days* as well as the WCA programs *Everyday Economics, Better Speech,* and *Social Problems.* Faville said the WCA program *Science at Work* was a big hit with the inmates, who, he said, "crowd my office at this time."[8]

In late 1935 WHA made an effort to extend the WCA offerings to formalized listening groups. The idea was being tried in Great Britain, where groups were getting together to discuss BBC programs under the direction of a local leader or teacher.[9] WHA managers thought the varied WCA offerings lent themselves to such formalized listening. Aiding WHA in the effort were the

National Youth Administration, the Wisconsin Works Progress Administration, the State Board of Vocational Education, the State Department of Public Instruction, and local education sponsors, with the NYA and WPA paying clerks in each county and support staff at Radio Hall. Although the afternoon hours of WCA programs were less desirable than evening hours for this purpose, the twice-daily WCA broadcasts (1 and 3 p.m.) allowed one leader to work with two groups per day. The plan called for a preparatory talk to the group to set up the session, listening to the program, then a directed follow-up discussion, including a critique of the broadcast and a short written quiz. During the first semester more than sixteen hundred people in ninety-one groups took part, with the participants located in seventeen Wisconsin counties. The average final exam grades for those in the group project were slightly higher than the average grade for all WCA listeners.[10]

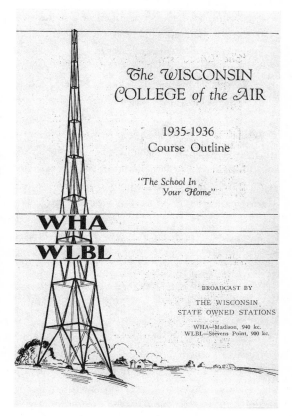

Wisconsin College of the Air bulletin
This graphic design was used in the mid-1930s for Wisconsin College of the Air bulletins as well as for the monthly mailings for the *Farm Program* and the *Homemakers' Program*. The slogan "The School in Your Home" was used throughout the first years of the series. (WHA Radio and Television Records/ University of Wisconsin Archives)

The WISCONSIN
COLLEGE *of the* AIR

1935-1936
Course Outline

"The School In
Your Home"

WHA
WLBL

BROADCAST BY

THE WISCONSIN
STATE OWNED STATIONS

WHA—Madison, 940 kc.
WLBL—Stevens Point, 900 kc.

The WCA offered these courses for the 1939–40 school year[11]:

Monday 1:30 p.m. *Soils and Men*—soil management taught by Milton Bliss of the Wisconsin College of Agriculture (and host of the WHA *Farm Program*).

Monday 3 p.m. *Your Job Outlook*—techniques for finding a job, hosted by John D. McClary of the University of Wisconsin Department of Vocational Guidance.

Tuesday 1:30 p.m. *Literature Then and Now*—books, drama, and poetry hosted by Charles Wedemeyer, teacher at Pulaski High School in Milwaukee and chair of the Wisconsin Education Association English Radio Committee. (This course was also offered as a Wisconsin School of the Air program, particularly for high school students.)

Tuesday 3 p.m. *Following Congress*—dramatizations of topics debated in Congress, taught by Jennie Turner of the State Board of Vocational and Adult Education, assisted by student actors from WHA. (This series in fact spawned a number of members of Congress: Glenn Davis participated in this program series on-air as a student at the university and was elected to the House of Representatives in 1946. In 1957 he was succeeded by Donald Tewes, who had also been a WHA student volunteer.[12] Tewes was defeated in his reelection bid by Robert Kastenmeier, who had participated in the WHA program as a student and who served in Congress until 1991.[13])

Wednesday 1:30 p.m. *Over at Our House*—dramatizations of problems in home economics encountered by a fictional young couple. The course was taught by Alice Hantke of the University of Wisconsin Department of Agricultural Journalism in cooperation with the home economics department. The program's producer was Vic Perrin, who later became known for his numerous appearances on the television series *Dragnet*.

Wednesday 3 p.m. *America through Books*—literature from different regions of the United States taught by Mary Devereaux of the University of Wisconsin Library School.

Thursday 1:30 p.m. *We, The Government*—citizenship, democracy, and public affairs taught by Richard Wilson of the University of Wisconsin's Extension Division.

Thursday 3 p.m. *Contemporary Economics*—roundtable discussions of various issues in modern economics led by Herschel Feldman of the University of Wisconsin Department of Economics under the auspices of Artus, the national honorary economics fraternity.

Friday 1:30 p.m. *World Youth Speaks*—featuring young people from around the world speaking their minds on war, racial problems, employment, government, and the future, hosted by James Flint, student religious leader at the University of Wisconsin. The course featured interviews that Flint had recorded with young people in Europe, as well as in-studio participation by foreign students attending the University of Wisconsin. The program was a follow-up to the previous year's offering, *American Youth Speaks,* which featured recordings that Flint had made throughout the country.

Friday 3 p.m. *Public Discussion Clinic*—advanced speech students demonstrating critical listening and effective discussion skills. The host was Edgar Willis of the University of Wisconsin's speech department.

A major step forward occurred in 1941 when the WHA schedule added several courses that were broadcast directly from classrooms on campus, although these were not technically a part of the WCA offerings at that time. By the fall of 1942 five such courses were in the schedule: *Introductory Sociology, United States at War, Social History of the United States, World Literature,* and *Haydn and Mozart Quartets.* Starting in the fall of 1943, WCA offered both studio programs and those live from university lecture halls. By the late 1940s the majority of WCA offerings were live from the classroom. For a time the 11 a.m. classes were live classroom presentations, while the 2 p.m. offerings were studio programs.

A WCA instructor who became a favorite of listeners' was Philo M. Buck, a professor of comparative literature. He arrived at the University of Wisconsin in 1926 from a teaching post at the University of Nebraska, and he had previously taught high school in St. Louis. Buck was a New Jersey native and a graduate of Gettysburg College, Ohio Wesleyan University, and Harvard. When he was a small child, his parents moved to India to work as missionaries, and the travels of his life provided a worldview for his lectures. He appeared on WHA as early as May 9, 1928, as the host of *Ten-minute Sermonettes on Great Literature;* these were part of the Wednesday evening educational broadcasts.[14] His skill as a teacher served him well in his new broadcasting role, and his studio-based WCA course closely mirrored his regular classroom course in world literature. WHA program director Bill Harley once remarked: "I've never seen Mr. Buck use a script in all the years I've been watching him broadcast. He sits down in a leather armchair before the microphone, lights up his pipe, and just talks. He is one of the best speakers, with one of the most delightful voices we have ever aired." Buck was so popular that when his retirement was announced (it was noted in WHA's January 1947 program guide), students and alumni requested that he stay on, and he continued to lecture in the classroom and through the WCA courses until the spring of 1949, when his health began to fail. When radio listeners learned that these broadcasts might be his last, hundreds wrote to WHA to say how much they enjoyed his lectures. Letters were said to have come "from octogenarians, no longer able to read print well, who were 'uplifted by listening regularly.' Some came from housewives, who 'find a quiet job like darning or dusting the radio,' at 11 o'clock on Fridays. Some came from men and women who had never entered a college, but who sat at their radios, notebooks in hand, storing up rich wisdom." One wrote: "When you finish each lecture I want to rush and write to you—and still I want to sit quietly lest I disturb the inner serenity and sense of beauty you

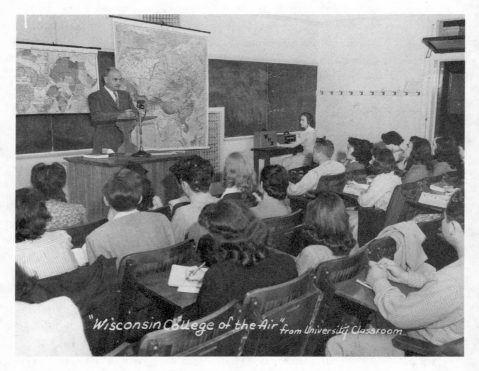

Wisconsin College of the Air live classroom broadcast
Dozens of regular University of Wisconsin classroom courses were offered as part of the Wisconsin College of the Air. This is professor Chester V. Easum lecturing to his history students in the classroom and to the WHA radio audience during an experimental broadcast from the 1941–42 school year. In the fall of 1943 the WCA offered Easum's course called *Backgrounds of World War II* at 11 a.m. on Monday, Wednesday, and Friday. (University of Wisconsin Archives series 23/24/3)

always bring. Thank you for every word—for every lecture."[15] Wisconsin Public Radio's large performance studio in Vilas Hall is named in his honor.

Another instructor who became a hit with listeners was Michael B. Petrovich. His classroom lecture series *The History of Russia* was first broadcast in the spring of 1953.[16] His numerous courses on communism and the Soviet Union were regular offerings, and calls continue to come in to Wisconsin Public Radio from listeners requesting rebroadcasts as well as from people asking to purchase tapes. Petrovich had appeared over the state stations in 1952 on the *Contemporary Trends* program with a lecture entitled "The Way the Communists Think in Russia." Requests for copies of the speech arrived at Radio Hall, some with donations. Two hundred copies were eventually printed and distributed. An army colonel at Wisconsin's Camp McCoy wrote: "This is the clearest explanation I have ever heard of the evolution of communism and the best definition of the communistic gobbledegook that has been presented to the public. Consequently, I would appreciate very much your sending me several copies of the talk for distribution to officers who are charged with presenting information and education lectures to troops on this subject."[17] The Petrovich series called *The Theory and Practice of Communism* aired in the summer of 1967 and generated so much positive mail response from listeners that manager Karl Schmidt said, "He must come close to being the best received lecturer we've ever had on the air."[18]

In the fall of 1945, WCA added the *Freshman Forum*. The University of Wisconsin had begun offering the course in 1940 "to stimulate interest in problems of the modern world and to aid students in orienting themselves to academic life in the university."[19] The format was a twice-weekly auditorium class. On Tuesdays a faculty specialist would lecture on one phase of the semester's topic. On Thursday the lecturer would return to lead a discussion and answer questions from the class, occasionally assisted by a student panel.[20] The program remained in the schedule for many years and was eventually offered for credit. In later years a similar forum from the University of Wisconsin–Milwaukee campus was carried by WHA and the state network. These programs were recommended for high school classes, adult groups, and civic organizations. The programs were also used in formal student listening groups at the University Extension Center campuses in Green Bay, Kenosha, Menasha, Racine, Sheboygan, and Wausau. The success of these groups prompted the Extension Division to organize adult nonstudent listening groups for the program, as had been tried with the WCA programs in 1936.[21]

Unlike the WSA programs, which were designed for use in school classrooms, the WCA programs were designed primarily for individual listening.

As a result, other stations were less interested in requesting the rights to rebroadcast the series, although some of the WCA programs were listed with WSA courses and recommended for use in high schools. WBNB in Beloit briefly carried WCA offerings and some WHA music features by rebroadcast.[22] The station was a commercial outlet originally owned by the *Beloit Daily News* and collaborated with Beloit College on many programs. The station was sold to Beloit College in September 1949 and operated only through the end of the following January.[23] In 1958 WBKV-FM in West Bend, then in the planning stage, applied to WHA to carry the WCA series by rebroadcast each weekday morning. The station highlighted these plans as part of its application before the FCC. It also carried the morning WSA series and the *Weather Roundup*, Monday through Friday.[24]

In later years other campuses began to participate in the series. In the fall of 1957 UW–Milwaukee furnished a course on children's literature and a series on the Indians of North America. The latter also aired during the summer of 1958 and the following fall semester.[25]

Although an early experiment in offering courses for extension credit was tried in 1942 for a series in elementary Spanish,[26] formal Wisconsin College of the Air courses were not offered for regular university credit until February 1966. The first was the ubiquitous freshman course American History: 1865 to the Present. A listener could obtain credit through the Articulated Instructional Media Program at the University of Wisconsin.[27]

The state stations realized another goal in October 1968, when they aired the first credit course in the series to originate at one of the campuses of the Wisconsin State University system. Professor Dean Paul Yambert of Wisconsin State University–Stevens Point offered a one-credit course, *Introduction to Natural Resources*. WSU also offered noncredit courses that fall, including *World Civilizations* from WSU–La Crosse and *History of Wisconsin* from WSU–Eau Claire.[28] (In 1971 the WSU campuses merged with the University of Wisconsin campuses in Madison, Milwaukee, and the UW–run group of two-year center institutions to form today's University of Wisconsin System.)

In 1978 the official name of the series was changed to the University of the Air. The network also explored how to use the network's new expertise in interactive call-in radio for a formal educational program. In the fall of 1981 one University of the Air series took this form. *Working: Changes and Choices* was hosted by UW–Extension faculty members who had in-studio guests and took calls from listeners. This series was part of a University of California extension program called *Courses by Newspaper*. Weekly articles accompanying the series appeared in newspapers around the state, and the course was offered for credit at several state institutions of higher education. Another series that semester was also broadcast live from the studio. An evening course, *A Comparative History of Childhood and Adolescence in Europe and America*, was presented live from the studios in Vilas Hall, reminiscent of the earliest College of the Air studio broadcasts.[29] Another live call-in was offered for credit in the fall of 1982, when Jurgen Herbst, an education professor at UW–Madison, hosted a twice-weekly evening program called *Classroom Conversations on the History of American Education*.[30]

The University of the Air series outlasted the School of the Air series. The University of the Air had to relinquish its weekday afternoon time slot in December 1991, when the Wisconsin Public Radio stations began carrying *Talk of the Nation* from National Public Radio, and the University of the Air programs moved to late evening. By then, taped broadcasts of classroom lectures had been reduced to three days a week, with the other weekdays given over to long-form public affairs programs such as *Cleveland City Club Forum, Alternative Radio, National Press Club*, and *Commonwealth Club of California*.

The University of the Air title was then applied to a weekly series of discussion programs featuring faculty members, and it continued to air over the network. WPR music host and novelist Norman Gilliland cohosts the series with UW–Madison English professor Emily Auerbach. These prerecorded one-hour programs on the guest's particular area of study air on Sunday afternoons over WPR's Ideas Network. On occasion, the shows are presented live and listeners are encouraged to call in.

CHAPTER 23

❧

Chapter a Day

Good books both old and new are read on a daily continued story basis.

The legend goes like this: one day in the late 1920s WHA staff members in Sterling Hall were in a panic as broadcast time approached and the scheduled guest had not appeared, which sometimes happened. The announcer on duty reached into his satchel for a book he had checked out of the library and simply read it on the air to fill the time. Listener response as to what happened next in the book led to the development of what became a signature program for WHA, *Chapter a Day.*

WHA had featured literature readings as early as the noontime educational broadcasts of 1922, when professors would appear on Fridays to read short passages from classical literature. However, these were one-time offerings and not the multiday serialization of entire books that characterizes the *Chapter a Day* program.

The earliest document found with the *Chapter a Day* title is the daily broadcast rundown for July 25, 1932. No book title was listed that first day, but the name of Marianne Smith appears in the listing.[1] It is likely that she was doing the reading: a woman of that name appears in the 1929 and 1931 Madison city directories as a University of Wisconsin student, and alumni records show she was a member of the class of 1932. The program aired for eight days, and the book may have been *David's Day* by Denis George Mackail, a title that appears with some of the daily listings.[2] Later that summer the schedule featured a series called *A Story a Day,* perhaps an error by the person compiling the program list or evidence of testing a different title for the series. It ran for four weeks with reader Helen Darrah.[3]

The program title at this early date seemed to alternate between *Chapter a*

Day and *A Chapter a Day,* but whether this was official or just a lack of precision by the person making out the daily schedule is not known. In the summer of 1932 the program aired at 3 p.m., and in the earliest years it was on in midafternoon in a slot held during the school year by the Wisconsin School of the Air or Wisconsin College of the Air programs. However, for most of its existence it has had a primary airing around midday for the convenience of lunchtime listeners. Its format has changed little: a reading from a book over the course of several weeks. The books usually are divided into a number of segments that is some multiple of five to allow for complete weeks of programming. Appropriate music is added at the end of the reading each day to fill the program out to the scheduled time. For most of its history the program has been thirty minutes long, but running times of fifteen and twenty minutes were also tried in the early days, and twenty-five minutes was the running time for a while in the 1980s to allow time for a National Public Radio newscast at the beginning of the hour. Nearly all the books are read by a single reader, rather than a cast.

The program was done live during its early years, as WHA did not get its first transcription recorder until 1935, and it probably continued as a live program for some time thereafter. A list of books read on the program from the prewar years seems to bear this out. Many of them were not divided in multiples of five and began or ended in midweek. This might indicate that the program was indeed done live with the readers unsure exactly how many days the reading would take. It also appears that in its earliest years, some readings were done by University of Wisconsin students rather than by the full-time staff at WHA.

Until 1939 the program was offered only during the summer, when School of the Air and College of the Air programs were not in production, and even then it was not offered continuously. Although the show aired in 1932, *Chapter a Day* was absent from the schedule during the summers of 1933 and 1934. It returned under that title again in June 1935, when Harold McCarty himself read the novel *The Great Hunger* by Norwegian author Johan Bøjer. Evidently, the 1932 experiment with the program had been forgotten, because in a 1935 letter to a listener, McCarty told of the current *Chapter a Day* offering and said, "We are trying now, for the first time, a program called 'A Chapter a Day' in which I shall read a complete novel during a two weeks period. It is Johan Bojer's 'The Great Hunger' and it is on the air each day at 2 for a 20 minute period. Perhaps you have already heard the reading Monday and today. We are anxious to know how our listeners react to a continuous program like this, and if you could conveniently listen to that period for two weeks and give us your comments on such a policy, we shall indeed appreciate it."[4]

After a midsummer gap in 1935 the program resumed on August 19, when Juanita Bauer, said to be "a reader of national fame," read the novel *The Lost Horizon* by James Hilton, again for a period of two weeks. In a letter to a listener WHA program assistant Leora Shaw said, "It is a pleasure to present such a fine reader as Mrs. Bauer, and we hope you can listen to her interpretations of this prize-winning book."[5] (The same book was also read in 1950, one of the very few times a title was presented years apart by different readers.) By the fall of 1935 the program had developed a following, as this excerpt from a reply to a reader's letter attests: "Your comments on the 'Chapter-a-Day' series were much appreciated. So much appreciation was shown for this series that we plan to resume it again next summer."[6] The program did return for the summer of 1936 but was not part of the schedule in 1937. It returned for the summer of 1938, and starting on April 3, 1939, *Chapter a Day* became a regular year-round feature on WHA. For its first decades *Chapter a Day* focused on current literature with the idea that the program would stimulate listeners to read the books themselves. Also, the standard reading was for ten episodes, one per weekday for a two-week period.[7]

Although some WHA programs were being simulcast over WLBL in Stevens Point by 1933, the central Wisconsin station did not carry *Chapter a Day* until May 27, 1936. Prior to that time, it had been preempting it with local programs.[8] Until WLBL's local programming ended in 1951, the Stevens Point station would usually preempt *Chapter a Day* with its own programs.

For a period in the 1930s a similar program called *Talking Book* appeared in the schedule, often alternating in the time slot with *Chapter a Day*. *Talking Book* was a thrice-weekly program that serialized classic literature for the benefit of the visually impaired and was produced in cooperation with the Wisconsin School for the Blind in Janesville and the American Federation for the Blind.[9] *Chapter a Day* itself played a role in serving this audience in later years. The Wisconsin Radio Reading Service began using the state network's SCA service in 1975. Their program schedule included *Chapter a Day* selections that had previously aired on the state network, and it proved to be the most popular program on the service.[10]

Recording technology gave WHA program managers additional flexibility, and some *Chapter a Day* readings were recorded on transcription discs as early as the mid-1940s. Prerecording the program allowed for some experimentation in the schedule. One of the first things the station tried was *Chapter at Night,* evening repeats of previously read books. Books read only a few weeks earlier would be rebroadcast in the evening on the state FM network. For a while the schedule followed a definite pattern, with the evening show repeating books that were first read exactly two months earlier. To this day, when producers acquire the broadcast rights for a book to be read on *Chapter a Day*, they ask permission for two airings. This allows a rebroadcast of the book sometimes years after its first run on the air. Many earlier selections are still available for rebroadcast; the shelves in WPR's Radio Operations Center are lined with tapes of previously aired *Chapter a Day* programs. These may yet be scheduled for an additional broadcast. In the Radio Hall years a collection of books read on the program was kept as sort of a lending library, and WHA staff members could check them out.

People known to have read for the program include Marianne Smith, Helen Darrah, Harold McCarty, Juanita Bauer, Marvin Bauer, Esther Hotton, Gerald Bartell, Karl Schmidt, Sherwin "Sherry" Abrams, Ray Stanley, Tom Detienne, Myron Curry, Ken Ohst, Jay Fitts, Fannie Frazier Hicklin, Sybil Robinson, Ed Burrows, Cliff Roberts, Carol Cowan, Kerry Frumkin, Jim Fleming, Judith Strasser, Norman Gilliland, and Catherine Brand.

Reader Karl Schmidt said he was always on the lookout for a book with a strong story line. "For that reason," he explained, "we sometimes have to exclude those books that are considered outstanding literature, because they don't lend themselves to serialized presentation."[11] In a 1985 interview Schmidt said he was reading ten to fifteen books a week, looking for titles suitable for the program. In novels he looked for a straightforward story with a simple plot and few characters. Once the publisher or literary agent granted permission for broadcast, Schmidt would block out the installments. He said, "I try to make each one have some unity within itself—a rise of action and a completion of action—and to avoid stops that are psychologically terrible. Then I edit to time. I also write a succinct synopsis of what's happened before the start of each episode." Schmidt said he delighted in the program: "It's such a loving thing to do because of the listener response." He said the program had a "fantastically loyal and passionate listenership. I love to have listeners call and fret that they missed the last chapter and want to know how it turned out." He said he also enjoyed hearing that bookstores have sold out of a book he had just finished reading and that libraries have waiting lists for it.[12]

In the 1950s and 1960s, some serialized books were done as *Chapter a Day* selections but were listed as having been recorded at the Canadian Broadcasting Corporation. These CBC transcription recordings fit the *Chapter a Day* format. The CBC continues to serialize books in fifteen-minute segments under the title *Between the Covers* on CBC Radio One. In 1961, the BBC dramatization of *Return of the Native* by Thomas Hardy was aired as a *Chapter a Day* selection.

In April 1961 Karl Schmidt read the 1959 novel *A Canticle for Liebowitz* by Walter M. Miller Jr. Listener response to this postapocalyptic work was positive (it was rebroadcast in 1967), and Schmidt thought for years about doing a radio play of the book. In 1981 he learned that a friend, John Reeves, a producer for the Canadian Broadcasting Corporation, was also interested in a radio play of the book. Reeves was a classics scholar and sometime playwright and had contributed to the WHA *Earplay* series. With funding from the Corporation for Public Broadcasting and the National Endowment for the Arts, Reeves and Schmidt wrote a fifteen-part radio adaptation of the book. The series was produced in New York and Madison with some Madison actors and a special score by two Milwaukee musicians. The series aired nationwide as part of *NPR Playhouse,* and to set the stage for its airing in Wisconsin, the WPR stations rebroadcast the 1961 *Chapter a Day* reading.[13]

During the first ten weekdays of October 1962, *Chapter a Day* featured *Silent Spring,* Rachel Carson's groundbreaking book on the dangers of pesticides. The following Monday the time slot was used to read reviews of the book. The inclusion of book reviews in the program was tried again in 1967, after Karl Schmidt completed his reading of *The Fixer* by Bernard Malamud and added

Chapter a Day *reader*
Karl Schmidt
One of the readers most closely associated with *Chapter a Day* for much of its history was Karl Schmidt. He joined the station as a student in 1940 and first read for the program in 1941. This photo was featured in the network's May–June 1962 program guide. (University of Wisconsin Archives series 23/24/1, negative 20353-C-1)

comments about the work from a number of noted reviewers.[14] From August 24 through September 11, 1964, *Chapter a Day* experimented with a slight change in format. Instead of reading a book over several weeks, the program featured short stories, either one per day or one over the course of two days.[15]

Sometimes the network would receive comments about the *Chapter a Day* reading from authors who tuned in to the program to hear their work read aloud. One such letter came from former Michigan Supreme Court justice John Voelker. Under the pseudonym Robert Traver, he had written the 1958 best-seller *Anatomy of a Murder,* and Karl Schmidt had excerpted Voelker's book *The Jealous Mistress* for *Chapter a Day* in April 1968. Voelker wrote to express his "vast delight" at Schmidt's reading and said, "I had no idea what added nuance and impact a sympathetic and artful reading can lend to one's prose. In fact, I am about to be converted to the belief that this is the way all books should be 'read.' My delight was not lessened by your own evident enjoyment of what your were doing."[16]

Chapter a Day *reader Jay Meredith Fitts*
Jay Fitts came to WHA after a career as an actor in network radio, appearing in the soap operas *Amanda of Honeymoon Hill* and *The Brighter Day,* as well as the dramatic series *By Kathleen Norris* and *The Mighty Show.* She read for *Chapter a Day* through the early 1980s. (University of Wisconsin Archives series 23/24/1, negative 4182-J-1-5A)

Some books read on *Chapter a Day* later become major Hollywood movies. Some well-known ones in recent years were *Shoeless Joe* (the basis for *Field of Dreams*), *The Pelican Brief,* and *Jurassic Park.* Also, the program has featured some nonfiction best-sellers such as the Lewis and Clark history *Undaunted Courage* by Stephen Ambrose and David McCullough's biography of Harry Truman. In the latter case, the book was excerpted for the program.

In the 1970s, a radio program of similar format was offered over the state stations: jazz host Michael Hanson produced a weekly series called *Mindwebs*. These were half-hour readings of what he called "speculative fiction," works of the supernatural and science fiction genres. Although Hanson never read for *Chapter a Day,* he remains in demand as a reader for commercial book recordings.

By the early 1980s, *Chapter a Day* was being offered at 12:05 p.m. on the FM network and WLBL. WHA in Madison would air a different title, beginning at 1 p.m. In the early 1990s, the schedule had only one book airing at a time. The program would air at 12:30 p.m. on WPR's talk service stations, repeat on all stations at 6:30 p.m., and then repeat again on the music service stations only at 10:30 p.m.; this schedule allowed two airings on each station per day. Also, some variations in form were tried. Karl Schmidt and Jim Fleming teamed up to read *My Old Man and the Sea* by David Hays and Daniel Hays, and Karl was joined by his wife, Jo, for a reading of *A Good Scent from a Strange Mountain* by Robert Olen Butler. One caller to WPR in the late 1990s, a factory worker in Burlington, Wisconsin, told of the unique appeal of the program. He said that he and a large group of fellow workers took their lunch period together and listened to *Chapter a Day.*

The 2005 schedule had airings at 12:30 p.m. and 11 p.m. on WPR's talk service stations. Since mid-2001 the program has been recorded digitally and played on the air from a compact disc; it was the last daily program on WPR to be played from reel-to-reel tape. The five most recent chapters are now archived in audio form on the WPR Web site as well. As with all WPR offerings, the broadcasts of the program are now streamed via the Internet, which has helped attract additional listeners. *Chapter a Day* reader Jim Fleming notes that his sister living in Japan would listen to the 11 p.m. (Central Time) rebroadcast of the program over the Internet during her lunch period.

Despite its longevity, the modern standard of public radio programs being an hour in length makes the half-hour *Chapter a Day* a difficult program to accommodate. This was less of a problem in its early years, when fifteen minutes was a typical program length. Another risk to the program came from the increasing popularity of books on audiotape; publishers have become more

Chapter a Day *reader Jim Fleming*
Fleming has been a *Chapter a Day* reader for decades, in addition to his work hosting classical music and the syndicated interview program *To the Best of Our Knowledge.* (University of Wisconsin Archives series 23/24/1)

reluctant to give permission for broadcast, fearing the *Chapter a Day* airings will cut into future sales of the audio format. Conversely, the quality of the *Chapter a Day* recordings has occasionally impressed authors and publishers enough that they allow edited versions of the *Chapter a Day* recordings to be sold as the audio version as well. Also, some regular *Chapter a Day* readers have been hired to do readings for these productions.

Although *Chapter a Day* has never been offered for syndication, a similar program called *The Radio Reader* has been available to other public radio stations. It's a production of WKAR at Michigan State University in East Lansing. Other public radio stations have done local readings similar *Chapter a Day* over the years.

As with all programs produced by WHA, commercial stations could apply for rebroadcasting permission for *Chapter a Day,* but rights to the program were requested only rarely. It is known that WRCO in Richland Center carried *Chapter a Day* in 1959 and 1960.[17]

Wisconsin Public Radio staffers have made the claim over the years that *Chapter a Day* is the longest continuously airing program on the state network, tracing it to 1927 and its title to 1929. However, it is obvious that the program has not enjoyed an unbroken run. The claim that the program began in 1927 is also unlikely. The schedule then in effect had WHA on the air one to three evenings per week, which does not lend itself to the known *Chapter a Day* format. It may indeed be that one evening in 1927, someone read a chapter from a book on air to fill time, but the time that elapsed between this event and the development of *Chapter a Day* as a regular program appears to have been years rather than days. The further claim that Harold B. McCarty was the person doing that first 1927 reading is also not possible because he did not arrive at WHA until October 1929. Years later McCarty told Schmidt that he read a book on air to fill time for a missing guest while WHA was still at Sterling Hall, dating the event to before December 1934.[18] Some have cited 1929 as the year when the *Chapter a Day* title was first used, but no program listings

Chapter a Day *reader Carol Cowan*
Long-time WHA employee Carol Cowan worked on everything from the Wisconsin School of the Air to call-in programs and for years was a reader on *Chapter a Day*. (University of Wisconsin Archives series 23/24/1, negative 7177C-1)

have been found from this era that mention the program. The schedule late that year had the *Homemakers' Program* at 10 a.m., *On Wisconsin* at noon, the *Farm Program* at 12:30 p.m., and little else, except specials and athletic events. A program listing from the fall of 1931 shows no *Chapter a Day* program, either. One reference says that Harold McCarty did indeed develop the program but in 1932,[19] which is the first year that the program appears in the daily WHA broadcast schedule documents. However, in McCarty's letter to a listener he says 1935 is when they were trying the program "for the first time." An in-house newsletter from January 1967 talks about the program and says it had enjoyed "more that thirty years of regular presentation."[20] It is worth noting that *Chapter a Day* is not mentioned in any of the WHA annual reports until the late 1940s. The annual report covering 1948 succinctly describes the program, saying: "Good books both old and new are read on a daily continued story basis."[21]

Given the available documents, it can be said *Chapter a Day* first appeared on WHA on July 25, 1932, and has been on continuously since April 3, 1939. Few broadcast programs have enjoyed such a long run. One that does predate *Chapter a Day* has also been carried by WPR although not since its debut. The Metropolitan Opera broadcast series first aired on December 25, 1931.[22]

CHAPTER 24

To Today

1979–

You're listening to Wisconsin Public Radio.

In the late 1970s and early 1980s, WHA and the state stations moved more toward NPR programming. In January 1979, the organizational title Wisconsin Public Radio was adopted, a more marketable name than state stations, Wisconsin Educational Radio Network, or Wisconsin State Broadcasting Service.

Two major developments occurred in late 1979. On November 5 National Public Radio unveiled *Morning Edition* as a morning drive-time companion to the afternoon program *All Things Considered.* That same month NPR began using the Westar IV satellite to distribute its programs instead of the land line loop in use since 1971. WPR activated its satellite receiver on December 13.[1]

Still, the development of local programs continued. One of the most notable was *Simply Folk,* which debuted in January 1979. In the 1970s the state network had carried some NPR folk offerings and a program called *Kicking the Dog Around,* produced at WLFM in Appleton. WHA had also produced a nine-part series called *Canadian Folk Songs* that aired in 1970. In 1978 WHA aired a local program called *Simple Folk,* the brainchild of producer Tom Martin-Erickson. For *Simply Folk* he was joined by producer Becca Pulliam. She had earlier coproduced a series called *Women-Made Music.* When Pulliam took a leave of absence in 1980, Judy Rose joined the program and remained after Pulliam's temporary return. Rose took over as the solo host of the program after Martin-Erickson became the network's operations director (he returned as program host after Rose's retirement in 2005). Rose also produced a series for incorporation in the program that drew on the recordings that folklorist Helene Stratman-Thomas had collected in the 1940s as part of a project for the University of Wisconsin and the Library of Congress. The new thirteen-part series,

The Wisconsin Patchwork, remastered the original 1940s recordings and was funded in part by a grant from the National Endowment for the Arts.[2] At its peak *Simply Folk* was on both Saturday and Sunday evenings, and over the years the program recorded and aired hundreds of live folk performances from venues throughout the Midwest.

In March 1979 the network's program guide listed the first on-air underwriters, short verbal statements acknowledging financial support from businesses and foundations. While some special programs had corporate support in earlier years, these underwriters were for the regular program schedule. Two of the underwriters from the first group remain supporters of WPR: American Family Insurance and the owners of Paisan's and Porta Bella restaurants in Madison.[3]

A format added in the late 1970s would become a central part of the WPR service: call-in/interview programs. The network had made some attempts at the format earlier. Starting in November 1967, a Saturday morning program called *Colloquy* featured university administrators and faculty members who fielded questions phoned in by listeners,[4] and the program ran through May 1968. That fall, some on-air candidate interviews included call-in segments, with distant listeners told to call collect.[5] WHA producer John Powell, who would become a state government reporter for WPR, also took calls from listeners during some weekend public affairs programs from Radio Hall in mid-1972.[6] Starting in September 1975, WHA had also carried *American Issues Radio Forum,* a National Public Radio call-in program that aired once a month on Saturdays.[7] The program was later carried on the entire state network. Listeners could also call in to a special series of programs over WHA for Health Week in November 1975.

The first regular statewide offering featuring the present-day call-in/interview format debuted on Sunday June 5, 1977. This public affairs program was called *Wisconsin Issues Forum* and was hosted by Richard Wexler. The show was originally one hour, noon to 1 p.m., and soon expanded to 12:15 to 2 p.m., and, later, to 10 a.m. to noon on Saturdays. The serious tone of the program was set from the outset: the first topic was "Public Employees: Should They Have the Right to Strike?" The other programs that first month looked at the taxation and regulation of mining in Wisconsin, the state's right-to-privacy laws, and the juvenile justice system.[8] In April 1978 Wexler had the two candidates for state supreme court on the air, in the tradition of WHA's *Political Education Forum.* Another innovation of this format that continues today was a monthly program that features the managers for WHA, WERN, and the FM network, fielding questions and complaints about the radio programs.[9] This also had roots in the past, serving the same function as the long-running program *Dear Sirs.*

Daily call-in programs began in early 1978. *Midday Report* host Larry Meiller was asked if he would like to do a regular daily call-in program. Meiller had hosted the *Farm Program* since the late 1960s and expressed interest in the experiment. He suggested a format that would continue to provide advice about agriculture but would also include topics that affect the daily lives of people, such as health and exercise, nutrition, and the outdoors. Meiller also envisioned that the program would draw on experts from the University of Wisconsin–Extension. The program combined the *Midday Report* (the name for the *Farm Program* since September 2, 1968) and *Accent on Living* (the name

Wisconsin Public Radio call-in host Larry Meiller
Meiller (left), former host of the *Farm Program,* has been a program host for the state network since the late 1960s. He continues to host the 11 a.m. to 12:30 p.m. time slot each weekday over Wisconsin Public Radio. This 1986 photograph shows him in the Wisconsin Public Radio's call-in studio in Vilas Hall. (University of Wisconsin Archives series 23/24/1)

for the *Homemakers' Program* since May 1, 1966) into a single program with the new title *Wisconsin Hear and Now*, which eventually included call-ins.

Meiller says he remembers the first program, which featured Dick Bristol and John Skinner from the College of Agricultural and Life Sciences. The topic was pet care, and the first call came in from a woman in Stevens Point who asked: "How do I tell if my cat is male or female?" Meiller says that Dick Bristol fielded the question and told her, "You pick up its tail."[10] The program eventually became *Conversations with Larry Meiller*, which continues today on WPR's talk stations.

More call-in programs were added to the schedule. Ronnie Hess, Jim Packard, Richard Hinchcliff, Ronda Allen, Roger Sarow, Steve Paulson, and Margaret Andreassen all had regular time slots. Host Dick Goldberg alternated between financial topics and relationship advice. Humanities producer Jean Feraca added to the call-in format with a weekday afternoon program, later moved to midmorning and expanded to two hours. Feraca later moved to weekend afternoons (and later still, back to weekday afternoons), with a new program title, *Here on Earth: Radio Without Borders.* The program has as partners the UW's Division of International Studies and Radio Netherlands. It was conceived to galvanize the world community by discussing the "gems" of the world, such as international movements, cross-cultural conversions, democracy-building initiatives, and the best world literature, movies, arts, food, and culture. Former news and public affairs director Tom Clark had a two-hour call-in slot after *Morning Edition,* but in 1990 the network decided to try the call-in format in drive time, with Clark on from 6 to 9 a.m., replacing *Morning Edition* during those hours on the talk service stations. The NPR newsmagazine then displaced the early morning classical program *Prelude* on the music stations. After Clark's retirement in 2003, Joy Cardin, WPR's director of talk programming, took over as host.

In July 1989 the network developed a formal bureau in Milwaukee and assigned classical music host Jan Weller to do a daily call-in program there that would be carried statewide. The late-morning offering was later moved to late afternoon and finally to the early evening and expanded to two hours. It remained on the air until Weller left the network; he later returned to classical music broadcasting at WFMT-Chicago. A business call-in program from the Milwaukee studio began airing in 1992 with host Ben Merens, and in 1993 former WTMJ talk show host Kathleen Dunn joined the Milwaukee staff. WPR put Dunn on in afternoon drive time, displacing NPR's *All Things Considered* on the talk stations, much like the earlier experiment of putting Tom Clark on during morning drive time in place of *Morning Edition.* One financial benefit of these moves was that these stations saw a reduction in their NPR affiliation fees, since they no longer had to pay the higher rates that NPR charges stations for carrying *Morning Edition* and *All Things Considered*. Dunn later moved to midmorning with Merens taking over the afternoon hours.

The state stations also offered network call-in programs. In December 1991 WPR's talk stations were among the first in the country to add NPR's *Talk of the Nation*. It had its roots in a national afternoon call-in program that NPR offered during the Persian Gulf War. Reporter John Hockenberry, former host of the late-evening NPR interview program *Heat*, had hosted the experimental wartime program. He was tapped to host the new offering, which ran Monday through Thursday; Friday was given over to *Talk of the Nation: Science Friday*, hosted by long-time NPR science reporter Ira Flatow.

Locally produced comedy came to Wisconsin Public Radio in 1981. A following had developed for a program called *The Breakfast Special* on Madison's community station, WORT. The show aired live each weekday morning from a Madison restaurant and was the station's most popular program.[11] The host was a former high school English teacher named Michael Feldman. His quick wit while bantering with the customers and guests caught the attention of WPR managers, who offered Feldman airtime on the network. Some humor segments he produced led to the development of a new program.[12] It premiered as *High Noon* on September 5, 1981, with a comedy-variety format from the Philo Buck Studio in Vilas Hall. The program underwent a change in time, format, and style and on July 24, 1982, debuted as *AM Saturday*. The new program aired from 9 to 11 a.m. live from the Café Palms in Madison's Hotel Washington, several blocks from the WPR headquarters. The new format was reminiscent of Feldman's successful WORT program but added a jazz quartet and telephone segment.[13] Feldman briefly left the program for a stint at WGN radio in Chicago and was replaced by George "Papa Hambone" Vukelich, a local radio host, newspaper columnist, and environmental essayist. Feldman later returned in an updated version of the program. The jazz and phone aspects of *AM Saturday* would be incorporated into the new program, *Whad'ya Know*, a two-hour comedy-quiz program that debuted in the summer of 1985. The Philo Buck Studio soon proved too small to accommodate the growing size of the audience, so the show was moved down three floors to the Parliamentary Room lecture hall on the fourth floor. The room has an audiovisual booth at the rear that served as a control room for the program. Beginning in January 1986, the program was distributed nationwide through National Public Radio and later moved to American Public Radio. It is now distributed by Public Radio International, successor to APR, and is carried by more than three hundred stations nationwide, making it the most successful syndicated program from WPR. It has changed locations again and now broadcasts from the Monona Terrace Convention Center on Madison's lakefront. It also goes on the road regularly at the invitation of the public radio stations that carry the program. Stations use the event as a fund-raiser and share the proceeds with the program.

Former *AM Saturday* host Vukelich continued to be heard on the WPR stations with his half-hour program *North Country Notebook*. It featured Vukelich's essays about Wisconsin's north woods, along with nature writings by the likes of John Muir, Aldo Leopold, and Sigurd Olson. It ran on weekends for several years and was known for featuring acoustic music and the sounds of loons. Its closing theme was "Wisconsin," sung by Glenn Yarborough.[14] The song remains one of the most requested selections on WPR's *Simply Folk* program.

A jazz program hosted by local musician Ben Sidran also began national distribution in early 1986. *Sidran on Record* was distributed through NPR and was heard in more than one hundred markets in the United States, as well as in Australia. Sidran had earlier served as artistic director and host of the National Public Radio series *Jazz Alive!*[15]

WPR offered other productions for national distribution. The network's Spanish language programming was offered through NPR under the name *Panorama Hispano* from 1984 to 1988. The program was funded in part by a grant from the NPR satellite Program Development Fund. The magazine-interview program *To the Best of Our Knowledge* began as a local program in 1990. It was accepted for national distribution through WFMT in Chicago and later moved to Public Radio International. In 2005 the series was honored with a Peabody Award, the fourth such accolade for the Wisconsin network.

WPR decided to capitalize on its expertise in the call-in format to produce several weekly programs for national distribution. Morning host Tom Clark cohosted the first two, joining a family physician for the medical advice program *Zorba Paster on Your Health* and sharing the studio with a psychologist for the parenting program *Sylvia Rimm on Raising Kids*. Rimm later left Wisconsin for a new professional position in psychology but continued to produce a version of her program at WCPN-Cleveland for several years. WPR also produced and syndicated *Calling All Pets*, a pet care program featuring pet expert Patricia McConnell, with Larry Meiller as cohost.

With two separate program services in Madison, the staff looked into the possibility of developing another FM station for the city to allow the news and information programs on WHA-AM to be heard in the FM band. Part of the impetus for this move was a desire to broadcast the WHA programs at night; the AM station was still signing off at sundown. In 1982, a committee looked at applying for an FM station at 89.1 mHz in Madison, with the call letters WHA-FM. This plan would also require that WERN move to 88.3 mHz. Had the plan gone forward, it's unclear what might have happened to WHA-AM. It could have been retained for simulcasting with the new FM outlet or sold to a commercial operator.[16] In December 1987, WHA-AM was finally granted authority to operate twenty-four hours a day, but at greatly reduced power at night.

The experiment of splitting off WHA from the rest of the network and having it present a separate program schedule led to the idea of two separate services. In 1990 the two services became known as the Ideas Network, featuring mostly call-in programs, with the other stations known as the NPR News and Classical Music Network, offering the NPR news magazines like *Morning Edition, All Things Considered,* and *Weekend Edition,* with the rest of the day given over primarily to classical music.

With the two network "streams" WPR was interested in having dual service for as much of the state as possible. With limited funds to build new facilities and with most of the non-commercial radio frequencies in Wisconsin already taken, WPR began seeking alliances with existing public and university stations. In October 1982 WYMS in Milwaukee joined WPR. The Milwaukee Public Schools–owned station had begun rebroadcasting some Wisconsin School of the Air programs in 1978 but now would carry regular WPR programs. At the very end of their affiliation, WYMS was airing only *Chapter a Day* and the network's afternoon jazz program, *Asylum,* which was by then being heard only on WPR stations in Madison and Wausau. When WPR ended its weekday jazz programming in the summer of 1989, WYMS reverted to independent operation with local Milwaukee hosts. The schedule was primarily jazz, with specialty ethnic programs on the weekends. In the early 1990s the station was facing financial difficulties, and a plan to re-affiliate with WPR was announced, making WYMS part of the network's talk service and dropping most of the jazz programming. This news prompted a local jazz fan to anonymously donate a substantial sum to WYMS to keep its jazz format intact. The station used the donation to kick off a successful fund drive, which gave the organization the financial means to remain independent. In 2002 the school board abruptly dismissed the staff, canceled all local programming, and began rebroadcasting the signal from public radio station WUWM at the University of Wisconsin–Milwaukee. Complaints from local jazz fans resulted in a change, and the station began carrying the syndicated satellite service *JazzWorks.* The school board solicited proposals for operating the station, and a nonprofit group called Radio for Milwaukee prevailed with a plan to offer a musically diverse format.

In 1983 two university-licensed stations joined the state network as affiliates. On September 12 WLSU-FM at the University of Wisconsin–La Crosse began carrying some WPR programs. It had been operating as an independent NPR station, with a professional staff augmented by student participation. The station briefly carried some WPR programming before once again becoming an independent operation. Later, the station rejoined the network as part of the NPR News and Classical Music Network and continued to offer much of its local news and jazz programming.

Also in September 1983, student station WRST at the University of Wisconsin–Oshkosh joined the network and began carrying NPR's *Morning Edition* by tape delay. The plan was for the station to record the program off the air from WPNE in Green Bay and play it back later in the morning when the local WPR stations had gone to classical music or call-in programs. In 1986 WPR approached officials at the University of Wisconsin–Oshkosh with a request that the station carry WPR material for more of the broadcast day, 5 a.m. to 1 p.m. daily. Oshkosh faculty members turned down the offer, saying the plan would take too much of the broadcast day and thereby deprive broadcasting students of on-air time. The network and WRST ended their affiliation agreement as of September 30, 1986. WRST went back to completely local programming until the fall of 1988, when it added Pacifica Radio News from Washington, D.C., via telephone. In 1990 WRST acquired a public radio satellite downlink, the only student-run station in Wisconsin (and one of the few in the country) to do so. The station used the equipment to replace the phone service from Pacifica News and to record the full-length symphony programs it had been carrying via tape from WFMT in Chicago. When WRST staffers were thinking about buying satellite equipment, the station was courted by American Public Radio (now Public Radio International). The national network was interested in WRST's becoming an affiliate and hoped the station would purchase programs that WPR was not then offering locally, such as *Monitoradio Early Edition, Saint Paul Sunday Morning, Soundprint, The Thistle and Shamrock,* and BBC World Service news programming. In February 1993 the station rejoined WPR and rebroadcasts the signal of the Ideas Network station in Green Bay for part of the day.

WPR also approached officials at Lawrence University in Appleton about rebroadcasting the WPR signal of the news and information service on their student station, WLFM. Lawrence officials agreed to the affiliation, and a WPR reporter-host was stationed in Appleton full time until 1990. One of the oldest college FM stations (on air in 1956), WLFM enjoyed national fame as home to one of the first radio trivia contests in the country. Begun in 1966 to keep students entertained during the midwinter semester break, it ran a full week-end, Friday evening through Sunday evening, with a question asked on air every few minutes. The prizes offered had almost no value, but dozens of teams would register to play, both on campus and off, and some former Lawrence students would even make a yearly pilgrimage to Appleton to participate. The affiliation agreement between WPR and WLFM ended in 2005, when Lawrence University sold the station to a religious broadcaster.

Other student stations joined the WPR network at various levels of involvement:

WGBW-FM at the University of Wisconsin–Green Bay went on the air in 1974. Ironically, it was able to apply for its 91.5 mHz frequency because the state network had recently abandoned its 91.5 station in the same area, WHMD-FM in Suring, which had gone on the air in 1965 in Marinette. WGBW joined WPR's talk service part time in 1986 and did some local programs with a WPR staff host in addition to student programs. WPR later operated the station full-time and applied to the FCC to actually reduce the station's power but increase its antenna height. Later, WPR built a new higher-powered FM station at 88.1 in Green Bay. The new outlet, with the call letters WHID, went on the air in April 1997 and carries the network's talk service. WGBW's frequency was transferred in 1998 to a religious broadcaster, which operates as WEMY-FM.

KUWS-FM originally was WSSU-FM, the student station at the University of Wisconsin–Superior that first went on the air in 1966. After affiliating with WPR, the station's power was dramatically increased from 940 watts to 83,000 watts, and the station's antenna was moved to a tower on a bluff across the river in Duluth. With the change came a different frequency and new call letters. The station carries WPR programming 75 percent of the time with the balance of the schedule operated locally by students, including broadcasts of University of Wisconsin–Superior hockey games. WPR hired former Superior student Mike Simonson to be the local bureau host and work with the student staff. Simonson also teaches journalism at the university. In 1997 he won the national Edward R. Murrow award from the Radio-Television News Directors Association in the radio documentary category for his series on the plight of HIV sufferers in rural areas. The station also rebroadcasts on a low-power translator station in Ashland.

WUEC-FM at the Eau Claire campus of the university went on the air in 1975. The station director had been searching for some program service to provide classical music and affiliated with WPR's music service in 1989. Originally, the station carried network programming from 8 a.m. to noon weekdays and noon to 5 p.m. on Sundays, with student-run programs on the remainder of the time. Except for one weekly student program, the station now carries the network feed full time.

WVSS-FM was originally the college station at the University of Wisconsin–Stout in Menomonie and went on the air in 1969. After an FCC field inspection in 1986 revealed some technical violations, WVSS contacted WPR about providing programming, and the station now carries the NPR News and Classical Music Network full time.

WRFW-FM is the student station at the University of Wisconsin–River Falls in far western Wisconsin and went on the air in 1968. It was briefly affiliated with WPR in 1990 and after a period as an independent station rejoined the network in 1999 as a half-time affiliate of the Ideas Network.

Three other stations, WSHS-FM, WGTD-FM, and WEPS-FM, are affiliates of WPR:

WSHS-FM is based at Sheboygan North High School and dates to 1971. It presents local programming from 9 a.m. to 6 p.m. weekdays during the school year and carry the Ideas Network off-air from WHID-FM in Green Bay the rest of the time.

WGTD-FM in Kenosha is licensed to Gateway Technical College. It had been an independent public radio station but joined WPR in 1993 as a member of the NPR News and Classical Music Network. It continues to provide some local programming and is the only non–Ideas Network station to air *Chapter a Day,* which it carries off-air from WHAD in Delafield.

WEPS-FM is licensed to School District U-46 in Elgin, Illinois. This was WPR's first affiliate licensed to a city outside Wisconsin (because of geography, the transmitters and towers for both of WPR's La Crosse stations and KUWS-Superior are in Minnesota but remain licensed to their Wisconsin communities). WEPS debuted in 1950, making it one of the oldest educational stations in Illinois, and it was once operated by a radio club at Elgin High School, where the studios remain. By 2000 student involvement had ended, and the station was operating with a single employee from 6 a.m. to noon weekdays. When up for license renewal in 2004, WEPS found it was one of several school-based stations in the Midwest that were facing a challenge from a Texas-based religious broadcaster. It wanted to force a sharing of the WEPS frequency in Elgin (when a non-commercial station operates less than half time, other organizations may apply to the FCC to share time on that frequency in that community). The FCC eventually dismissed the challenge, but school officials and WPR had already begun working on an affiliation agreement. While the program signal was available off the air from WHAD in

Delafield, about seventy-five miles away, sound quality dictated another solution. A new piece of technology, normally used as a studio-to-transmitter link, feeds the station a broadcast-quality signal via the Internet, with the over-the-air signal used as a backup. WEPS continues to provide its local schedule of school news and announcements and a wide variety of syndicated non-commercial radio programs. It carries WPR's Ideas Network the rest of the time and extends the network's service to the far western suburbs of the Chicago metropolitan area.

Wisconsin Public Radio also secured funding to build new stations. In 1988 the first new state FM station in more than twenty years was constructed in Park Falls, Wisconsin. Its call letters, WHBM, kept the tradition of the *WH* call signs while honoring long-time manager Harold B. McCarty, who had died the previous year. In 1996 WLBL-FM went on the air in Wausau; this outlet shares its time with independent public radio station WXPR in Rhinelander. In 1997 a low-power translator station began serving the Madison area, repeating the signal from WHHI in Highland. In 1998 FM stations WHDI and WHND began operation on Wisconsin's Door Peninsula, providing that area with a clearer signal for each network service. Also, low-powered translator stations for each WPR service were built in Ashland in 1999.

The addition of computer automation equipment in the late 1990s allowed WHA and the FM network to operate twenty-four hours a day. Starting in April 1998, the NPR News and Classical Music stations began offering classical music overnight from the Beethoven Satellite Network, a service of WFMT-Chicago. The Ideas Network stations carried World Service programming from the BBC, distributed by Public Radio International.

For much of the history of WHA and the FM network, the only news coverage was provided by Roy Vogelman and the staff in Madison. The expansion of the news staff allowed for more sophisticated news offerings. State government reporter John Powell rejoined WHA as a public affairs producer in 1972; he had been a WHA-TV newscaster in the late 1960s before serving in the military. In 1976 he covered both the Democratic National Convention in New York and the Republican National Convention in Kansas City.[17] In 1984 Powell accompanied Wisconsin's governor on a trade mission to the Far East, filing stories by telephone throughout the trip.

In late 1979 the network began to explore the idea of having news bureaus in other locations. Ronnie Hess became the network's first Milwaukee-based reporter, sharing space at WUWM.[18] The network also benefited by being allowed to air reports done by local WUWM reporters. Later, reporters at WLSU in La Crosse began feeding news stories by phone to Madison, also for statewide broadcast. Chuck Quirmbach was later sent from the Madison office to Milwaukee as the local reporter, sharing space at WUWM and later at WYMS, the station run by the Milwaukee Public Schools. The sharing arrangement lasted until WPR established its own facility in Milwaukee in 1989. Throughout the 1980s WUWM was able to access WPR stories by phone and used them in its own newscasts.

In 1986 the network began to establish more bureaus, with reporters hired for Green Bay, Stevens Point, Eau Claire, Appleton, and Superior. These reporters would also be on air in the early morning, reading local announcements during Madison-originated programs. and for a time they also presented local newscasts tailored to their region. They would spend the late morning and afternoon hours generating news reports to feed to Madison for statewide use. The Stevens Point bureau was on the university's Stevens Point campus, sharing space with college station WWSP in the former WLBL studio facility. The central Wisconsin bureau was later moved to Wausau. More reporting strength was added as WLSU in La Crosse, and WGTD in Kenosha joined the network as affiliates. Their local news staffers feed stories to WPR for statewide airing.

WHA, WLBL, and the original network of FM stations continue to operate as Wisconsin Public Radio. Although they have much in common with other modern public radio broadcasters, remnants of the organization's rich history survive.

Chapter a Day, which began using that title in July 1932, has been on continuously since April 3, 1939.

The University of the Air stopped airing classroom lectures in the early 1990s, but the service remains in a new form as a weekly conversation with professors about their particular area of academic study. WPR's Gilliland and UW–Madison English professor Emily Auerbach cohost the program. The new incarnation is reminiscent of the educational talks presented on 9XM and WHA in the early years. Still, callers regularly ask WPR whether Michael Petrovich's lecture series on the history of Russia will be repeated (WPR still has the tapes).

Classical music has been featured continuously since the first experimental telephonic broadcasts on 9XM in 1917–20 and the regular Friday evening *Radiophone Concerts* on 9XM in 1921. Remote broadcasts of classical concerts also continue with the regular Sunday afternoon series of live concerts from the Chazen Museum of Art across the street from the WPR headquarters. The audio for these events is transmitted to the station over broadcast lines in the steam tunnels under the university, just as it was for early 9XM live concerts.

Larry Meiller, who took over as host of the *Farm Program* in 1968, continues on the air with a weekday program called *Conversations with Larry Meiller* that is the direct descendant of both the *Farm Program* and the *Homemakers'* *Program*. Since 1978 it has had a call-in format, and it continued to offer farm market reports until 1991. In recent years, the Friday topic has been gardening, which had been a regular weekly topic on the *Homemakers' Program* as early as 1935 and part of the *Farm Program* in the 1960s. The program also draws heavily on the expertise of UW–Extension personnel in areas such as housing, wildlife ecology, horticulture, and entomology, and other experts on computers, cooking, pet care, taxes, lawn care and weather.

The standard set by the *Political Education Forum* of 1932 has continued: all candidates for national or statewide office are offered airtime on WPR call-in programs in the weeks leading up to the election. Special election night broadcasts, which were done as early as 1928 on WLBL, also continue. Like that early broadcast, some civic journalism offerings on WPR are done in association with other news organizations. The current partnership is known as We the People, and the consortium includes Wisconsin Public Television, the *Wisconsin State Journal,* commercial television station WISC in Madison, and the Wood Communications Group.

News began as a weekly program in March 1922 and has continued and evolved, becoming the substantial news efforts that characterize today's offerings from Wisconsin Public Radio. Roy Vogelman, the first (and longest-serving) WHA news director, set the tone in a news policy he developed in 1947. Much of what he set forth in terms of types of coverage, presentation style, and reporting is still in effect today. WLBL appears to have had access to a wire service in 1939; both WLBL and WHA gained access to broadcast wire service by Teletype in 1942. WPR now has reporters around the state, and the network presents nearly five thousand local newscasts per year. In 2000 the news operation was named best in the state by the Wisconsin Associated Press. Also, WPR continues to have its own studio at the State Capitol building, in the same room it has occupied since 1931.

Broadcasting the state's weather forecast continues on all stations, as it has since the very beginning of 9XM broadcasts. In early 2003 the National Weather Service alerted WPR of its plans to stop generating a statewide forecast in text form, as nearly everyone using the weather service text material prefers forecasts specific to regions or metro areas. WPR staff met with weather service officials and explained that although they might indeed have the only agency that still needed the statewide forecast, it was the only forecast that the organization could use. Moreover, they pointed out that the organization had used the forecast continuously since 1916. The arguments convinced the weather service officials to continue producing a state forecast for Wisconsin.

Postscript

The Oldest Station in the Nation

This work would not be complete without addressing WHA's claim as "the oldest station in the nation." The claim is often repeated, and it was made early in the station's history. In 1927, a newspaper report headlined "U.W. Station Nine Years a Broadcaster" said the station had "begun its programs in 1919."[1] In 1938 the publication *Education by Radio* also named 1919 as the start of 9XM broadcasts and said the station is "the oldest broadcasting station in the country."[2] Also in 1938 the entertainment publication *Variety* awarded WHA its Showmanship Award, and the citation said, "This station, by the way, will be 22 years old next spring," pushing back the beginnings of the station to 1917.[3] WHA managers through the years were only too happy to make this claim, and for a time some were unwilling to even consider any evidence that challenged the station's status as "oldest."

At the annual WHA Family Dinner on November 24, 1958, a marker from the State Historical Society proclaiming WHA as the "oldest station in the nation" was unveiled near Radio Hall, outside the window of what had been Earle Terry's basement laboratory in Science Hall (when WHA moved to Vilas Communication Hall in 1972, the marker moved there as well). Harold Engel had approved the text of the marker, titled "9XM-WHA 'The Oldest Station in the Nation.'" It reads:

On this campus, pioneer research and experimentation in "wireless" led to successful transmissions of voice and music in 1917, and the beginning of broadcasting on a scheduled basis in 1919.

Experimental station 9XM transmitted telegraphic signals from Science Hall

315

until 1917, when it was moved to Sterling Hall. In that year, Professor Earle M. Terry and students built and operated a "wireless telephone" transmitter.

In 1918, during World War I, when other stations were ordered silenced, 9XM operated under special authorization to continue its telephonic exchange with U.S. Navy stations on the Great Lakes. After the war, programs were directed to the general public.

The WHA letters replaced the 9XM call on January 13, 1922. Thus, the University of Wisconsin station, under the calls 9XM and WHA, has been in existence longer than any other.

The marker makes no mention of the 1916 telegraphic weather broadcasts or the original wireless ban of 1917. Most important, it appears to be incorrect about the year when scheduled broadcasting began.

"Oldest" and "First"

In this context, the definitions of *oldest* and *first* are best explained by researchers Joseph E. Baudino and John M. Kitross. In a 1977 article in the *Journal of Broadcasting,* they examined the claims of WHA and three other pioneer broadcast stations with regard to being oldest or first. They say *first* means having primacy, being the first ever, while *oldest* refers to seniority among those still existing. They make a distinction between the two words, noting that the first broadcaster may no longer be on the air or has not been on continuously. For this analysis of radio broadcasting, *first* means the very first station, whether it is on the air today or not or has had long periods when it was not in operation. *Oldest* means the oldest of the stations on the air today that have had continuous service, with exceptions allowed for equipment failures, acts of God, or events beyond the control of the operator. For broadcasting, one such event is the World War I ban on non-military wireless transmission from April 7, 1917, to October 1, 1919.

It's a bit more difficult to define what constitutes radio broadcasting. Many academic researchers, along with Baudino and Kitross, agree with the criteria set down by R. Franklin Smith. While working on a doctoral degree at the University of Wisconsin in 1959, he wrote an article about the term for the *Journal of Broadcasting.* His accepted definition says a broadcast station is one that "(1) utilizes radio waves (2) to send noncoded sounds by speech or music (3) in the form of a continuous patterned program service, (4) intended to be received by the public, and (5) is licensed by the government."[4] The first condition eliminates from consideration wired systems like the telephone "newsteller" service in Budapest and some early experiments by inventor Nathan

Harold B. McCarty and Harold Engel at the 9XM/WHA historical marker
This Wisconsin historical marker was originally installed outside Science Hall, near
Radio Hall. Behind the marker is the building's original room 5, the office and
laboratory of Earle Terry. The marker is now near the entrance to Vilas
Communication Hall, the current home of Wisconsin Public Radio. (University
of Wisconsin Archives series 23/24/1, negative 18465-C-1)

Stubblefield. In 1892 he transmitted voice without wires, but he used ground induction. The second condition eliminates telegraphic and other coded services. The third eliminates experimental unscheduled broadcasts, and the fourth eliminates point-to-point, or private, transmissions.

Smith said that only the first four conditions need be present for establishing the "first" station, because some voice transmissions were made before the Radio Act of 1912 required all radio operations to have a government license. The two December 1906 "broadcasts" by Reginald Fessenden satisfy some of the requirements, as do some experimental transmissions by Lee de Forest during the years 1907–10. However, in both cases the irregular and experimental nature of the transmissions keeps them from rising to the level of regular broadcasting.

Using Smith's definitions, Baudino and Kitross examined the claims from WHA and several other early broadcasters and analyzed documentary evidence that had then only recently come to light. They limited their analysis to WHA and three other stations that have strong claims to being oldest or first: KDKA-Pittsburgh, KCBS–San Francisco, and WWJ-Detroit.[5]

The analysis that follows has benefited from access to the papers of Harold McCarty, which were not available in public archives until 1987. Also, a recent book by Gordon Greb and Mike Adams about the history of the KCBS ancestor includes much new information. However, the story of WHA is unchanged: all available evidence shows that regularly scheduled voice broadcasts on 9XM/WHA began in the first week of 1921, with some "regular" music broadcasts perhaps a few weeks earlier. Still, a discussion of "oldest" and "first" is a useful exercise.

The First Station

Baudino and Kittross concluded that the first U.S. broadcast station was located in San Jose, California, and was operated by Charles David Herrold. "Doc" Herrold opened his College of Engineering and Wireless in the Garden City Bank Building in San Jose on January 1, 1909, and it was the location of his wireless operation. There is evidence of live instrumental music broadcasts later that year and of regular daily broadcast of phonograph records in 1910, albeit primarily for testing purposes. A regular program schedule was established in 1912. The station even predates the concept of call letters, referring to itself on-air as "the Herrold station" and later using a variety identifiers through 1917, sometimes unofficially. These included FN, SJN (a call sign at the time reserved for use in Sweden), and the experimental license designations 6XE and 6XF. In late 1921 Herrold received a license for his San Jose station with the call letters KQW, which is the ancestor of station KCBS–San Francisco.

Herrold started the station as a way to build interest in his college and, much as 9XM's Earle Terry would do later, went so far as to distribute crystal sets to help build an audience. There is evidence Herrold operated on a regular schedule on Wednesday evenings early on and eventually operated daily. One listener recalled that the early weekly broadcasts started off fine but became "mushy" as the program progressed, caused by the microphone overheating and ultimately burning out. The next week the program would begin with Herrold's apology for how the previous week's program ended and then the same thing would often occur.[6] Herrold eventually developed a water-cooled microphone.[7] In addition to playing phonograph records, the announcers read news from the *San Jose Mercury-Herald*.[8] Herrold's wife, Sybil, was on the air as well, which probably makes her the first female disk jockey in the United States. She was the announcer for a show she called the *Little Hams Program,* and she played records to attract teenage amateur wireless enthusiasts. She even held the couple's new son before the microphone so listeners could hear his cries. Herrold found a local record store willing to provide records for broadcast in exchange for an on-air mention, a practice that KDKA predecessor 8XK near Pittsburgh and 9XM in Madison would adopt in the future. The San Jose store's owners found that the selections played on the radio would sell out. Herrold also helped another store outfit a listening room with comfortable chairs, two radio receivers, and two dozen sets of headphones.[9] Herrold broadcast special programs from San Jose for six to eight hours a day during the 1915 Panama-Pacific International Exposition in San Francisco. Visitors to the fair could hear the program at the de Forest wireless exhibit. Herrold's broadcasts were a boon for inventor Lee de Forest. He was there to demonstrate his new Audion vacuum tube, but the transmitter he had brought along for demonstrations failed to work.[10]

Like nearly all other wireless operators, Herrold was forced to shut down in 1917 with the entry of the United States into World War I, although he did unsuccessfully offer his station for government service. However, after the ban on wireless transmitting was lifted in October 1919, the station did not return to the air as soon as possible, partly because Herrold's prewar "arc phone" technology was not capable of sending efficiently on the new 360-meter wavelength. The government authorized Herrold's return to the air under his old experimental call 6XF on March 9, 1920, and some of his former students recalled that he was on air with voice broadcasts and using a new tube transmitter before May 1920. Herrold received a limited commercial license for his station on December 9, 1921, with the call letters KQW, but details are sketchy as to exactly how regular the programming was between March 1920 and December 1921. The KQW license was later held jointly by Herrold and the

First Baptist Church and later by the church alone. However, the new owners seemed uninterested in the station's origins, as evidenced by an annual report covering the station's "first" year of operation, January 15, 1926 to January 15, 1927.[11] The church later transferred the license to CBS. The network moved the station to San Francisco and in 1949 changed the call letters to KCBS, which remain to this day. However, some historians maintain that the gap in program service after World War I negates the claim that KCBS is the oldest station, because it did not operate continuously. It can, however, claim descent from the nation's first radio station by virtue of Herrold being the licensee for KQW through the mid-1920s.

The Oldest Station

Baudino and Kittross give KDKA-Pittsburgh the nod as the oldest continuously operating radio station on the air. Its predecessor was experimental wireless station 8XK operated by Westinghouse engineer Dr. Frank Conrad, and it was first licensed in 1916. He originally set up the station to receive the telegraphic time signals in order to settle a bet about the accuracy of his watch. When the wireless ban went into effect in 1917, the Westinghouse Company was issued two special licenses to continue radio experimentation during the war. The stations were designated 2WM and 2WE. One was near the Westinghouse plant in east Pittsburgh and the other was at Conrad's home.[12]

After the war Conrad put his personal station back on the air as soon as he could. While amateurs were not allowed to resume transmitter operation until October 1, 1919, Conrad got around this restriction by applying to have 8XK relicensed as a "special land station." This occurred sometime between June 15 and August 1 of that year.

On the evening of October 17, 1919, Conrad played a phonograph record in place of his occasional on-air conversations about wireless equipment. Radio hobbyists flooded Conrad with so many requests for specific pieces of music that he announced he would broadcast records for two hours on Wednesday and Saturday evenings. Conrad's two young sons would sometimes serve as announcers or play the piano or sing, and there is evidence of other live music performances as well. The bulk of the programming was phonograph records, but there were some spoken-word presentations, including sports scores, and the broadcasts were reported in the local newspapers. Conrad kept the programs going on a regular basis throughout 1920, and the operation in his garage took on the characteristics of a radio broadcasting station.[13]

Interest in these early programs prompted a local department store to advertise in the *Pittsburgh Sun* on September 29, 1920, that it had a supply of simple radio receivers on hand and was offering them for sale so members of the public could "receive the programs sent out by Dr. Conrad." H. P. Davis, a Westinghouse vice president, saw the ad. The interest in the Conrad broadcasts by the general public (i.e., nonhobbyists) had already suggested to Davis the possibility of using Westinghouse's manufacturing capability to build receiving sets. The company also had excess factory capacity for building wireless gear, now that the war was over. The advertisement planted in Davis's mind the idea for "broadcasting."[14]

The next day Davis assembled a team of Westinghouse employees, including Conrad, to discuss the possibility of "broadcasting" on a regular basis, so people would acquire the habit of listening "just like they do of reading a newspaper." Davis wanted to know whether it would be possible to have a transmitter built and licensed in time to report the results of the presidential election on November 2, 1920. Westinghouse filed an application with the Department of Commerce on October 16, 1920, saying overtly that they "wished to have a license to broadcast regularly scheduled programs." The agency granted a "limited commercial license" on October 27, 1920, with the call letters KDKA, in the same license category as the one that 9XM/WHA would receive in December 1921. Because the election was fast approaching, the Department of Commerce called a week later and informally assigned the temporary call letters 8ZZ to the station, just in case the license did not arrive in time. Some references say the 8ZZ calls were used for the first two days' broadcasts, although other sources say the license arrived at Westinghouse on October 27, and the station used the KDKA call letters from the outset. Still other references say the KDKA and 8ZZ call letters were used interchangeably for the first few days. Audio clips from the "first broadcast" using the KDKA call letters don't settle the question: they're all reenactments and have fooled many radio historians (some of these clips are also now on the Internet).

The election night broadcast went as scheduled, from the new broadcasting "studio" at the Westinghouse plant in East Pittsburgh. Dr. Conrad was not there, however; he was nervously standing by in his garage, ready to take over the broadcast with his reliable 8XK transmitter, should the new KDKA equipment fail. The next day KDKA began a daily program from 8:30 to 9:30 p.m., and the station has been on the air ever since.

WWJ—The Other Competitor

Another station that claims the title of oldest station is WWJ in Detroit. The station traces its history to amateur station 8MK and its first broadcast to August 20, 1920. WWJ was owned by the *Detroit News,* and the first 8MK broadcast

came from a makeshift "radio phone room" in its building, but the station was
not licensed to the paper. Rather, it was licensed to the Radio News and Music
Company, a sales subsidiary of Lee de Forest's firm. In his autobiography de
Forest said he and a friend established the company to sell radio transmitters
to newspaper owners. They convinced *Detroit Daily News* owner William E.
Scripps that the paper should be the first in the country to own a radio transmitter. In his autobiography de Forest also gives the original date of broadcast
as August 20, 1920, and says it was the first commercial radio station in the
United States to broadcast regular daily programs. He seemed to have forgotten
the broadcasts by Charles Herrold that were so useful to his demonstrations
at the 1915 Panama-Pacific International Exposition in San Francisco.

However, the paper did not hold a radio license in its name during this early
period and did not acquire one until October 13, 1921. The paper had requested a special amateur license, but this was changed, perhaps by the radio
inspector, to a limited commercial class license, and the call letters WBL were
assigned. The next license for WBL was dated February 11, 1922, and was in
effect for three months. On it the *WBL* is crossed out and *WWJ* written in its
place with a notation initialed *D. C.* that says that the call letters were changed
on March 3, 1922. D. C. is believed to be D. B. Carson, then the commissioner of navigation.

The broadcast of August 20, 1920, did indeed occur, but tracing this broadcast on 8MK to today's WWJ is problematic. Baudino and Kittross say the "evidence of a direct relationship between the licensee of 8MK and the licensee
of WBL is very tenuous, particularly when compared to the relationship of
8XK and KDKA." Baudino and Kittross dismiss the "tortured reasoning" that
Lee de Forest uses to say WWJ was first. They also note that there is natural
chauvinism on de Forest's part because 8MK was using a de Forest–brand
transmitter.[15]

Nonetheless, when WHA celebrated its "fiftieth" anniversary in 1969, WWJ
officials sent a variety of publicity materials to Madison to bolster their claim
to being the oldest station.

9XM/WHA

What, then, of the claim made by 9XM and WHA? WHA's claim, that it is
descended from 9XM, is the most solid of all the competitors', even more so
than the link between 8XK and KDKA, which clearly were two separate enti-
ties because they existed simultaneously. Quite simply, WHA was just the new
name for 9XM. It had the same transmitter, same address, and same licensee,
and when the new license and call letters went into effect on January 13, 1922,

WHA's voice programming was in all respects identical to the programming heard on 9XM the day before. However, given Baudino and Kittross's criteria, it is clear that 9XM/WHA cannot claim the title of oldest station. It can trace its beginning of regular broadcasting service to January 3, 1921, and perhaps a few weeks earlier.

Most of the early 9XM/WHA historical records do not survive. In 1930 former WHA program director W. H. Lighty wrote a letter to former WHA student operator Malcolm Hanson, who by this time was a radio engineer with the Antarctic expedition of Admiral Byrd. Lighty wrote: "I am endeavoring to gather up some of the background facts in connection with the radio station development in the University of Wisconsin. With the sudden death of Professor Terry last year, and your absence from all means of communication, it has not been possible to collect any data as to the earliest dates of broadcasting from the University of Wisconsin."[16] As John Stanley Penn began researching his dissertation in 1946, WHA personnel privately hoped that he would unearth documents that would "nail down" some of the important dates in the station's history.[17] This indicates that perhaps the exact date existed only in Terry's memory or was among the papers that his wife discarded after his death in May 1929.

WHA published histories that have often claimed January 3, 1919, as the first day of broadcasting, which is puzzling. When former wireless squad member C. M. Jansky Jr. delivered the main address at the 1958 WHA family dinner, he gave this date as the beginning of regular telephonic broadcasting and daily weather reports. This is unlikely on several counts. Of particular significance is that the ban on civilian wireless was still in effect, so "broadcasting" to the general public was in theory not possible, although a regular transmission to government wireless operators could be considered a form of "broadcasting," particularly if it was intended for multiple recipients rather than as a point-to-point message. However, the date Jansky gave is before the *Press Bulletin* of March 5, 1919, that said the first successful point-to-point speech transmission was made the previous month, timing that is borne out by a February 17, 1919, letter to Terry from a district superintendent of the U.S. Naval Communication Service at the Great Lakes Naval Station.[18] Some of Harold Engel's publicity material states that "regular programs were broadcast for the Great Lakes Naval Station and two-way communication was maintained with that point,"[19] but it makes no mention of the type of programs or how much of a "broadcast" this might have been.

Terry's correspondence with Charles Culver at Beloit College should also be considered. The letter from Terry to Culver of March 25, 1919, says: "We are still working on radio telephony problems," and the June 4, 1919, letter from Culver says the telephonic "test" of that date was "not at all satisfactory."[20] Neither statement would be likely if the station was regularly broadcasting by voice, nor does Terry mention anything about a regular schedule.

Years later, Jansky maintained there was a regular schedule of voice weather broadcasts over 9XM in 1919. What makes his argument difficult to dismiss is that he left the Madison campus for a position at the University of Minnesota in January 1920.[21]

Some histories, notably Kenneth Gapen's, cite February 1920 as the beginning of regular voice broadcasts. However, it is clear that this date applies only to the telegraphic weather broadcast; records show that this service was in operation by February 1, 1920.[22]

By May 1920 local weather bureau chief Eric Miller was writing: "Prof. Terry is planning to experiment with the sending of the forecast by wireless telephone, using a vacuum tube of his own invention, *but up to this time,* the necessary auxiliary apparatus has been needed for other purposes. Prof. Terry's vacuum tube has been successfully used in talking to Great Lakes, Ill., *and when applied to the sending of the forecast should be audible* in the apparatus ordinarily used by amateurs in wireless telegraphy, throughout the southern half of Wisconsin" (emphasis added).[23] Throughout the rest of the summer of 1920, Miller was responding to queries from people eager to hear the telephonic weather broadcasts. In a letter of September 20, 1920, Miller says: "Wireless phone is still in the experimental stage. It can be received, *when in operation,* with the ordinary set used for wireless telegraphy (head phone etc.)." He went on to say he'd keep the letter on file and would let the listener know "*when we are ready to begin sending by wireless phone.*"[24]

Through the late summer and early fall of 1920, Malcolm Hanson continued work on the new telephonic transmitter. As late as September 27, 1920, he was telling his mother this about the wireless telephone transmitter: "I expect to have it done in about three weeks."[25] Miller wrote to another listener on October 15, 1920, that the voice broadcasts were not yet in operation.[26] The new transmitter was completed sometime after he sent this letter.

Hanson reported that some regular programs of phonograph music were offered beginning about November 1920, "about the same time that the Westinghouse station KDKA in East Pittsburgh commenced broadcasting."[27] As mentioned earlier, WHA operator Burton Miller remembered Hanson saying to him on several occasions that the University of Wisconsin station missed being the first in the regular broadcasting field by only five days.[28] This would put the first day of regular noncode broadcasts as November 7, 1920. Again, these 9XM programs (probably music) may have been only once-a-week efforts and perhaps primarily for testing purposes. Two letters that Terry wrote to listeners in December 1920 survive in the WHA records. The listeners had to asked about telephonic weather broadcasts, and Terry responded that they'd start after the holidays. In both he mentioned the ongoing telegraphic service but made no mention of any telephonic service at all, further evidence that he may have been unaware of any late night programs.[29]

Jansky's statements are also contradicted by Eric Miller. In several communications with his superiors, Miller gave the date of January 3, 1921, as the beginning of regular telephonic weather broadcasts, and he repeated it in letters to graduate student John Penn and others.[30] January 1921 is also the date that Hanson remembered. In February 1922 he wrote his "Elementary Circular on Radio Telephone Communication." It was mailed out in response to requests for information about radio. In it Hanson says that January 1921 was when voice broadcasts began on 9XM.[31] January 1921 is also listed as the beginning of regular telephonic broadcasting on the WHA/9XM "QSL" card from 1922–23.

Hanson said, "If there were telephone broadcasts as early as March, 1920, they were highly experimental and lasted only a short time,"[32] but Hanson was not in Madison at the time. In a 1933 journal article T. M. Beaird, the program director of educational radio station WNAD at the University of Oklahoma, said "fall 1920" was the date for the first 9XM telephonic broadcast but offered no evidence for the statement.[33]

The strongest argument for 9XM's beginning regular broadcasting after KDKA's debut comes from someone who was in a position to know: Earle Terry himself. On two different occasions in the 1920s, he gave the honor of being the first broadcaster to KDKA. In a 1924–25 lecture series called Significant Lines of Progress during the Past Quarter Century, Terry gave a speech on progress in radio. In it he says: "The past four years have seen the development of radio broadcasting by which is transmitted for the benefit of whoever cares to listen to scheduled programs of music, lectures, news bulletins and other recreational and instructive material. This began November 4 [*sic*], 1920, when the Westinghouse Company from its radiophone station at East Pittsburgh broadcasted the returns of the presidential election of that year."[34] Terry was well known for his humble streak when it came to his own accomplishments, but he was also a man of science, and it is unlikely that in this formal context he would say KDKA was first if 9XM could honestly make the claim.

Several years later Terry wrote to the Federal Radio Commission to defend WHA's right to remain on the 570 kHz frequency. The letter dated October

31, 1928, says in part: "The University of Wisconsin insists that, because of its long record in broadcasting work, it is entitled to a desirable channel. It desires to point out to the Commission that it has been a pioneer in the broadcasting field. Of the broadcasting stations now in operation in the United States, KDKA alone anidates [*sic*] WHA, and that by a few months only."[35]

Other documents dispute WHA's claim over KDKA. In a 1924 history of the station composed by Lighty in response to a request from the *Milwaukee Journal,* he gives January 3, 1921, as the date that radio telephone broadcasting began. He adds that regular voice broadcasting "has been carried on regularly and consecutively since."[36] In a 1929 article the *Wisconsin Alumni Magazine* after Terry's death, L. R. Ingersoll said the Wisconsin radio station was "the first university station and, so far as known, the second broadcasting station in the entire country."[37] An article about program changes in the *Daily Cardinal* from October 1929 said WHA is "the oldest station in the middle-west and the second oldest station in the United States."[38] It appears that WHA's unqualified claims as "oldest" begin about the same time that Harold McCarty became WHA's manager. He was a staunch defender of WHA's right to the title, heavily relying on Jansky's statement about regular programming in 1919 and dismissing as "phony" the claims of KQW.[39]

One small complication that is overlooked is the short period in mid-1924 when WHA's license expired and the call letters were deleted (see chapter 6). WHA's Class C limited commercial license, dated April 3, 1924, expired on July 6, 1924, but WHA programming continued through Monday, July 28. On the face of the April 3 license is a penciled notation: "Delete per LSR Chicago 9/8/24." A new Class A limited commercial license was issued to the University of Wisconsin on October 4, 1924. In the section called "Report and Recommendation" is the recommendation that "*former call WHA be re-assigned*" (emphasis added).

This is a minor point because the period without a license closely corresponds to when the station would have been off the air anyway, and this brief period is not something that detracts from the station's record of continuous operation. This is particularly true when one considers that WHA in its early years had much longer "gaps" in continuous programming during university vacations and because of equipment failures. One notable period of silence lasted from July 29, 1922, to January 8, 1923, 162 days when the station operated for only a few days (in November 1922). WHA's Harold Engel must also have regarded the expiration of the license and deletion of the call letters to be of no consequence, as he is forthright about it in the history of the station that he provided for the book *Education's Own Stations* in 1937.[40]

Clearly, WHA/9XM is not the oldest continuously operating station in the United States, but it does have a fairly solid claim to being the second oldest. The slogan on the WHA letterhead from the 1930s is also valid: "America's Oldest Educational Station." Among the stations claiming to be first or oldest, WHA/9XM is the only non-commercial educational candidate.

APPENDIXES

NOTES

BIBLIOGRAPHY

INDEXES

Appendix A

9XM/WHA Time Line

1909   Wireless experiments begin at the University of Wisconsin

1914   UW Professor Edward Bennett issued experimental wireless license 9XM

1915   9XM license transferred to the University of Wisconsin (June)

       9XM in daily operation for receiving and point-to-point transmitting (November)

1916   Telegraphic reception of basketball results from Iowa City station 9YA (January 10)

       Telegraphic reception of "war news from Berlin" from station POZ (March 3)

       Telegraphic reception of general message for mobilization of Wisconsin National Guard (June 18)

       First regular telegraphic broadcast of weather forecast (December 4)

1917   First telegraphic broadcast of college basketball game (February 17)

       First clear telephonic transmission of phonograph music (after mid-January/before March 21)

       President Wilson puts wireless ban into effect (April 7)

       9XM allowed back on air for wartime experimentation (May 16)

1918   9XM moves from Science Hall to basement of Sterling Hall (January)

       Semiregular telephonic transmission exchanges with the U.S. Army (summer-fall)

1919   First clear transmission of human speech between Madison and Great Lakes Naval Training Station (February 17)

       Semiregular evening telephonic music broadcasts (summer-fall)

       Semiregular telegraphic market and weather reports (fall)

1920   Irregular telephonic broadcasts of weather forecast? (February–June)
       Telegraphic relay of election returns? (November 2)
       Regular broadcasts of phonograph records? (November 7)
       9XM telephonic transmitter receives new license (December)
1921   Regular schedule of telephonic weather broadcasts begins (January 3)
       Evening music broadcasts begin? (January 28)
       First remote broadcast, University Glee Club at Music Hall
           (March 11)
       First telephonic reports of farm markets (September 19)
       First concert remote from University Armory, soprano Mabel
           Garrison (October 20)
       First typewritten program guide issued (October 28)
       First live symphony concert broadcast, Cincinnati Symphony
           (November 1)
       Application for limited commercial license (December 23)
1922   9XM relicensed as WHA (January 13)
       First regular news program, *University Press Bureau Radiophone
           Report* (March 10)
       First educational broadcast, *Appreciation of Music* (March 24)
       Daily educational broadcasts begin (May 29)
1923   WHA makes its last regular Morse code broadcast (February)
       First? college basketball play-by-play, Minnesota at Wisconsin
           (February 19)
       Pablo Casals "test" broadcast (February 20)
       First? broadcast of state high school basketball tournament
           (March 24)
       First? broadcast by a Wisconsin governor (June 4)
       First? play-by-play of college football, Coe at Wisconsin (October 6)
1924   WHA moves to 1090 kHz (October)
1925   WHA moves to 560 kHz (January)
       WHA studio moves from basement to first floor of Sterling Hall
           (May?)
1926   WHA power increased to 750 watts (summer)
1927   WHA granted use of 590 kHz for basketball games and specials
           (January)
       WHA moves to 940 kHz (May)
       WHA moves to 900 kHz (November)
       First professionally printed program guide, the *University Antenna*
           (December 1)

1928   Daily transmission of road conditions from Wisconsin Highway
        Department (January)
        University political science department begins monthly political
        review program (March)
        WHA moves to 570 kHz (September)

1929   WHA moves to 940 kHz (April 2)
        Farm Program and *Homemakers' Program* split into separate
        programs (April 2)
        Farm Program begins tri-weekly simulcast over WTMJ-Milwaukee
        (April 3)
        Earle Terry dies in Madison (May 1)
        Edward Bennett appointed manager (June)
        Harold B. McCarty joins staff as part-time announcer (October 9)
        What's Back of the News news analysis program debuts (October 11)

1930   Experimentation with use of radio for classroom instruction begins
        (March 17)
        Homemakers' Hour rebroadcast by WIBA-Madison (August)
        First WHA origination for national network (NBC) (October 8)
        First airing of programs from Ohio-based shortwave educational
        network (October 14)

1931   Harold McCarty appointed part-time program director (February)
        First course broadcast from college classroom, C. H. Mills's course
        on music appreciation (September 29)
        Wisconsin School of the Air debuts (October 5)

1932   Daily typewritten program schedule for in-house use begins
        (January 1)
        Regular daily broadcasts by legislators from capitol studio (March 21)
        First broadcasts from new transmitter location at former WISJ site
        (July 20)
        Earliest documented reference to *Chapter a Day* (July 25)
        Political Education Forum debuts (August 22)
        WSA program *Creative Art* (predecessor of *Let's Draw*) debuts
        (October 6)

1933   WHA power increased to 1,000 watts (January 13)
        Rebroadcast of selected WLBL market programs begins (February 6)
        All Wisconsin Old-Time Fiddlers Contest aired (February 25)
        Aline Watson Hazard begins hosting the *Homemakers' Program*
        (June 20)

On-air typing class begins (June 26)

Afield with Ranger Mac debuts on Wisconsin School of the Air
(September 25)

Wisconsin College of the Air debuts (October 2)

1934   Monthly bulletins issued for *Farm Program* and *Homemakers'
Program (July 1)

WHA issues program guide booklet (November)

WHA moves to Radio Hall (December 3)

1935   WHA power increased to 2,500 watts (April 23)

First transcription disc recorder acquired (summer/fall?)

1936   WHA power increased to 5,000 watts (September 22)

Let's Draw debuts on Wisconsin School of the Air (September 30)

1937   First Ohio State award for WHA, for WSA's *Let's Draw*

WHA transferred to Department of Agriculture budget

1938   Broadcast line installed to Eric Miller's weather bureau office
(January)

WHA applies for 670 kHz (September 2)

1939   *Chapter a Day* returns to schedule and begins continuous run
(April 3)

WHA makes first remote broadcast using call letters WDAC and
shortwave equipment (August 15)

1941   WHA moves from 940 kHz to 970 kHz (March 29)

Operation of WHA returned to University of Wisconsin (July 1)

1942   WHA begins regular Sunday broadcasts (February 1)

WHA installs Associated Press news wire service (July 18)

1943   College of the Air begins regular classroom offerings (spring)

New WHA program bulletin debuts (June 1)

WHA-produced program airs on NBC Blue network (October 22)

WHA offers monthly music listings (December 1)

1944   WHA originates four-part music series for Mutual Broadcasting
System

1945   Regular monthly program bulletins begin (January)

WHA begins airing some Mutual Broadcasting System network
programs (August 20)

WHA music performance series begins on Mutual network
(December 9)

Last Christmas Day off the air (December 25)

Appendix B

WPAH/WCP/WLBL Time Line

1922   Construction of WPAH-Waupaca begins (November)

        License issued for WPAH-Waupaca (December 12)

1923   On-air testing of WPAH begins (February 3)

        WPAH debuts broadcast schedule (February 5)

        WPAH begins live evening band concert broadcasts (June)

        WPAH triweekly evening "community" talent programs begin
           (September 26)

        WPAH Sunday evening religious programs begin (November 11)

1924   WPAH discontinues service (January 19)

        WPAH dismantled and equipment moved to Stevens Point
           (February 26)

        U.S. Department of Commerce deletes WPAH call letters
           (February 28)

        WCP–Stevens Point begins postmidnight tests (March 9)

        First *Enemies of Sleep* postmidnight program (March 30)

        Badger State Crier daily news program begins (April 23)

        WLBL call letters replace WCP, operating with 500 watts at 1080
           kHz (May 12)

        Frank R. Calvert becomes manager of WLBL (June)

        WLBL introduces postcard program guide/reception
           acknowledgement (summer)

1925   First cooperation with Central State Teachers College (September?)

1927   WLBL airs regional high school basketball tournament (March 10)

        WLBL granted power increase to 750 watts (April 8)

        New transmitter in operation (April 19)

WLBL shifted to 940 kHz (June 1)

WLBL relays boxing match action from wire reports (July 21)

Governor Fred Zimmerman vetoes $12,000 WLBL appropriation
bill (July 23)

WLBL shifted to 900 kHz (October 31)

1928   WLBL "booster" broadcasts from southern train trip (February)

Election night broadcasts with *Stevens Point Daily Journal*
(September 4/November 5)

WLBL limited to daytime-only operation (November 11)

1929   WLBL applies for power increase to 3,000 watts (November 14)

1930   WLBL begins live weekly band concerts from high school
(February 25)

WLBL begins broadcasting lost-and-found items from local paper
(March 19)

First? high school football broadcast, Wausau at Stevens Point
(October 10)

First? college football broadcast, Oshkosh Normal at Central State
(October 11)

1932   WLBL ends operation in Whiting Hotel (March 2)

WLBL begins studio operation from Fox Theatre with transmitter
in Ellis (May 2)

Political Education Forum debuts/first regular WHA retransmission
(August 22)

1933   Bidirectional broadcast line connects WLBL to WHA for governor's
inaugural (January 2)

Broadcast line in daily use (February 6)

State floats plan to lease out WLBL frequency (July)

Green Bay Packers broadcasts debut, fed from WTMJ-Milwaukee
(November?)

University of Wisconsin football broadcasts debut, fed from
WTMJ-Milwaukee? (November 25)

Stevens Point Daily Journal begins printing daily program listings for
WLBL (December 6)

1935   Broadcast lines installed to Central State Teachers College campus
(fall)

1936   WLBL first airs *Chapter a Day* from WHA (May 27)

1937   WLBL moves transmitter to Auburndale (June 18)

1938   WLBL studios and offices move to Central State Teachers College
(September 6)

Final Green Bay Packers broadcast, Packers at New York Giants
(November 20)

1939   Central State course *This Land of Ours* airs as part of WHA School
of the Air (fall)

WLBL begins newscasts with Associated Press content (October 3)

WLBL resumes regular local broadcasts of Central State football
games (October 21)

1940   "Cheese for Christmas" promotion to gauge audience (December)

1941   WLBL moves from 900 kHz to 930 kHz (March 29)

1942   Associated Press broadcast wire service installed (April 15)

1943   WLBL studio A vacated for use as military barracks (May 1)

1944   WLBL transcriptions air on WIBA-Madison (October)

1947   WLBL tower collapses (February 12)

New tower in operation (December 22)

1949   WLBL network feed from FM stations in Chilton (spring) and Rib
Mountain (summer)

1950   Vern Varney appointed program director for college offerings
(May 29)

Last local (noncollege) WLBL program airs (June 17)

1951   Vern Varney resigns from program director position (March)

Last local WLBL program from Central State (June 8?)

Line from college to transmitter discontinued (June 8)

WLBL license transferred to State Radio Council (July 1)

1952   WLBL transmitter engineers begin contributing to *Weather
Roundup* (December 1)

1956   WLBL adds Sunday broadcasting for the first time since 1938
Packers games (May 7)

1961   New RCA transmitter replaces 1937-era university-built "Old
Betsy" (December 31)

1968   Consultant's report recommends sale or other disposal of WLBL
(October 15)

1973   Last daily *Weather Roundup* report from WLBL (August 20)

1976   Final *Weather Roundup* report from WLBL (July 7)

1986   WPR central Wisconsin news bureau established in old WLBL
studio, feeds WLBL (fall)

1993   WPR central Wisconsin news bureau moves to University of
Wisconsin–Marathon County Center in Wausau (fall)

1994   WLBL local weekly programs begin from Wausau WPR bureau
(fall)

1996   WLBL-FM begins service at 91.9 mHz (February 23)
2004   Local talk show *Route 51* debuts over WLBL-AM/FM and
          WHBM–Park Falls (October 7)
2005   Reduced-power post-sunset operation allowed for twenty-four-hour
          service (January)

Appendix C

FM Network Time Line

1932   First simulcast of WHA and WLBL (May 2)
1933   Broadcast line connects WHA and WLBL for inauguration
            broadcast (January 2)
        WLBL programs debut on WHA (February 6)
1945   State Radio Council is formed
1946   FCC issues FM construction permit for WIUN-Madison
            (February 13)
        FCC issues FM construction permit for WIUV-Delafield
            (February 13)
1947   First FM station, WHA-FM, goes on the air: (March 30)
        Farm Program adds weather live from weather bureau (September)
        First full-time news director hired (September)
        First Wisconsin College of the Air course aired direct from the
            classroom (fall)
1948   WHA-FM changes frequency from 91.5 mHz to 88.7 mHz (May)
        WHAD-Delafield goes on the air (May 30)
1949   WHKW-Chilton goes on air (January 1)
        Dr. John Schindler gives "How to Live a Hundred Years Happily"
            broadcast (February 3)
        WHSF–Rib Mountain goes on the air (June 10)
1950   WHWC-Colfax goes on the air (June 28)
        WHLA–West Salem goes on the air (November 21)
1951   Wisconsin Good Neighbor Day chronicled on *Homemakers' Program*
            (September 11)
1952   WHHI-Highland and WHSA-Brule go on the air (September 14)
        Weather Roundup debuts (December 1)

1954   Last episode of *Afield with Ranger Mac* (May 25)
1955   Edgar Gordon retires from *Journeys in Music Land* (May 4)
       Budget cuts force suspension of Saturday broadcasting except for
           WHA (October 1)
1956   Experimental two-station "stereo" broadcasts (June)
1958   Last broadcast of high school basketball tournament (March 22)
       First regular jazz programs, hosted by Ken Ohst (May)
       WHA historical marker dedicated (November 24)
1960   Last college basketball game broadcast, Purdue at Wisconsin
           (March 5)
1963   WHA-FM begins stereo broadcasts (January 13)
       State stations use NBC feed from WIBA for coverage of Kennedy
           assassination (November 22)
       Metropolitan Opera broadcasts debut on state stations (December 7)
1964   WHAD-Delafield begins stereo broadcasts (January 19)
1965   WHMD-Marinette goes on the air (January 12)
       Aline Watson Hazard retires from *Homemakers' Program* (July 1)
       FM network's Saturday hours partially restored (September)
1966   First Wisconsin College of the Air course for credit airs (February 8)
       Homemakers' Program renamed *Accent on Living* (May 1)
       All FM stations now broadcast in stereo (May)
       Fannie Steve retires from *Rhythm and Games* (May 13)
       SCA FM multiplex "second service" begins (summer)
       Last college football broadcast, Minnesota at Wisconsin
           (November 19)
1967   State Radio Council becomes the Educational Broadcasting Board
           of the Coordinating Council for Higher Education
       Colloquy begins, marking first regular use of listener call-in
           programming (November 4)
1968   United Press International audio service added (June?)
       Farm Program renamed *Midday Report* (September 2)
       First for-credit course airs from a Wisconsin State University campus
           (October 3)
       First use of listener call-in programming for broadcasts featuring
           political candidates (October 3)
1970   Last broadcast of *Let's Draw* (May 5)
       Station break chimes eliminated (June 15)
1971   *All Things Considered* debuts, marking first live NPR program
           (May 3)

Educational Broadcasting Board becomes the Educational
     Communications Board
Proposal made to split WHA programming from FM network and
     WLBL (September)
1972   Radio operation moved to Vilas Communication Center from
     Radio Hall (October)
Election night special carried statewide from WUWM-Milwaukee
     (November 7)
First local broadcast from a state FM station, *Programa Cultural en
     Español,* on WHAD (December 8)
1973   WHMD-Suring abandoned (January 6)
WHKW-Chilton moves to Green Bay and becomes WPNE-FM
     (January 6)
1974   Full Saturday service restored (January 1)
WHWC-FM moves transmitter from Colfax to television tower at
     Wheeler (February 9)
WHLA-FM moves transmitter from Holmen to television tower in
     La Crescent, Minnesota (February 9)
Last broadcast of *Let's Sing* (May 8)
WHA-FM changes call letters to WERN (September 9)
1975   WHRM changes frequency from 91.9 to 90.9 (October)
1977   *Wisconsin Issues Forum* debuts, marking first regular call-in/interview
     public affairs program (June 5)
1978   *Wisconsin Hear and Now* replaces *Midday Report* and *Accent on Living*
     (January)
First on-air pledge drive, WHA only (April 1–2)
WYMS-Milwaukee begins airing some Wisconsin School of the Air
     programs (fall)
1979   WHA, WERN, and WHHI start using Wisconsin Public Radio
     name (January 1)
Simply Folk debuts (January 6)
First network pledge drive (September 27–October 1)
NPR's *Morning Edition* debuts (November 5)
WPR begins satellite reception of NPR programs (December 13)
1980   First news bureau established in Milwaukee (January)
WPR begins airing *A Prairie Home Companion* from Minnesota
     Public Radio (May 3)
1981   Michael Feldman begins hosting *High Noon,* predecessor of
     Whad'ya Know (September 5)

1982   WYMS-Milwaukee begins airing some WPR programs (October 4)
1983   WLSU–La Crosse begins airing some WPR programs (September 12)
        WRST-Oshkosh begins tape delay airing of *Morning Edition*
            (September)
1984   Last School of the Air programs air over FM network (May)
1985   *Whad'ya Know* debuts (June 1)
1986   NPR distributes *Whad'ya Know* and *Sidran on Record* (January)
        WPR begins carrying *As It Happens* from the CBC (August 4)
        WPR News bureaus established in four cities (September 1)
1987   Broadcast schedule expanded to 1 a.m. daily (September)
1988   WHBM–Park Falls goes on the air (November 11)
1989   Milwaukee bureau opens (July 1)
1990   WPR News and Information service now called Ideas Network
            (September)
        WPR Music and Arts service now called NPR News and Classical
            Music Network (September)
1995   Last School of the Air programs transmitted by SCA service (May)
1996   WLBL-FM begins operation from Wausau (February 23)
1997   WHID–Green Bay begins operation, replacing WGBW (April 26)
1998   WHA and FM Network now on twenty-four hours a day (April 7)
1999   WHND and WHDI begin service from Sister Bay (September 24)
2005   WLFM-Appleton ends affiliation when Lawrence University sells
            station (September 15)
        WEPS-Elgin, Illinois, joins WPR as an affiliate of the Ideas Network
            (September 28)

Notes

Prologue: Voices through the Air

1. Shurick, *First Quarter Century of American Broadcasting.*

2. David L. Woods, "Semantics versus the 'First' Broadcasting Station," *Journal of Broadcasting,* Summer 1967, 199.

3. G. C. B. Rowe, "Broadcasting in 1912," *Radio News,* June 1925, 2219, cited in Thomas White, *United States Early Radio History,* http://earlyradiohistory.us.

4. Archer, *History of Radio to 1926,* 55.

5. Barnouw, *History of Broadcasting,* 1:10–15; "Guglielmo Marconi, 1874–1937," *Ballycastle,* www.northantrim.com/Marconi.htm.

6. Archer, *History of Radio to 1926,* 92–93.

7. Fessenden, *Fessenden: Builder of Tomorrows,* 153.

8. Harkness, Higgins, Rideout, and Skiles, *Electrical Engineering,* 36.

Chapter 1. Early Wireless Experiments at the University of Wisconsin

1. de Anguera, *Ethereal Messages,* 6.

2. U.S. Navy, Bureau of Equipment, *List of Wireless Telegraph Stations of the World,* corrected to September 1, 1909 (Washington, D.C.: U.S. Government Printing Office, 1909).

3. L. R. Ingersoll, "Earle Melvin Terry, 1879–1929," *Wisconsin Alumni,* May 1929, 255.

4. Penn, "Earle Melvin Terry, Father of Educational Radio," *Wisconsin Magazine of History,* Summer 1961, 253.

5. Lloyd L. Call to Penn, April 24, 1947, Penn Papers.

6. C. T. Schrage to Penn, September 18, 1946, Penn Papers.

7. Arthur H. Ford to M. C. Beebe, December 30, 1915, WHA Radio and Television Records.

Chapter 2. Early Broadcasts from 9XM

1. Baker, *Farm Broadcasting*, 5–6.

2. Michael Friedewald, "Beginnings of Radio Communication in Germany," *Journal of Radio Studies*, Winter 2000, 458.

3. *Wisconsin State Journal*, March 6, 1916, 2.

4. *Press Bulletin*, March 15, 1916.

5. *Wisconsin State Journal*, June 19, 1916, 4.

6. L. Hanson, *Story of Malcolm Hanson*, 49.

7. *Daily Cardinal*, November 18, 1916, 11.

8. Penn, "Origin and Development of Radio Broadcasting," 74.

9. Michael Penn, "Tuning in to a Legacy," *On Wisconsin*, Fall 1998, 37.

10. E. B. Calvert, "History of Radio in Relation the Work of the Weather Bureau," *Monthly Weather Review* 51, no. 1 (January 1923): 1.

11. Ibid.

12. Frost, *Education's Own Stations*, 237.

13. Ibid., 233.

14. Miller to U.S. Weather Bureau, September 30, 1915, McCarty Papers.

15. E. Miller, letter to the editor, *Milwaukee Journal*, December 4, 1916 (copy), WHA Radio and Television Records.

16. *New York Times*, December 11, 1916, 5.

17. Calvert, "History of Radio," 1.

18. Kenneth Gapen, "Pioneering in Educational Broadcasting," *Wisconsin Alumni*, May 1932, 241.

19. Penn, "Origin and Development of Radio Broadcasting," 77–81.

20. Mrs. I. F. Thompson to H. B. McCarty, May 2, 1949, Penn Papers.

21. Malcolm Hanson to Andrew Hopkins, June 17, 1931, bound in Gapen, "Agricultural Broadcasting."

22. Penn, "Origin and Development of Radio Broadcasting," 110.

23. "Radio News from Wisconsin," *Education by Radio*, November 22, 1934, 54–55.

24. Stanley Rutter Manning, "Reminiscences," 2–5, quoted in Barnouw, *History of Broadcasting*, 1:30.

25. Norman Michie, "Tuning In," *Radio Guide*, Wisconsin Public Radio, September 1983, 13.

26. *Radio Service Bulletin*, March 1, 1917, 27.

27. Howard to Terry, March 8, 1917, WHA Radio and Television Records.

Chapter 3. Wartime Radio Experiments at the University of Wisconsin

1. Taussig, *Book of Radio*, 191–202, cited in Thomas White, *United States Early Radio History*, http://earlyradiohistory.us.

2. Elizabeth McLeod, posting to old.time.radio@broadcast.airwaves.com, a listserv (July 8, 1998).

3. Dillon to 9XM, April 7, 1917, WHA Radio and Television Records.

4. Frost, *Education's Own Stations,* 368. 3XJ was notable because its experimental license from the Department of Commerce carried the serial number 1, the first such license issued after the passage of the Radio Act of 1912.

5. *Daily Cardinal,* May 15, 1917, 8.

6. Dillon to Terry, April 26, 1917, WHA Radio and Television Records.

7. Taylor to Van Hise, May 8, 1917, Van Hise Papers.

8. Hise to Taylor, May 9, 1917 (copy), Van Hise Papers.

9. A. Hoyt Taylor, "Short Wave Reception and Transmission on Ground Wires, Submarine and Subterranean," *Proceedings of the Institute of Radio Engineers,* August 1919, 351, quoted in Penn, "Origin and Development of Radio Broadcasting," 95.

10. Frost, *Education's Own Stations,* 263.

11. M. Hanson to Lida Hanson, May 15, 1917 (English translation from Danish), Hanson Papers.

12. M. Hanson to L. Hanson, April 21, 1917 (English translation from Danish), Hanson Papers.

13. M. Hanson to L. Hanson, August 28, 1917 (English translation from Danish), Hanson Papers.

14. M. Hanson to L. Hanson, October 18, 1917 (English translation from Danish), Hanson Papers.

15. Penn, "Origin and Development of Radio Broadcasting," 96.

16. Penn, "Earle Melvin Terry, Father of Educational Radio," *Wisconsin Magazine of History,* Summer 1961, 255.

17. Penn, "Origin and Development of Radio Broadcasting," 100.

18. Ibid., 101.

19. Ibid., 102.

20. Ibid., 81.

21. Ibid., 104.

22. Ibid., 105.

23. Shurick, *First Quarter Century of American Broadcasting,* 12.

24. Van Hise to Snow, August 8, 1917 (copy), Van Hise Papers.

25. Penn, "Origin and Development of Radio Broadcasting," 106.

26. Mildred Frazier Bruff to Penn, June 2, 1947, and Helen Fairburne Jones to Penn, June 5, 1947, both in Penn Papers.

27. Penn, "Origin and Development of Radio Broadcasting," 114.

28. Culver to Terry, May 27, 1918, WHA Radio and Television Records.

29. Terry to Culver, July 3, 1920, WHA Radio and Television Records.

30. Burton M. Miller to Penn, June 15, 1953, Penn Papers.

31. E. J. Knapp to Penn, August 4, 1949, Penn Papers.

32. Nolte to Penn, June 19, 1947, Penn Papers.

Chapter 4. Telephonic Broadcasting by 9XM

1. *Press Bulletin,* March 5, 1919.

2. McPherson to Terry, February 19, 1919, WHA Radio and Television Records.

3. Terry to Culver, March 25, 1919 (copy), WHA Radio and Television Records.

4. Culver to Terry, June, 4, 1919, WHA Radio and Television Records.

5. Miller to Chief, Weather Bureau, May 31, 1919, McCarty Papers.

6. *Milwaukee Journal,* November 29, 1942, sec. 6, p. 11.

7. William F. Steuber, "It's Wireless!" *Airwaves Magazine,* February 1982, 37.

8. Greenslade to Harold Engel, April 24, 1937, McCarty Papers.

9. Wisconsin State Broadcasting Service News Release, November 23, 1958, WHA Radio and Television Records.

10. Michael Penn, "Tuning in to a Legacy," *On Wisconsin,* Fall 1998, 41.

11. L. L. Nettleton to Julian Mack, November 13, 1958, McCarty Papers.

12. Nettleton to Penn, April 30, 1947, Penn Papers.

13. Wisconsin Department of Markets Annual Report, 1919–1920, Madison, January 1, 1921, 8–9. On file at Wisconsin Historical Society.

14. Harold B. McCarty, lecture before University of Wisconsin communication arts class, September 28, 1971 (audiotape), Wisconsin Public Radio Collection.

15. *Daily Cardinal,* January 22, 1920, 1.

16. W. H. Lighty to Malcolm Hanson, March 12, 1930, Hanson Papers.

17. *Press Bulletin,* March 10, 1920.

18. E. Miller to Chief, U.S. Weather Bureau, May 12, 1920, McCarty Papers.

19. E. Miller to A. W. Hopkins, June 8, 1920 (copy), McCarty Papers.

20. Miller to Chief.

21. Yorkson to Miller, June 11, 1920, McCarty Papers.

22. Miller to Yorkson, quoted in *Wisconsin Public Broadcasting,* 5.

23. Department of Commerce, Bureau of Navigation, Commercial First Grade Radio License, serial 16935, issued to Malcolm Hanson, June 20, 1919, Washington, D.C., Hanson Papers.

24. Penn, "Origin and Development of Radio Broadcasting," 122.

25. Miller to Dr. F. B Jewett, June 22, 1920 (copy), McCarty Papers.

26. Miller to Penn, May 27, 1950, Penn Papers.

27. Harold A. Engel, "WHA, Wisconsin's Radio Pioneer," *Badger History,* March 1949, 15.

28. Penn, "Origin and Development of Radio Broadcasting," 122.

29. Miller to H. M. Baldwin, September 20, 1920 (copy), McCarty Papers.

30. M. Hanson to L. Hanson, September 27, 1920 (English translation from Danish), Hanson Papers.

31. E. Miller to R. E. Rogers, October 15, 1920 (copy), McCarty Papers.

32. E. Miller to U.S. Weather Bureau, Department of Agriculture, Washington, D.C., October 12, 1921 (copy), Andrew Hopkins Papers.

33. Malcolm Hanson to Andrew Hopkins, June 17, 1931, bound in Gapen, "Agricultural Broadcasting."

34. *Sandusky (Ohio) Star-Journal,* November 6, 1920, 6.

35. Malcolm Hanson to Andrew Hopkins, June 17, 1931, bound in Gapen, "Agricultural Broadcasting."

36. B. Miller to J. E. Mack, March 14, 1950, McCarty Papers.

37. Terry to Frank D. Urie December 11, 1920, and Terry to Victor Fink, December 11, 1920, both in WHA Radio and Television Records.

38. Penn, "Origin and Development of Radio Broadcasting," 490.

Chapter 5. Regular Voice Broadcasts on 9XM

1. E. B. Calvert, "History of Radio in Relation the Work of the Weather Bureau," *Monthly Weather Review* 51, no. 1 (January 1923): 1.

2. Terry to Frank D. Urie, December 11, 1920; Terry to Victor Fink, December 11, 1920, both in WHA Radio and Television Records.

3. *Daily Cardinal,* January 19, 1921, 3.

4. Penn, "Origin and Development of Radio Broadcasting," 141.

5. Ibid.

6. Smith to Penn, March 25, 1950, Penn Papers.

7. Barnouw, *History of Broadcasting,* 1:67.

8. Archer, *History of Radio to 1926,* 199.

9. Greb and Adams, *Charles Herrold,* 99.

10. *Capital Times,* January 28, 1921, 3.

11. *Daily Cardinal,* January 29, 1921, 1.

12. Shurick, *First Quarter Century of American Broadcasting,* 123.

13. John H. O'Connor to 9XM, February 17, 1921, WHA Radio and Television Records.

14. M. Hanson to L. Hanson, February 21, 1921 (English translation from Danish), Hanson Papers.

15. Malcolm Hanson to Andrew Hopkins, June 17, 1931, bound in Gapen, "Agricultural Broadcasting."

16. *Press Bulletin,* March 2, 1921.

17. *Wisconsin State Journal,* March 3, 1921, 1.

18. *Press Bulletin,* March 2, 1921.

19. *New York Times,* February 26, 1921.

20. *Capital Times,* March 12, 1921, 3.

21. Eric Miller to Weather Bureau, October 12, 1921 (copy), McCarty Papers.

22. *Press Bulletin,* April 20, 1921.

23. Calvert, "History of Radio," 9.

24. Eric R. Miller to Dr. Edwin B. Frost, April 25, 1921 (copy), McCarty Papers.

25. *Press Bulletin,* June 8, 1921.

26. Eric Miller to W. P. Stewart, June 10, 1921 (copy), WHA Radio and Television Records.

27. George W. Curran to Radio 9XM, September 23, 1921, WHA Radio and Television Records.

28. M. Hanson, "Elementary Circular on Radio Telephone Communication," mimeograph, February 1922, Harold Engel Papers.

29. Miller to Weather Bureau, December 3, 1921 (copy), WHA Radio and Television Records.

30. Ibid.

31. Miller to Weather Bureau, October 12, 1921 (copy), McCarty Papers.

32. M. Hanson to L. Hanson, October 2, 1921 (English translation from Danish), Hanson Papers.

33. Ibid.

34. W. H. Lighty, "A Sketch of the Revivification of University Extension at the University of Wisconsin," mimeograph, Department of Debating and Public Discussion, University of Wisconsin Extension Division, Madison, September 1938, 6. In his history of the Wisconsin Idea, Jack Stark defines it as "the University's direct contributions to the state: to the government in the forms of serving in office, offering advice about public policy, providing information and exercising technical skill, and to the citizens in the forms of doing research directed at solving problems that are important to the state and conducting outreach activities" (see Stark's "The Wisconsin Idea: The University's Service to the State," in Legislative Reference Bureau, *1995–1996 Wisconsin Blue Book;* Stark's chapter is available at www.legis.state.wi.us/lrb/pubs/feature/wisidea.pdf).

35. Paul Lighty, interview by author, October 10, 2003, Hackettstown, N.J.

36. Michael Penn, "Tuning in to a Legacy," *On Wisconsin,* Fall 1998, 41; Russell Lighty, unpublished manuscript, Wisconsin Public Radio Collection.

37. P. Lighty interview.

38. Strock to Harold Engel, November 11, 1958, Engel Papers.

39. W. H. Lighty, "Notes on the University of Wisconsin Radio Station, WHA Madison, Wisconsin" (copy), May 22, 1924, McCarty Papers.

40. Harold B. McCarty, lecture before University of Wisconsin communication arts class, September 28, 1971 (audiotape), Wisconsin Public Radio Collection.

41. Malcolm Hanson to Andrew Hopkins, June 17, 1931, bound in Gapen, "Agricultural Broadcasting."

42. *Press Bulletin,* November 2, 1921.

43. Radio Station 9XM Operating Schedule, 1921–1922, WHA Radio and Television Records.

44. M. Hanson, "Elementary Circular."

45. *Milwaukee Sentinel,* December 18, 1921, sec. 3, p. 10.

46. 9XM Circular 1, October 28, 1921, WHA Radio and Television Records.

47. Shurick, *First Quarter Century of American Broadcasting,* 66.

48. Penn, "Origin and Development of Radio Broadcasting," 157.

49. *New York Times,* February 9, 1922.

50. *Press Bulletin,* November 9, 1921.

51. *New York Times,* November 2, 1921, 20; *Milwaukee Sentinel,* December 18, 1921, sec. 3, p. 10.

52. *Press Bulletin,* December 14, 1921.

53. H. N. Stenen to University of Wisconsin, November 30, 1921 (copy), WHA Radio and Television Records.

54. Holmes News Service to Malcolm Hanson, November 29, 1921, WHA Radio and Television Records.

55. J. G. Crownhart, "Campaigning by Wireless Telephone," *La Follette's Magazine,* November 1921, 165.

56. *Milwaukee Journal,* November 20, 1921.

57. Crownhart, "Campaigning by Wireless Telephone," 165.

58. *Wisconsin Farmer,* November 24, 1921, 1.

59. Ibid., 13.

60. *Wisconsin State Journal,* May 11, 1969, sec. 6, p. 1.

61. Boyd Nestlerode to E. Miller, November 30, 1921, McCarty Papers.

62. E. Miller to Penn, May 27, 1950, Penn Papers.

63. Edwin B. Frost to E. Miller, December 22, 1921, McCarty Papers.

64. *Wisconsin Farmer,* November 24, 1921, 1.

65. Schmitt to Terry, December 14, 1921, WHA Radio and Television Records.

66. Terry to Schmitt, December 16, 1921 (copy), WHA Radio and Television Records.

67. E. Miller to Schmitt, December 16, 1921 (copy), WHA Radio and Television Records.

68. Schmitt to Terry, December 17, 1921, WHA Radio and Television Records.

69. Department of Commerce, Bureau of Navigation, Radio Service "Applicant's Description of Apparatus" serial 276, December 23, 1921 (copy), Wisconsin Public Radio Collection.

70. Jean Nelson, interview by author, February 1, 2004, Fitchburg, Wisconsin.

71. Terry to Schmitt, December 19, 1921 (copy), WHA Radio and Television Records.

72. Department of Commerce, Bureau of Navigation, Commercial First Class Radio Operator's License for Malcolm Hanson, Serial 2866, Chicago, December 23, 1921, Hanson Papers.

73. *Milwaukee Sentinel,* December 18, 1921, sec. 3, p. 10.

Chapter 6. WHA Begins

1. *Radio Service Bulletin,* February 1, 1926, 2.

2. *Press Bulletin,* September 22, 1926; *Radio Service Bulletin,* January 20, 1926, 4;

Kenneth Gapen, "Pioneering in Educational Broadcasting," *Wisconsin Alumni,* May 1932, 241.

3. Malcolm Hanson to Andrew Hopkins, June 17, 1931, bound in Gapen, "Agricultural Broadcasting."

4. Hazard, "History of WHA *Homemakers' Hour,*" 4.

5. Paul Lighty, interview by author, October 10, 2003, Hackettstown, N.J.

6. Steven Abrams, *Online Discographical Project,* www.honkingduck.com.

7. M. Hanson to Whittemore, January 16, 1922, Hanson Papers.

8. M. Hanson, to L. Hanson, March 9, 1922 (English translation from Danish), Hanson Papers.

9. Terry to Birge, February 2, 1922 (copy), WHA Radio and Television Records.

10. Terry to Grant, February 8, 1922 (copy), WHA Radio and Television Records.

11. Grant to Terry, February 14, 1922, WHA Radio and Television Records.

12. M. Hanson, "Elementary Circular on Radio Telephone Communication," mimeograph, February 1922, Engel Papers.

13. *Capital Times,* March 10, 1922, 1.

14. *Press Bulletin,* March 15, 1922.

15. *Wisconsin State Journal,* April 16, 1922, 14.

16. Penn, "Origin and Development of Radio Broadcasting," 188.

17. Ibid., 188–90.

18. Ibid., 193.

19. Ibid., 170.

20. Noon-Day Educational Radio Broadcasts/Evening University Lectures, week of May 29, 1922, Penn Papers.

21. P. Lighty interview.

22. *Press Bulletin,* April 19, 1922.

23. Penn, "Origin and Development of Radio Broadcasting," 224.

24. Milford Witts to E. B. Gordon, March 21, 1922; I. E. Burtis to WHA, March 23, 1922, both in Lighty Papers.

25. Penn, "Origin and Development of Radio Broadcasting," 226.

26. Edgar B. Gordon, audiotaped interview, September 19, 1969, Wisconsin Public Radio Collection.

27. *Press Bulletin,* March 22, 1922.

28. Penn, "Origin and Development of Radio Broadcasting," 221.

29. Ibid., 229.

30. *Press Bulletin,* September 13, 1922.

31. Penn, "Origin and Development of Radio Broadcasting," 168.

32. *Press Bulletin,* October 4, 1922.

33. *Wisconsin State Journal,* April 16, 1922, 14.

34. Ibid.

35. Earle M. Terry, manuscript, June 24, 1922, WHA Radio and Television Records.

36. *Press Bulletin,* July 12, 1922.

37. *Daily Cardinal,* July 21, 1922, 1.

38. Lighty to M. Hanson, March 12, 1930 (copy), Hanson Papers.

39. Jones to Terry, July 5, 1922, WHA Radio and Television Records.

40. Terry to Jones, August 23, 1922 (copy), WHA Radio and Television Records.

41. Penn, "Origin and Development of Radio Broadcasting," 207.

42. L. R. Ingersoll, "Earle Melvin Terry, 1879–1929," *Wisconsin Alumni,* May 1929, 255.

43. *Daily Cardinal,* May 3, 1929, 2.

44. *Press Bulletin,* January 10, 1923.

45. Orangeville Radio Club to WHA, undated postcard (1922), WHA Radio and Television Records.

46. Orangeville Radio Club to Gordon, postcard, July 5, 1922, WHA Radio and Television Records.

47. Schumaker to WHA, January 8, 1923, WHA Radio and Television Records.

48. M. Hanson to Shumaker, January 9, 1923 (copy), WHA Radio and Television Records.

49. Schumaker to WHA.

50. University of Wisconsin Educational Radio Broadcast Program for the week of March 5–10, 1923, Penn Papers.

51. University of Wisconsin Educational Radio Broadcast Program for the week of March 26–31, 1923, Penn Papers.

52. *Press Bulletin,* April 25, 1923.

53. M. Hanson, "Introduction to Radio Lecturers," February 16, 1923, Lighty Papers.

54. *Press Bulletin,* March 14, 1923.

55. Arlin P. Craig to WHA, March 25, 1923, WHA Radio and Television Records.

56. Malcolm Hanson to Andrew Hopkins, June 17, 1931, bound in Gapen, "Agricultural Broadcasting"; Ross M. Herrick to James Robertson, April 28, 1969, McCarty Papers.

57. Penn, "Origin and Development of Radio Broadcasting," 269.

58. "Radio Broadcast Program of the University of Wisconsin Radio Station WHA Prepared by the University Extension Division of Better Homes Week, June 4–9, 1923," Penn Papers.

59. University of Wisconsin Educational Radio Broadcast (various dates 1923), Penn Papers.

60. Ibid.

61. J. M. McBride to University of Wisconsin Broadcasting Station, October 25, 1923, WHA Radio and Television Records.

62. Mauer, "History of Station WHA," 53.

63. W. E. Rogers to Station WHA, October 27, 1923, WHA Radio and Television Records.

64. A. A. Lundgren to Radio Department, University of Wisconsin, WHA Radio and Television Records.

65. *Janesville Gazette,* October 27–28, 1923, 14.

66. *Daily Cardinal,* March 15, 1924, 7.

67. University of Wisconsin Educational Radio Broadcast Program for the week of October 22–26, 1923, Penn Papers.

68. University of Wisconsin Educational Radio Broadcast Program for the week of December 10–14, 1923, Penn Papers.

69. Shurick, *First Quarter Century of American Broadcasting,* 266.

70. Archer, *History of Radio to 1926,* 324.

71. *Press Bulletin,* February 6, 1924.

72. Ibid.

73. Penn, "Origin and Development of Radio Broadcasting," 270.

74. Ibid., 272.

75. *Press Bulletin,* May 28, 1924.

76. University of Wisconsin Educational Radio Broadcast Program for the week of June 16–22, 1924, Penn Papers.

77. Edward Bennett to L. Hanson, February 23, 1922, Hanson Papers.

78. M. Hanson to L. Hanson, November 15, 1922 (English translation from Danish), Hanson Papers.

79. L. Hanson, *Story of Malcolm Hanson,* 94–95.

80. *Press Bulletin,* October 3, 1923, and June 27, 1923.

81. B. Miller to Penn, June 15, 1953, Penn Papers.

82. de Anguera, *Ethereal Messages,* 13–14.

83. Department of Commerce, Bureau of Navigation, Radio Service, License for Land Radio Station, Class "C" Limited Commercial, Serial 887, April 3, 1924 (copy), Wisconsin Public Radio Collection.

84. Department of Commerce, Bureau of Navigation, Radio Service, License for Land Radio Station, Class "A" Limited Commercial, Serial 887, October 4, 1924 (copy), Wisconsin Public Radio Collection.

85. University of Wisconsin Educational Radio Broadcast Programs for the week of October 13–17, 1924, Penn Papers; Penn, "Origin and Development of Radio Broadcasting," 244.

86. Penn, "Origin and Development of Radio Broadcasting," 244.

87. E. Miller to Penn, May 27, 1950, Penn Papers.

88. *Press Bulletin,* February 4, 1925.

89. *Press Bulletin,* January 14, 1925.

90. Penn, "Origin and Development of Radio Broadcasting," 259.

91. *Press Bulletin,* May 13, 1925.

92. *Radio Service Bulletin,* February 2, 1925, 22.

93. Penn, "Origin and Development of Radio Broadcasting," 266.

94. *Capital Times,* April 7, 1925, 1.

95. *Daily Cardinal,* October 1, 1925, 4.

96. Penn, "Origin and Development of Radio Broadcasting," 280.

97. Hazard, "History of WHA *Homemakers' Hour,*" 7.

98. Mike Murray, interview by author, October 24, 2002.

99. Wood, "First Decade of the 'Fourth Network.'"

100. Penn, "Origin and Development of Radio Broadcasting," 258.

101. *Press Bulletin,* August 1, 1926.

102. Penn, "Origin and Development of Radio Broadcasting," 310.

103. Ibid., 293.

104. Ibid., 310.

105. *Daily Cardinal,* February 4, 1927, 3.

106. Penn, "Origin and Development of Radio Broadcasting," 310.

107. Ibid., 295.

108. Ibid., 322.

109. *Daily Cardinal,* October 9, 1927, 1.

110. WHA Transmission Log, October 1, 1927, WHA Radio and Television Records.

111. *Capital Times,* October 1, 1927, 11.

112. Penn, "Origin and Development of Radio Broadcasting," 296.

113. Shurick, *First Quarter Century of American Broadcasting,* 304.

114. *University Antenna,* December 1, 1927, WHA Radio and Television Records.

115. Penn, "Origin and Development of Radio Broadcasting," 296.

116. *Press Bulletin,* January 18, 1928.

117. *Press Bulletin,* March 21 and March 14, 1928.

118. Penn, "Origin and Development of Radio Broadcasting," 314.

119. *Press Bulletin,* June 6, 1928.

120. Mallory to Penn, December 6, 1951, Penn Papers.

121. *Daily Cardinal,* February 24, 1929, 1.

122. *Press Bulletin,* October 31, 1928.

123. *Daily Cardinal,* November 18, 1928, 12.

124. *Daily Cardinal,* October 30, 1928, 12.

125. *Press Bulletin,* November 7, 1928.

126. *Daily Cardinal,* January 5, 1929, 1.

127. Penn, "Origin and Development of Radio Broadcasting," 306.

128. Ibid., 305.

129. Ibid., 296.

130. Ibid., 318.

131. *Press Bulletin,* January 9, 1929.

132. Penn, "Origin and Development of Radio Broadcasting," 303.

133. *Daily Cardinal,* April 2, 1929, 5.

134. *Daily Cardinal,* April 25, 1929, 11.

135. H. L. Russell, "Around the Campus," *Wisconsin Country Magazine,* May 1929, 11.

136. Penn, "Origin and Development of Radio Broadcasting," 304.

137. Ingersoll, "Earle Melvin Terry," 255.

138. *Capital Times,* May 2, 1929, 1.

139. *Capital Times,* May 3, 1929, 7.

140. Gapen, "Agricultural Broadcasting."

Chapter 7. WHA Comes into Its Own

1. H. L. Ewbank, memorandum to H. B. McCarty, May 15, 1946, Engel Papers.

2. Quoted in Penn, "Origin and Development of Radio Broadcasting," 235.

3. Ibid., 327.

4. *Daily Cardinal,* April 21, 1929, 1.

5. Harold B. McCarty, lecture before University of Wisconsin communication arts class, September 28, 1971 (audiotape), Wisconsin Public Radio Collection.

6. *Press Bulletin,* July 10, 1929.

7. *Press Bulletin,* June 12, 1929.

8. This program was known by a variety of titles. *Homemakers' Program* seems to have been the one preferred and is what will be used here unless the original source uses one of the variants.

9. *Daily Cardinal,* October 8, 1927, 7.

10. Penn, "Origin and Development of Radio Broadcasting," 331.

11. *Daily Cardinal,* October 8, 1929, 1.

12. *Daily Cardinal,* October 15, 1929, 5.

13. *Daily Cardinal,* November 1, 1929, 9.

14. *Press Bulletin,* October 16, 1929.

15. Penn, "Origin and Development of Radio Broadcasting," 328.

16. *Daily Cardinal,* November 21, 1929, 12.

17. *Daily Cardinal,* March 21, 1931, 1.

18. *Press Bulletin,* May 13, 1931.

Chapter 8. The WHA–WLBL Merger

1. Penn, "Origin and Development of Radio Broadcasting," 327.

2. Ibid., 379.

3. Ibid.

4. G. T. Barnes, Inc., to E. Bennett, April 23, 1929, McCarty Papers.

5. Penn, "Origin and Development of Radio Broadcasting," 380.

6. *Stevens Point Daily Journal,* March 15, 1927, 9.

7. *Stevens Point Daily Journal,* January 27, 1930, 4.

8. Hill to Kohler, March, 28, 1930 (copy), McCarty Papers.

9. Penn, "Origin and Development of Radio Broadcasting," 380.

10. *Capital Times,* May 26, 1930, 1.

11. Penn, "Origin and Development of Radio Broadcasting," 386.

12. *Daily Cardinal,* November 18, 1930.

13. Frost, *Education's Own Stations,* 194.

14. Penn, "Origin and Development of Radio Broadcasting," 390.

15. Federal Radio Commission Docket 984, November 19–21, 1930, Washington, D.C., McCarty Papers.

16. "Radio During May and June," *Education by Radio,* July 16, 1931, 90.

17. Penn, "Origin and Development of Radio Broadcasting," 394.

18. Bennett to J. P. Brahany (copy), McCarty Papers.

19. *Daily Cardinal,* January 7, 1933, 8.

20. Penn, "Origin and Development of Radio Broadcasting," 399.

Chapter 9. More Hours on the Air

1. Penn, "Origin and Development of Radio Broadcasting," 333.

2. *Daily Cardinal,* December 11, 1930, 1.

3. *Wisconsin State Journal,* December 31, 1931, sec. 3, p. 5.

4. *Daily Cardinal,* September 26, 1930, 1.

5. *Wisconsin State Journal,* September 23, 1930, 1.

6. *Daily Cardinal,* September 28, 1930, 1–2.

7. *Daily Cardinal,* October 14, 1930, 6.

8. *Daily Cardinal,* October 24, 1930, 12.

9. de Anguera, *Ethereal Messages,* 18.

10. *Wisconsin State Journal,* September 2, 1930, 20.

11. Penn, "Origin and Development of Radio Broadcasting," 366.

12. Harold B. McCarty, lecture before University of Wisconsin communication arts class, September 28, 1971 (audiotape), Wisconsin Public Radio Collection.

13. Ibid.

14. *Wisconsin State Journal,* December 31, 1931, sec. 3, p. 5; WHA Broadcast Schedule, March 30, 1935, WHA Radio and Television Records.

15. WHA Broadcast Schedule, May 14, 1932, January 7, 1933, June 8, 1933, January 12, 1935, WHA Radio and Television Records.

16. *Daily Cardinal,* March 24, 1931, 5.

17. *Press Bulletin,* May 30, 1931.

18. *Daily Cardinal,* October 2, 1931, 1.

19. Penn, "Origin and Development of Radio Broadcasting," 347–48.

20. *Daily Cardinal,* July 21, 1932, 2.

21. WHA Broadcast Schedule, August 22, 1932, WHA Radio and Television Records.

22. Engel to Edward Skelton, March 1, 1933 (copy), WHA Radio and Television Records.

23. WHA Broadcast Schedule, December 30, 1933, WHA Radio and Television Records.

24. WHA Broadcast Schedule, April 21, 1934, WHA Radio and Television Records.

25. Harold A. Engel, "Typewriting Lessons by Radio," in *Education on the Air, Fifth*

Yearbook of the Institute for Education by Radio (Columbus: Ohio State University, 1936), 100–103.

26. "Gleanings from Various Sources," *Education by Radio,* May 24, 1934, 24.

27. WHA Broadcast Schedule, November 1, 1933, WHA Radio and Television Records.

28. WHA Broadcast Schedule, August 8, 1932, WHA Radio and Television Records.

29. Jay Rath, "WHA's Early Voices: Where Are They Now?" *Airwaves Magazine,* October 1982, 8.

Chapter 10. More Challenges from Commercial Stations

1. Penn, "Origin and Development of Radio Broadcasting," 401.

2. Ibid., 402.

3. Ibid., 404.

4. *Sheboygan Press,* July 26, 1933, 13.

5. *Stevens Point Daily Journal,* November 16, 1933, 10.

6. *Sheboygan Press,* October 13, 1933, 1.

7. Penn, "Origin and Development of Radio Broadcasting," 405.

8. Ibid., 406.

9. *Press Bulletin,* December 27, 1933.

10. *Press Bulletin,* December 6, 1933.

11. *Stevens Point Daily Journal,* December 12, 1933.

12. *Press Bulletin,* January 3, 1934.

13. Penn, "Origin and Development of Radio Broadcasting," 407.

14. H. L. Ewbank, *Conservation of Radio Resources,* pamphlet of material presented October, 1, 1934, before the Federal Communications Commission, Washington, D.C., Wisconsin Public Radio Collection.

15. *Sheboygan Press,* October 13, 1933, 12.

Chapter 11. The *Political Education Forum*

1. *Press Bulletin,* March 21, 1928.

2. *Stevens Point Daily Journal,* September 4, 1928, 1.

3. *New York Times,* December 21, 1930, sec. XX, p. 13.

4. Penn, "Origin and Development of Radio Broadcasting," 363.

5. WHA Broadcast Schedule, March 21, 1932, WHA Radio and Television Records.

6. "Public Stations Enlighten Wisconsin Citizens," *Education by Radio,* September 15, 1932, 95.

7. F. R. Calvert to Harold B. McCarty, August 22, 1932; McCarty to Calvert, September 10, 1932 (copy), both in WHA Radio and Television Records.

8. McCarty to Calvert.

9. Penn, "Origin and Development of Radio Broadcasting," 364.

10. O. A. LaBudde to James W. Baldwin, undated (1932, copy), WHA Radio and Television Records.

11. WHA Broadcast Schedule, February 6, 1933, WHA Radio and Television Records.

12. Penn, "Origin and Development of Radio Broadcasting," 423.

13. Harold Engel, "Radio in the Wisconsin Legislature," *Education by Radio,* April 27, 1933, 23.

14. *InterCom,* newsletter, Wisconsin State Broadcasting Service, August 2, 1965, 1, Engel Papers.

Chapter 12. A New Home

1. Penn, "Origin and Development of Radio Broadcasting," 343.

2. Hazard, *For the Love of Mike,* 5.

3. Penn, "Origin and Development of Radio Broadcasting," 412.

4. A. E. Bell, "WHA—Leader in the Technical Development of Broadcasting," *Wisconsin Engineer,* November 1936, 24.

5. *Milwaukee Journal,* November 29, 1942, sec. 6, p. 11.

6. *Daily Cardinal,* June 30, 1934, 5.

7. *Cathedral Echoes* postcard, undated (ca. 1935), McCarty Papers.

8. Penn, "Origin and Development of Radio Broadcasting," 413.

9. Marcia Beane Baird, "The ABCs of Interactive Communication," *Wisconsin Alumnus,* May–June 1981, 8.

10. Lillian Schoephoerster, "A Quarter Century with WHA," *Wisconsin Country Magazine,* November 1944, 11.

11. Penn, "Origin and Development of Radio Broadcasting," 414.

12. "Annual Report of the University Radio Committee," Document 1031, January 7, 1952, 10, Engel Papers.

Chapter 13. Budget Woes and New Programs

1. Penn, "Origin and Development of Radio Broadcasting," 416.

2. *Daily Cardinal,* January 19, 1935, 1.

3. Penn, "Origin and Development of Radio Broadcasting," 417.

4. *Daily Cardinal,* January 19, 1935, 1.

5. *Sheboygan Daily Press,* October 24, 1935, 5.

6. McCarty to "Life in the U.S." editor, *Readers' Digest,* January 3, 1980 (copy), McCarty Papers.

7. *Wisconsin State Journal,* October 24, 1943, 22.

8. E. Miller to Richard Vesey, February 23, 1951 (copy), McCarty Papers.

9. WHA Broadcast Schedule, various dates 1938–40, WHA Radio and Television Records.

10. "University Activities," *Wisconsin Alumnus,* April 1940, 249, http://digital.library.wisc.edu/1711.dl/UW.v41i3 (December 12, 2005).

11. Randall Davidson, unpublished inventory of WHA transcription recordings at Wisconsin Historical Society Archives, completed on September 23, 2003.

12. Penn, "Origin and Development of Radio Broadcasting," 418.

13. Ibid., 419.

14. Ibid.

15. Ibid., 440.

16. Ibid., 441.

17. *Chicago Tribune,* October 2, 1938, editorial.

18. Harold B. McCarty, lecture before University of Wisconsin communication arts class, September 28, 1971 (audiotape), Wisconsin Public Radio collection.

19. Penn, "Origin and Development of Radio Broadcasting," 441–42.

20. Ibid.

21. "First Annual Report of the Committee on Radio Broadcasting," Document 564, February 1939, 2–7, Harold Engel Papers.

22. WHA Broadcast Schedule, February 19, 1939, WHA Radio and Television Records.

23. *Oshkosh Daily Northwestern,* November 27, 1940, 13.

24. Baker, *Farm Broadcasting,* 285.

25. "Third Annual Report of the University Radio Committee," Document 629, October 1941, 1, Engel Papers.

26. Ibid.

Chapter 14. The War Years and After

1. "Annual Report of the University Radio Committee," Document 641, December 1943, 6–7, Engel Papers.

2. "Fourth Annual Report of the University Radio Committee," Document 662, December 1942, 4, Engel Papers.

3. Jean Fleming, "Radio . . . WHA," in "University Activities," *Wisconsin Alumnus,* July 1943, 325, http://digital.library.wisc.edu/1711.dl/UW.v44i4.

4. *Press Bulletin,* January 19, 1927.

5. Press Association wire copy, message code GH313PEW 15, from Tom O'Neil to WHA, July 18, 1942, McCarty Papers.

6. Wisconsin College of the Air Course Outline 1942–43, 15, WHA Radio and Television Records.

7. "Annual Report of the University Radio Committee," December 1943, 1.

8. *This Is Truax Field,* radio script, March 27, 1943, 6–7, McCarty Papers.

9. "Annual Report of the University Radio Committee," December 1943, 2.

10. Ibid., 6.

11. Wisconsin State Broadcasting Service, Radio Programs, July–August 1961, WHA Radio and Television Records.

12. WHA Classical Music Program Schedule, December 1943, WHA Radio and Television Records.

13. WHA Classical Music Program Schedule, May 1944, WHA Radio and Television Records.

14. "Annual Report of the University Radio Committee," University Document 722, February 5, 1945, 5, Engel Papers.

15. Ibid., 3. The Mutual Broadcasting System, originally owned by the Bamberger Broadcasting Service, was founded in 1934 so that WOR–New York, WGN-Chicago, WLW-Cincinnati, and WXYZ-Detroit could share programs; by 1947 it had four hundred affiliates nationwise (see Barry Mishkind, "MBS Section," *Broadcast Archive,* http://www.oldradio.com/archives/prog/mutual.htm).

16. *Wisconsin State Journal,* August 19, 1945, sec. 2, p. 11.

17. WHA Radio Program Guide, September 1945, WHA Radio and Television Records.

18. WHA Radio Program Guide, October 1945, WHA Radio and Television Records.

19. "Eighth Annual Report of the University Radio Committee," Document 755, March 4, 1946, 5, Engel Papers.

20. "Annual Report of the University Radio Committee," Document 878, January 3, 1949, 5, Engel Papers.

21. *Pro-Arte Quartet of the University of Wisconsin,* in RadioGoldIndex, the Definitive Database of Old Time Radio Programs, http://radiogoldindex.com/frame1.html (December 12, 2005).

22. McCarty to Principals of Schools in the District Basketball Tournaments, March 7, 1947 (copy), WHA Radio and Television Records.

23. Scott Anderson, interview by author, November 3, 2003, Neenah, Wisconsin.

24. Wirth to Harley, March 12, 1947, WHA Radio and Television Records.

25. Wirth to Harley, April 1, 1947, WHA Radio and Television Records.

26. Harley to Wirth, April 3, 1947 (copy), WHA Radio and Television Records.

27. "Annual Report of the University Radio Committee," Document 838, January 12, 1948, 3, Engel Papers.

Chapter 15. The FM Network

1. "Annual Report of the University Radio Committee," Document 722, February 5, 1945, 6–8, Engel Papers.

2. "Eighth Annual Report of the University Radio Committee," Document 755, March 4, 1946, 8, Engel Papers.

3. Ibid., 9.

4. Ibid.

5. "Annual Report of the University Radio Committee," Document 790, January 13, 1947, 1, Engel Papers.

6. "Annual Report of the University Radio Committee," Document 838, January 12, 1948, 10, Engel Papers.

7. FM Dedication Broadcast, March 30, 1947 (audiotape), Wisconsin Public Radio Collection.

8. "Annual Report of the University Radio Committee," 1948, 9–11.

9. WHA Radio Program Guide, June–July 1947, WHA Radio and Television Records.

10. "Annual Report of the University Radio Committee," Document 935, February 6, 1950, 12, Engel Papers.

11. "Annual Report of the University Radio Committee," Document 878, January 3, 1949, 11, Engel Papers.

12. "Annual Report of the University Radio Committee," Document 1031, January 7, 1952, 4, Engel Papers.

13. Sanger, *Rebel in Radio,* 161–68.

14. State Radio Council, "State Radio Report," August 1, 1950, 3, Engel Papers.

15. State Radio Council, "State Radio Report," December 20, 1951, 1, Engel Papers.

16. *InterCom,* March 26, 1952, 1, Engel Papers.

17. *WHA Radio-TV Program Preview,* April 1968, 21. On file at Wisconsin Historical Society.

18. State Radio Council, "State Radio Report," December 20, 1951, 1, Engel Papers.

19. State Radio Council, "Review of Educational Broadcasting in Wisconsin," September 15, 1952, 8, Engel Papers.

20. *InterCom,* January 23, 1952, 2, Engel Papers.

21. *WHA Radio-TV Program Preview,* November 1968, 24.

22. *InterCom,* July 1, 1957, 2, Engel Papers.

23. *Wisconsin State Journal,* May 11, 1969, sec. 6, p. 1.

24. Norstrand, *First 35 Years,* 6.

25. *InterCom,* March 12, 1952, 3, Engel Papers.

26. *InterCom,* June 1, 1965, 3, Engel Papers.

27. Arthur Hove, "WHA, Not So Much a Radio Station as a Way of Life," *Wisconsin Tales and Trails,* Spring 1967, 36.

28. *Wisconsin Alumnus,* December 1964, 17.

29. *InterCom,* March 1, 1961, 2, Engel Papers.

30. "Unsung Heroes of WPR's Weather Roundup," *Radio Guide and Broadcasting News,* December 1980, 2, Wisconsin Public Radio Collection.

31. *InterCom,* March 1, 1958, 3, Engel Papers.

32. *InterCom,* December 1, 1958, 4, Engel Papers.

33. *InterCom,* January 4, 1956, 2, Engel Papers.

34. Ibid.

35. *InterCom,* May 1, 1963, 1, Engel Papers.

36. *InterCom,* April 1, 1965, 4, Engel Papers.

37. "Annual Report of the Division of Radio-Television Education," 1963, 7, Engel Papers; Wisconsin State Broadcasting Service, Radio Programs, May–June 1966, on file at Wisconsin Historical Society.

38. "Annual Report of the Radio-Television Committee and the Staff of the Division of Radio-Television Education," 1964, 24, Engel Papers.

39. *InterCom,* February 1, 1965, 2, Engel Papers.

40. *WHA Radio-TV Program Preview,* November 1968, 19–21.

41. Jansky and Bailey, Consulting Broadcast Engineers, "Educational Broadcast Communications for Wisconsin," October 15, 1968, Washington, D.C.

Chapter 16. From Educational Radio to Public Radio

1. A copy of Vogelman's memo survives in the Engel Papers.

2. *State Radio Service Program Guide,* January 1948, WHA Radio and Television Records.

3. *State Radio Service Program Guide,* May 1948, WHA Radio and Television Records.

4. "The Amazing Case of Dr. Schindler," *Wisconsin Alumnus,* December 1949, 34.

5. Tamminga, "A Radio Arts Building."

6. McCarty to Audio Devices, December 9, 1949, McCarty Papers.

7. *State Radio Service Program Guide,* October 1949, WHA Radio and Television Records.

8. Wood, "First Decade of the 'Fourth Network,'" 456.

9. State Radio Council, "State Radio Report," August 1, 1950, 3, Engel Papers.

10. State Radio Council, "State Radio Report," August 10, 1951, 2, Engel Papers.

11. *InterCom,* January 23, 1952, 2, Engel Papers.

12. State Radio Council, "State Radio Report," September 1, 1950, 2, Engel Papers.

13. Harold Engel, memorandum to Transmitter Operators re: Rebroadcasting, October 10, 1962, WLBL Auburndale documents.

14. *InterCom,* April 1, 1960, 2, Engel Papers.

15. "Annual Report of the University Radio Committee," Document 1031, January 7, 1952, 3–4, Engel Papers.

16. Ibid., 4.

17. Ibid., 9.

18. Ibid., 10.

19. Wisconsin State Broadcasting Service memorandum re: Operation Penetration, October 10, 1951, WLBL Auburndale Documents.

20. "Annual Report of the University Radio Committee," Document 1031, January 7, 1952, 10, Engel Papers.

21. Ibid., 11–12.

22. *Wisconsin Public Broadcasting,* 30–36.

23. "Television in the Classroom and Beyond," *Wisconsin Alumni,* January 1965, 13.

24. *InterCom,* June 1, 1961, 1, Engel Papers.

25. *InterCom,* April 1, 1964, 1, Engel Papers.

26. *InterCom,* June 1, 1965, 1, Engel Papers.

27. "Biography of Senator S. I. Haykawa," *U.S. English, Inc.,* www.us-english.org/inc/about/hayakawa.asp.

28. Wisconsin State Broadcasting Service Radio Programs, May 1954, WHA Radio and Television Records.

29. Wisconsin State Broadcasting Service Radio Programs, August 1954, WHA Radio and Television Records.

30. *InterCom,* October 1, 1955, 1, Engel Papers.

31. "It's FM for Me, Says Joe," *Lawrence Alumnus,* Fall 1955, 14.

32. *InterCom,* January 4, 1956, 1, Engel Papers.

33. "The Gremlins Gamboled," *Lawrence Alumnus,* Spring 1956, 6–9.

34. *InterCom,* January 6, 1958, 3, Engel Papers.

35. *Wisconsin State Journal,* June 8, 1956, sec. 2, p. 13.

36. "Annual Report of the University Radio-Television Committee," Document 1249, February 11, 1957, 9, Engel Papers.

37. Norman Michie to State Radio Council transmitter operators, October 2, 1956, WLBL Auburndale Documents.

38. *InterCom,* April 1, 1957, 3, Engel Papers.

39. *InterCom,* January 2, 1957, 2, Engel Papers.

40. Jaker, Sulek, and Kanze, *Airwaves of New York,* 155.

41. Ray Norstrand, *First 35 Years,* 8.

42. Wisconsin State Broadcasting Service Radio Programs, October 1956, WHA Radio and Television Records.

43. Robert J. Ball, "Gilbert Highet and Classics at Columbia," *Columbia Alumni Magazine,* Fall 2001, columbia.edu/cu/alumni/Magazine/Fall2001/Highet.html (accessed March 9, 2006).

44. *InterCom,* July 2, 1956, 1, Engel Papers.

45. *InterCom,* May 1, 1957, 3, Engel Papers.

46. *InterCom,* December 2, 1957, 1, Engel Papers.

47. *InterCom,* April 1, 1965, 4, Engel Papers.

48. Tom Martin-Erickson, interview by author, November 11, 2003.

49. *InterCom,* April 1, 1958, 2, Engel Papers.

50. Wisconsin State Broadcasting Service Radio Programs, March–April 1959, WHA Radio and Television Records.

51. "Etc.," *Wisconsin Alumnus,* December 1964, 17–18.

52. Radio Listings, *Airwaves Magazine,* March 1984, 37.

53. "Thanks from Weyauwega Airlines," *Airwaves Magazine,* September 1982, 4.

54. "Annual Report of the Radio-Television Committee," Document 1466a, February 6, 1961, 2, Engel Papers.

55. "Annual Report of the Radio-Television Committee and the Staff of the Division of Radio-Television Education," 1964, pt. 2, p. 2, Engel Papers.

56. *InterCom,* August 1, 1960, 1, Engel Papers.

57. McCarty to Fuller, December 21, 1960 (copy), McCarty Papers.

58. McCarty to Ellis H. Dana, November 13, 1961 (copy), McCarty Papers.

59. McCarty, memorandum, April 9, 1965, McCarty Papers.

60. "Good Shepherd Lutheran Church History," Good Shepherd Lutheran Church, www.gslcwi.com.

61. Wisconsin State Broadcasting Service Radio Programs, March–April 1961, 3.

62. Milam, *Original Sex and Broadcasting*, 232.

63. *InterCom*, March 1, 1961, 1, Engel Papers.

64. *InterCom*, November 1, 1962, 2, Engel Papers.

65. Ibid., 1.

66. *InterCom*, February 1, 1963, 3, Engel Papers.

67. "Annual Report of the Division of Radio-Television Education," 1963, pt. 2, p. 8, Engel Papers.

68. WLBL log, October 13, 1963–December 31, 1965, WLBL Auburndale Documents.

69. Dunning, *On the Air*, 455–57.

70. *InterCom*, February 1, 1964, 3, Engel Papers.

71. *InterCom*, December 1, 1964, 1, Engel Papers.

72. "Annual Report of the Division of Radio-Television Education," 1963, pt. 2, p. 12, Engel Papers.

73. "Annual Report of the Radio-Television Committee," 1964, pt. 2, p. 10, Engel Papers.

74. Wisconsin State Broadcasting Service Radio Programs, January–February 1964, WHA Radio and Television Records.

75. Collins, *National Public Radio*, 20.

76. Wisconsin State Broadcasting Service Radio Programs, May–June 1964, WHA Radio and Television Records.

77. Lari Fanlund, "Music and Memories: Don Voegeli," *Airwaves Magazine*, October 1982, 9.

78. *InterCom*, July 17, 1967, 1, Engel Papers.

79. University of Wisconsin Extension Division of Educational Communications, "Annual Radio-Television Report," 1967, 13.

80. *State of Wisconsin Blue Book, 1993–1994* (Madison: Wisconsin Legislative Reference Bureau, 1994), 424.

81. *Wisconsin State Journal*, October 19, 1967, 1.

82. Karl Schmidt to Radio Staff, October 30, 1967, 1, WLBL Auburndale Documents.

83. Wisconsin State Broadcasting Service Radio Programs, March–April 1967, WHA Radio and Television Records.

84. *WHA Radio-TV Program Preview*, April 1968, 8–64. On file at Wisconsin Historical Society.

85. *Wisconsin Public Broadcasting*, 36.

86. *WHA Radio-TV Program Preview*, December 1968, 19–22. On file at Wisconsin Historical Society.

87. *WHA Radio-TV Program Preview,* October 1968, 16. On file at Wisconsin Historical Society.

88. Ibid., 8.

89. Engel, *Wisconsin Place Names,* preface.

90. *Wisconsin State Broadcasting Service Radio Guide,* April 1969, WHA Radio and Television Records.

91. *InterCom,* March 2, 1959, 3, Engel Papers.

92. *Wisconsin State Broadcasting Service Radio Guide,* September 1969, WHA Radio and Television Records.

93. *Wisconsin State Broadcasting Service Radio Guide,* November 1969, WHA Radio and Television Records.

94. Ibid.

95. *Wisconsin State Broadcasting Service Radio Guide,* December 1969, WHA Radio and Television Records.

96. Ralph W. Johnson, memorandum to state station transmitter operators, June 9, 1970, WLBL Auburndale Documents.

97. "WHA-FM Late Night Programming," *Radio Guide and Broadcasting News,* Wisconsin State Broadcasting Service, November 1970, Wisconsin Public Radio Collection.

Chapter 17. The Era of Public Radio

1. *Earplay* Project, first quarterly report, 1972, WHA Radio and Television Records.

2. David Mamet, *Writing in Restaurants* (New York: Penguin, 1986), 14.

3. Application for Radio Drama Production Unit, Board of Regents, University of Wisconsin System, March 30, 1977, WHA Radio and Television Records.

4. "Earplay 1980," *Radio Guide,* Wisconsin Public Radio, January 1980, 5, Wisconsin Public Radio Collection.

5. Harold B. McCarty, lecture before University of Wisconsin communication arts class, September 28, 1971 (audiotape), Wisconsin Public Radio Collection.

6. Vilas Communication Hall Dedicatory Ceremony program, September 20, 1974, Wisconsin Public Radio Collection.

7. Tony Moe, memorandum to Educational Communications Board staff, October 6, 1972, WLBL Auburndale Documents.

8. "Election '72: Day of Decision," *Radio Guide and Broadcasting News,* Wisconsin Educational Radio Network, November 1972, Wisconsin Public Radio Collection.

9. Educational Communications Board, *Update,* May 1973, 1, Wisconsin Public Radio Collection.

10. "Chapter a Day," *Radio Guide and Broadcasting News,* July–August 1973, Wisconsin Public Radio Collection.

11. John Powell, interview by author, September 14, 2004, Madison, Wisconsin.

12. "ECB to Establish New Network Operations Center," *Radio Guide and Broadcasting News,* September 1974, Wisconsin Public Radio Collection.

13. *970 Radio Guide,* November 1974, Wisconsin Public Radio Collection.

14. Jean Nelson, interview by author, February 1, 2004, Fitchburg, Wisconsin.

15. "Who's Who on Your Board of Directors," *Radio Guide,* Wisconsin Public Radio, January 1980, 20, Wisconsin Public Radio Collection.

16. *New York Times,* November 11, 2001, sec. 2, p. 1.

17. *970 Radio Guide,* April 1978, 3, Wisconsin Public Radio Collection.

18. "Member Update," *Radio Guide,* Wisconsin Public Radio, December 1979, 20, Wisconsin Public Radio Collection.

Chapter 18. WPAH/WLBL, the Other State Station

1. Wisconsin Department of Markets, Annual Report, 1921–22, Madison, February 28, 1923, 35. On file at Wisconsin Historical Society.

2. Terry to B. B. Jones, August 22, 1922 (copy), WHA Radio and Television Records.

3. Wisconsin Department of Markets, press release, August 30, 1922, WHA Radio and Television Records.

4. *Radio Service Bulletin,* no. 64, August 1, 1922, 3.

5. *Waupaca County Post,* November 2, 1922, 1.

6. *Wausau Pilot,* February 8, 1923, 5.

7. *Waupaca County News,* January 11, 1923, 1.

8. Ibid.

9. *Radio Service Bulletin,* no. 69, January 2, 1923, 3.

10. *Wausau Pilot,* February 8, 1923, 5.

11. *Waupaca County Post,* January 18, 1923, 1.

12. *Waupaca County Post,* February 8, 1923, 1.

13. WPAH Acknowledgment letter, February 6, 1923 (copy), Wisconsin Educational Communications Board Archives.

14. *Waupaca County News,* March 8, 1923, 1.

15. *Appleton Post-Crescent,* June 9, 1923, 14.

16. *Waupaca County News,* October 4, 1923, 1.

17. *Waupaca County Post,* September 6, 1923, 1.

18. *Waupaca County Post,* November 1, 1923, 1.

19. *Waupaca County Post,* November 29, 1923, 1.

20. *Waupaca County News,* December 13, 1923, 1.

21. *Waupaca County News,* September 27, 1923, 1.

22. *Waupaca County News,* November 1, 1923, 1.

23. *Waupaca County News,* October, 18, 1923, 1.

24. *Clintonville Tribune,* October 26, 1923, 1.

25. *Waupaca County Post,* November 8, 1923, 1.

26. *Waupaca County Post,* November 15, 1923, 1.

27. Ibid.

28. *Oshkosh Daily Northwestern,* November 19, 1923, 10.

29. *Waupaca County News,* November 15, 1923, 1.

30. *Waupaca County News,* November 22, 1923, 1.

31. *Waupaca County Post,* November 29, 1923, 1.

32. *Waupaca County News,* November 22, 1923, 1.

33. *Waupaca County News,* December 6, 1923, 1.

34. *Ripon Commonwealth,* December 14, 1923, 1.

35. *Waupaca County News,* December 13, 1923, 1; *Appleton Post-Crescent,* December 17, 1923, 7.

36. *Waupaca County News,* December 13, 1923, 1.

37. *Appleton Post-Crescent,* February 4, 1924, 2.

38. *Waupaca County News,* December 13, 1923, 1.

39. *Waupaca County News,* October 25, 1923, 1.

40. *Fond du Lac Daily Commonwealth,* November 26, 1923, 2.

41. *Fond du Lac Daily Commonwealth,* November 30, 1923, 2.

42. *Clintonville Tribune,* November 2, 1923, 6.

43. *Clintonville Tribune,* November 9, 1923, 1.

44. *Waupaca County News,* December 6, 1923, 15.

45. *Waupaca County News,* December 27, 1923, 1.

46. *Waupaca County News,* January 24, 1924, 1.

47. *Iola Herald,* January 31, 1924, 1.

48. *Stevens Point Daily Journal,* February 5, 1924, 1.

49. *Decatur Review,* February 5, 1924, 1.

50. *Iola Herald,* February 28, 1923, 1.

51. *Stevens Point Daily Journal,* February 27, 1924, 6.

52. *Stevens Point Daily Journal,* February 22, 1924, 3.

53. *Stevens Point Daily Journal,* February 4, 1924, 3.

54. *Stevens Point Daily Journal,* February 22, 1924, 3.

55. *Stevens Point Daily Journal,* March 10, 1924, 1.

56. *Stevens Point Daily Journal,* March 13, 1924, 2.

57. *Stevens Point Daily Journal,* April 3, 1924, 3.

58. *Stevens Point Daily Journal,* May 12, 1924 1.

59. *Stevens Point Daily Journal,* March 4, 1924, 1.

60. *Stevens Point Daily Journal,* April 23, 1924, 1.

61. *Stevens Point Daily Journal,* May 12, 1924, 1.

62. Ibid.

63. *Stevens Point Daily Journal,* May 28, 1924, 1, and June 17, 1924, 1.

64. Morgan Chase, "Well, Well, Good Evening Everyone! This Is WLBL, Wisconsin Land of Beautiful Lakes," *See America First,* June–July–August 1924, 65.

65. *Stevens Point Daily Journal,* April 30, 1924, 1.

66. Chase, "Well, Well, Good Evening Everyone!" 64–65.

67. *Stevens Point Daily Journal,* November 13, 1924, 1.

68. *Stevens Point Daily Journal,* November 15, 1924, 1.

69. *Stevens Point Daily Journal,* January 29, 1925, 1.

70. *Stevens Point Daily Journal,* March 22, 1924, 1.

71. *Stevens Point Daily Journal,* March 29, 1924, 1.

72. *Stevens Point Daily Journal,* March 21, 1925, 1.

73. *Stevens Point Daily Journal,* January 8, 1925, 1.

74. *Stevens Point Daily Journal,* January 23, 1924, 1.

75. WLBL schedule postcard, undated (ca. 1925), Wisconsin Public Radio Collection.

76. *Appleton Post-Crescent,* January 7, 1926, 19.

77. *Stevens Point Daily Journal,* February 1, 1927, 1.

78. *Stevens Point Daily Journal,* February 2, 1927, 8.

79. *Stevens Point Daily Journal,* March 15, 1927, 2.

80. *Stevens Point Daily Journal,* March 1, 1927, 7.

81. *Stevens Point Daily Journal,* March 10, 1927, 7.

82. *Wisconsin Rapids Daily Tribune,* January 12, 1928, 5.

83. *Stevens Point Daily Journal,* April 19, 1927, 1.

84. *Radio Service Bulletin,* no. 122, May 31, 1927, 10.

85. *Radio Service Bulletin,* no. 127, October 31, 1927, 9.

86. *Stevens Point Daily Journal,* July 12, 1927, 1.

87. *Stevens Point Daily Journal,* July 13, 1927, 5.

88. *Stevens Point Daily Journal,* July 23, 1927, 1.

89. *Stevens Point Daily Journal,* July 22, 1927, 4.

90. *Stevens Point Daily Journal,* July 23, 1927, 1.

91. *Stevens Point Daily Journal,* July 22, 1927, 1.

92. *Stevens Point Daily Journal,* December 23, 1927, 2.

93. *Stevens Point Daily Journal,* January 27, 1928, 6.

94. *Stevens Point Daily Journal,* February 8, 1928, 1.

95. *Stevens Point Daily Journal,* February 22, 1928, p. 1.

96. *Stevens Point Daily Journal,* July 5, 1928, 7.

97. *Stevens Point Daily Journal,* September 4, 1928, 1.

98. Frost, *Education's Own Stations,* 194.

99. *Stevens Point Daily Journal,* November 6, 1928, 1.

100. *Stevens Point Daily Journal,* February 17, 1930, 1.

101. Wisconsin Department of Agriculture and Markets, Activity Report–Stevens Point, February 1930, McCarty Papers.

102. *Stevens Point Daily Journal,* January 7, 1930, 1.

103. Wisconsin Department of Agriculture and Markets, Activity Report–Stevens Point, February 1930, McCarty Papers.

104. *Stevens Point Daily Journal,* March 19, 1930, 11.

105. *Stevens Point Daily Journal,* April 4, 1930, 13.

106. Wisconsin Department of Agriculture and Markets, Activity Report–Stevens Point, October 1930, McCarty Papers.

107. Department of Agriculture and Markets, Biennial Report, 1930–32, January 1933, 65. On file at Wisconsin Historical Society.

108. Comments from listeners/WLBL, undated (ca. 1933), Engel Papers.

109. T. M. Beaird, "Wisconsin Struggles to Prevent Complete Commercial Control of Radio Broadcasting," *Education by Radio,* August 3, 1933, 37–38.

110. F. R. Calvert to O. J. Thompson, January 3, 1934, McCarty Papers.

111. *Stevens Point Daily Journal,* May 2, 1932, 1.

112. Leo S. Turner to Calvert, September 15, 1932, WLBL Auburndale Documents.

113. Calvert to McCarty, August 22, 1932, WHA Radio and Television Records.

114. H. O. Brickson to O. J. Thompson, October 25, 1933, McCarty Papers.

115. *Sheboygan Press,* October 13, 1933, 12.

116. *Stevens Point Daily Journal,* September 22, 1933, 1.

117. "Announcers Schedule," undated (1933), McCarty Papers.

118. Harold A. Engel, "Wisconsin's State Radio Chain," *Education by Radio,* February 2, 1933, 12.

119. *Stevens Point Daily Journal,* August 17, 1933, 1.

120. *Sheboygan Press,* July 26, 1933, 13.

121. *Stevens Point Daily Journal,* November 16, 1933, 10.

122. Frost, *Education's Own Stations,* 384–85.

123. *Stevens Point Daily Journal,* November 16, 1933, 10.

124. *Sheboygan Press,* October 13, 1933, 2.

125. Engel to Hyer, December 14, 1933, McCarty Papers.

126. Calvert to Thompson, January 3, 1934, McCarty Papers.

127. Hill to Bennett, January 9, 1934, McCarty Papers.

128. Calver to Hill, January 12, 1934, McCarty Papers.

129. McCarty to Bennett, January 8, 1934 (copy), McCarty Papers.

130. McCarty, to Bennett, February 26, 1934 (copy), McCarty Papers.

131. *DePere Journal-Democrat,* December 14, 1933, 1.

132. Frost, *Education's Own Stations,* 384.

133. *Iola Herald,* September 16, 1937, 1.

134. "Comments on Operating Log of WLBL," November 26 and December 3, 1933, McCarty Papers.

135. *Stevens Point Daily Journal,* November 24, 1933, 1.

136. *Stevens Point Daily Journal,* October 5, 1934, 4.

137. *Stevens Point Daily Journal,* November 19, 1938, 4.

138. *Stevens Point Daily Journal,* October 2, 1936, 5; *Sheboygan Press,* November 14, 1933, 13.

139. *Stevens Point Daily Journal,* October 1, 1937, 9.

140. *Sheboygan Press,* October 13, 1933, 12.

141. Torinus, *Packer Legend,* 85.

142. *Stevens Point Daily Journal,* October 2, 1936, 5.

143. *Stevens Point Daily Journal,* November 23, 1935, 10.

144. *Stevens Point Daily Journal,* June 11, 1934, 5.

145. *Stevens Point Daily Journal,* September 24, 1937, 1.

146. F. R. Calvert, Activity Report for Stevens Point, Wisconsin, May 1935, McCarty Papers.

147. *Pointer,* September 10, 1935, 1.

148. *Pointer,* September 26, 1935, 1.

149. *Stevens Point Daily Journal,* February 28, 1936, 2.

150. *Stevens Point Daily Journal,* September 26, 1936, 4.

151. Wisconsin Department of Agriculture, "Radio Station WLBL—Twenty-Five Years of Markets and Agricultural Information by Radio in Wisconsin," Special Circular 100, February 1948. On file at Wisconsin Historical Society.

152. *Stevens Point Daily Journal,* May 8, 1936, 1.

153. *Stevens Point Daily Journal,* June 29, 1937, 1.

154. *Stevens Point Daily Journal,* June 22, 1937, 12.

155. *Stevens Point Daily Journal,* June 18, 1937, 1.

156. *Stevens Point Daily Journal,* June 29, 1937, 1.

157. *Stevens Point Daily Journal,* July 2, 1937, 5.

158. WLBL Guest Register, 1937–72, WLBL Auburndale Documents.

159. *Sheboygan Press,* February 15, 1938, 16.

160. Wisconsin Department of Agriculture, "Radio Station WLBL."

161. "Suggestions to Be Incorporated in WLBL–Central State Teachers' College Agreement," undated (1938), WLBL Files, University of Wisconsin–Stevens Point Archives.

162. Robert Wundrock, interview by author, December 2, 2002, Madison, Wisconsin.

163. *Stevens Point Daily Journal,* June 22, 1937, 12.

164. Calvert to Engel, June 21, 1939, WLBL Auburndale Documents.

165. *Stevens Point Daily Journal,* September 25, 1938, 12.

166. *Stevens Point Daily Journal,* October 20, 1939, 4; *Pointer,* September 25, 1940, 6.

167. Wisconsin College of the Air Course Outlines, 1939–40, 14, WHA Radio and Television Records; *Pointer,* September 20, 1939, 1, 5.

168. *Stevens Point Daily Journal,* September 25, 1940, 6.

169. Federal Communications Commission, application for consent to assignment of radio broadcast station construction permit or license, FCC form 314, July 21, 1939, WLBL Auburndale Documents.

170. *Stevens Point Daily Journal,* September 30, 1939, 3.

171. "History of AP Broadcast," Associated Press, www.apbroadcast.com/AP+Broadcast/About+Us/Miscellaneous/History.htm.

172. Wisconsin Department of Agriculture, Biennial Report, 1939–40, December 1940, 22. On file at Wisconsin Historical Society.

173. Wisconsin Department of Agriculture, Biennial Report, 1945–46, August 1946, 32. On file at Wisconsin Historical Society.

174. *Stevens Point Daily Journal,* July 22, 1939, 4.

175. *Stevens Point Daily Journal,* April 2, 1943, 4.

176. *Stevens Point Daily Journal,* April 26, 1940, 4.

177. *Stevens Point Daily Journal,* December 2, 1947, 4.

178. *Stevens Point Daily Journal,* March 7, 1950, 4.

179. Wisconsin Department of Agriculture, Biennial Report, 1941–42, December 1942, 74. On file at Wisconsin Historical Society.

180. Ibid.

181. "History of AP Broadcast."

182. Wisconsin Department of Agriculture, Biennial Report, 1941–42, 75.

183. Ibid.

184. Agreement between Wisconsin State Department of Agriculture and Board of Normal School Regents, April 21, 1943, WLBL Files, University of Wisconsin–Stevens Point Archives.

185. F. R. Calvert, Memorandum, April 22, 1943, WLBL Files, University of Wisconsin–Stevens Point Archives.

186. Wisconsin Department of Agriculture Biennial Report, 1943–44, December 1944, 57. On file at Wisconsin Historical Society.

187. *Stevens Point Daily Journal,* February 22, 1947, 1.

188. Milton Button, director of the Wisconsin Department of Agriculture, radio address over WHA on "FM Dedication Broadcast," March 30, 1947 (audiotape), Wisconsin Public Radio Collection.

189. *Stevens Point Daily Journal,* March 3, 1947, 1; "Quarter Century of Markets and Agricultural Information by Radio in Wisconsin," radio script, broadcast over WLBL February 5, 1948, 3, Wisconsin Educational Communications Board Archives.

190. *Stevens Point Daily Journal,* March 14, 1950, 1.

191. *Stevens Point Daily Journal,* March 16, 1950, 4.

192. D. N. McDowell, "General Statement Regarding the Expanded Services for Radio Station WLBL," March 1950, Engel Papers.

193. Walter L. Bohman to Hansen, March 14, 1950, University of Wisconsin–Stevens Point Archives.

194. Hansen to Bohman, March 16, 1950 (copy), WLBL Files, University of Wisconsin–Stevens Point Archives.

195. *Stevens Point Daily Journal,* March 18, 1950, 1.

196. Ibid.

197. *Stevens Point Daily Journal,* March 21, 1950, 1.

198. *Stevens Point Daily Journal,* March 24, 1950, 1.

199. *Stevens Point Daily Journal,* April 1, 1950, 1, and March 28, 1950, 4.

200. McCarty to Kostuck, March 29, 1950 (copy), McCarty Papers.

201. Eugene R. McPhee to Hansen, March 28, 1950, WLBL Files, University of Wisconsin–Stevens Point Archives.

202. Hansen, to McDowell, April 18, 1950 (copy), WLBL Files, University of Wisconsin–Stevens Point Archives.

203. Central State Teachers College news release, May 25, 1950, WLBL Files, University of Wisconsin–Stevens Point Archives.

204. *Stevens Point Daily Journal,* June 16, 1950, 1.

205. Vern Varney, Memorandum, July 7, 1950, Radio Files, University of Wisconsin–Stevens Point Archives.

206. Hansen to McDowell, July 13, 1950 (copy), WLBL Files, University of Wisconsin–Stevens Point Archives.

207. D. N. McDowell to William C. Hansen, October 3, 1950, Radio Files, University of Wisconsin–Stevens Point Archives.

208. Don E. Wilkinson to Wisconsin Telephone Company, August 2, 1950 (copy), Radio Files, University of Wisconsin–Stevens Point Archives.

209. McPhee to Hansen, October 13, 1950, Radio Files, University of Wisconsin–Stevens Point Archives.

210. Hansen to McPhee, October 24, 1950 (copy), Radio Files, University of Wisconsin–Stevens Point Archives.

211. Central State Teachers College Radio Schedule, January 15–20, 1951, mimeograph, McCarty Papers.

212. *Pointer,* January 25, 1951, 2.

213. *Pointer,* March 15, 1951, 4.

214. *Pointer,* April 19, 1951, 3.

215. Hansen to James Whitinger, Virgil Martinson, James Miller, and L. M. Sasman, June 14, 1951 (copy), Radio Files, University of Wisconsin–Stevens Point Archives.

216. WLBL Weather Reports, April 1, 1971–July 7, 1976, 134, WLBL Auburndale Documents.

217. Michie to Transmitter Operators, June 18, 1956, WLBL Auburndale Documents.

218. WLBL Weather Reports, October 1, 1967–March 31, 1971, and April 1, 1971–July 7, 1976 (two volumes), WLBL Auburndale Documents.

219. Selner to Michie, May 18, 1956 (copy), WLBL Auburndale Documents.

220. WLBL log, June 25, 1961–October 12, 1963, WLBL Auburndale Documents.

221. Jack G. McBride, Nebraska Educational Television Commission, "Report to the Wisconsin Educational Communications Board on a Wisconsin Educational Radio and Television Management Study," October 15, 1968. On file at Wisconsin Historical Society.

222. Alpine to Jack Stiehl, September 20, 1971 (copy), WLBL Auburndale Documents.

Chapter 19. The *Farm Program*

1. *Press Bulletin,* July 12, 1922.

2. University of Wisconsin Educational Radio Broadcast for the week of July 10–15, 1922, Penn Papers.

3. University of Wisconsin Educational Radio Broadcast Program for the week of January 15–20, 1923, Penn Papers.

4. Hazard, "History of WHA *Homemakers' Hour,*" 9.

5. Ibid., 15.

6. *University Antenna,* December 1, 1927, WHA Radio and Television Records.

7. *Press Bulletin,* March 14, 1928.

8. *Press Bulletin,* April 10, 1929.

9. *Press Bulletin,* October, 2, 1929.

10. H. L. Russell, "Around the Campus," *Wisconsin Country Magazine,* May 1929, 11.

11. Harold B. McCarty, lecture before University of Wisconsin communication arts class, September 28, 1971 (audiotape), Wisconsin Public Radio Collection.

12. Gapen, "Agricultural Broadcasting," 40.

13. Baker, *Farm Broadcasting,* 186.

14. Ibid., 138.

15. Gapen, "Agricultural Broadcasting," 38.

16. Farm Radio Programs, January 1935, Extension Service, College of Agriculture, University of Wisconsin. On file at Wisconsin Historical Society.

17. Gapen, "Agricultural Broadcasting," 50.

18. Frederick Boyd, "Ken Gapen, Farm Editor, Puts on Realistic Broadcasts," *Wisconsin Country Magazine,* March 1934, 12.

19. "Radio News from Wisconsin," *Education by Radio,* November 22, 1934, 55.

20. Baker, *Farm Broadcasting,* 29–39.

21. Wisconsin College of the Air, Course Outlines, 1935–36, WHA Radio and Television Records.

22. Wisconsin College of the Air, Course Outlines, 1939–40, WHA Radio and Television Records.

23. "Third Annual Report of the University Radio Committee," Document 629, October 1941, 4, Engel Papers.

24. "Eighth Annual Report of the University Radio Committee," Document 755, March 4, 1946, 4, Engel Papers.

25. "Annual Report of the University Radio Committee," Document 838, January 12, 1948, 5, Engel Papers.

26. "Annual Report of the University Radio Committee," Document 935, February 6, 1950, 6, Engel Papers.

27. "Annual Report of the University Radio Committee," Document 983, January 8, 1951, 6, Engel Papers.

28. Baker, *Farm Broadcasting,* 51.

29. Ibid., 238.

30. Maurice White, personnel file, October 29, 1953, McCarty Papers; Baker, *Farm Broadcasting,* 286.

31. *InterCom,* December 2, 1957, 3, Engel Papers.

32. *InterCom,* September 1, 1959, 4, Engel Papers.

33. "Annual Report of the University Radio-Television Committee," Document 1121, February 1, 1954, 9, Engel Papers.

34. Wisconsin State Broadcasting Service Radio Programs, January–February 1964, WHA Radio and Television Records.

Chapter 20. The *Homemakers' Program*

1. Evening University Lectures, June 6–9, 1922, Penn Papers.

2. University of Wisconsin Educational Broadcast, programs for the weeks of February 5–10, 1923, and April 2–7, 1923, both in Penn Papers.

3. Hazard, "History of WHA *Homemakers' Hour*," 16.

4. Ibid., 19.

5. Ibid., 20.

6. Ibid., 29–36.

7. Hazard, *For the Love of Mike*, v.

8. Hazard, "History of WHA *Homemakers' Hour*," 70–77.

9. Ibid., 39.

10. "Annual Report of the University Radio Committee," Document 878, January 3, 1949, 4, Engel Papers.

11. Hazard, "History of WHA *Homemakers' Hour*," 41.

12. Ibid., 46–48.

13. Ibid., 56.

14. Hazard, "Competition for Soap Operas," *Education on the Air, the Second Yearbook of the Institute for Education by Radio* (Columbus: Ohio State University, 1933), 311.

15. Broadcast Facilities and Reliability Questionnaire, January 29, 1942, for station WHA, Engel Papers; Hazard, "History of WHA *Homemakers' Hour*," 41.

16. Randall Davidson, Awards Master List (unpublished), Wisconsin Public Radio Collection.

17. "Third Annual Report of the University Radio Committee," Document 629, October 1941, 4, Engel Papers.

18. "Annual Report of the University Radio Committee," Document 641, December 1943, 4, Engel Papers.

19. Hazard, *For the Love of Mike*, 26–28.

20. "Annual Report of the Radio-Television Committee," Document 1312a, February 3, 1958, 7, Engel Papers.

21. "Annual Report of the Radio-Television Committee," Document 1530a, February 5, 1962, 16, Engel Papers.

22. Hazard, *For the Love of Mike*, 16–17.

23. *InterCom*, August 2, 1965, 1, Engel Papers.

Chapter 21. The Wisconsin School of the Air

1. Frost, *Education's Own Stations*, 145.

2. Shurick, *First Quarter Century of American Broadcasting*, 303.

3. Barnouw, *History of Broadcasting*, 1:250.

4. Dunning, *On the Air,* 29.

5. "Around the State," *Wisconsin Journal of Education,* November 1928, 160.

6. Mauer, "History of Station WHA," 35–36.

7. *New York Times* December 21, 1930; Mauer, "History of Station WHA," 36.

8. Harold B. McCarty, lecture before University of Wisconsin communication arts class, September 28, 1971 (audiotape), Wisconsin Public Radio Collection.

9. Harold B. McCarty, "The Wisconsin School of the Air," *Wisconsin Journal of Education,* November 1931, 136–38.

10. Wisconsin School of the Air bulletin, October 1931, McCarty Papers.

11. *Capital Times,* October 5, 1931, 6.

12. State Department of Public Instruction, "Education in Wisconsin—Biennial Report, 1930–1932," 1932, 10–18. On file at Wisconsin Historical Society.

13. Wisconsin Research Project, *Radio in the Classroom,* 84.

14. Lester Ward Parker, "The Wisconsin Study of School Broadcasts," *Education on the Air, the Ninth Yearbook of the Institute for Education by Radio* (Columbus: Ohio State University, 1940), 92.

15. Apps, *One-Room Country Schools,* 90.

16. Harold A. Engel, "Wisconsin School of the Air Approved by Listeners," *Wisconsin Journal of Education,* May 1932, 429.

17. Harold A. Engel, "School Program Broadcasts and Schools of the Air," *Education on the Air, the Fifth Yearbook of the Institute for Education by Radio* (Columbus: Ohio State University, 1936), 112.

18. Wisconsin School of the Air bulletin, second semester, 1937–38, McCarty Papers.

19. "Afield with Ranger Mac," *Wisconsin Country Magazine,* November 1944, 14 (reprinted from *Coronet Magazine,* August 1944).

20. "Annual Report of the University Radio Committee," University Document 722, February 5, 1945, 2, Engel Papers.

21. "Fourth Annual Report of the University Radio Committee," Document 662, December 1942, 2, Engel Papers.

22. WHA Broadcast Schedules, August 11–September 18, 1941, WHA Radio and Television Records.

23. Wisconsin Research Project, *Radio in the Classroom,* 135.

24. Randall Davidson, unpublished inventory of WHA transcription recordings at Wisconsin Historical Society Archives, completed on September 23, 2003.

25. Wisconsin Research Project, *Radio in the Classroom,* 197.

26. "Annual Report of the University Radio Committee," Document 838, January 12, 1948, 3, Engel Papers.

27. Wisconsin Research Project, *Radio in the Classroom,* 14.

28. "Annual Report of the University Radio Committee," Document 935, February 6, 1950, 4, 16, Engel Papers.

29. *InterCom,* March 1, 1958, 3, Engel Papers.

30. "Annual Report of the Radio-Television Committee," Document 1578a, March 4, 1963, 1962, 14, Engel Papers.

31. Educational Communications Board, *Parade of Programs, 1978–1979,* 5, Wisconsin Educational Communications Board Archives.

32. *WHA Radio TV Program Preview,* September 1968, 19. On file at Wisconsin Historical Society.

33. Apps, *One-Room Country Schools,* 90–101.

34. Wisconsin Research Project, *Radio in the Classroom,* 85.

35. "Annual Report of the University Radio Committee," Document 983, January 8, 1951, 4, Engel Papers.

36. "Annual Report of the University Radio Committee," Document 790, January 13, 1947, 4, Engel Papers.

37. Kelly, "Art Education by Radio," 58.

38. *InterCom,* October 1, 1955, 3, Engel Papers.

39. "Afield with Ranger Mac," 14.

40. "Annual Report of the University Radio-Television Committee," Document 1073, February 2, 1953, 6, Engel Papers.

41. Wisconsin School of the Air bulletin, October 1931, McCarty Papers.

42. Walter Krulevitch, "1945 Reports of School Visits," January 24, 1945, WHA Radio and Television Records.

43. Wisconsin College of the Air bulletin, 1939–40, 14, WHA Radio and Television Records.

44. "Annual Report of the University Radio Committee," Document 838, January 12, 1948, 3, Engel Papers.

45. "Annual Report of the University Radio Committee," Document 935, February 6, 1950, 6, Engel Papers.

46. "Annual Report of the University Radio-Television Committee," Document 1121, February 1, 1954, 5, Engel Papers.

46. "Annual Report of the University Radio-Television Committee," Document 1167, February 7, 1955, 4, Engel Papers.

48. Wisconsin School of the Air bulletin, 1954–55, Wisconsin Public Radio Collection.

49. "Annual Report of the University Radio-Television Committee," Document 1249, February 11, 1957, 4, Engel Papers.

50. *InterCom,* April 1, 1960, 1, WLBL Auburndale Documents.

51. *InterCom,* March 1, 1962, 3, WLBL Auburndale Documents.

52. "Annual Report of the University Radio Committee," Document 1121, January 13, 1947, 3, Engel Papers.

53. "Annual Report of the University Radio-Television Committee," Document 1167, February 7, 1955, 4, Engel Papers.

54. State Radio Council, "Outline of Functions, Responsibilities, Membership, Facilities, Services and Staff," April 1, 1966, 2, Wisconsin Public Radio Collection.

55. *WHA Radio-TV Program Preview,* July–August 1968, 6. On file at Wisconsin Historical Society.

56. H. B. McCarty, "Development and Dissemination of Educational Materials Directly Related to the AID/OPERATION NINOS Program, Dealing with Problems of Malnutrition in Latin America," April 14, 1971 (copy), McCarty Papers.

57. Karl Schmidt to Radio Staff, August 11, 1967, mimeograph, WLBL Auburndale Documents.

58. *The Darker Brother,* listing in the Wisconsin School of the Air bulletin, 1969, McCarty Papers.

59. WHA fiftieth anniversary script, 1969, mimeograph, 13, Wisconsin Public Radio Collection.

60. National Public Radio Program Library Catalog, April 1974, McCarty Papers.

61. *Conversations with Carol Cowan,* November 11, 1988 (audiotape; includes recordings made in April 1986), Wisconsin Public Radio Collection.

62. Educational Communications Board, *Parade of Programs, 1983–1984,* Wisconsin Educational Communications Board Archives.

63. Educational Communications Board, *Parade of Programs, 1984–1985,* 6, Wisconsin Educational Communications Board Archives.

64. Educational Communications Board, *Parade of Programs, 1994–1995,* Wisconsin Educational Communications Board Archives.

Chapter 22. The Wisconsin College of the Air

1. Penn, "Origin and Development of Radio Broadcasting," 254.

2. Frost, *Education's Own Stations,* 235.

3. Harold B. McCarty, lecture before University of Wisconsin communication arts class, September 28, 1971 (audiotape), Wisconsin Public Radio Collection.

4. *Daily Cardinal,* July 21, 1932, 2.

5. Penn, "Origin and Development of Radio Broadcasting," 373.

6. Undated (ca. 1934) description of the Wisconsin College of the Air, Engel Papers.

7. Frost, *Education's Own Stations,* 282.

8. Faville to Engel, December 7, 1934, Engel Papers.

9. Briggs, *BBC,* 116.

10. "Survey and Analysis of Radio Study Groups for the Wisconsin National Youth Administration and the Wisconsin Works Progress Administration in Cooperation with Wisconsin State Station WHA," 1936, Engel Papers.

11. Wisconsin College of the Air bulletin, 1939, WHA Radio and Television Records.

12. *InterCom,* November 1, 1956, 4, Engel Papers.

13. Jay Rath, "WHA's Early Voices: Where Are They Now?" *Airwaves Magazine,* October 1982, 8.

14. *Press Bulletin,* May 2, 1928.

15. Hazel McGrath, "Prof. Philo Buck: An Inspiring Teacher," *Badger Quarterly,* June 1949, 6.

16. "Annual Report of the University Radio-Television Committee," Document 1121, February 1, 1954, 7, Engel Papers.

17. *InterCom*, March 5, 1952, 1, Engel Papers.

18. Karl Schmidt to Radio Staff, September 15, 1967, 1, WLBL Auburndale Documents.

19. Wisconsin State Broadcasting Service, Radio Programs, November–December 1958, WHA Radio and Television Records.

20. *Freshman Forum* bulletin, Fall 1951, Wisconsin Public Radio Collection.

21. State Radio Council, "State Radio Report," September 1, 1950, 1, Engel Papers.

22. "Annual Report of the University Radio Committee," Document 935, February 6, 1950, 13, Engel Papers.

23. de Anguera, *Ethereal Messages,* 25.

24. *InterCom*, March 1, 1958, 3, Engel Papers.

25. *InterCom*, October 1, 1957, 1, and "Annual Report of the Radio-Television Committee," 1958, Document 1363a, February 2, 1959, 7, both in Engel Papers.

26. "Fourth Annual Report of the University Radio Committee," Document 662, December 1942, 3, Engel papers.

27. WHA fiftieth anniversary script, 1969, mimeograph, 13, Wisconsin Public Radio Collection.

28. *WHA Radio-TV Program Preview,* October 1968, 10. On file at Wisconsin Historical Society.

29. "Two Live on U of Air," *Radio Guide,* Wisconsin Public Radio, September 1981, 4, Wisconsin Public Radio Collection.

30. *Airwaves Magazine,* December 1982, p. 14.

Chapter 23. *Chapter a Day*

1. WHA Broadcast Schedule, July 25, 1932, WHA Radio and Television Records.

2. WHA Broadcast Schedule, August 1, 1932, WHA Radio and Television Records.

3. WHA Broadcast Schedule, August 8–September 9, 1932, WHA Radio and Television Records.

4. McCarty to Dorothy C. Rice, June 18, 1935 (copy), WHA Radio and Television Records.

5. Shaw to Alma E. Mueller, August 14, 1935 (copy), WHA Radio and Television Records; the book won Britain's Hawthornden Prize.

6. Shaw to Amy Richardson, October 16, 1935 (copy), WHA Radio and Television Records.

7. *InterCom,* January 10, 1967, 3, Engel Papers.

8. *Stevens Point Daily Journal,* May 26, 1936, 4.

9. *Talking Book* scripts, 1938 (various dates), McCarty Papers.

10. Loberger, "Wisconsin Radio Reading Service," iii–iv.

11. Arthur Hove, "WHA, Not So Much a Radio Station as a Way of Life," *Wisconsin Tales and Trails,* Spring 1967, 34.

12. Marianne Goss, "Guru of Exellence," in Davis, *Scrapbook,* 42.

13. Carol Cohen, "A Canticle for the Apocalypse," *Airwaves Magazine,* October 1982, 15.

14. *InterCom,* January 10, 1967, 3, Engel Papers.

15. "*Chapter a Day*—Books Presented in 1964," Wisconsin Public Radio Collection.

16. John Voelker to Wisconsin State Broadcasting Service, undated (1968), quoted in *WHA Radio/TV Program Preview,* September 1968, 1. On file at Wisconsin Historical Society.

17. H. D. Peebles to Engel, July 11, 1959, McCarty Papers.

18. Jim Fleming, interview by author, September 29, 2003, Madison, Wisconsin.

19. Michael Penn, "Tuning in to a Legacy," *On Wisconsin,* Fall 1998, 38.

20. *InterCom,* January 10, 1967, 3, Engel Papers.

21. "Annual Report of the University Radio Committee," Document 878, January 3, 1949, 5, Engel Papers.

22. Dunning, *On the Air,* 455.

Chapter 24. To Today

1. *Radio Guide,* Wisconsin Public Radio, November 1979, 2, Wisconsin Public Radio Collection.

2. *Airwaves Magazine,* August 1983, 48–49.

3. "Wisconsin Public Radio Underwriters," *Radio Guide,* Wisconsin Public Radio, March 1979, 20, Wisconsin Public Radio Collection.

4. Wisconsin State Broadcasting Service Radio Programs, November–December 1967. On file at Wisconsin Historical Society.

5. *WHA Radio-TV Program Preview,* November 1968, 8. On file at Wisconsin Historical Society.

6. John Powell, interview by author, April 1, 2003, Madison, Wisconsin.

7. *970 Radio Guide,* September 1975, 1, Wisconsin Public Radio Collection.

8. *Educational Communications Board Radio Guide,* June 1977, Wisconsin Public Radio Collection.

9. *Radio Guide,* Wisconsin Public Radio, February 1981, Wisconsin Public Radio Collection.

10. Apps, *People Came First,* 242.

11. WORT March 1980 Listener Survey results, in Quinn, *WORT-Madison,* 76.

12. Judith Heise-Kovalic, interview by author, January 15, 2004, Madison, Wisconsin.

13. Sandra-Jeanne Peterson, "Feldman Creates a Scene," *Airwaves Magazine,* August 1982, 12.

14. *Radio Guide,* Wisconsin Public Radio, March 1984, 1, Wisconsin Public Radio Collection.

15. Dan DeVany, "Ben Sidran Moves to Jazz Alive!" *Airwaves Magazine,* November 1982, 10.

16. "WHA: AM to FM," *Airwaves Magazine,* June 1982, 32.

17. "Politics '76: The Conventions," *Radio Guide and Broadcasting News,* Wisconsin Educational Radio Network, July–August 1976, Wisconsin Public Radio Collection.

18. "Hess in Milwaukee," *Radio Guide,* Wisconsin Public Radio, January 1980, 4, Wisconsin Public Radio Collection.

Postscript: The Oldest Station in the Nation

1. *Capital Times,* October 1, 1927, 3.

2. "On Wisconsin!" *Education by Radio,* August–September 1938, 25.

3. *Education by Radio,* January 1939, 1.

4. R. Franklin Smith, "Oldest Station in the Nation?" *Journal of Broadcasting,* Winter 1959–60, 41–43.

5. Joseph E. Baudino and John M. Kittross, "Broadcasting's Oldest Stations: An Examination of Four Claimants," *Journal of Broadcasting,* Winter 1977, 61–83.

6. Barnouw, *History of Broadcasting,* 1:34.

7. Shurick, *First Quarter Century of American Broadcasting,* 11.

8. Greb and Adams, *Charles Herrold,* 98.

9. Ibid., 105.

10. Ibid., 101–2.

11. KQW Annual Report, January 15, 1926–January 15, 1927, San Jose, California, McCarty Papers.

12. Baudino and Kittross, "Broadcasting's Oldest Stations," 65.

13. Ibid., 66.

14. Ibid.

15. Ibid., 79

16. Lighty to Hanson, March 12, 1930, Hanson Papers.

17. H. L. Ewbank, memorandum to H. B. McCarty, May 15, 1946, Engel Papers.

18. *Press Bulletin,* March 5, 1919; R. D. McPherson to E. M. Terry, February 19, 1919, WHA Radio and Television Records.

19. Frost, *Education's Own Stations,* 464.

20. Terry to Culver, March 25, 1919 (copy), and Culver to Terry, June 4, 1919, both in WHA Radio and Television Records.

21. C. M. Jansky, "The Beginnings of Radio Broadcasting," speech given at the WHA family dinner at the University of Wisconsin, November 24, 1958, Wisconsin Public Radio Collection.

22. Eric R. Miller to Chief, U.S. Weather Bureau, May 12, 1920, McCarty Papers.

23. Ibid.

24. Miller to H. M. Baldwin, September 20, 1920 (copy), McCarty Papers.

25. M. Hanson to Lida Hanson, September 27, 1920 (English translation from Danish), Hanson Papers.

26. Miller to R. E. Rogers, October 15, 1920 (copy), McCarty Papers.

27. Malcolm Hanson to Andrew Hopkins, June 17, 1931, bound in Gapen, "Agricultural Broadcasting."

28. B. Miller to J. E. Mack, March 14, 1950, McCarty Papers.

29. Terry to Frank D. Urie, December 11, 1920, and Terry to Victor Fink, December 11, 1920, both in WHA Radio and Television Records.

30. Miller to Penn, May 27, 1950, Penn Papers; Miller to Richard Vesey, February 23, 1951 (copy), McCarty Papers.

31. M. Hanson, "Elementary Circular on Radio Telephone Communication," mimeograph, February 1922, Engel Papers.

32. Malcolm Hanson to Andrew Hopkins, June 17, 1931, bound in Gapen, "Agricultural Broadcasting."

33. T. M. Beaird, "Wisconsin Struggles to Prevent Complete Commercial Control of Radio Broadcasting," *Education by Radio,* August 3, 1933, 37–38.

34. Earle M. Terry, speech as part of series Significant Lines of Progress during the Past Quarter Century, Penn Papers.

35. Penn, "Origin and Development of Radio Broadcasting," 296.

36. W. H. Lighty, "Notes on the University of Wisconsin Radio Station, WHA Madison, Wisconsin" (copy), May 22, 1924, McCarty Papers.

37. L. R. Ingersoll, "Earle Melvin Terry, 1879–1929," *Wisconsin Alumni,* May 1929, 255.

38. *Daily Cardinal,* October 13, 1929, 13.

39. Harold B. McCarty, lecture before University of Wisconsin communication arts class, September 28, 1971 (audiotape), Wisconsin Public Radio Collection.

40. Department of Commerce, Bureau of Navigation, Radio Service, License for Land Radio Station, Class "C" Limited Commercial, Serial 887, April 3, 1924 (copy), Wisconsin Public Radio Collection; Frost, *Education's Own Stations,* 466.

Bibliography

Books, Dissertations, and Theses

Apps, Jerold W. *One-Room Country Schools: History and Recollections from Wisconsin.* Amherst, Wisc.: Amherst Press, 1996.

————. *The People Came First.* Madison: Wisconsin Epsilon Sigma Phi Foundation, 2002.

Archer, Gleason L. *History of Radio to 1926.* 1938. Reprint, New York: Arno Press and the New York Times, 1971.

Baker, John C. *Farm Broadcasting: The First Sixty Years.* Ames: Iowa State University Press, 1981.

Barnouw, Eric. *A History of Broadcasting in the United States,* vol. 1, *A Tower in Babel.* New York: Oxford University Press, 1966.

Briggs, Asa. *The BBC: The First Fifty Years.* Oxford: Oxford University Press, 1985.

Collins, Mary. *National Public Radio: The Cast of Characters.* Washington, D.C.: Seven Locks Press, 1993.

Davis, Margaret E., ed. *The Scrapbook: The Wisconsin Public Radio Family, 1917–1986.* Madison: Wisconsin Public Radio, 1986.

de Anguera, Dave. *Ethereal Messages: A History of Beloit College Radio, 1907–1994.* Beloit, Wisc.: Beloit College Press, 1994.

Dunning, John. *On the Air: The Encyclopedia of Old-Time Radio.* New York: Oxford University Press, 1998.

Engel, Harold A., comp. *Wisconsin Place Names; a Pronouncing Gazetteer.* Madison: University of Wisconsin, University Extension, WHA, 1968.

Fessenden, Helen M. *Fessenden: Builder of Tomorrows.* New York: Howard-McCann, 1940.

Frost, S. E. Jr. *Education's Own Stations.* 1937. Reprint, New York: Arno Press and the New York Times, 1971.

Gapen, Kenneth M. "Agricultural Broadcasting by Educational Institutions." Master's thesis, University of Wisconsin–Madison, 1931.

Greb, Gordon, and Mike Adams. *Charles Herrold, Inventor of Radio Broadcasting*. Jefferson, N.C.: McFarland, 2003.

Hanson, Lida S. *The Story of Malcolm Hanson*. Milwaukee: privately published, 1946.

Harkness, Jon M., Thomas J. Higgins, Vincent C. Rideout, and James J. Skiles. *Electrical Engineering at the University of Wisconsin in Madison, 1891–1991*. Madison: Department of Electrical and Computer Engineering, University of Wisconsin, 1991.

Hazard, Aline Watson. *For the Love of Mike*. Madison: privately published, n.d. (1970?).

———. "History of WHA *Homemakers' Hour*." Bachelor's thesis, University of Wisconsin–Madison, 1940.

Jaker, Bill, Frank Sulek, and Peter Kanze. *The Airwaves of New York: Illustrated History of 156 AM Stations in the Metropolitan Area, 1921–1996*. Jefferson, N.C.: McFarland, 1998.

Kelly, Mary Francis. "Art Education by Radio: A Historical Study of *Let's Draw*." Ph.D. diss., University of Wisconsin–Madison, 1990.

Loberger, Mary Ellen. "The Wisconsin Radio Reading Service: An Assessment of Its Role in Providing News and Information to Wisconsin's Print-Handicapped Population." Master's thesis, University of Wisconsin–Madison, 1979.

Mauer, Barbara Joan. "History of Station WHA, 1926–1931." Master's thesis, University of Wisconsin–Madison, 1957.

Milam, Lorenzo Wilson. *The Original Sex and Broadcasting: A Handbook on Starting a Radio Station for the Community*. San Diego: Mho & Mho Works, 1988.

Norstrand, Ray. *The First 35 Years*. Chicago: WFMT-Chicago, 1987.

Penn, John Stanley. "The Origin and Development of Radio Broadcasting at the University of Wisconsin to 1940." Ph.D. diss., University of Wisconsin–Madison, 1959.

Quinn, George, ed. *WORT-Madison: 25 Years of Community Radio*. Madison, Wisc.: Back Porch Radio Broadcasting, 2000.

Sanger, Elliot M. *Rebel in Radio: The Story of WQXR*. New York: Hastings House, 1973.

Shurick, E. P. J. *The First Quarter Century of American Broadcasting*. Kansas City, Mo.: Midland, 1946.

Tamminga, William. "A Radio Arts Building for the University of Wisconsin." Master's thesis, Massachusetts Institute of Technology, 1949. Engel Papers.

Taussig, Charles William. *The Book of Radio*. New York: D. Appleton, 1922.

Torinus, John B. *The Packer Legend: An Inside Look*. Neshkoro, Wisc.: Laranmark Press, 1982.

Wisconsin Public Broadcasting—Seventy-Five Years of Service. Madison: Educational Communications Board, 1992.

Wisconsin Research Project in School Broadcasting. *Radio in the Classroom*. Madison: University of Wisconsin Press, 1942.

Wood, Donald Neal. "The First Decade of the 'Fourth Network': An Historical, Descriptive Analysis of the National Educational Television and Radio Center." Ph.D. diss., University of Michigan, Ann Arbor, 1963.

Newspapers

Appleton (Wisc.) Post-Crescent
Cambridge (Wisc.) News
(Madison, Wisc.) Capital Times
Chicago Tribune
Clintonville (Wisc.) Tribune
(University of Wisconsin–Madison) Daily Cardinal
Decatur (Ill.) Review
DePere (Wisc.) Journal-Democrat
Iola (Wisc.) Herald
Janesville (Wisc.) Gazette
Juneau (Wisc.) Independent
La Crosse (Wisc.) Tribune and Leader-Press
Milwaukee Journal
Milwaukee Sentinel
New York Times
Oshkosh (Wisc.) Daily Northwestern
(Central State Teachers College) Pointer, Stevens Point, Wisc.
Ripon (Wisc.) Commonwealth
Sheboygan (Wisc.) Press
Stevens Point (Wisc.) Daily Journal
Stoughton (Wisc.) Daily Courier-Hub
Waupaca County (Wisc.) News
Waupaca County (Wisc.) Post
Wausau (Wisc.) Pilot
Wisconsin Rapids (Wisc.) Daily Tribune
(Madison) Wisconsin State Journal

Magazines and Periodicals

Airwaves Magazine, Friends of Channel 21, Madison, Wisc.
Badger History, State Historical Society of Wisconsin
Badger Quarterly, University of Wisconsin–Madison
Education by Radio, National Committee on Education by Radio, Washington, D.C.
Journal of Broadcasting, Association for Professional Broadcasting Education, University of Southern California
Journal of Broadcasting and Electronic Media, Broadcast Education Association, Washington, D.C.
Journal of Radio Studies, Nassau Community College, Garden City, N.Y.

La Follette's Magazine, Robert M. La Follette Co., Madison, Wisc.

Lawrence Alumnus, Lawrence College Alumni Office, Appleton, Wisc.

Monthly Weather Review, U.S. Department of Agriculture/Weather Bureau, Washington, D.C.

970 Radio Guide, WHA Radio Association, Madison, Wisc.

On Wisconsin, University of Wisconsin–Madison

Radio News, Experimenter Publishing Co., Jamaica, N.Y.

Radio Service Bulletin, U.S. Department of Commerce, Bureau of Navigation, Washington, D.C.

See America First, Bureau of American Travel, Sheboygan, Wisc.

Technical World, Technical World Co., Chicago

University of Wisconsin Press Bulletin, University of Wisconsin–Madison

WHA Radio-TV Program Preview, University of Wisconsin–Extension, Madison

Wisconsin Alumni, University of Wisconsin–Madison

Wisconsin Alumnus, University of Wisconsin–Madison

Wisconsin Country Magazine, University of Wisconsin–Madison College of Agriculture and Home Economics

Wisconsin Engineer, Wisconsin Engineering Journal Association, Madison

Wisconsin Farmer, Wisconsin Farmer Co., Madison

Wisconsin Journal of Education, Wisconsin State Teachers' Association, Madison

Wisconsin Magazine of History, State Historical Society of Wisconsin, Madison

Wisconsin Tales and Trails, Wisconsin Tales and Trails, Madison

Manuscript Collections

Wisconsin Historical Society Archives
    Harold A. Engel Papers, 1922–68 (U.S. Mss 138AF)
    Malcolm Hanson Papers, 1906–47 (Wis Mss RI and PH 683)
    Andrew W. Hopkins Papers, 1880–1973 (M72–437)
    W. H. Lighty Papers (M61–148)
    Harold B. McCarty Papers, 1933–86 (M87–183)
    John Stanley Penn Papers, 1922–53 (U.S. Mss 8AF/11)
University of Wisconsin Archives
    Edward Bennett Papers, 1919–48 (series 8/6/6)
    Henry L. Ewbank Papers, 1925–52 (series 7/35/12/1–5/M9i7)
    WHA Radio and Television Records, 1915–84 (series 41/6/2/4 and 41/6/2/5)
University of Wisconsin–Stevens Point Archives/Chancellor's Office Collection
    WLBL Radio Station, 1935–51, archival/manuscript collection
    Radio, 1948–55, archival/manuscript collection
Wisconsin Public Radio Collection
Wisconsin Educational Communications Board Archives
WLBL Auburndale Documents, 1932–76 (now part of Wisconsin Educational Communications Board Archives)

Index

Information about specific stations can be found in the Station Index following the main index on page 402. Page numbers in *italic* indicate illustrations.

Station Index